A 'New' Woman in Verga and Pirandello
From Page to Stage

LEGENDA

LEGENDA is the Modern Humanities Research Association's book imprint for new research in the Humanities. Founded in 1995 by Malcolm Bowie and others within the University of Oxford, Legenda has always been a collaborative publishing enterprise, directly governed by scholars. The Modern Humanities Research Association (MHRA) joined this collaboration in 1998, became half-owner in 2004, in partnership with Maney Publishing and then Routledge, and has since 2016 been sole owner. Titles range from medieval texts to contemporary cinema and form a widely comparative view of the modern humanities, including works on Arabic, Catalan, English, French, German, Greek, Italian, Portuguese, Russian, Spanish, and Yiddish literature. Editorial boards and committees of more than 60 leading academic specialists work in collaboration with bodies such as the Society for French Studies, the British Comparative Literature Association and the Association of Hispanists of Great Britain & Ireland.

The MHRA encourages and promotes advanced study and research in the field of the modern humanities, especially modern European languages and literature, including English, and also cinema. It aims to break down the barriers between scholars working in different disciplines and to maintain the unity of humanistic scholarship. The Association fulfils this purpose through the publication of journals, bibliographies, monographs, critical editions, and the MHRA Style Guide, and by making grants in support of research. Membership is open to all who work in the Humanities, whether independent or in a University post, and the participation of younger colleagues entering the field is especially welcomed.

ALSO PUBLISHED BY THE ASSOCIATION

Critical Texts
Tudor and Stuart Translations • New Translations • European Translations
MHRA Library of Medieval Welsh Literature

MHRA Bibliographies
Publications of the Modern Humanities Research Association

The Annual Bibliography of English Language & Literature
Austrian Studies
Modern Language Review
Portuguese Studies
The Slavonic and East European Review
Working Papers in the Humanities
The Yearbook of English Studies

www.mhra.org.uk
www.legendabooks.com

ITALIAN PERSPECTIVES

Editorial Committee
Professor Simon Gilson, University of Warwick (General Editor)
Dr Francesca Billiani, University of Manchester
Professor Manuele Gragnolati, Université Paris-Sorbonne
Dr Catherine Keen, University College London
Professor Martin McLaughlin, Magdalen College, Oxford

Founding Editors
Professor Zygmunt Barański and Professor Anna Laura Lepschy

In the light of growing academic interest in Italy and the reorganization of many university courses in Italian along interdisciplinary lines, this book series, founded by Maney Publishing under the imprint of the Northern Universities Press and now continuing under the Legenda imprint, aims to bring together different scholarly perspectives on Italy and its culture. *Italian Perspectives* publishes books and collections of essays on any period of Italian literature, language, history, culture, politics, art, and media, as well as studies which take an interdisciplinary approach and are methodologically innovative.

APPEARING IN THIS SERIES

20. *Ugo Foscolo and English Culture*, by Sandra Parmegiani
21. *The Printed Media in Fin-de-siècle Italy: Publishers, Writers, and Readers*, ed. by Ann Hallamore Caesar, Gabriella Romani, and Jennifer Burns
22. *Giraffes in the Garden of Italian Literature: Modernist Embodiment in Italo Svevo, Federigo Tozzi and Carlo Emilio Gadda*, by Deborah Amberson
23. *Remembering Aldo Moro: The Cultural Legacy of the 1978 Kidnapping and Murder*, ed. by Ruth Glynn and Giancarlo Lombardi
24. *Disrupted Narratives: Illness, Silence and Identity in Svevo, Pressburger and Morandini*, by Emma Bond
25. *Dante and Epicurus: A Dualistic Vision of Secular and Spiritual Fulfilment*, by George Corbett
26. *Edoardo Sanguineti: Literature, Ideology and the Avant-Garde*, ed. by Paolo Chirumbolo and John Picchione
27. *The Tradition of the Actor-Author in Italian Theatre*, ed. by Donatella Fischer
28. *Leopardi's Nymphs: Grace, Melancholy, and the Uncanny*, by Fabio A. Camilletti
29. *Gadda and Beckett: Storytelling, Subjectivity and Fracture*, by Katrin Wehling-Giorgi
30. *Caravaggio in Film and Literature: Popular Culture's Appropriation of a Baroque Genius*, by Laura Rorato
31. *The Italian Academies 1525-1700: Networks of Culture, Innovation and Dissent*, ed. by Jane E. Everson, Denis V. Reidy and Lisa Sampson
32. *Rome Eternal: The City As Fatherland*, by Guy Lanoue
33. *The Somali Within: Language, Race and Belonging in 'Minor' Italian Literature*, by Simone Brioni
34. *Laughter from Realism to Modernism: Misfits and Humorists in Pirandello, Svevo, Palazzeschi, and Gadda*, by Alberto Godioli
35. *Pasolini after Dante: The 'Divine Mimesis' and the Politics of Representation*, by Emanuela Patti

Managing Editor
Dr Graham Nelson, 41 Wellington Square, Oxford OX1 2JF, UK
www.legendabooks.com

A 'New' Woman in Verga and Pirandello

From Page to Stage

Enza De Francisci

LEGENDA
Italian Perspectives 40
Modern Humanities Research Association
2018

*Published by Legenda
an imprint of the Modern Humanities Research Association
Salisbury House, Station Road, Cambridge CB1 2LA*

*ISBN 978-1-78188-783-7 (HB)
ISBN 978-1-78188-784-4 (PB)*

First published 2018

All rights reserved. No part of this publication may be reproduced or disseminated or transmitted in any form or by any means, electronic, mechanical, photocopying, recording or otherwise, or stored in any retrieval system, or otherwise used in any manner whatsoever without written permission of the copyright owner, except in accordance with the provisions of the Copyright, Designs and Patents Act 1988, or under the terms of a licence permitting restricted copying issued in the UK by the Copyright Licensing Agency Ltd, Saffron House, 6–10 Kirby Street, London EC1N 8TS, England, or in the USA by the Copyright Clearance Center, 222 Rosewood Drive, Danvers MA 01923. Application for the written permission of the copyright owner to reproduce any part of this publication must be made by email to legenda@mhra.org.uk.

Disclaimer: Statements of fact and opinion contained in this book are those of the author and not of the editors or the Modern Humanities Research Association. The publisher makes no representation, express or implied, in respect of the accuracy of the material in this book and cannot accept any legal responsibility or liability for any errors or omissions that may be made.

Trademark notice: Product or corporate names may be trademarks or registered trademarks, and are used only for identification and explanation without intent to infringe.

© Modern Humanities Research Association 2018

Copy-Editor: Dr Anna J. Davies

CONTENTS

	Acknowledgements	ix
	List of Translations and Abbreviations	x
	Introduction: A New Voice	1
1	From Page to Stage	8
2	Women Centre Stage	34
3	The Sicilian Voice	53
4	The Silent Voice	90
5	The Sexual Voice	120
	Conclusion: Visibility and Voice	159
	Bibliography	166
	Index	182

To Mum, Dad, Anna Laura and Giulio Lepschy.

In loving memory of Vera, my nonni, Mrs Lyons, and Terry d'Alfonso

ACKNOWLEDGEMENTS

I would like to express my deepest gratitude to my supervisors for their expert guidance which has made this all possible: Anna Laura Lepschy and Shirley Vinall — thank you for inspiring me to reshape my book and for painstakingly going through my final edits. I wish to thank my examiners Emanuela Tandello and Ursula Fanning for their invaluable insight into my PhD, and express my deepest gratitude to Susan Bassnett, Ian Short, Guido Bonsaver, and Susan Rutherford for their comments on earlier drafts of my work. My thanks go to members of staff at Glasgow University and University College London, especially Giulio Lepschy, David Forgacs, Axel Körner, Catherine Keen, Florian Mussgnug, Vieri Samek, Barbara Burns, Laurence Grove, and Duncan Maclennan. I should also like to thank Marina Warner, Loredana Polezzi, Sonia Massai, and Anna Sica for all their support over the years.

I gratefully acknowledge UCL for funding several research periods abroad, including to the Scuola Normale di Pisa which saw the start of this project; Il circolo for funding my research at the Istituto di Studi Pirandelliani and the Biblioteca nazionale in Rome; and to the Italian Embassy for supporting my studies at the University of Bologna (DAMS). I am particularly grateful to Alfredo Stussi and Marco De Marinis for mentoring me during these periods, and to Dina Saponaro and Lucia Torsello for welcoming me at the Pirandello Institute. I am also indebted to the library staff at Glasgow, UCL, Senate House, and the British Library, as well as to Simon Gilson, Graham Nelson, and the peer reviewers at Legenda.

Finally a *grazie di cuore* to my family, especially my father whose endless stories about our Sicilian heritage have always been at the heart of my life-long fascination with Sicily. I wish to thank my cousins Daniele and Alessio for all their hard work on my cover, Luca for having introduced me to Pirandello's fiction, and my *nipotina* Siena for her bubbly company. Special thanks go to Adam Greenwood for checking my translations, Lily Kahn, Tom and Edward Holberton, Chiara Boldrini, Belinda John-Baptiste, Mariam Curzon, Chris Stamatakis, Geraldine Brodie, Daniela Cerimonia, Davide Messina, Carlo Pirozzi, Simone Caffari, Brían Doonan, Nicola Ibba, Gabrielle Oropallo, Marco Gambino, Simon Sleight, Marco Santello, George Whitmore, the Ramsay Hall crowd, my English language colleagues, and my friends in Agrigento: a city which continues to inspire me today.

E.D.F., Glasgow, September 2018

LIST OF TRANSLATIONS AND ABBREVIATIONS

The following editions of Verga's works and translations are referred to here using the abbreviations shown:

GIOVANNI VERGA, *Carteggio Verga-Capuana*, ed. by Gino Raya (Rome: Edizioni dell'Ateneo, 1984) [*CVC*]
GIOVANNI VERGA, *Lettere a Luigi Capuana*, ed. by Gino Raya (Florence: Le Monnier, 1975) [*LC*]
GIOVANNI VERGA, *Lettere al suo traduttore*, ed. by Fredi Chiappelli (Florence: Le Monnier, 1954) [*Lt*]
GIOVANNI VERGA, *Lettere sparse*, ed. by Giovanna Finocchiaro (Rome: Bulzoni, 1980) [*Ls*]
GIOVANNI VERGA, *I Malavoglia* (Milan: Mondadori, 1998) [*I Mala.*]
GIOVANNI VERGA, *Mastro don Gesualdo* (Milan: Mondadori, 2000) [*MDG*]
GIOVANNI VERGA, *Tutte le novelle*, 2 vols (Milan: Mondadori, 1982) [*Tn* I, *Tn* II]
GIOVANNI VERGA, *Tutto il teatro* (Milan: Mondadori, 1980) [*Tt*]
GIOVANNI VERGA, *Cavalleria rusticana and Other Stories*, trans. with an intro. by G. H. McWilliam (Harmondsworth: Penguin, 1999) [*CROS*]

The following editions of Pirandello's works and translations are referred to here using the abbreviations shown:

LUIGI PIRANDELLO, *Novelle per un anno*, ed. by Manlio Costanzo, 3 vols (Milan: Mondadori, 1985–1990) [*Na* I, *Na* II, *Na* III]
LUIGI PIRANDELLO, *Tutti i romanzi*, ed. by Giovanni Macchia and Manilo Costanzo, 2 vols (Milan: Mondadori, 1973) [*Tr* I, *Tr* II]
LUIGI PIRANDELLO, *Maschere nude*, ed. by Alessandro D'Amico, 4 vols (Milan: Mondadori, 1986–2007) [*Mn* I, *Mn* II, *Mn* III, *Mn* IV]
LUIGI PIRANDELLO, *Saggi, poesie, scritti varii*, ed. by Manilo Lo Vecchio-Musti (Milan: Mondadori, 1960) [*Spsv*]
LUIGI PIRANDELLO, *Saggi e interventi*, ed. and with an introductory essay by Ferdinando Taviani, and a testimony by Andrea Pirandello (Milan: Mondadori, 2006) [*Si*]
LUIGI PIRANDELLO, *Short Stories*, selected and trans. from the Italian by Fredrick May (London-New York: Quartet Encounters, 1987) [*SS*]
LUIGI PIRANDELLO, *Collected Plays*, ed. by Robert Rietty, 4 vols (London: John Calder, 1987–1992) [*CP* I, *CP* II, *CP* III, *CP* IV]
LUIGI PIRANDELLO, *Tonight We Improvise and '"Leonora, addio!"'*, trans. with an intro. and notes by J. Douglas Campbell and Leonard G. Sbrocchi (Ottawa: The Canadian Society for Italian Studies, 1987) [*TWI*]

Unless specified, all translations are my own.

INTRODUCTION

A New Voice

Various theoretical and critical approaches have been adopted when examining the notion of theatre translation.[1] The present volume aims to contribute to this area, in the context of Italian nineteenth- and twentieth-century literature, by offering a comparison between Giovanni Verga's and Luigi Pirandello's methods of transposing certain of their *novelle* to the stage. Both authors shared a common Sicilian background and wrote for similar readerships and audiences, composing a range of short stories, novels, and plays. Throughout their long careers, Verga published eight plays in total, four of which are based on short stories, and Pirandello published forty-three plays, twenty-nine of which are adapted from his narratives. While some critics and scholars have considered several aspects of the transformation from short story to play in the work of the Sicilian authors, none has ever explored their literary techniques on a comparative basis.[2] Most have taken a comprehensive view of the modifications made to the dramatic adaptations, prioritising *what* changes have been made over *how* and *why* such changes have been made.

Through close textual analysis, this book evaluates the processes involved when the two authors transform their oeuvre in the narrative and theatrical genres, illustrating what occurs when the role of the narrator is replaced by the exchanges of the characters on stage. The chapters focus on each at the peak of their careers (for Verga from 1880 to 1901 and for Pirandello from 1917 to 1928) and offer a diachronic overview of how they adapt four of their *novelle* for the stage.[3] By assessing the authors together rather than separately, the volume will be able to introduce a new perspective with which to consider the pair.

The intention here is to analyse the ways in which a *new voice* emerges when the authors develop their short stories into plays, an analysis especially relevant to the representation of women. Indeed, as soon as Verga and Pirandello shift their tales from the narrative genre to the theatrical (a genre which predominantly relies on speech), more emphasis is inevitably placed on their characters' ability to articulate their thoughts and as a result, their individual voices (taken to mean not simply the ability to speak, but the right to express an opinion) get 'louder'. Whereas in the *novelle* the narrator can speak on behalf of the characters, in the dramatic versions the characters are forced to speak for themselves. Certain male characters inevitably undergo similar transformations. Lollo in 'La caccia al lupo' is described as a '[u] omo di poche parole' [[m]an of few words] (*Tn* II, 451) and as a '[u]omo di poche chiacchiere' [[m]an with little small talk] (*Tt*, 131) in the corresponding play, and yet, despite his nature, on stage he is forced to articulate the details of his wolf hunt for the benefit of the audience. Likewise, the essentially silent Verri in '"Leonora, addio!"' is turned into an extremely vocal character in *Questa sera si recita a soggetto* (1928–29). However, what is significant about this shift in emphasis is how, while men have been typically associated with words (logic and reason) and women with silence (nature and emotion), the additional use of dialogue introduced in the theatrical adaptations enables the female protagonists to break away from their traditional identification as the antithesis of logocentrism and become 'new' women on stage.

While the two authors cannot be classed as feminist writers, they nonetheless seem to adopt a feminist approach. According to Gayle Austin, a feminist approach 'means paying attention when women appear as characters and noticing when they do not. It means making some "invisible" mechanisms visible'.[4] In terms of the female roles analysed here, the volume will engage with their absence as much as their presence. In fact, the authors pay much attention to women in their fiction, portraying a wide range and a considerable number of female characters in their narratives and plays. With regard to Verga, Susan Amatangelo stresses his 'particular talent for portraying women', postulating that 'Verga consistently depicts women's lives with a mixture of compassion and pessimism that suggests his awareness of the female experience'.[5] In fact, Verga's *Storia di una capinera* (1871) was considered by his contemporaries as 'una tesi sociale' [a social theory].[6] In a letter of 2 March 1872, his fellow author Caterina Percoto praised him for bringing to public attention the custom of obliging unmarried women to observe forced enclosure, thus calling him a 'campione' [champion] of women's rights.[7] So despite admitting to being 'poco [...] feminista' [not much of a feminist] (*Ls*, p. 95) in a letter to a friend Adelaide Bernardini in 1900, and confessing to another friend Paolina Greppi in a letter of 21 February 1890 to having 'poca fede nelle donne scrittrici' [little faith in women writers], describing Matilde Serao as 'eccettuata perch'è ermafrodita' [excepted because she is a hermaphrodite],[8] it would seem that his own portrayal of women actually contradicts these views. Indeed, Verga's use of free indirect speech in his Sicilian countryside tales enables him to witness the events of his stories through the eyes of the villagers, creating a strong sense of empathy with all his characters, including the women. Though Verga essentially is a male author who lacked first-hand experience of the hardship many women faced at the time, his fiction nonetheless delves under the skin of the female characters and enables them to tell their *own* stories in their *own* words, particularly when transposed on stage.

As for Pirandello, he also shows great empathy for his women characters. In fact, it has been observed by Maria Antonietta Grignani that 'le figure femminili di Pirandello sono più numerose di quelle maschili' [the female characters in Pirandello are more numerous than the male],[9] and many critics have noted that this abundance of female roles, particularly after 1925, was a direct result of the influence of Marta Abba who became Pirandello's leading lady in his theatre company, *Teatro d'Arte*. Daniela Bini has claimed that 'it was Marta Abba's entrance into Pirandello's life that galvanized the writer's ideas and gave birth to plays centred on female characters',[10] and Leonardo Bragaglia has argued that, '[s]oltanto con l'avvento di Marta Abba, determinante, queste figure prenderanno un volto, *una voce*, un nome' [[o]nly with the decisive arrival of Marta Abba would these characters gain a face, *a voice*, and a name] (my italics).[11] According to Susan Bassnett, in the plays that Pirandello dedicates to Marta Abba, 'although the female protagonists do not avoid pain, they nevertheless fight against it',[12] and, similarly, Ann Caesar underlines that in these plays, 'Pirandello depicts women who are, for all their neuroses, strong-willed and uncompromising, much more so than his male protagonists who are altogether more vacillating'.[13]

My analysis, however, focuses predominantly on the female characters that Pirandello portrays prior to his encounter with the actress, with the exception of *Questa sera si recita a soggetto*. In so doing, I show that Pirandello's early women also have a strong and powerful voice, above all on stage. Indeed, even when they appear to accept their suffering, such as Mommina in the early short story '"Leonora, addio!"', they implicitly resist it. For example, Bassnett regards *Liolà* (1916) as a 'distastefully misogynistic' play which exemplifies 'not so much a love of life as a hatred of women'.[14] Bassnett's argues against Eric Bentley who considers Liolà to be the only positive character in the play: 'By positive I mean morally positive, being an agent, not merely a victim; hammer, not merely anvil.'[15] Despite this, it could just as well be argued that the true agent of the play is the 'meek' Mita — she is the character who gets what she wants not only by manipulating Tuzza's flawed plan to her advantage, but by using Liolà as *her* sexual object. By seducing Liolà and becoming pregnant, Mita is essentially able to win her wealthy husband back by falsely maintaining that her unborn child is the legitimate heir to his 'throne'.

What, then, is striking about the 'new' women on stage is how they are now placed in a position where they need to express their thoughts and opinions for themselves, independently of the narrator and, as a result, they challenge the traditional male subject in literature. In the words of Sue-Ellen Case:

> For feminists, gender is the crucial encoding of the subject that has made it historically a position unavailable for women to inhabit. The traditional subject has been the male subject, with whom everyone must identify. Scanning the 'masterpieces' of the theatre, with their focus on the male subject, one can see that women are called upon to identify with Hamlet, Oedipus, Faust and other male characters.[16]

According to Pam Morris, by observing the action through the focal lens of the male subject, readers are made to empathise with the author's male-centred perspective:

> The construction of narrative point of view is one of the most powerful means by which readers are imperceptibly brought to share the values of the text [...]. By assuming that place we assume also the viewpoint and attitudes that go with it. Not surprisingly, in male-authored texts the attitudes and values are predominantly male-orientated.[17]

As a result of this process, Judith Fetterley has argued that readers are taught to *think as men*:

> [A]s readers and teachers and scholars, women are taught to think as men, to identify with a male point of view, and to accept as normal and legitimate a male system of values, one of whose central principles is misogyny.[18]

The viewpoint that the traditional subject has been typically reserved for the male gender certainly rings true in *all* of Verga's and Pirandello's narratives. The case is very different, nonetheless, when the tales are adapted for the stage. For instance, in Verga's collections of short stories, such as his *Vita dei campi* (1880) and *Per le vie* (1883), the storyteller articulates the patriarchal voice of society through free indirect speech, a kind of blend between direct and indirect speech which was first identified by Charles Bally in his *Style indirect libre* (1912).[19] On stage, however, this patriarchal voice grows more muted as individual voices take centre stage, especially the female voice which, in the case of Verga, was symptomatic of the influence of the *divina* Duse, the actress who inspired his first two plays — *Cavalleria rusticana* (1884) and *In portineria* (1885).

Pirandello adopts a similar approach. While patriarchal society is articulated through the voice of the narrator in his short stories, such as in '"Leonora, addio!"' and 'La Signora Frola e il Signor Ponza, suo genero', the women in the dramatic rewritings are ultimately given their say. Mommina's dialogues are extended in *Questa sera si recita a soggetto*, and Signora Ponza in *Così è (se vi pare)* (1917) reveals the mystery of her identity. As for 'Quando si è capito il giuoco' (1913) and *Il giuoco delle parti* (1918), while the narrative prioritises the male protagonist's point of view, in the dramatic version his wife is given a chance to express herself.

But what about the female characters who remain silent? One of the most intriguing voices to emerge here is the silent voice. Adriana Cavarero's *For More Than One Voice* (2005), on the recuperation of the vocalic and the distinction between voice and meaning, examines a number of silent female voices, such as those articulated by the Muse and the Siren in classical literature. The Muse in Plato's *Ion*, for instance, is the poet's source of inspiration, but her actual voice is silent to common mortals: 'For the audience, the poet is the audible form of the inaudible inspiration; it is the sonorous voice of the mute Muse'.[20] Similarly, the Siren, who lures sailors to their death through her seductive singing, is also to some extent silenced. With the exception of the Homeric Sirens, who musically narrate the events they witnessed in Troy and essentially 'speak' through their singing, variations of this story, namely by Max Horkheimer and Theodor Adorno in their *Dialectic of Enlightenment* (1944), have emphasised the Siren's ability to *sing* rather than *speak*. As Cavarero puts it: 'For Horkheimer and Adorno, the Sirens in fact represent "pure" voice; they sing, but they say nothing, recount nothing. They do not belong to the world of Homeric orality'.[21] Consequently, the Sirens conform to what Cavarero considers an object of masculine desire where 'the woman appears first of all as a body and as an inarticulate voice. She must be beautiful, but she must not speak'.[22]

Contrary to this, I want to show that, even when a female character remains silent, she nonetheless is still able to *say something*. Take, for instance, the Muse. Though she is silent to the human ear, she is the only one able to articulate what the poet cannot. It is her inspiration which leads to his poetry — he writes because of *her*. The Muse might not therefore have an actual sound for those other than the poet, but it is her non-verbal voice which changes the lives of others for better (as is the case here) or for worse (as is the case with the Siren). In line with this, it will be demonstrated here that, even when the authors create women characters who remain silent or are physically absent from the plots, they are still able to say something: Màlia in *In portineria* expresses her complex psychology through her non-verbal communication; Signora Ponza never appears in 'La Signora Frola e il Signor Ponza, suo genero' and yet her metaphorical presence rivals the logic of Pirandello's mouthpiece character Laudisi; and the late Silvia's physical absence in *Tutto per bene* is transformed into a re-created presence by her husband whose present-day and self-perception are determined by his memory of her. A further illustration of this tendency emerges in Pirandello's critical essay 'Femminismo'.[23] Though Bassnett deems the essay 'distasteful both in its attack on feminism (the old, "all-feminists-are-too-ugly-to-get-themselves-a-man" line) and its attack on women in general',[24] what is noteworthy is how the main debate is centred on the woman question, an issue which takes precedence over and above everything else, despite the fact that the female voice remains predominantly silent.

By drawing attention to women and therefore allowing the women to have their say (albeit a 'silent' say), the two writers continue to share further common ground with a feminist perspective. According to Case, the aim of feminist critics and theatre historians is

> to make women visible, to find their voice, to recover the works that the dominant history suppressed and to explain the historical process of the suppression of women and its effect on their achievements. At the same time, critics used these political strategies to create new ways to read a play, to view a production and to deconstruct the canon of dramatic criticism.[25]

This is precisely where I believe we can establish a dialogue between the two authors and feminist thought. As this book will illustrate, Verga and Pirandello also *make women visible* and enable the women to *find their voices* on stage, even when the characters are physically absent or verbally silent. After an assessment of the different paths which could have led the pair to adapt their narratives for the stage in Chapter 1, Chapter 2 discusses what could have inspired Verga to produce his female stage roles, including the influence of tragic opera, the rising popularity of the *prima donna* and the *grande attrice*, and the emergent 'donne nuove' debates epitomised by the heroines in Henrik Ibsen's *A Doll's House* (1879) and later Sibilla Aleramo's *Una donna* (1906). Chapters 3 to 5 then examine how the new female voices in Verga's and Pirandello's theatre break away from three archetypal images of women: the innocent persecuted heroine, the silent obedient wife, and the mad sexual adulteress. By pointing out similar patterns inherent in the treatment of women in writings by both male and female authors, within and outside Italy, these chapters will shed light on how the dramatic adaptations pose a challenge to the way in which women have been traditionally portrayed in literature. In so doing, this approach will create new ways to read plays when examining the shift from the narrative genre to the theatrical, further deconstructing the canon of dramatic and feminist criticism. Moreover, it will illuminate how the newly vocalised female figures paved the way for a 'new' kind of woman who upset, problematised, and indeed complicated popular images typically associated with her gender and, through her agency — mainly her capacity to change her own circumstances or those of others — really was radical for her time.

By revealing the evolution of the new dramatic female roles and the added enrichment which results from the transfer to the stage, Chapter 6 concludes that Verga was one of the first playwrights to introduce New Italy to a 'new' woman on stage. It is proposed here that Verga's deliberate choice to place his female roles centre stage was symptomatic of an era which was providing fruitful grounds for such characters to flourish. To finish, I highlight how the characterisation of this 'new' woman was later developed by Verga's successor. As the different masks are peeled off, what we find in Pirandello is that the role of women is an ever-present constant. New light is thus thrown on his portrayal of the female voice, and this is seen as one of the key innovative factors that differentiates him from his predecessor, particularly in his theatrical revisionings where Pirandello seizes the opportunity of further articulating these voices and of deepening their resonances. This book therefore opens up new parameters, addressing questions such as why the narrative genre is so well suited to Verga's preoccupations, why the dramatic form is more effective in articulating Pirandello's *umorismo*, and what Pirandello's adaptations reveal about the ways in which he came to negotiate the transition from *verismo* to *umorismo*.

Notes to the Introduction

1. See in particular *Page to Stage: Theatre as Translation*, ed. by Ortrun Zuber-Skerritt (Amsterdam: Rodopi, 1984); *Constructing Culture: Essays on Literary Translation*, ed. by Susan Bassnett and André Lefevere (Clevedon: Multilingual Matters, 1996); Linda Hutcheon, *A Theory of Adaptation* (London and New York: Routledge, 2006); and more recently *Adapting Translation for the Stage*, ed. by Geraldine Brodie and Emma Cole (London and New York: Routlegde, 2017).
2. The main critical literature to consider Verga's transpositions includes Siro Ferrone, *Il teatro di Verga* (Rome: Bulzoni, 1972); Anna Barsotti, *Verga drammaturgo* (Florence: La nuova Italia, 1974); Francesca Malara, *Copioni e drammaturgie di fine ottocento* (Milan: Edizioni universitarie di Lettere Economia Diritto, 2000); and Guido Baldi, *Reietti e superuomini in scena* (Naples: Liguori, 2009). As for Pirandello, see above all Emanuele Licastro, *Luigi Pirandello dalle novelle alle commedie* (Verona: Fiorini, 1974); and Domenico Maceri, *Dalla novella alla commedia pirandelliana* (New York: Peter Lang Publishing, 1991).
3. The four pairs of text by Verga are 'Cavalleria rusticana' (1880) and *Cavalleria rusticana* (1884); 'Il canarino del n. 15' (1883) and *In portineria* (1885); 'La Lupa' (1880) and *La Lupa* (1896); and 'La caccia al lupo' (1897) and *La caccia al lupo* (1901). Those by Pirandello are: 'La Signora Frola e il Signor Ponza, suo genero' (1917) and *Così è (se vi pare)* (1917); 'Quando si è capito il giuoco' (1913) and *Il giuoco delle parti* (1918); 'Tutto per bene' (1906) and *Tutto per bene* (1919–1920); and '"Leonora, addio!"' (1910) and *Questa sera si recita a soggetto* (1928–1929).
4. Gayle Austin, *Feminist Theory for Dramatic Criticism* (Michigan: University of Michigan Press, 1990), p. 1.

5. Susan Amatangelo, *Figuring Women: A Thematic Study of Giovanni Verga's Female Characters* (Massachusetts: Rosemont Publishing and Printing Corp, 2004), p. 11.
6. See Giulio Cattaneo, *Giovanni Verga* (Turin: UTET, 1963), p. 95.
7. Ibid., p. 110.
8. Giovanni Verga, *Lettere a Paolina*, ed. by Gino Raya (Rome: Fermenti, 1980), p. 157
9. Maria Antonietta Grignani, 'Incursioni al femminile nei romanzi di Pirandello', in *La donna in Pirandello*, ed. by Stefano Milioto (Agrigento: Centro Nazionale Studi Pirandelliani, 1988), pp. 23–35 (p. 24).
10. Daniela Bini, 'Enacting the Dissolution of the Self: Woman as One, No One, and One Hundred Thousand', in *Luigi Pirandello: Contemporary Perspectives*, ed. by Gian-Paolo Biasin and Manuela Gieri (Toronto: University of Toronto Press, 1999), pp. 163–88 (p. 169).
11. Leonardo Bragaglia, *Interpreti pirandelliani (1910–1969): vita scenica delle commedie di Luigi Pirandello dalle origini ai giorni nostri* (Rome: Trevi, 1969), p. 259.
12. Susan Bassnett, 'Female Masks: Luigi Pirandello's Plays for Women', in *Twentieth-Century European Drama*, ed. by Brian Docherty (Basingstoke: Macmillan, 1994), pp. 13–25 (p. 14).
13. Ann Caesar, 'The Branding of Women: Family, Theatre and Female Identity in Pirandello', *Italian Studies*, 70 (1990), 48–63 (p. 63).
14. Bassnett, *Twentieth-century European Drama*, p. 15.
15. Eric Bentley, *The Pirandello Commentaries* (Evanston, Illinois: Northwestern University Press, 1986), pp. 11–12.
16. Sue-Ellen Case, *Feminism and Theatre* (London: Macmillan, 1988), pp. 121–22.
17. Pam Morris, *Literature and Feminism* (Oxford: Blackwell, 1993), p. 28.
18. Judith Fetterley, *The Resisting Reader: A Feminist Approach to American Fiction*, 1st Midland Book edn (Bloomington and London: Indiana University Press, 1978), p. xx.
19. See Giulio Herczeg, *Lo stile indiretto libero in italiano* (Florence: Sansoni, 1963); and Roy Pascal, *The Dual Voice: Free Indirect Speech and its Functioning in the Nineteenth-Century Novel* (Manchester: Manchester University Press, 1977).
20. Adriana Cavarero, *For More Than One Voice: Towards a Philosophy of Vocal Expression*, trans. with an intro. by Paul A. Kottman (Stanford: Sanford University Press, 2005), p. 95.
21. Ibid., p. 113.
22. Ibid., p. 107.
23. See Maggie Günsberg, 'Parla pure, papà: non ti sento', *The Yearbook of the British Pirandello Society*, 18–19 (1988–1989), 91–101; and Maggie Günsberg, *Patriarchal Representations: Gender and Discourse in Pirandello's Theatre* (Oxford: Berg, 1994), pp. 196–204.
24. Bassnett, *Twentieth-century European Drama*, p. 17.
25. Case, p. 113.

CHAPTER 1

From Page to Stage

Short Story, Stage, and Star

Many different paths might have led Verga and Pirandello to write for the theatre. One such may be traced to the part played by particular actresses. This chapter will explore the significant influence on the process of Eleonora Duse and Marta Abba, the muses who offered the authors, respectively, the means to transform their stories from page to performance. Verga, for example, experienced a number of challenges when writing for the stage and it was not until he met Duse that his plays began to gain notable critical attention. It is argued here that without the *grande attrice*, Verga might not have pursued his career as a playwright, nor created the kind of female voice to emerge from his dramatic adaptations. As for Pirandello, though Duse never performed in any of his plays, she nonetheless had a crucial impact on his developing views of the role of the actor and the merging of art and reality, embodying the ideal fusion of fiction and non-fiction which he came to see in Abba — a fusion that would later be at the heart of his groundbreaking metatheatre.

A Suitable Pairing

After finishing his doctoral studies at the University of Bonn in 1893, Pirandello took up residence in Rome and it was here that he first became acquainted with a variety of different writers, including the *veristi* Verga and Capuana, both of whom wrote largely about their native Sicily.¹ Verga was a major figure in this realist literary movement, and Pirandello would certainly have had to accommodate to his influence when he began writing his own fiction. From his arrival in Rome to approximately 1916, Pirandello, like the *veristi*, also drew his subject matter from his motherland, with the publications during this year of *Il berretto a sonagli*, *La giara*, and *Liolà*, which was considered by Antonio Gramsci as 'la migliore delle commedie che il teatro dialettale siciliano sia riuscito a creare' [the best play that Sicilian dialect theatre has managed to create].² But unlike Verga, Pirandello was not reluctant to employ dialect in his plays. He originally wrote *Liolà* in his local *Agrigentino* dialect in 1916 and produced a literal Italian translation which he placed alongside the original text, a parallel text he published a year later in 1917. However, dissatisfied with his translation,³ and in line with his earlier view in 'Teatro siciliano?' (1909)

that dialect literature 'è fatta per restare entro i confini del dialetto' [is made to remain within the confines of the dialect] (*Spsv*, p. 1168), Pirandello kept revising his use of Italian in 1928 and shortly before his death in 1936, leaving the Sicilian original untouched.[4]

Interestingly, Pirandello began writing in the wake of Verga's popularity. By the late nineteenth century, Verga had enjoyed considerable success for his narratives, namely for his *Vita dei campi* (1880), *I Malavoglia* (1881) and *Mastro don Gesualdo* (1888). What is more, Pirandello's popularity began to spread as Verga's writing was gradually coming to an end. In one of their final encounters, Pirandello offered Verga a copy of his new novel *Il fu Mattia Pascal* (1904) and, as the biographer Gaspare Giudice has pointed out:

> Verga, dopo qualche tempo, cortesemente e modestamente, gliene aveva scritto dicendo che la propria luce era quasi spenta e si accendeva all'orizzonte quella del giovane scrittore girgentano.[5]
>
> [Verga, after some time, obligingly and modestly, wrote to him saying that his own light would soon disappear, while that of the young writer from Agrigento was lighting up the horizon.]

As he matured as a writer, Pirandello broke away from the *verista* movement and its focus on the Sicilian peasantry to concentrate mainly on the Italian bourgeoisie. Perhaps this new choice of community offered him the possibility of adding an intellectual dimension to his fiction. He subsequently placed his protagonists in difficult situations, forcing them to use their reason — as opposed to their instinct — in order to find a solution. For example, instead of portraying the traditional husband-wife-lover triangular relationship, a popular subject among the *veristi* writers, Pirandello was keen to explore more ambiguous triangles, such as one involving husband, *late* wife, and lover, as is the case in *Tutto per bene*.

The first time that Pirandello publicly expressed his views about his predecessor was on 2 September 1920, when he was invited to deliver a speech at the Teatro Massimo Vincenzo Bellini in Catania in honour of Verga's eightieth birthday ('Discorso di Catania' in *Spsv*, pp. 409–26), and once more at the Reale Accademia d'Italia ('Discorso alla Reale Accademia d'Italia' in *Spsv*, pp. 391–406), on 3 December 1931, this time to commemorate the fiftieth anniversary of the publication of *I Malavoglia*. In the latter speech, Pirandello identified two groups of authors in Italy: those who adopted a 'stile di cose' [a style of things] (*Spsv*, p. 391), such as Dante, Machiavelli, Ariosto, Manzoni, and Verga, and those who adopted a 'stile di parole' [a style of words] (*Spsv*, p. 391), like Petrarch, Guicciardini, Tasso, Monti, and D'Annunzio. The authors who wrote in a 'stile di parole' employed an antiquated 'high', Petrarchan variety of Italian, what Pirandello had earlier called '[lo] scriver *bello*' [[w]riting *beautifully*] in his 1906 critical essay 'Soggettivismo e oggettivismo' (*Spsv*, p. 202), while those who employed a 'stile di cose' allowed their characters to speak in their natural, 'low', regional variety of Italian, what Pirandello this time referred to as '[lo] scriver *bene*' [writing *well*] (*Spsv*, p. 202). This is what Pirandello specifically admired about Verga. He praised Verga for allowing his Sicilian characters to speak in their idiosyncratic register and thus considered him 'il più "antiletterario" degli scrittori' [the most 'anti-literary' of writers] (*Spsv*, p. 394 and p. 415).

In typically Pirandellian manner, however, beneath these commendations lie some acid remarks:

> Fu detto anche che il Verga 'vede nella realtà il mondo quale esso è, e si spiega che non può essere diverso da quello che è' [...]. Bisognerebbe diffidare di noi stessi, della realtà del mondo posta da noi. Per sua fortuna il Verga non ne diffida; e perciò appunto non è, né può essere, nel senso vero e proprio della parola, un umorista. (*Spsv*, p. 399)
>
> [It was also said that Verga 'sees in reality the world as it is, and it is clear that it cannot be different from that which it is' [...]. We ought to doubt ourselves and the reality of the world as we see it. Fortunately for him, Verga has no such doubts, which is precisely why he is not — nor can he ever be, in the true and proper sense of the word — a humorist.]

These closing remarks stress a significant point of divergence between Pirandello and his predecessor. Pirandello here argues that Verga, along with the French Naturalists and the *veristi* writers, aimed at portraying only one view of reality in his fiction, without ever questioning what this view actually consisted of. Pirandello, on the other hand, mistrusted objective truth, and was more concerned with portraying a relativistic perspective in his fiction — one only has to think of the emergence of this perspective in *Il fu Mattia Pascal* and *Uno, nessuno e centomila* (1926). It was Pirandello's doubts about objective reality that led to his deviation from the *verista* movement, a deviation which was taken one step further as soon as he adapted his narratives into plays.

Verga's Passage to the Theatre

While the two authors differed in approach, both chose to transpose a large number of their short stories to the stage. In the case of Verga, it would seem that his dialogic narrative technique, his so-called 'racconto dialogato' [dialogued narrative] or 'dialogo raccontato' [narrated dialogue],[6] inspired him to write for the theatre which largely relies on speech. Indeed, Capuana, in his *Per l'arte* (1885), declared that 'gli scrittori che verranno dietro a noi ci accenderanno qualche cero, se non per altro, per l'esempio di *aver parlato* scrivendo' [the writers who will follow on after us will light a candle or two for us, if only for the example provided of *having spoken* while writing].[7]

What is, in fact, striking about Verga's short stories and novels are the different narrative voices. The narrative is mainly composed through free indirect speech. According to the linguist Giulio Herczeg: 'La novità del Verga consiste nel fatto che egli osa adoperare un discorso indiretto libero più vicino al diretto che non all'indiretto' [Verga's originality consists in the fact that he dares to use a type of free indirect speech which is closer to direct speech than to indirect speech].[8] Indeed, the popular narrator in Verga's short stories represents the choral voice of the villagers, as Gaetano Ragonese puts it: 'Chi parla non è più l'autore ma uno del popolo' [The person speaking is no longer the author but one of the people],[9] what Antonio Silvestro calls a 'portavoce dell'anima folclorica del villaggio' [spokesperson of the village's folkloristic spirit].[10] Moreover, to mimic the characters' spoken language, Verga employed a type of 'Sicilianised Italian': a form of Italian with a heavy dialectal imprint superimposed, like a sort of 'popular' or 'Regional' Italian.[11] This idiosyncratic register allowed Verga to both retain the local colour and enable his readers to taste the Sicilian flavour of his stories. In this way, the newly united Italian readership would be able to gain an understanding of Sicilian without having to read dialect.

In addition, what might have also contributed to Verga's move towards the theatre was his use of impersonality, a technique he outlines in the prelude to his short story 'L'amante di Gramigna' (1880) where he exposes the principles of *verismo*. Here, Verga sheds light on his intention to create his narratives as though they were a 'documento umano' (*Tn* I, p. 191) [human document], composed of 'parole semplici e pittoresche della narrazione popolare' (*Tn* I, p. 191) [simple and picturesque terms of popular narrative (*CROS*, p. 93)] so that the reader is 'faccia a faccia col fatto nudo e schietto, senza stare a cercarlo fra le linee del libro, attraverso la lente dello scrittore' (*Tn* I, p. 191) [confronted by the plain and simple facts rather than having to go searching for them between the lines with the lens of the writer (*CROS*, p. 93)]. According to Verga, 'il trionfo del romanzo' (*Tn* I, p. 192) [the triumph of the novel (*CROS*, p. 94)] lies in 'la sincerità della sua realtà' (*Tn* I, p. 192) [the sincerity of its reality (*CROS*, p. 94)] — the harsh realities seen through the eyes of the characters:

> [L]a mano dell'artista rimarrà assolutamente invisibile, e il romanzo avrà l'impronta dell'avvenimento reale, e l'opera d'arte sembrerà *essersi fatta da sé*, aver maturato ed esser sorta spontanea come un fatto naturale, senza serbare alcun punto di contatto col suo autore. (*Tn* I, p. 192)
>
> [[T]he hand of the artist will remain completely invisible. When that happens it will carry the imprint of the real event, the work of art will seem to have created itself, to have grown spontaneously and come to fruition as though it were part of nature, without preserving any point of contact with its author.] (*CROS*, p. 94)

By removing the author's hand, Verga strove to create the illusion that he was absent from the narrative and that the characters were recounting their own stories in their own words. It is therefore not by chance that his use of impersonality has been associated with the dramatic form. Federico De Roberto underlined in 1890 that '[l]'impersonalità non può conseguirsi che nel puro dialogo, e l'ideale della assoluta rappresentazione obbiettiva consiste nella *scena* come si scrive pel teatro' [impersonality cannot be accomplished except in pure dialogue, and the ideal of absolute objective representation consists in the *scene* as is written for the theatre].[12] In relation to Verga, Silvio D'Amico adds:

> Per naturale forza di cose il Verga narratore, raccontando e commentando sempre meno, e dando ai suoi personaggi una libertà sempre maggiore, vale a dire lasciando ch'essi vivessero e dicessero tutto da sé, s'è trovato necessariamente alle soglie del Teatro.[13]

[By natural force of circumstance Verga the storyteller, narrating and commenting less and less, and giving his characters an even greater freedom, that is to say leaving them to live and speak independently, unavoidably found himself at Theatre's doorstep.]

Verga himself associated his impersonal narrative technique with the theatre. In a letter to Nicola Scarano of 12 March 1915 about *I Malavoglia*, he explained the aim of the *veristi*: 'Dipingere il quadro coi colori adatti, in una parola, da cima a fondo, nella parlata degli attori e nella descrizione delle *scene* com'essi lo vedono, per vivere in loro e con loro' (*Ls*, p. 404, my italics) [To paint the picture with suitable colours, in other words, from top to bottom, in the actors' spoken language and in their description of the *scenes* as they see them, in order to live in them and with them]. By withdrawing 'la mano dell'artista' (*Tn* I, 192) [the hand of the artist (*CROS*, p. 94)] from the narrative and enabling what he calls the 'actors' to execute their scenes independently, Verga thus produced a kind of '*effetto della rappresentazione*' [*theatrical effect*].[14]

What is more, once the characters become autonomous, Verga also appeared to anticipate Pirandello's meta-theatre. As Pierluigi Pellini has observed:

> Portare alle estreme conseguenze il principio dell'impersonalità 'teatrale' significa aprire la strada ai più moderni esperimenti pirandelliani: quelli di Verga sono già, in parte, personaggi 'senza autore', che non trovano un giudice autorevole in grado di dare senso alla loro esistenza.[15]

> [Taking the principle of 'theatrical' impersonality to the extreme means opening the road to more modern Pirandellian experiments. Verga's characters are already, in part, 'without an author'; there is no authoritative judge to give meaning to their existence.]

To cite a few examples, in the opening extract from 'Nedda' (1874), Verga depicts himself sitting in his armchair in front of the fireplace, reminiscing about the olive picker, in the same way as Pirandello depicts himself meeting the peculiar character Dottor Fileno in 'La tragedia di un personaggio' (1911), one of the stories considered as the basis for *Sei personaggi in cerca d'autore* (1921) — others include 'Personaggi' (1906) and 'Colloquii coi personaggi' (1915). A similar impression is conveyed in 'Fantasticheria' (1880) where Verga reappears as a character as he recollects a trip to the fishing village of Aci Trezza with his aristocratic lady friend. The fishermen later return in *I Malavoglia*, forming a kind of story-within-a-story, just as other characters from his *Novelle rusticane* re-emerge in the short story 'Di là del mare'.[16]

Although in these examples, character and author are distinctly separate, Verga simultaneously intended to convey the impression that he was *at one* with the Sicilian community in his literature. Indeed, though he claimed to be impartial in his works, this does not necessarily make him a dispassionate writer. As he confided in a letter to his translator and close friend Édouard Rod on 14 July 1899, again about *I Malavoglia*: 'Ho cercato di mettermi nella pelle dei miei personaggi, vedere le cose coi loro occhi ed esprimerle colle loro parole' [I have tried to put myself in my characters' skin, to see things with their own eyes and to express them in their own words] (*Lt*, pp. 130–31). Verga continued to reveal to Rod the nostalgia he felt for Vizzini once his family left the fishing village following the cholera epidemic, illustrating his attempt to recapture his fond memories in his fiction:

> Così mi mescolai alla vita dei contadini [...] mi affezionavo alle brave persone che vedevo tutti i giorni: cercavo istintivamente di comprenderle. Più tardi queste impressioni della giovinezza mi ritornarono con una forza vivissima; fu allora che tentai di fissarle.[17]
>
> [And so I mingled with the country-folk [...] I grew fond of the honest people I saw every day: I instinctively tried to understand them. Later these impressions I had during my younger years came back to me very vividly; it was then that I tried to pin them down.]

Even though Verga's approach to his narrative seems to have naturally led him to write for the dramatic genre, overall he had a problematic relationship with the theatre. He clearly felt that transposing his *novelle* into plays compromised the artistic value of his work, as he confided to Capuana on 24 February 1888: '[C]'è sempre una diminuzione dell'opera d'arte, nel passare per un'altra interpretazione' [[T]here is always a diminution in the work of art, in passing through another interpretation] (*CVC*, p. 291). Verga, in fact, had a long history of unsuccessful attempts at staging plays well before the unprecedented success of *Cavalleria rusticana* in 1884. There has been much debate about when exactly Verga wrote his first play. According to Luigi Russo, this was *Rose caduche* (based on the novel *Una peccatrice* (1866)), which he believes was written between 1873 and 1875.[18] Lina Perroni, on the other hand, has argued that *Rose caduche* was composed several years earlier in 1869.[19] More recently, Lina Jannuzzi and Ninfa Leotta have documented all of Verga's published and un-published theatrical works, starting from his *Onore* also produced in 1869.[20] Giuseppe Petronio, however, has traced Verga's initial theatrical attempt to *I nuovi tartufi*, which he maintains was written in 1865.[21]

Perhaps Verga's struggle with the theatre was more of a struggle to write for a theatre audience. This was a time when the theatre, above all for the élite, was still considered a main source of entertainment. The problem for Verga, however, was that his theatre was not conventionally 'entertaining'. In *Cavalleria rusticana*, for example, he risked making contemporary audiences feel uncomfortable through his depiction of Sicily's fight for survival shortly after political unification in 1861 when, to some extent, the island was arguably left to govern itself. This is what might have led Verga in a letter to Rod of 10 January 1884 to expose his hesitations just before the première of the play. While he was composing his narratives, he was, as he put it, 'faccia a faccia col lettore' [face-to-face with the reader], but now, writing for the stage, 'le mie idee devono passare per degli interpreti né convinti né audaci forse come me' [my ideas have to pass through interpreters who are not as convinced or as bold as I am] (*Lt*, p. 80).

Again, in a letter of 22 May 1884 this time to his French contemporary Émile Zola, who shared a similar opinion in his critical essay 'Le naturalisme au théâtre' (1880),[22] Verga argued that 'le théâtre, comme œuvre littéraire, est de beaucoup inférieur au roman' [the theatre, as a work of literature, is far inferior to the novel] (*Ls*, p. 163), a viewpoint he continued to assert four years later on 15 June 1888 to the *verista* Felice Cameroni: '[A]llora basta — e torneremo ai nostri personaggi d'inchiostro e di carta che parlano meglio, dicono di più e sono quello che sono' [[E]nough is enough — and so we'll return to our characters in ink and paper who speak better, say more and are what they are] (*Lt*, pp. 203–04). Several years after that, in 1894, Verga elaborated on his doubts about writing for a theatre audience during an interview with Ugo Ojetti about his play *Dal mio al tuo*:

> Ho scritto pel teatro, ma non lo credo certamente una forma d'arte superiore al romanzo, anzi lo stimo una forma inferiore e primitiva, sopra tutto per alcune ragioni che dirò meccaniche. Due massimamente: la necessità dell'intermediario tra autore e pubblico, dell'attore; la necessità di scrivere non per un lettore ideale come avviene nel romanzo, ma per un pubblico radunato a folla così da dover pensare a una media di intelligenza e di gusto, a un *average reader*, come dicono gli inglesi.[23]

> [I have written for the theatre, but I certainly do not believe that it is a form of art superior to the novel. On the contrary, I consider it an inferior and primitive form, above all for several reasons which I will call mechanical. Namely two reasons: the need to have an intermediary between the author and public, that is the actor; and the need to write not for an ideal reader as occurs with the novel, but for an audience brought together in a crowd, in such a way that one must think of an average level of intelligence and taste, of an *average reader* as the English say.]

In the preface of *Dal mio al tuo* in 1906, he expressed a similar view:

> [Il] lettore [è] miglior giudice spesso, certo più sereno, faccia a faccia colla pagina scritta che gli dice e gli fa vedere assai più della scena dipinta, senza suggestione di folla e senza le modificazioni — in meglio o in peggio poco importa — che subisce necessariamente l'opera d'arte passando per un altro temperamento d'artista onde essere interpretata.[24]

> [Readers are often better judges, certainly more impartial, when confronted with the written page, which speaks to them and enables them to see a lot more than a painted set, without any persuasion from a crowd and without any of the changes — whether for better or for worse it does not matter — which the work of art inevitably undergoes when it passes through another artistic temperament to be interpreted].

Consequently, it would appear that the main cause of Verga's problematic relationship with the theatrical genre was intrinsically linked with his use of language. As Natalino Sapegno points out: 'Il Verga sentì sempre i problemi della sua arte molto concretamente come problemi di linguaggio, e cioè di rapporto con un pubblico determinato' [Verga always perceived the problems of his art in concrete terms, as problems of language; a problem therefore of his relationship with a specific audience].[25] Indeed, Verga knew well that his innovative Sicilianised-Italian could not be so easily adopted in his plays. The average spectator would not have expected to decode the dialectal register on a night out at the theatre, and if Verga targeted a purely Sicilian audience by writing in dialect, he would have considerably reduced his number of spectators.

As a result of his reservations, it has been agreed that Verga did not have a vocation for the theatre. As Silvana Monti has concluded: 'La "vocazione" del Verga per il teatro è condizionata dal fatto che tutta la borghesia italiana dell'Ottocento era legata al mondo dello spettacolo' [Verga's 'calling' for the theatre is conditioned by the fact that all of Italy's bourgeoisie in the nineteenth century was wedded to the world of theatre].[26] Similarly, according to Carmelo Musumarra:

> Il Verga non ebbe la vocazione del teatro, e se scrisse per le scene lo fece quasi per un dovere d'ufficio come avevano fatto i suoi amici Giacosa e Capuana e altri, in quanto uno scrittore degno di questo nome, a quei tempi, doveva affrontare direttamente il pubblico delle platee.[27]

> [Verga did not have a calling for the theatre; he wrote for the stage almost as an official duty just as his friends Giacosa and Capuana and others had done, in that a writer worthy of the name, at that time, had to directly confront the spectators in the auditoriums.]

In fact in the nineteenth and early twentieth century, the popularity of the theatre soared and subsequently the need for material prevailed. Perhaps as a thriving writer, Verga felt obliged to write for this popular medium, even for financial reasons. As he mentioned to Capuana in a letter of 29 October 1883: 'Quello che ti potrebbe interessare per un altro verso è che il teatro è la sola cosa che possa fruttare materialmente alla letteratura' [What might interest you, on the other hand, is that the theatre is the one thing that can yield a return, materially speaking, in literature] (*CVC*, p. 208). But if Verga really had no vocation for the theatre, considering the dramatic genre an inferior form of art, why would he continue to adapt his narratives into plays? Was it simply for financial reasons?

Arguably, some of the answers to these questions can be traced in his correspondence. In one of his letters to Felice Cameroni on 20 April 1890 composed several years after *Cavalleria rusticana* (1884) and *In portineria* (1885), Verga wrote:

> Ahimè!, mi tenta ancora il sogno di questa forma dell'arte comunicativa ed efficacissima, la realizzazione di un pubblico intelligente e di una collaborazione perfetta tra autore e comici. (*Ls*, p. 244)

> [Alas! The dream of this communicative and very effective form of art still tempts me: the realisation of an intelligent audience and of a perfect collaboration between author and actors.]

From this, it seems that what tempted Verga to write for the theatre was the collaboration between author, actors, and what he calls an 'intelligent' audience. In a letter to Capuana of 7 July 1885, only a year after the success of *Cavalleria rusticana* and just before the première of *In portineria*, Verga had already thought carefully about what he meant by an intelligent audience, describing his ideal spectators as 'un pubblico scelto e intelligente, non numeroso, non guastato dalle coltellate della *Cavalleria rusticana* e che non è venuto in teatro per vedere mordere l'orecchio a compare Alfio' [a select and intelligent audience, not great in number, not tainted by the terrible stabbing in *Cavalleria rusticana* and which has not come to the theatre to see Compare Alfio's ear being bitten] (*CVC*, p. 242). Verga here not only preferred to write for a select few, but seemed to reproach his own art, mainly his *coup de théâtre* in *Cavalleria rusticana*, for having 'played the game' by satisfying this average spectator.

Moreover, Verga details in the above letter to Capuana what kind of actor would participate in his ideal collaboration, an interpretation 'dalla Duse o da una Duse maschio — l'Andò è troppo attore ancora' [by Duse or a male version of Duse — Andò is still too much of a theatrical actor] (*CVC*, p. 242). And this brings us closer to understanding what actually tempted Verga to write for the theatre. If, as Verga revealed to Cameroni, the main temptation was that of writing for 'un pubblico intelligente' [an intelligent audience] and forming 'una collaborazione perfetta tra autore e comici' [a perfect collaboration between author and actors] (*Ls*, p. 244), what Verga was really saying — drawing from his letter to Capuana — was that a small-sized 'intelligent' audience tempted him to produce plays, together with a 'perfect collaboration' between himself and his actors, or, more specifically, Duse.

Such collaborations were particularly desirable because of the especially powerful role played by actors in the theatre system in late nineteenth-century Italy. The influence of the actor was exceptionally strong during this period, arguably because of Italy's socio-linguistic history. Prior to unification, Italy had been dismissed by Prince Metternich at the 1815 Congress of Vienna as no more than a 'geographical expression',[28] an agglomeration of unstable regions and states: the Austrian-controlled North, the Papal States of Central Italy, and the Kingdom of the Two Sicilies in the South. Political fragmentation was also mirrored linguistically. Despite efforts by the Cinquecento humanist Pietro Bembo to establish the Florentine of the *tre corone* (Dante, Boccaccio, and Petrarch) as the Italian literary standard, after 1861 the majority of Italians spoke in dialect. Tullio De Mauro has estimated that, in the wake of Italy's relatively late unification, approximately 2.5% of the population was able to speak Italian.[29] This political and linguistic disunity had inevitable implications for Italian theatre. For a medium so reliant on speech, the lack of a common spoken language would seem to inhibit the growth of an early national theatre, a growth hindered further following the collapse of public subsidies for the performing arts in unified Italy.[30] In fact, many *mattatore* companies of the nineteenth century favoured touring abroad, in theatres around Europe and in North and South America.[31] As a result, only two forms of Italian drama met with any notable success in and outside Italy when, subsequently, they were taken out into a global market. These were the *commedia dell'arte* and opera, both of which subordinate the importance of the spoken word to, respectively, body language and music.[32] Though, like Verga, there was some early attempt to fill in this gap, particularly by Paolo Giacometti's *La morte civile* (1861), Achille Torelli's *I mariti* (1875), and later by Marco Praga, Giuseppe Giacosa, Vittorio Bersezio, as well as Giacinto Gallina,[33] ultimately, nineteenth-century Italy was not generating its own major playwrights in this period, equivalent to Dumas, for example.[34]

The lack of a common tongue consequently lent added importance to gesture over speech on stage, and helped cultivate an actor's theatre, 'il teatro dell'attore' [the Theatre of the Actor], in which audiences were drawn not by the play *per sé* but by the star actors, especially Adelaide Ristori, Ernesto Rossi, and Tommaso Salvini, whose performances became the central ingredient of any production. According to Cesare Molinari, 'parlando di teatro di attore ci si riferisce a quel genere di teatro in cui la funzione progettuale è affidata all'attore' [speaking about the theatre of the actor one refers to that dramatic genre where the main responsibility falls on the actor].[35] Hence, more importance was placed on the *actions* of the actors to convey the meaning of the play, as opposed to the actual *words* of their script, a dramatic technique for which Duse became renowned.

Verga's Muse: Eleonora Duse

From Verga's correspondence, we can confirm that Duse was at the heart of his decision to adapt *Cavalleria rusticana* for the stage. In fact, he already had the actress in mind to interpret the lead role well before the première at the Teatro Carignano in Turin on 14 January 1884. In a letter to Giacosa of 8 October 1883, he asked whether Duse '[v]orrà e potrà recitare una mia cosa in un atto o due a Roma nel prossimo novembre' [would want and able to perform something of mine in one or two acts in Rome next Novermber] (*Ls*, pp. 146–47). Giacosa certainly played the intermediary and encouraged Verga to include a part for Duse: 'Ti giuro che con un'attrice come la Duse si possono far meraviglie, meraviglie' [I promise you that with an actress like Duse, one can do wonders, wonders].[36] Later, in a letter of 15 November 1883, Giacosa informed Verga of the director Cesare Rossi's doubts about the play, highlighting that 'la Duse ha subito l'influenza del suo capocomico ed anch'essa presagisce una caduta' [Duse has been influenced by her director and she also forsees a fiasco], and that she was 'timidissima nel giudicare dell'opera finché non è rappresentata e d'altronde teme, incoraggiandoti, di assumere responsabilità' [very reluctant to judge the play until it has been performed and, moreover, is afraid that, by encouraging you, she will be held responsible].[37] In spite of her reservations, Duse eventually accepted the part of Santuzza. The biographer Alfred Alexander has argued that once she took on this role, Verga felt the need to develop Santuzza's character, which was only thinly sketched in the narrative, so as to give the star actress 'the opportunity to show her art'.[38]

Following Duse's acceptance of the role, Verga worked closely with the actors to ensure a convincing amalgamation of the Sicilian countryside community and the bourgeois world of the theatre. He was very much aware that the diva's interpretation of the village girl had to be kept simple in order to reflect the nature of her character. As he revealed in a letter to Capuana on 18 August 1884:

> [Q]uesta commediola va *recitata male* per essere *resa bene*, cioè senza enfasi né effetti teatrali. Io voglio la stessa semplicità e la stessa naturalezza della gente che parli e si muova come i contadini e non sappia di recitare. (*CVC*, p. 227–28)

> [[T]his short play has to be *performed badly* in order to be *conveyed well*, that is without any embellishments or theatrical effects. I want the same simplicity and naturalness of the people who speak and move like country-folk and do not know that they are acting.]

In fact, for the première Verga took a hands-on approach to directing the play in order to ensure what he called in a letter to Giacosa of 18 November 1883 'quella fusione ch'è indispensabile a rendere il *quadro* come lo vedo io' [that fusion which is indispensable in order to convey the *picture* as I see it] (*Ls*, p. 151). He even personally took charge of the actors' costumes with the help of Capuana and his brother Mario, specifying in letters what each actor, including Duse, should wear and giving specific measurements for all of the costumes.[39]

Following the opening night, Giacosa's predictions came true. Eugenio Torelli-Viollier congratulated Verga in the *Corriere della sera* on his unprecedented success and attributed a large part of the triumph to Duse, '[chi] fece fremere e piangere gli spettatori' [[who] made the spectators shiver and weep].[40] Audiences in Italy, and later around the world, reacted so positively to Duse that Verga once said to her: '*Cavalleria rusticana* appartiene più a te che a me' [*Cavalleria rusticana* belongs more to you than it does to me].[41]

Different from other actresses, such as Aliprandi Pieri and Annetta Campi who were criticized for their lack-lustre interpretations of Santuzza,[42] Duse, by contrast, gave a more passionate rendition, particularly during the scene in which she reveals the truth about the adultery. According to a review in the *Corriere della sera*, on 30–31 October 1888, Duse became over-expressive and ran around the stage in an agitated and desperate way.[43] During her performance in Paris, she was described in *Le Gaulois* on 1 July 1897 as being 'humble, douce, timide, puis ardente, sauvage d'une sauvagerie farouche, désespérée, furieuse, puis écrasée sous le remords' [humble, gentle, shy, then ardent, wild to a ferocious degree, desperate, furious, then crushed with remorse].[44]

Her performances, however, were not as 'wild' as those of her Sicilian contemporaries, in particular the actress Mimì Aguglia.[45] As the British theatre critic, Arthur Symons, pointed out, 'to see her [Aguglia] after the Santuzza of Duse [...] is to realise the difference between this art of the animal and Duse's art of the soul'.[46] Symons goes on to describe Aguglia's 'furious wrestle with her lover' and her 'unanticipated knife into his heart',[47] actions which are not included in the original script. Indeed, the Sicilian troupes worked in a mostly oral tradition, improvising their lines from one scene to the next,[48] and from the description above, it seems that Aguglia, like her co-star Giovanni Grasso, took this tradition to the extreme, something which evidently irritated Verga. During Grasso's 1908 tour in Paris, for instance, Verga was so horrified by his 'bloody' performances in both *Cavalleria rusticana* and *La Lupa* that he withdrew all his plays from the actor.[49] In fact, though Verga never produced an official version of the play in dialect (unlike Mascagni who, in his operatic adaptation, retained the use of dialect only in the prelude 'La Siciliana'), and adamantly believed that targeting a purely Sicilian audience in dialect would be 'una diminuzione' [a diminution],[50] he nonetheless gave directors and leading actors permission to translate his plays into Sicilian,[51] to which contemporary audiences responded extremely well: '*Cavalleria rusticana*, recitato in dialetto, acquistava maggiore umanità e colore della celebrata esecuzione in italiano' [*Cavalleria rusticana*, performed in dialect, acquired more humanity and colour compared to the famed version in Italian].[52] Despite the success, Verga always insisted that he had no intention of composing the play in dialect, as he explained in an interview in Palermo for the newspaper *L'ora* on 12 February 1909 where he spoke of 'quella *Cavalleria* che mai sognai scrivere per Teatro dialettale' [that *Cavalleria* which I never dreamt about writing for Dialect Theatre].[53]

Unlike the Sicilian troupes, Duse, instead, was said to personify the role of Santuzza, moving her body just as the character would have done herself. Symons in his review shed light on her 'unconscious hand',[54] which appeared to instinctively fold over Turiddu's sleeve.[55] Another critic, the German Herman Bang, also recollected how Duse in the role of Santuzza seemed to spontaneously twist her handkerchief while leaning against a wall.[56] Duse herself admitted that, at the end of her performances, the most tired parts of her body were her hands.[57] In his article 'Eleonora Duse: Actress Supreme', first published in *The Century Magazine* shortly after the actress's death in 1924, Pirandello (known by his contemporaries as 'una Duse coi pantaloni' [a Duse in trousers]),[58] called her hands 'divine hands, that seemed to talk'.[59]

Several others stressed how Duse appeared so fused within her roles that her physiological features allegedly changed during her performances. Her facial expressions powerfully conveyed Santuzza's profound remorse as she betrays Turiddu. Her fellow actor Luigi Rasi remembered her '*faccia convulsiva*' [*contorted face*], '[l]'occhio agitato da tremiti impercettibili' [her eye flickering with imperceptible tremors], and 'le guancie [che] passavano con incredibile rapidità dal rossore al pallore' [her cheeks [that] changed colour with incredible speed from red to pallor], which enabled her to give an authentic portrayal 'dei personaggi *a temperamento isterico*' [of characters of *a hysterical temperament*].[60] As a result, Molinari has argued that it was the actress herself who created the role,[61] and Susan Bassnett has concluded that the actress's seemingly natural responses on stage represented how she felt 'totally at one with her character'.[62]

Anna Sica has proposed that Duse's 'one-ness' with her roles was based on the declamation system *La drammatica*.[63] Indeed, many other of the actress's contemporaries pointed to Duse's careful 'study' of her roles. According to the British critic William Archer in 1894, her dramatic technique was deliberately controlled: '[W]hile it has the appearance of absolute nature — while for the moment it is nature — [it] is at the same time the outcome of conscious, deliberate study and art'.[64] *The Era* on 26 May 1894 also attributed Duse's acting to an actual study: '[H]er conception of the character is truthful, simple and natural — a study, in fact, of lower class life in Italy worked out in every detail, with artistic conscientiousness'. Likewise, *The Pall Mall Gazette* on 24 May stressed Duse's 'mechanical' style:

> Signora Duse's acting has this much of the mechanical underlying all its marvellous appearance of simplicity that it is almost unvarying in its fineness, unaltered in its subtlety. Her creation of any given character never seems to vary; it is always a work of genius.[65]

A *verista*, though, who was unconvinced by Duse's interpretation was Capuana. Recalling a production he had seen in Sicily, he argued that the non-professional actress, performing the role of Santuzza in her mother-tongue dialect, appeared more genuine and authentic than the star actress: 'Ebbene, "Santuzza-Duse", ai miei occhi di siciliano, era risultata una specie di falsificazione della appassionata creatura di Giovanni Verga, nei gesti, nella espressione della voce, nei vestiti' ['Santuzza-Duse', therefore, seemed to my Sicilian eyes to be a sort of falsification of Giovanni Verga's passionate creature, in her gestures, in the expression of her voice, in her costume].[66]

Verga was nevertheless pleased with Duse's interpretation, praising how she 'prese a cuore le mie parti' [took my roles to heart] in a letter to Gegè Primoli of 24 January 1884 (*Ls*, p. 156). Indeed, it was only a matter of time before one of the most naturalistic writers in nineteenth-century Italy would meet one of the most naturalistic actresses to emerge from the Italian stage. Both aimed to convey a sort of mimesis in their art, seeing the action through the characters' eyes and expressing the characters' suffering in their own words, engaged in what Donatella Orecchia has called a 'ricerca parallela';[67] that is, a 'parallel search' for portraying reality on stage.

In the same way as *Cavalleria rusticana* was written for the interpretation of Duse, so was *In portineria*, which premièred on 16 May 1885 at the Teatro Manzoni in Milan. In a letter cited earlier to Giacosa in 1883 — 'Vorrà e potrà recitare una mia cosa in un atto *o due* a Roma nel prossimo novembre?' [Will [Duse] want and be able to perform a thing of mine in one *or two* acts in Rome next November?] (*Ls*, pp. 146–47, my italics) — Verga appeared to imply that his second play was also written for the star actress.[68] Suspicions are confirmed when, in a further letter to Primoli of 8 March 1885, he admitted: 'Figurati se vorrei dare la Duse il mio lavoro [*In portineria*]! L'ho avuta sempre dinanzi agli occhi, nello scriverla' [Of course I would like Duse to interpret my work [*In portineria*]! I had her before my eyes the whole time I was writing it] (*Ls*, p. 174). Verga clearly valued her acting, as he revealed to Capuana on 5 June 1885: '[D]'interpreti adatti sinora non ne abbiamo che una: La Duse. Certo il secondo atto di *In portineria* non può essere fatto accettare che da lei' [[S]o far we have only one suitable interpreter: Duse. Of course the second act in *In portineria* will not be well-received unless it is performed by her] (*LC*, p. 209).

Just as Santuzza became identified with Duse, so did the role of Màlia, as Orecchia has pointed out:

> Un ritratto questo di Màlia e insieme, crediamo, un ritratto di quella Duse che Verga ha visto e che immagina, che in parte ha conosciuto e che in parte desidera: la Duse dell'attenzione al dettaglio, che si sottrae all'effetto scenico, che esprime solo con la mobilità del volto e degli occhi turbamenti, pensieri, gioie e dolori che l'attraversano.[69]

> [This is a portrait of Màlia and also — we believe — a portrait of that Duse whom Verga had seen and imagined, whom in part he had met and in part desired: the Duse characterised by attention to detail, who does not deal in stage effects, who gives expression to moods, thoughts, joys and griefs merely with the movement of her face and eyes].

In portineria, however, did not open with Duse but with the actress Olga Lugo, who starred as Màlia alongside Enrico Reinach. Unlike in the case of *Cavalleria rusticana*, early performances of *In portineria* were generally unsuccessful. Following its première, Torelli-Viollier in the *Corriere della sera* on 17 May 1885 pointed to the overall dissatisfaction among audiences: 'Ci furono risate ironiche e perfino qualche voce di "basta". L'ultima scena, nella quale gli amici dell'autore fidavano molto, parve crudele; il sipario calò tra le disapprovazioni' [There was ironic laughter and even the odd 'enough!'. The last scene, in which the author's friends very much had faith, seemed cruel; the curtain fell amidst expressions of disapproval].[70] Similarly, Cameroni, also in the *Corriere della sera*, wrote: 'Il primo atto passò in silenzio. Il secondo destò più volte segni di stanchezza e di disapprovazione' [The first act was greeted in silence. The second aroused on various occasions signs of boredom and disapproval],[71] concluding that it was a '[b]rutta serata quella di ieri per l'indirizzo della letteratura drammatica' [[b]ad night, last night, for the development of dramatic literature].[72] Verga himself acknowledged the poor reception. Writing to Capuana on 7 July 1885, he mentioned how the spectators 'hanno riso a quella informe' [laughed at the disabled character] (*CVC*, p. 245).

Duse performed the role a year later on 1 December 1886 at the Teatro Valle in Rome with Flavio Andò. What was significant about her interpretation was how she altered the predominantly negative reviews. Critics and audiences were struck, above all, by her interpretation of Màlia's death. On 2 December 1886, the *Corriere della sera* praised the way in which 'la Duse si abbandonò con inerte mollezza in braccio alla sorella' [Duse let herself fall into her sister's arms lifelessly] and the following day, Boutet, in the same newspaper, wrote: '[M]orì come si muore [...] non si va più oltre' [[S]he died as people do die [...] one cannot get better than this].[73] A few days later, on 4 December, in the *L'arte drammatica*, a further review revealed that Duse 'è stata una tisichella incantevole [...] per i suoi sguardi, per i suoi sorrisi che morivano sulle labbra pallide' [was an enchanting consumptive girl [...] with her gaze, with her smiles which died on her pale lips].[74]

In changing the audience's unenthusiastic response, Duse was able momentarily to 'rescue' the play. As Raffaello Barbiera puts it: '*In portineria* ebbe in Eleonora Duse un'interprete somma e una salvatrice almeno momentanea' [*In portineria* had in Eleonora Duse an outstanding interpreter and a saviour, albeit temporary].[75] Indeed, as Cesare Levi observed, Duse's performance 'piacque al pubblico, ma non ebbe la forza da rimanere a lungo sulle scene' [was liked by the public, but did not have the strength to remain on stage for long].[76] In fact, after this Duse never played *In portineria* again, something which inevitably disappointed Verga. As he confided to Cameroni on 4 January 1890: '[M]i duole dell'ingiustizia dei molti verso la povera *Portineria*, e mi duole che ingiusta le sia pure la Duse che pure dovrebbe avere senso d'artista' [I am saddened by how unjust many people have been to my poor *Portineria*, and by the fact that Duse too is unjust towards it, even though she should have more artistic sense] (*Ls*, p. 236). In Molinari's biography, he claims that 'il personaggio di Màlia, troppo monodico e privo di spessore, non deve aver affascinato in modo particolare la Duse [the character of Màlia, too monotone and lacking in substance, cannot have particularly charmed Duse],[77] and even suggests that *In portineria* brought to life one of Duse's personal fears of being 'morta prima di morire' [dead before her death].[78]

Though Duse kept the role of Santuzza in her early national and international repertoire, her interest in Verga's theatre soon came to an end. Several biographers have offered different reasons for this. According to William Weaver, 'Duse's tastes did not coincide with the harsh realism of this literary movement'.[79] Similarly, Giovanni Pontiero explains that following the triumph of *Cavalleria rusticana*, 'Duse soon lost interest in plays with a regional flavour'.[80] Indeed, Duse was constantly looking out for new roles and innovation: by the late-1880s, she was beginning to collaborate with Arrigo Boito on his experimental adaptation of *Antony and Cleopatra*, after which she began working for Gabriele D'Annunzio, both engaged in developing a new type of non-realistic, Symbolist, Italian theatre.

So in contrast to the unanimous view that Verga lacked a vocation for the dramatic form, it seems that he *did* have a vocation — thanks to Duse. Without her, his theatre might not have developed in the way it did. Had the actress continued to perform Verga's roles, arguably the critical response to his subsequent plays, in particular *La Lupa*, would have been different. As Natale Tedesco concludes: '[S]e il personaggio della Gnà Pina fosse stato impersonato dalla Duse, si sarebbe meglio capita la funzione del protagonismo femminile nella drammaturgia verghiana' [[I]f the character of Gnà Pina had been interpreted by Duse, it would have been easier to understand why Verga gives leading roles to women in his plays].[81]

Pirandello's Passage to the Theatre

Unlike Verga, Pirandello took to the theatre more smoothly, despite identifying himself more as a narrative prose writer in the early stages of his career. After completing the play '*U cuccu*, Pirandello in a letter of 18 August 1916 confided to his son Stefano, who was by now a prisoner of war in Mauthausen, that he wanted to close 'questa parentesi teatrale per rimettermi al mio più naturale lavoro di narratore' [this theatrical aside in order to get back to my more natural work as a narrator].[82] Writing again to his son, on 24 October 1916, he described *Liolà* simply as his 'villeggiatura' [holiday].[83] Indeed, the number of his publications supports his early preference for narrative: during his lifetime, he wrote 44 plays and 246 *novelle*, now collected in his *Novelle per un anno* (1922).[84] However, as Jørn Moestrup has noted, once Pirandello began to establish his name as a playwright, his narrative production declined considerably.[85]

Having written a series of articles on the nature of the *novella*, including his early essays 'Romanzo, racconto, novella' (1897) and 'Fede e bellezza' (1898), Pirandello thought carefully about the narrative genre. He clearly valued the *novella*, as he expressed in 'Novelle e novellieri' (1906): 'Una buona novella può dare, alla lettura, più squisita e più intensa soddisfazione anche d'un bel romanzo' [A good short story can, when read, give a more exquisite and more intense feeling of satisfaction than a good book] (*Si*, p. 515), but was aware that 'una buona novella è rara appunto per la sua brevità' [a good short story is rare precisely because of its succinctness] (*Si*, p. 515).

Interestingly, Pirandello's views on the dialogic *novella* are very different. In 'Soggettivismo e oggettivismo nell'arte narrativa', and later in 'Novelle e novellieri', he argued that

> la novella dialogata, quantunque più vicina esteriormente alla forma drammatica, è però la più lontana che si possa immaginare dal rigor sintetico della tragedia unitaria. Sì, essa vorrebbe condensare, anche troppo: tutta una novella, in una sola scena. Ma riesce spesso una scena staccata e quasi inorganica. Non sorretta più dal congegno narrativo, va su i lievi trampoli descrittivi delle didascalie, pestando un po' troppo in vero quel volgare tappeto che è lo stile conversativo alla francese. E per voler troppo condensare da una parte è costretta a diluirsi soverchiamente dall'altra. (*Spsv*, p. 203, and *Si*, p. 517, with slight rewordings)
>
> [the dialogic *novella*, however closer it is outwardly to the dramatic form, is nonetheless the furthest away that one can imagine from the synthetic rigour of tragedy with its three unities. Yes, it would like to condense the events, even too much: condensing the entire *novella* into just one scene. But often this results in a detached and almost inorganic scene. No longer sustained by the narrative structure, the dialogic *novella* relies on the descriptive support of stage directions and comes too close, in fact, to the conversational style of the French. And by striving for too much condensing in one area, it is forced to dilute excessively in another.]

This viewpoint is perhaps an indirect critique of the *veristi* writers, whose narratives took their synthetic stamp from the conversational style of the French Naturalists and condensed the main action to 'una sola scena' [just one scene]. However, Pirandello's attitude towards the *novella dialogata* is somewhat ambivalent, as certain features he criticises can be found in his own short stories. In 'Quando si è capito il giuoco', for example, Pirandello does not offer any background information on the protagonists, nor does he develop their characterisations. Instead, he seems to portray the course of events in 'una sola scena' [just one scene], and it is not until he transforms the narrative to a play that he expands on the antecedent facts and provides a detailed account of all the main characters.

Also ambivalent are Pirandello's views on the tradition of transposing works from narrative to theatre, which, as he knew well, was another practice used by many writers in the nineteenth century, including the Naturalists and *veristi*. In the opening paragraph of 'L'azione parlata' (1899), he underlines that 'una favola d'indole narrativa, in generale, mal si lascia ridurre e adattare al congegno delle scene' [a tale of a narrative nature, in general, is not easily reduced and adapted to the mechanisms of the stage] (*Spsv*, p. 981). This point of view might have further complicated his decision to transpose his *novelle* into plays, but it could equally well be argued that in these critical essays, he was actually experimenting with the possibility of exploiting the dramatic aspect of his narrative in his later stage adaptations.

Pirandello was also concerned with the finding the right spoken word for his characters,[86] that is 'la frase unica, che non può esser che quella, propria a quel dato personaggio in quella data situazione' [the unique phrase, which cannot be but that, suited to the given characters in the given situation] (*Spsv*, p. 982), as he continues to explain in 'L'azione parlata'. Later, in 'Teatro e letteratura' (1918), Pirandello elaborates on this notion: 'Bisogna far parlare i personaggi come, dato il loro carattere, dato le loro qualità e condizioni, nei varii momenti dell'azione, *debbono* parlare' [One needs to make characters speak as they *should* speak, given their personality, qualities and conditions in various moments of the action] (*Spsv*, p. 986). Moreover, not only was he concerned with finding appropriate spoken words, but with making these words explode on stage, something he was unable to achieve when writing prose.[87] As he maintained in an interview for the Parisian journal *Le Temps* on 20 July 1925 where he talked about the war inspiring him to adapt his work for the stage: 'Les mots ne pouvaient plus demeurer écrits sur le papier, il fallait qu'ils éclatassent dans l'air, dits ou criés' [My words could no longer remain written on paper, it was necessary for them to explode in the air, spoken or cried out aloud].[88]

Pirandello's 'explosive' approach to drama would seem to further develop his *umorista* views expressed in 'L'umorismo', originally published in 1908 but revised in 1920. As he illustrates in this critical essay, the *umorista* seeks to investigate what lies beneath the exterior mask, challenging the realist concept that what is on the outside corresponds to what is in the inside. Through what is called '[il] *sentimento del contrario*' [[the] *feeling of the opposite*] (*Spsv*, p. 127), the *umorista* is aware that what is exposed on the surface may reveal the opposite of what is concealed underneath and thus attempts to gain an understanding of the hidden suffering, a notion crystallised by the description of the 'vecchia signora' [elderly lady] (*Spsv*, p. 127) which was introduced into the second edition of the essay. Pirandello here gives the example of an elderly lady, heavily made up to look much younger than she is, so that the ambiguity of her appearance arouses laughter in the comic. The *umorista*, on the other hand, pays close attention to *why* she is parading herself like this and, through '[il] *sentimento del contrario*' [[the] *feeling of the opposite*] (*Spsv*, p. 127), acknowledges that she dresses in such a way because she is afraid of losing her younger husband. As a result, the *umorista* cannot react in the same way as the comic.

Another 'humorist' concept enhanced on stage is what Pirandello's contemporary critic, Adriano Tilgher, calls *vedersi vivere* [*seeing oneself live*]:[89]

> Che cosa, secondo Pirandello, distingue l'uomo dagli altri esseri della natura? Questo, e questo soltanto: che l'uomo vive e si sente vivere, e gli altri esseri della natura, invece, vivono puramente e semplicemente.[90]
>
> [What, according to Pirandello, distinguishes man from other beings in the natural world? This, and only this: that man lives and is aware of living, and the other beings from the natural world, by contrast, live purely and simply.]

As Tilgher indicates, through 'la coscienza, la riflessione, il pensiero' [consciousness, reflection, and thought],[91] one is made to acknowledge '[l]'essenziale di essere e di sapere di essere, di vivere e di sapere di vivere' [[t]he basics of existing and the awareness of existing, and of living and the awareness of living].[92] Interestingly, the concept of *vedersi vivere* can be associated with another important passage to emerge in 'L'umorismo' to do with interior silence. In Pirandello's words, it is during these moments of 'interior silence' that we begin to see ourselves more clearly: 'In certi momenti di silenzio interiore, in cui l'anima nostra si spoglia di tutte le finzioni abituali, e gli occhi nostri diventano più acuti e più penetranti, noi vediamo noi stessi nella vita' [In certain moments of interior silence, in which our souls strip themselves of our usual fictions, and our eyes become more acute and penetrating, we see ourselves in our own lives] (*Spsv*, p. 152), a notion which pays just as much attention to silence as to words, as Chaper 4 will show.

Largely because of his critical writings, Pirandello has become recognised as an intellectual writer. Pirandello, in the preface to *Sei personaggi in cerca d'autore* (1921), ironically considered himself as having the 'disgrazia' (*Mn* II, 655) [misfortune (*CP* II, xiii)] of being a philosophical writer. As Tilgher puts it, '*Umorismo e cerebralità*: tutta l'arte di Pirandello è chiusa in queste parole' [*Umorismo* and the cerebral: all of Pirandello's art is embodied in these words].[93] Likewise, Gianni Grana has argued that 'Pirandello mette in gioco una psicologia più complessa, un'urgenza umana più risentita, ma anche un più esasperato intellettualismo' [Pirandello puts into play a more complex psychology, a more intense human urgency, but also a more sharpened intellectualism],[94] and Nicola Chiaromonte has claimed that '[f]or the main characteristic of Pirandello's plays, the presence of the intellect as the prime mover of the dramatic action, is to be found as the basis of every important development in the contemporary theatre'.[95] In spite of the tendency to stress the intellectual aspect of his writing, it would appear that the cerebral content of Pirandello's work does not overshadow the emotional substance, especially so following his encounter with Marta Abba.

Pirandello's Muse: Marta Abba

Just as Verga deliberated over the relationship between author, actors, and audience, so did Pirandello. Overall, critics have tended to emphasise Pirandello's early views of actors whom he deemed to be incapable of truly embodying their characters. Indeed, he always claimed that art and reality were separate from each other: '[L]a vita o si scrive o si vive' [[L]ife is either written or lived] (*Spsv*, p. 1003). As exemplified in *Sei personaggi in cerca d'autore*, characters are physically separate from actors. The Father argues that it is only the protagonists themselves who can genuinely bring their drama to life. In comparison with actors, characters are, in his words: 'Meno reali, forse; ma più veri!' [Less real, perhaps, but more true!] (*Mn* II, 681). Pirandello's scepticism towards the role of the actor is encapsulated in the early critical essay, 'Illustratori, attori e traduttori' (1908). Here, he stresses the distinction between actors and their characters, arguing that actors' interpretations do not always correspond with the playwright's original creation, leading a hypothetical author present at a rehearsal to want to shout out to the actor:

> 'No! così no!' torcendosi come a un supplizio, per il dispetto, per la rabbia, per il dolore di non veder rispondere la traduzione in realtà materiale, che dev'essere per forza altrui, alla concezione e a quell'esecuzione ideale che son sue (*Spsv*, p. 216).

> ['No, not like that' [...] writhing in agony, contempt, rage, and pain because the translation into material reality (which is necessarily someone else's) does not correspond to the ideal conception and execution that had begun with him and belongs to him alone.][96]

In spite of this, in this essay Pirandello also recognised the potential of 'un grande attore' [a great actor] capable of becoming 'l'incarnazione piena e perfetta' [the full and perfect incarnation] of a character (*Spsv*, p. 215), an incarnation he first witnessed in Duse. In fact, in *The Century Magazine* addressed earlier, Pirandello opened his discussion by stressing that '[f]rom the very beginning of her long career Eleonora Duse had the one controlling thought — the ambition to disappear, to merge herself as a real person, in the character she brought to life on the stage', what he considers to be 'the first duty of the actor — that supreme renunciation of self'.[97] He recalled the actress's physiological transformations when performing the women in her early repertoire, such as the lead roles in *La Dame aux camélias*, *Frou-Frou*, *Fedora*, and *Cavalleria rusticana*, noting her 'facial expression free from every conventional device, and changing only in direct correspondence with real inner transformations of the soul',[98] thus immersing herself entirely in her character.

Following his encounter with Abba, Pirandello came to recognise in her the artistic fusion he had initially noticed in Duse. Abba became Pirandello's leading lady in his theatre company, *Teatro d'Arte*, when she interpreted the main role in Massimo Bontempelli's *Nostra Dea*, which premièred at the Odescalchi theatre in Rome on 22 April 1925. The architect Virgilio Marchi, who at the time was working at the theatre, noticed that during her performances, '[l]'attrice apparve particolarmente adatta alla interpretazione multiforme degli stati d'animo del personaggio protagonista' [[t]he actress seemed particularly suited to the multiform interpretation of the lead character's dispositions],[99] a viewpoint also put forward by the scholar Olga Ragusa: 'More than anyone else she succeeded in achieving Pirandello's wish for complete identification between actor and role'.[100]

Several others have drawn parallels between Duse and Abba. As Claudio Vicentini has explained:

> La Duse aveva formato la propria arte lavorando sui testi di Verga, di Dumas e di Ibsen, diventandone l'attrice esemplare. E nello stesso modo, ora, Marta Abba avrebbe potuto sviluppare i modi della propria recitazione misurandosi con le opere di Pirandello, realizzandosi compiutamente come interprete ideale delle nuove forme della sua drammaturgia.[101]

> [Duse had learnt her craft by working on the writings of Verga, Dumas and Ibsen, becoming their exemplary actress. And now, in the same way, Marta Abba could develop her own acting technique by pitting herself against the works of Pirandello, realising her potential entirely as the ideal interpreter of the new forms associated with his drama.]

Similarly, Mirella Schino has pointed out that Abba 'riprenderà una gestualità inarrestabile, una intensità fisica e vocale inquietante' [would carry on with an unrelenting use of gestures, a physical and vocal intensity which unsettles], concluding (rather negatively) that '[s]arà un'arma, però, che ella non riuscirà a dominare se non sotto il controllo di direttori rigorosi ed esigenti come Talli o Pirandello' [[i]t would become a weapon, however, that she would not be able to dominate unless under the control of rigorous and demanding directors such as Talli or Pirandello].[102]

Abba's mimetic acting technique appears to have been heavily inspired by

Pirandello as a director. During rehearsals, he urged his actors to *become* their characters on stage. In his words during a rehearsal for *Sei personaggi in cerca d'autore* in 1921:

> Quando io dirigerò, gli attori dovranno studiare e imparare a memoria le loro parti [...]. E quando verranno sul palcoscenico, non dovranno più essere gli attori, ma i personaggi stessi della commedia o del dramma che dovranno recitare.[103]

> [When I direct, the actors will have to study and memorise their parts [...]. And when they go on stage, they no longer should be actors, but the characters themselves from the comic or tragic play that they have to perform.]

Pirandello was known to recite his plays for the benefit of his actors by reading aloud all the various parts. As Giudice indicates:

> Egli era il primo a 'calarsi' nei personaggi propri e altrui. Come alcuni grandi autori-attori del passato (si pensi a Shakespeare e a Molière) egli fu infatti anche, a modo suo, attore. Attore mentre leggeva i copioni, attore mentre dirigeva e mentre assisteva alle opere di teatro, anche non sue.[104]

> [He was the first to 'inhabit' the characters, his own as well as those of others. Just as some of the great author-actors in the past were (consider Shakespeare and Molière), he was also, in his own way, an actor. He was an actor whenever he read through the scripts, whenever he was directing and whenever he co-operated in theatrical works, even those which were not his own.]

According to the actor Anton Giulio Bragaglia, 'nessun attore riuscirà, così in pieno, a trasferirsi nei personaggi' [no other actor will ever be able to fully transfer himself into the characters in the way that he did],[105] no other actor, perhaps, except for Abba. In the same way as Duse signed her letters with her character's name, Abba, during her performances, wanted her character's name on the door of her dressing room rather than her own.[106] As she confided in a letter to Pirandello of 26 February 1932:

> Soltanto sul palcoscenico, il mio coraggio, che è pur tanto, si mostra senza timori e senza pudori. Ma forse perché lassù non è 'Marta Abba' che parla, che grida, che sorride, ma questo o quel personaggio.[107]

> [Only on stage does my courage, which is anyway great, show itself without fear and shame. But probably because up there it is not 'Marta Abba' who speaks, shouts, smiles, but this or that character.]

Pirandello was, in turn, inspired by Abba, and as a result he dedicated a number of plays to her. Although some of his best-known plays had been composed for Angelo Musco and Ruggero Ruggeri, what was different about the way Pirandello based his female roles on Abba was how they seemed to re-evoke *her*. As Daniela Bini shows, in the first play written for Abba, *Diana e la Tuda* (1926), Tuda physically resembled her, and in the second, *L'amica delle mogli* (1926), the protagonist is called Marta.[108]

Among the plays Pirandello wrote for Abba was *Questa sera si recita a soggetto*.[109] During the rehearsals of this play in Berlin before the première, Pirandello was disappointed with the interpretation of the lead actress Elizabeth Lennartz, and expressed in his correspondence with Abba on 30 May 1930: 'Ci vuole un'attrice *potentissima*, una Marta Abba, per far la scena finale' [It takes a *very powerful* actress, a Marta Abba, to perform the final scene].[110] Indeed, Vicentini has argued that Pirandello based the collapse of the fictional *prima attrice* on Abba. Following the première of *La nuova colonia* on 24 March 1928 at the Teatro Argentina in Rome, Abba, so immersed in her character, allegedly fainted just as the *prima attrice* later does in *Questa sera si recita a sogetto*.[111] Others, such as Paolo Puppa, have continued to link Abba with Mommina: 'È a ridosso della Abba [...] la stessa Mommina dolente in *Questa sera si recita a soggetto*' [Behind Abba [...] is the suffering Mommina in *Tonight We Improvise*].[112]

The last play Pirandello dedicated to her was *Trovarsi*, which premièred in 1932 at the Teatro dei Fiorentini in Naples with Abba in the lead role. The protagonist, Donata Genzi, herself an actress, is made to choose between her profession and her lover Elj who cannot accept the fictitious roles she performs on stage. In the closing scene, she prioritises her career by confidently declaring her devotion to her art as she evokes an image of the stage while fully immersed in the character she is performing.[113] Although Donata is very different from the character she is interpreting (a sexually confident woman who lures a married man away from his wife),[114] it is through the roles she plays that she is able to *find herself*: 'E questo è vero... E non è vero niente... Vero è soltanto che bisogna crearsi, creare! E allora soltanto, ci si trova' [This is true... And at the same time it is not true at all... What is true is only that we must create ourselves, create! Only then do we find ourselves] (*Mn* IV, 614).

Significantly, all through rehearsals Pirandello kept writing to Abba so as to inspire her performance. In his letters, he repeatedly associates her with the role of Donata. On 13 April 1936, he states: '[N]ativamente "Donata Genzi" sei Tu e come Te non potrà essere nessun'altra' [[B]y birth You are 'Donata Genzi', and there will never be another one like You],[115] and a few years earlier, on 4 September 1932:

> È proprio unicamente per Te, per la Tua arte fatta tutta di fervore e d'intelligenza, luminosa e chiara, vibrante e penetrante: nessuna, all'infuori di Te, potrà *viverla* sulla scena: è cosa assolutamente Tua, senza la minima possibilità che possa farla sua una qualsiasi altra attrice.[116]
>
> [It is really uniquely for You, made for Your art, which consists wholly of fervour and intelligence — luminous and clear, vibrant and penetrating. Nobody except You will be able *to live her role* on stage; it is absolutely Yours, without the slightest possibility that any other actress might make it her own.]

What is exceptional about Donata is how she brings to life what Pirandello called above 'l'incarnazione piena e perfetta' [the full and perfect incarnation] (*Spsv*, p. 215) of the theatre, similar to the way in which the *prima attrice* in *Questa sera si recita a soggetto* embodies the character of Mommina. However, while the ideal fusion of fiction and non-fiction in the play ends the moment the *prima attrice* is taken off stage following her collapse, the suggestion at the end of *Trovarsi* is that Donata will for evermore *be* her character. So, in conclusion, if Donata represents the utopian union between character and actor, and Donata is actually based on Abba — the only non-fictional actress Pirandello deemed worthy of the interpretation of the fictional actress — this suggests that Pirandello considered Abba to be 'l'incarnazione piena e perfetta' [the full and perfect incarnation] of his own (post-1925) theatre.

The Heart of the Stage

Both Duse and Abba occupied a central position in motivating the two authors to write for the stage. In the case of Verga, he might not have even adapted his narratives into plays had it not been for Duse. Though Duse never performed in any of Pirandello's plays, she nevertheless affected his developing views of the actor, which he later came to see in Abba. The two actresses thus became crucial in the evolution of both writers' theatre: as soon as Duse abandoned her early realist roles, the success of Verga's theatre came to an end, and as for Abba, once she entered Pirandello's theatre company, he was able to take his ideal fusion of art and reality one step further in his pioneering meta-theatrical plays. Duse and Abba subsequently became the perfect embodiment of the authors' key female protagonists, inspiring 'new' women stage roles, which might have never developed without them.

Notes to Chapter 1

1. For more background, see Gaspare Giudice, *Luigi Pirandello* (Turin: UTET, 1963).
2. Antonio Gramsci, *Letteratura e vita nazionale* (Rome: Editori Riuniti, 1991), p. 341.
3. For evidence of his dissatisfaction, see Enza De Francisci, 'Liolà Lost in (its Literal) Translation?', *Pirandello Studies*, 34 (2014), 55–65; and Enza De Francisci, 'Translating *Sicilianità* in Pirandello's Dialect Play *Liolà*', in *Adapting Translation for the Stage*, ed. by Geraldine Brodie and Emma Cole (London and New York: Routlegde, 2017), pp. 223–35.
4. For more on Pirandello's method of translating Sicilian, see Alberto Vàrvaro, '*Liolà* di Luigi Pirandello fra il dialetto e la lingua', *Bollettino del Centro di studi filologici e linguistici siciliani*, 5 (1957), 346–51; Anna Laura Lepschy, 'On Pirandello's Versions of *Liolà*', *Cuadernos de filología italiana*, 16 (2009), 263–73; and Sarah Zappulla Muscarà, 'Pirandello traduttore e autotraduttore', in *Pirandello e la parola*, ed. by Enzo Lauretta (Agrigento: Centro Nazionale Studi Pirandelliani, 2000), pp. 133–42.
5. Gaspare Giudice, 'Pirandello e Verga', *Galleria*, 15.1–2 (1965), 19–32 (p. 21).
6. Luigi Russo, *Giovanni Verga* (Rome: Laterza, 1995), p. 107. Similarly, Edoardo Scarfoglio concluded that in Verga's narrative, 'il dialogo è raccontato, il racconto invece è parlato' [his dialogue is narrated, and his narrative is instead spoken]; see Edoardo Scarfoglio, *Il libro di Don Chisciotte*, ed. by Carlo Alberto Madrignani (Naples: Liguori, 1990), p. 98. Luigi Capuana also described Verga's style of writing as 'quel suo dialogo narrato [...] quella sua narrazione parlata dal personaggio' [his narrated dialogue [...] his narrative spoken by the character]; see Luigi Capuana, *Per l'arte*, ed. by Riccardo Scrivano (Naples: Edizioni Scientifiche, 1994), p. 44. For more on this technique, see Roberto Bigazzi, *Le risorse del romanzo: componenti di genere nella narrativa moderna* (Pisa: Nistri-Lischi, 1996), pp. 187–96.
7. Capuana, *Per l'arte*, p. 28.
8. See Giulio Herczeg, *Lo stile indiretto libero in italiano* (Florence: Sansoni, 1963), p. 28.
9. Gaetano Ragonese, *Interpretazione del Verga: saggi e ricerche*, 2nd edn (Rome: Bulzoni, 1977), p. 166.
10. Antonio Di Silvestro, *Le intermittenze del cuore: Verga e il linguaggio dell' interiorità* (Catania: Biblioteca della Fondazione Verga, 2000), p. 62.
11. For a definition of regional Italian, see Anna Laura Lepschy and Giulio Lepschy, *The Italian Language Today*, 2nd edn (London: Routledge, 1991), pp. 13–14.
12. Federico De Roberto, *Processi verbali* (Palermo: Sellerio, 1976), p. 4.
13. Silvio D'Amico, *Il teatro italiano* (Milan: Treves, 1932), p. 9.

14. Sergio Blazina, *La mano invisibile: poetica e procedimenti narrativi del romanzo verghiano* (Turin: Tirrenia, 1989), p. 67.
15. Piero Pellini, *Naturalismo e verismo* (Florence: La Nuova Italia, 1998), p. 161.
16. See Anna Laura Lepschy, *Narrativa e teatro fra due secoli: Verga, Invernizio, Svevo, Pirandello* (Florence: Olschki, 1984), pp. 9–23.
17. Quoted in Russo, p. 80.
18. Ibid., p. 201.
19. See Siro Ferrone, *Il teatro di Verga* (Rome: Bulzoni, 1972), p. 55.
20. *Verga e il teatro europeo: prove d'autore*, ed. by Lina Jannuzzi and Ninfa Leotta (Lecce: Milella, 1992).
21. Giuseppe Petronio, 'Teatro e narrativa in Verga', in *Giovanni Verga e il teatro: atti del convegno Catania, 13–15 aprile, Teatro Stabile di Catania* (Catania: Assessorato regionale ai beni culturali e P. I., 1986), pp. 9–16 (p. 10).
22. '[L]e roman, grâce à son cadre libre, restera peut-être l'outil par excellence du siècle, tandis que le théâtre ne fera que le suivre et en compléter l'action' [[T]he novel, thanks to its free form, will remain perhaps the perfect tool of the century, whereas the stage will follow it and complete its action]; see Émile Zola, *Le roman expérimental*, ed. by François-Marie Maurad (Paris: Flammarion, 2006), p. 160.
23. Ugo Ojetti, *Alla scoperta dei letterati*, postface by Nicola Merola (Milan: Fratelli Dumolard editori, 1895), pp. 70–71.
24. Giovanni Verga, *Dal mio al tuo* (Milan: Treves, 1906), p. vii.
25. Natalino Sapegno, *Ritratto di Manzoni* (Bari: Laterza, 1961), p. 273.
26. Silvana Monti, 'Il teatro di Verga e la società della "Nuova Italia"', *Problemi*, 4–5 (1967), 174–86 (p. 174).
27. Carmelo Musumarra, 'Verga', in *Dizionario critico della letteratura italiana* (Turin: UTET, 1973), pp. 584–89 (p. 588).
28. Giuseppe Fumagalli, *Chi l'ha detto?* (Milan: Ulrico Hoepli, 1989), pp. 361–62.
29. Tullio De Mauro, *Storia linguistica dell'Italia unita* (Rome: Laterza, 1995), p. 41.
30. See Axel Körner, *Politics of Culture in Liberal Italy: From Unification to Fascism* (New York: Routledge, 2009).
31. See Marvin Carlson, *The Italian Shakespearians: Performances by Ristori, Salvini, and Rossi in England and America* (Washington: The Folger Shakespeare Library, 1985).
32. See Pietro Trifone, *Malalingua: l'italiano scorretto da Dante a oggi* (Bologna: Il Mulino, 2007), pp. 51–65.
33. See *La commedia e il dramma borghese dell'ottocento*, ed. by Siro Ferrone, Il teatro italiano, 5 (Turin: Einaudi, 1979).
34. For more on this 'gap', see Roberto Alonge, *Teatro e spettacolo nel secondo Ottocento* (Rome: Laterza, 1988), p. 3.
35. Cesare Molinari, 'Teorie della recitazione: gli attori sull'attore. Da Rossi a Zacconi', in *Teatro dell'Italia unita: atti dei convegni Firenze 10–11 dicembre 1977, 4–6 novembre 1978*, ed. by Siro Ferrone (Milan: il Saggiatore, 1980), pp. 75–100 (p. 77).
36. In Federico De Roberto, *Casa Verga e altri sagi verghiani*, ed. by Carmelo Musumarra (Florence: Le Monnier, 1964), p. 196.
37. Ibid., p. 198.
38. Alfred Alexander, *Giovanni Verga: A Great Writer and his World* (London: Grant and Cutler, 1972), p. 110.
39. See Giulio Cattaneo, *Giovanni Verga* (Turin: UTET, 1963), pp. 228–29.
40. Quoted in De Roberto, *Casa Verga*, pp. 209–10.
41. Quoted in Clemente Fusero, *Eleonora Duse* (Milan: Dall'Oglio editore, 1971), p. 102.
42. Cesare Molinari, *L'attrice divina: Eleonora Duse nel teatro italiano fra i due secoli* (Rome: Bulzoni, 1985), p. 72.
43. Ibid., p. 73.
44. Félix Duquesnel, 'Les Premières', *Le Gaulois*, 1 July 1897.
45. See *Le donne del teatro siciliano da Mimì Aguglia a Ida Carrara*, ed. by Sarah Zappulla Muscarà and Enzo Zappulla (Acireale: La Cantinella, 1995).

46. Arthur Symons, *Eleonora Duse* (London: Elkin Mathews, 1926), p. 131.
47. Ibid., p. 131.
48. See Antonio Scuderi, 'Sicilian dialect theatre', in *A History of Italian Theatre*, ed. by Joseph Farrell and Paolo Puppa (Cambridge: Cambridge University Press, 2006), pp. 257–65.
49. As Verga wrote to Rod on 29 January 1908: 'Io non mi spiego ancora il successo della Compagnia Grasso a Parigi; ma mi spiego benissimo l'insuccesso, o quasi, della *Lupa*, specialmente data a quel modo e con quei *mutamenti*... Basta, ho telefontato a Praga di ritirare al Grasso tanto *La Lupa* che *Cavalleria*, nella quale il Grasso mi torna in scena fra i carabinieri, dopo aver ucciso Turiddu, all'ultima scena! Questo è l'attore e l'interprete che avete applaudito a Parigi senza parlar del resto, che è caricatura grottesca del carattere siciliano' [I cannot understand the success Grasso's company received in Paris, but I can well understand the lack of success, more or less, of *The She-Wolf*, when it was performed in this way and with those *changes*... Enough, I have telephoned Praga giving orders to remove from Grasso both *The She-Wolf* and *Cavalleria* where he returns on stage among the police, after having killed Turiddu, in the final scene! This is the actor and interpreter that you applauded in Paris, without even speaking about the rest, which is a grotesque caricature of the Sicilian character] (*Lt*, pp. 245–46). Similarly, a year later, Pirandello in 'Teatro Siciliano?' would refer to 'la meravigliosa, bestialità di Giovanni Grasso' [the wonderful bestiality of Giovanni Grasso] (*Spsv*, p. 1168).
50. De Roberto, *Casa Verga*, p. 295.
51. See D'Amico, 'Il teatro verista e il *grande attore*', pp. 25–46.
52. Francesco De Felice, *Storia del teatro siciliano* (Catania: Gianotta, 1956), p. 78.
53. Quoted in Sarah Zappulla Muscarà and Enzo Zappulla, *Giovanni Grasso: il più grande attore tragico del mondo* (Acireale, Catania: Cantinella, 1995), p. 133.
54. Symons, p. 131.
55. For more on Duse's so-called 'gesto "inutile"' ['unnecessary' gesture], known by Stanislawskij as objectivisation, see Mirella Schino, *Il teatro di Eleonora Duse* (Bologna: Il Mulino, 1992), pp. 55–100.
56. Herman Bang, 'Menschen und Masken', in *Eleonora Duse: Bildnisse und Worte*, ed. by Bianca Segantini and Francesco von Mendelssohn (Berlin: Kaemmerer, 1926), pp. 64–75 (p. 66).
57. See Giulio Piccini (Jarro), 'I nervi della Duse', in *Eleonora Duse*, ed. by Leonardo Vergani with the collaboration of Luigi Pizzinelli (Milan: Aldo Martello, 1958), pp. 93–101 (p. 98).
58. See Guido Lopez, *Marco Praga e Silvio d'Amico: lettere e documenti (1919–1929)* (Rome: Bulzoni, 1990), p. 95.
59. Luigi Pirandello, 'Eleonora Duse: Actress Supreme', *The Century Magazine*, June 1924, pp. 244–51 (p. 247).
60. Luigi Rasi, *La Duse: con 55 illustrazioni* (Florence: R. Bemporad & Figlio, 1901), p. 38.
61. Molinari, *L'attrice divina*, p. 72.
62. Susan Bassnett, 'Eleonora Duse', in *Bernhardt, Terry, Duse: The Actress in her Time*, ed. by John Stokes, Michael R. Booth, and Susan Bassnett (Cambridge: Cambridge University Press, 1988), pp. 119–70 (pp. 142–43).
63. See *La drammatica metodo italiano: trattati normative e testi teorici*, ed. by Anna Sica (Milan: Mimesis, 2013). Trans. in Anna Sica, *The Italian Method of La Drammatica* (Milan: Mimesis, 2014).
64. William Archer, *The Theatrical 'World' of 1894*, with an intro. by George Bernard Shaw, and a synopsis of playbills of the year by Henry George Hibert (London: Walter Scott, LTD, 1895), p. 164.
65. Quoted in Enza De Francisci, 'Eleonora Duse in *Cavalleria rusticana*: Santuzza on the London Stage', *Italian Studies*, 69.1 (2014), 95–110 (p. 106).
66. Luigi Capuana, *Teatro dialettale siciliano*, 3 vols (Palermo: Alberto Reber, 1911–1912), I, pp. x–xi.
67. Donatella Orecchia, *La Prima Duse: nascita di un'attrice moderna (1879–1886)* (Rome: Artemide, 2007), p. 127.
68. See Aurelio Navarria, *Annotazioni verghiane e pagine staccate* (Caltanissetta-Rome: Edizioni Salvatore Sciascia, 1976), p. 173.
69. Orecchia, p. 135.
70. Quoted in Ferrone, *Il teatro di Verga*, p. 182, n. 69.

71. Ibid., p. 182, n. 70.
72. Ibid., p. 183.
73. Molinari, *L'attrice divina*, p. 74.
74. Ibid., p. 74.
75. See Raffaello Barbiera, *Polvere di palcoscenico: note drammatiche*, 2 vols (Catania: N. Giannotta, 1908), II, p. 125.
76. Cesare Levi, 'Il teatro di Giovanni Verga', *Nuova Antologia di lettere, scienze ed arti*, 6th series (July-August 1920), 141–47 (p. 144).
77. Molinari, *L'attrice divina*, p. 73.
78. Ibid., pp. 73–74.
79. William Weaver, *Duse: A Biography with 53 illustrations* (London: Thames and Hudson, 1984), p. 43.
80. Giovanni Pontiero, *Eleonora Duse: In Life and Art* (Frankfurt a.M.: Peter Lang, 1986), p. 53.
81. Natale Tedesco, '*La Lupa*: la contestualità della novella e delle "scene drammatiche"', in *Giovanni Verga e il teatro*, pp. 101–05 (p. 102).
82. Luigi Pirandello, *Il figlio prigioniero: carteggio tra Luigi e Stefano Pirandello durante la guerra 1915–1918*, ed. by Andrea Pirandello (Milan: Mondadori, 2005), p. 144.
83. Luigi Pirandello, 'Lettere al figlio Stefano di Luigi Pirandello', in *Almanacco letterario Bompiani* (Milan: Bompiani, 1937), p. 40.
84. See Enzo Lauretta, 'Le novelle per un anno', in *Le novelle di Pirandello: atti del 6° convegno internazionale di studi pirandelliani*, ed. by Stefano Milioto (Agrigento: Centro Nazionale Studi Pirandelliani, 1980), pp. 19–32 (p. 21).
85. Jørn Moestrup, 'La diversa funzione di novella e dramma nell'opera di Luigi Pirandello', *Analecta Romana Instituti Danici*, 5 (1969), 199–239 (p. 199).
86. See Maria Luisa Altieri Biagi, 'La lingua in scene: dalle novelle agli atti unici', in *Gli atti unici di Pirandello (tra narrativa e teatro)*, ed. by Stefano Milioto (Agrigento: Centro Nazionale Studi Pirandelliani, 1979), pp. 259–315.
87. For more on Pirandello's 'explosive' use of dialogue and its possible roots in the Futurist movement, see Enza De Francisci, 'Pirandello's (Futurist?) War of Words', *Pirandello Studies*, 35 (2015), 27–40.
88. Luigi Pirandello, 'En confiance', trans. by Benjamin Crémieux, *Le Temps*, 20 July 1925.
89. For more on the distinction between *vivere* [living] and *vedersi vivere* [seeing oneself live], see Adriano Tilgher, *Studi sul teatro contemporaneo*, 3rd edn (Rome: Libreria di scienze e lettere, 1928), pp. 186–258. See also Tilgher's article, 'Le estetiche di Luigi Pirandello', originally in *Raccolta* (January 1940), now in the appendix of Adriano Tilgher, *Il problema centrale: cronache teatrali 1914–1926*, ed. by Alessandro D'Amico (Genova: Edizioni del teatro stabile, 1973), p. 391.
90. Adriano Tilgher, *Studi sul teatro contemporaneo*, pp. 187–88.
91. Ibid., p. 188.
92. Ibid., p. 188.
93. Ibid., p. 190.
94. Gianni Grana, *Profili e letture di contemporanei* (Milan: Marzorati, 1962), p. 28.
95. Nicola Chiaramonte, 'Pirandello and the Contemporary Theatre', *World Theatre*, 16.3 (1967), 224–37 (p. 224).
96. Trans. in *Luigi Pirandello: A Documentary Record*, ed. by Susan Bassnett and Jennifer Lorch (Chur, Switzerland: Harwood Academic Publishers, 1993), p. 28.
97. Luigi Pirandello, *The Century Magazine*, p. 244. Although Duse never starred in any of his plays, Pirandello valued her art throughout his life. From as early as 1887, he had attempted to persuade her to perform some of his early theatrical works, such as *Fatti che or son parole* (1887) and *Le popolane* (1888) — two plays which are now lost — but his hopes were not fulfilled. Years later, as a mature writer, after seeing her performance in the film *Cenere* (1916), based on the 1904 novel by Grazia Daledda and directed by the actor Febo Mari, he was, once again, inspired to ask her to interpret the role of the mother in his *La vita che ti diedi* (1923). Duse, however, declined the offer because she felt unable to identify with the mother who, instead of grieving for her son, continues to see him alive in herself as well as in his partner expecting his child.

As she confessed to a close companion and biographer Olga Signorelli: '[S]e a me muore una persona cara io devo piangere, disperarmi, ma poi a poco a poco la ritrovo *su piano spirituale*' [[I]f somebody close to me dies, I have to cry, tear myself apart, but then, very slowly, I find them again *on a spiritual level*]; quoted in Vittorio Branca, 'Divina Duse, reciti per me; Suo Pirandello', *Corriere della sera*, 8 October 1986. For more on Duse and Pirandello, see Alessandro D'Amico, 'Rendez-vous manqué: Eleonora Duse, Luigi Pirandello', *Théâtre en Europe*, 10 (1986), 98–105; and Elio Gioanola, *Pirandello's Story: la vita o si vive o si scrive* (Milan: Jaca Book, 2007).

98. Pirandello, *The Century Magazine*, p. 274.
99. Virgilio Marchi, 'Ricordi sul Teatro d'Arte', in *Pirandello capocomico*, ed. by Alessando D'Amico and Alessandro Tinterri (Palermo: Sellerio, 1987), pp. 407–34 (p. 413).
100. Olga Ragusa, *Luigi Pirandello: An Approach to his Theatre* (Edinburgh: Edinburgh University Press, 1980), p. 175.
101. Claudio Vicentini, *Pirandello: il disagio del teatro* (Venice: Marsilio, 1993), p. 159.
102. Schino, p. 141.
103. See Andrea Camilleri, 'Pirandello e la regia teatrale', in *Atti del congresso internazionale di studi pirandelliani* (Florence: Le Monnier, 1967), pp. 311–15 (pp. 311–12).
104. Giudice, *Luigi Pirandello*, p. 474.
105. Anton Giulio Bragaglia, 'Pirandello, l'uomo', in *Almanacco letterario Bompiani*, pp. 87–88 (p. 88).
106. Vicentini, p. 168.
107. Marta Abba, *Caro Maestro... Lettere a Luigi Pirandello 1926–1936*, ed. by Pietro Frassica (Milan: Mursia, 1994), pp. 252–53 (p. 253).
108. Daniela Bini, *Pirandello and his Muse: The Plays for Marta Abba* (Florida: University Press of Florida, 1998), p. 36 and p. 50. See also Carlo Ferrucci, 'Marta recita Marta', in *La musa ritrosa: Pirandello e Marta Abba* (Bologna: CLUEB, 2010), pp. 45–56.
109. For more on how the *prima attrice* in *Questa sera si recita a soggetto* might have been inspired by both Duse and Abba, see Enza De Francisci, 'Generations (Duse-Abba), Gender (The Performing Female Artist), and Genre (from *Leonora, addio!* to *Questa sera si recita a soggetto*)', *Pirandello Studies*, 32 (2012), 58–70.
110. Luigi Pirandello, *Lettere a Marta Abba*, ed. by Benito Ortolani (Milan: Mondadori, 1995). p. 493.
111. Vicentini, p. 153.
112. Paolo Puppa, 'Prefazione', in Luigi Pirandello, *Così è (se vi pare), Il giuoco delle parti, Come tu mi vuoi*, intro. by Nino Borsellino, preface and note by Paolo Puppa (Milan: Garzanti, 1995), pp. lvi–lxxii (p. lxvi).
113. In the same way as Donata evokes the theatre in her mind, Pirandello's grandson Andrea recalls that Abba, when reciting plays together with Pirandello, recreated the theatre 'in uno spazio irreale' [in an unreal space]; see Andrea Pirandello, 'Ricordo', in *Pirandello: l'uomo, lo scrittore, il teatrante*, ed. by Fabio Battistini, Maria G. Gregori, and Mario Sculatti (Milan: Mazotta, 1987), pp. 144–51 (p. 147).
114. For more on Donata and her fictional roles, see Anna Laura Lepschy, 'Notes on the Figure of the Actor in Pirandello', *The Yearbook of the British Pirandello Society*, 1 (1981), 1–18.
115. Luigi Pirandello, *Lettere a Marta Abba*, p. 1307 (original capitalisation).
116. Ibid., p. 1020 (original capitalisation).

CHAPTER 2

Women Centre Stage

A New Beginning

While the previous chapter illustrated the different paths which could have led Verga and Pirandello to adapt their narratives into plays, and the influence both Duse and Abba exerted on them in facilitating their passage to the theatre, the purpose here is to trace the origins of Verga's 'new' female stage roles. The first part will consider what kind of roles for women were emerging on the dramatic and operatic stages in the nineteenth century and who their interpreters were. The second part will address what came to be called 'la donna nuova' [new woman],[1] a term often applied to star actresses such as Adelaide Ristori and Duse, who performed unconventional roles like Ibsen's Nora in *A Doll's House* (1879) — a play whose protagonist abandons her children to seek emancipation, similar to Sibilla Aleramo's anonymous narrator in her autobiographical novel *Una donna* (1906). The Italian reception of Nora is then explored, a role first performed by Emilia Aliprandi Pieri in 1889 followed closely by Duse in 1891. By examining Nora's reception in Italy, the chapter illuminates the wider cultural context which saw the rise of a 'new' type of female role, and helps assess how Ibsen might have influenced the development of Verga's theatre.

Women in Italy

Verga produced his dramatic works during a critical time in women's history. In the nineteenth century, women remained 'defraudat[e] della pienezza dei diritti umani' [cheated out of their full human rights],[2] and by the late 1880s many positivist studies were arguing that women were inferior, such as Cesare Lombroso's *La donna delinquente, la prostituta e la donna normale* (1893) and Paolo Mantegazza's *Fisiologia della donna* (1893). Despite this, it was during these decades that women's active involvement in the public sphere was increasing. Women, for instance, had already played an important role in the struggle for Italy's political independence.[3] In unified Italy, many educational changes were subsequently introduced. Official statistics show that female illiteracy declined from 84% in 1861 to 54.5% in 1901. From 1876, women were admitted to universities for the first time,[4] and by 1899, there were 19,864 women taking teacher training courses compared to a mere 1,323 male trainees.[5] Moreover, women were participating in the workforce as never before, notwithstanding the tensions this caused. Though divisions between northern and southern Italy prevailed, working-class women played a crucial role. As Perry Willson explains: 'By far the largest group of "economically active" females were peasants'.[6] Indeed, women continued to contribute to the workforce throughout the Great War, one of the causative factors responsible for suffrage in 1946 shortly after the Second World War, in spite of Mussolini's efforts in the early twentieth century to suppress women's rights.[7]

As a result of women's growing participation in the workforce, a number of feminist unions and leagues emerged in Italy, such as the Lega Promotrice degli Interessi Femminili, which was associated with the Unione delle Lavoranti and set up by both Anna Maria Mozzoni and Paolina Schiff in Milan. Their political campaigns lobbied for equal pay, the introduction of legal rights for unmarried women, and the right to female suffrage. The majority of the early activists were of aristocratic descent or from the upper-middle classes and campaigned in socialist movements. Mozzoni, who published in journals founded by women such as in *La donna* (1868), notably joined the Milanese Socialist League in 1889, though she was often not supported by the male-dominated movement.

Verga's theatre was also developing at a time when many Italian women writers were committed to giving voice to the female condition. These include, to name a few, Neera (pseudonym for Anna Radius Zuccari), who valued Verga's opinion of her attempt to write for the theatre;[8] Matilde Serao, who, like Verga, was concerned with the condition of women in Southern Italy;[9] Maria Messina, who was in close correspondence with Verga about her Sicilian literature;[10] and Aleramo.

In Saveria Chemotti's view, what differentiated Italian nineteenth-century women writers from the male tradition was largely their use of a female narrator, who recounted events from her point of view, as the 'pulsione, riflesso ed eco della propria interiorità, della propria identità, dei propri valori' [impulse, reflection and echo of her own inner life, identity, and values].[11] Unlike their male contemporaries, these writers could convey their first-hand knowledge of womanhood in their fiction and journalism.[12] Examples of such first-person narration emerge in the work of La Marchesa Colombi, particularly in her highly successful book, *La gente per bene* (1887) and her epistolary novel *Prima morire* (1887), which recounts the story of an adulterous mother, Eva, who leaves her husband and daughter for a musician, only to return following the discovery of her daughter's illness — a vastly different woman from Ibsen's Nora and Aleramo's narrator, neither of whom leave their children for a lover, nor return home having done so.

According to Ann Caesar, it is the very fact that Italian women writers made their authorial presence visible in their works which distinguished them from their *veristi* contemporaries like Verga who claimed to remove 'la mano dell'artista' (*Tn* I, p. 192) [the artist's hand] from his fiction:

> Where *veristi* writers look to create the appearance of truth, *vraisemblance*, by giving readers the illusion that they are looking directly on the world without having to recourse to an authorial lens, the women writers [...] develop an aura of truth by making very visible their own hand in the development of the narrative and by documenting it with letters, diaries and memoirs.[13]

But what happened when the *veristi* writers turned their narratives into plays? Once Verga placed the female subject at the forefront of his theatre, owing largely to the influence of Duse, he also prioritised the female voice. The women on stage displace the role of the (male) narrator and, in the first person, recount their *own* stories in their *own* words, similar to the diary entries and correspondence of the women writers.

Verga's theatre also flourished alongside Italy's rich operatic tradition. As was usual at the time, many French narrative roles inspired Italian composers to concentrate their female roles on the demi-monde. One only needs to think of Violetta in Giuseppe Verdi's *La traviata* (1853), based on Dumas's novel-turned-play *La Dame aux camélias* (1848 and 1852) and the renowned singer in Giacomo Puccini's *Tosca* (1900), taken from Sardou's homonymous play (1887). Though a number of women in standard operatic repertoires occupy a central position in the plots, admittedly, many of them die. Rebecca Meitlis has argued that '[i]t seems inevitable that Violetta and Tosca have to die'.[14] However, as Susan Rutherford has pointed out, 'these heroines do not die simply because they are women but because they are tragic protagonists'.[15] Indeed, in Ralph Locke's words, despite being tragic, 'the heroines are not as spineless as we have been led to believe',[16] as exemplified in operas reflecting national traditions, in particular Verdi's Joan of Arc.

But why were women characters placed centre stage? Women were often positioned at the emotional centre of a play for quite pragmatic reasons. Spectators — especially female spectators — demanded female roles.[17] As Verga's contemporary critic Giacinto Battaglia concluded, the 'fonte principale del così detto interesse drammatico, senza del quale verun componimento che si destini al teatro, per quanto profondamente concepito ed eruditamente svolto, riuscirà sempre freddo e sterile di risultato, è la donna' [principal source of dramatic interest, without which any theatrical work (however profoundly conceived and eruditely wrought) will be cold and sterile, is woman].[18] According to Rutherford, '[t]here were hard, economic reasons for providing characters who would speak to the interests of women spectators and offer performance opportunities for the most potent element at the box office, the prima donna',[19] something Verga would have also been well aware of given the popular tradition of the *grande attore*. Indeed, during Duse's early tours where she included *Cavalleria rusticana* in her repertoire, her performances caused ticket prices to escalate. Max Beerbohm, in his review of the actress at the Lyceum on 26 May 1900, was clearly shocked that the 'English public' had to pay 'higher prices than it pays for a play in its own language'.[20]

The popularity of the star actress and soprano thus challenged a range of gender norms. Sopranos, such as Giuditta Pasta in the early nineteenth century, earned considerably more than male singers, often running their own business, influencing scores, interpretations, and taking managerial decisions. In addition, the high register of the soprano's voice, together with her capacity to match or even outsing men, placed women singers on an 'absolutely equal footing' in many love duets,[21] underlining what Carolyn Abbate has called 'opera's capacity to disrupt male authority on stage',[22] a capacity which spoken theatre is unable to match as the dramatic actress cannot exploit her 'vocal assertiveness' in the same way.[23]

Despite this, stage actresses like Ristori and Duse also earned more than their male co-stars and directed their own theatre companies. Duse, for instance, founded the *Drammatica Compagnia della Città di Roma* in 1887 with her fellow actor, Flavio Andò. As the *capocomica*, it was her role to hire actors, choose which plays to include in the company's repertoire, and decide in which theatres to perform.[24]

The nineteenth century also saw the celebrity soprano and star actress adopt transgressive approaches to their operatic and theatrical repertoires. Some even rebelled against conventional female roles by interpreting male roles *en traversti*. Pasta, for example, performed the title role in Rossini's *Otello* in 1828.[25] Ristori and Duse, on the other hand, kept performing female roles, unlike Duse's French rival Sarah Bernhardt who, during her international tours in America from 1880 to 1916, performed the role of Hamlet in a translation by Eugène Morand and Marcel Schwob, a role which did not go down too well with contemporary (female) critics.[26] But while Ristori performed more majestic roles, like her ground-breaking Lady Macbeth translated by Giulio Carcano, Duse preferred to interpret female roles with whose '*compianto femminile*' [*female sorrow*] she could empathise, as she revealed in her well-known letter to Francesco d'Arcais in 1886,[27] hence performing what Lucia Re has called a range of 'daring stage roles'.[28]

Verga's decision, then, to cast Duse as the central role in his first two plays begins to make sense when considered in the context of Italy's longstanding operatic tradition. Presumably what attracted Verga to Duse was, to some degree, the opportunities she afforded him to disseminate his plays widely, and therefore he needed to create principal female characters who would not only appeal to her dramatic technique, but would also fit in with the kind of roles she included in her repertoire. But how 'daring' were his roles? By placing his female characters on stage, releasing them to the living interpretations of actresses through inflection, gesture and *mise-en-scène*, Verga (and later Pirandello) undoubtedly remade his characters 'anew', but just how new and radical were they? We know Verga specifically wrote his early female roles for Duse, the actress who came to represent for some an embodiment of the so-called 'donna nuova'. Thus, in order to assess whether we can align Verga's roles with this new image of women, we need to know what the 'donna nuova' actually meant and how she made her way onto the Italian stage.

La donna nuova

As Michela De Giorgio observes, the term 'donna nuova' was used in various ways in Italy at the start of the nineteenth century, including 'collocazioni plurime e utilizzazioni differenti, dal discorso politico, alla narrazione letteraria' [multiple contexts and different uses, from political discourse to literary narrative].[29] Annarita Buttafuoco explains that, during the Risorgimento, the 'donna nuova' was still closely associated with her traditional representation as mother or rather as mother of the eventual nation-state, arguably a woman devoted not to her own personal emancipation but that of her country and her sons who would go on to protect the *patria*:

> [A]lla 'donna nuova' veniva affidata la funzione essenziale di regolare e di garantire l'ordine sentimentale e materiale nel premio organismo sociale, la famiglia, base e al tempo stesso specchio della nazione intera.[30]
>
> [[T]o the 'new woman' was assigned the essential function of regulating and guaranteeing emotional and material order in the prized social organism, the family, the basis and at the same time the mirror of the entire nation.]

Following political unification, however, the 'donna nuova' distanced herself from her domestic role and became a woman who was intrinsically linked with the workforce as a result of industrialisation. Teachers, in particular, who could help mould future law-abiding citizens, were considered to be what Buttafuoco has labelled 'la "donna nuova" per eccellenza' [the 'new woman' par excellence].[31]

What is curious here, however, is the extent to which the definitions of the 'donna nuova' provided by the early emancipationists were not particularly 'new'. In 1899, the journal *Italia Femminile* introduced its upcoming director Rina Pierangeli Faccio (Aleramo's name by birth) and the description of Faccio is very different from the 'donna nuova' she would later come to represent:

> [G]iovane d'anni ma nel pensiero matura, Rina Pierangeli Faccio è una *donna nuova* nel senso migliore della parola, poiché è anzitutto sposa e madre modella ed ha per prima religione la famiglia.[32]
>
> [[Y]oung in age but mature in thought, Rina Pierangeli Faccio is a *new woman* in the best sense of the word, since she is, above all, a model wife and mother who considers the family to be her first religion.]

Similarly, according to Gabriella Spalletti, the president of the Consiglio Nazionale delle Donne Italiane, during a congress in Rome in 1907, the 'donna nuova' was personified in the star actress Ristori, who balanced her family roles with her role as an artist:

> La vita di Adelaide Ristori è la prova che la donna può essere artista e occuparsi della sua famiglia, girare il mondo per sedurlo e meravigliarlo con suo genio, pure rimanendo moglie e madre incomparabile.[33]
>
> [Adelaide Ristori's life is proof that a woman can be an artist and take care of her family, travel around the world to seduce and stun it with her genius, while also remaining an incomparable wife and mother.]

This description, however, did not accurately apply to other prominent actresses, specifically Duse. Unlike Ristori, Duse left her husband, Tebaldo Checchi, during her first tour of South America in 1885, and led a nomadic, financially independent life, at the cost of living separately from her daughter who was placed in a boarding school, the Collegio Margherita in Turin. While performing in London, Duse confided in a letter of 8 June 1894 to her lover, Arrigo Boito, referring to herself in the third person: 'Lenor per guadagnarsi di *che vivere* per Enrichetta e per lei, è andata lontana' [Lenor in order to earn enough *to live* for Enrichetta and for herself, had to travel far].[34] Duse, in fact, spent many years of her career performing abroad with her theatre company.[35] By virtue of her alternative lifestyle, Duse, before the outbreak of World War One, became 'a feminist icon',[36] as Re explains:

> [F]or many women especially (but not only) in Italy and Europe, Duse was a living symbol of the 'new woman', and of a woman's potential to free herself, to take centre stage, to be independent, and professionally successful, and to challenge patriarchal norms.[37]

Indeed, despite not being entirely in line with the suffragette movement in the *Giornale d'Italia* (1913),[38] considering issues like the right to an equal education more important than the right to vote, Duse made a substantial contribution to the women's cause in Italy. In 1914, she founded the Libreria delle attrici in Rome which was meant to house a rich collection of books for actresses. Many of the books were from her own personal collection (parts of which have recently been uncovered at the Murray Edwards Collection in Cambridge),[39] but, owing to a number of financial difficulties and the outbreak of war, the library eventually closed in 1915.

Ristori and Duse differed further in terms of repertoire. While Ristori favoured historical and regal roles, such as Schiller's *Mary Stuart* translated by Andrea Maffei, *Queen Elizabeth* and *Marie Antoinette* by Paolo Giacometti, Duse exhibited a more transgressive approach, interpreting roles like Ibsen's Nora despite the somewhat foreseeable critical backlash. In the words of Anna Laura Mariani, the role of Nora came for many feminists to represent 'una "donna nuova", che non rifiuta la maternità ma non vuole neppure sacrificare ad essa il suo processo di emancipazione' [a 'new woman', who does not reject motherhood but neither wants to sacrifice to it her own path to emancipation].[40] In fact, to some extent, Nora does not reject motherhood by failing to show affection for her children (she loves them and leaving them causes her great pain) but instead compromises it in order to avoid sacrificing her emancipation.[41] Though it could be argued that the character of Nora was constructed by a male author convinced that a woman who rejected the role of a wife would also abandon her children, then what about Aleramo, who was influenced by Ibsen in reworking her own story for her novel? As Caesar reminds us, 'this was no Ibsen writing about a fictitious Nora, but a woman writing about her own recent past'.[42]

So why was Duse not defined as a 'donna nuova' at the Consiglio Nazionale delle Donne Italiane? It would appear that, while campaigning for a wide range of issues, early feminists overlooked women's sexual liberation and anyone who did not adhere to their conventional views of their own gender. Willson has described the emancipationists as 'sexual puritans' who 'believed that women's primary role was motherhood, and sexuality itself was inherently bad'.[43] This position was, above all, endorsed by Ersilia Majno, the president of the Unione Femminile which was founded in Milan in 1899. Perhaps because of the prevailing cultural tendency to categorise 'non-traditional' women as loose or lesbian, Majno might have deliberately been inclined to portray herself in a puritanical light as a strategic means of deflecting criticism and asserting 'good' conduct, particularly to her residents at the Asilio Mariuccia, a residential home which she set up with her husband in Milan in 1902 in order to shelter and re-educate former prostitutes. In various periodicals and supplements, such as *Unione femminile* and *Schiave bianche*, she published a series of articles opposed to *libero amore*. For example, in her preface to the Swedish feminist writer Ellen Key's *Love and Marriage* (1911), which placed importance on physical relationships, Majno entirely ignored this aspect and limited herself to a more eugenic discourse. As Buttafuoco points out:

> Il rapporto sessuale di per sé sembra non avesse alcun valore per la Majno: era un aspetto necessario della vita di coppia — legale o non che questa fosse — che si riscattava dalla sua quasi 'bestialità' e si sublimava, per la donna, nella maternità.[44]
>
> [A sexual relationship per se seemed not to have any value for Majno: it was a necessary aspect in the life of a couple — legal or not — redeemed of its quasi 'bestiality' and sublimated, for the woman, in her maternity.]

Aleramo's *Una donna* was another work which sat uncomfortably with Majno. In 1902, after leaving her husband Ulderico Pierangeli and son Walter in Porto Civitanova in Le Marche, Aleramo moved to Rome to live with her father and started to recall her ordeal in her novel.[45] What is noteworthy is that Ibsen's Nora had such a profound effect on Aleramo that she actually includes a passage about the character in one of her chapters. Just before the narrator leaves her son, she is taken to the theatre to watch *A Doll's House* and here she describes the audience's reaction to Nora's exit: 'La verità semplice e splendente nessuno, nessuno voleva guardarla in faccia!' [The simple and shining truth, nobody, absolutely nobody, wanted to look at it directly in the face!].[46] According to Marina Zancan, it was this particular passage which offered the narrator the 'momento giusto' [the right moment] to leave her unhappy marriage.[47] As Aleramo noted in a diary entry of 24 November 1940, had it not been for Ibsen's Nora, she might never have turned into the woman she became: '[S]enza quella voce "ottocentesca", forse non sarei "divenuta quella che sono"' [[W]ithout that 'nineteenth-century' voice, I might not have 'become what I am'].[48]

Majno, however, considered the protagonist of the novel to be self-indulgent and selfish, the wrong role model for young girls.[49] Significantly, as Aleramo was completing the final draft, she was in close correspondence with Majno (whose husband represented the author unsuccessfully during the legal battle for custody of her son). It was during this time that Majno exerted her influence on the development of *Una donna*, particularly Aleramo's initial idea to end her novel in a way which resembled more closely the events in her own life. While the protagonist leaves her son for no other reason than herself, in Aleramo's own life a man was partially involved — Felice Damiani. As Aleramo later wrote in another novel, *Il Passaggio* (1919): '[N]on era per amore d'un altr'uomo ch'io mi liberavo: ma io amavo un altr'uomo' [[I]t was not for the love of another man which led me to free myself: but I did love another man].[50] However, when Aleramo, in a letter of 30 June 1903, informed Majno of her decision to include the presence of her lover in the concluding chapter of her book, Majno, in her response, reacted unfavourably to this choice:

> Ti rimando il tuo manoscritto e ti chiedo: Hai tu pensato che tuo figlio

leggerà un giorno il tuo libro e ti giudicherà? Senza dire di altre persone che lo leggeranno e vi ravviseranno, si ravviseranno in tutti i particolari che esponi intorno a te e alla tua famiglia e potranno pensare che se un orgoglio sconfinato ha potuto farti credere interessante e ragione d'un'opera artistica denudarti così davanti al pubblico, v'è però una misura anche per certe confessioni.[51]

[I return your manuscript and ask you: have you not thought that your son will one day read your book and judge you? Not to mention that other people will read it and will recognise you, will recognise themselves in all the details that you reveal regarding yourself and your family, and they might think that while unbounded pride might indeed have persuaded you to think that it would be interesting and appropriate material for an artistic work to reveal yourself in such manner before the eyes of the public, nevertheless there is a limit even for certain confessions].

What is striking here is how Aleramo's novel, just like Ibsen's play, was also being turned into what Alessandra Cenni has called 'l'incarnazione del modello della *donna nuova*' [the incarnation of the model of the *new woman*],[52] an incarnation driven by a woman's independence rather than by a man.

Though there were evident discrepancies in the way in which the 'donna nuova' was viewed, what remained consistent among the rising emancipationists was how each was committed to introducing a different kind of woman to New Italy: a woman who fought for the right to self-determination, no longer the typical 'angelo del focolare' [domestic angel]. According to Aleramo (still at the time called Rina Pierangeli Faccio) in the journal she edited, *Italia femminile* (1899), women had to re-assess the way in which they viewed themselves: 'Noi dobbiamo rifarci, ricostruire su basi di tanto più solide delle passate, la nostra educazione e il nostro sentimento' [We have to re-make ourselves, reconstruct our education and our sensibility on bases which are much more solid than in the past].[53] Likewise, in the words of Paola Lombroso in her *Caratteri della femminilità* (1909):

> Lo sviluppo del suo *io* è diventato il pensiero dominante della donna, e le par che questo sviluppo debba consistere nel far tutto quello che le era proibito o impedito di fare altra volta.[54]
>
> [The development of her *sense of self* has become the dominant thought for the woman, and it seems to her that this development must consist in doing everything that she was previously prohibited or prevented from doing.]

This viewpoint was shared by other emancipationists, including Teresa Labriola in her *La quistione feminista* (1910):

> Nel gran quadro della vita umana apparisce con contorni sufficientemente chiari, il tipo nuovo della donna che già per il carattere dello spirito è quasi precorritrice dell'avvenire [...]. La donna che contiene in sé il significato del proprio essere, ha superata la cerchia nella quale era stata rinchiusa da secoli. Essa ha superato il vecchio tipo femminile, che aveva fuori di sé il proprio significato.[55]
>
> [In the grand scheme of human life there appears, with sufficiently clear outlines, a new type of woman who, owing to the nature of her spirit of character, is already almost a forerunner of the future [...]. The woman who

contains in herself the meaning of her own being has risen above the cycle in which she had been enclosed for centuries. She has risen above the old female archetype, whose meaning lay outside of her.]

It is intriguing, then, that during this very process of regeneration, in the midst of early discussions about the 'donna nuova', Verga should also be regenerating his female stage roles. Instead of creating his characters *ab ovo*, he transposes them from the narrative genre into the theatrical, and it is the new voice that women gain on stage which enables them to express their new sense of self. Ibsen's Nora was one of the first heroines to inspire this revolutionary period for women on stage, 'quella voce "ottocentesca"' [that 'nineteenth-century' voice] which Aleramo so admired.[56] Could, therefore, the figure of Nora have influenced Verga as he was refashioning his new female stage roles for Duse, and, if so, how exactly was Nora received on the Italian stage?

Casa di bambola

According to Andrea Camilleri in his entry in the *Enciclopedia dello spettacolo* (1959), Duse was the first actress in Italy to play Nora: '[A] lei si dovett[e] la prima rappresentazione di *Casa di bambola*' [[T]o her we owe the première of *A Doll's House*].[57] But in actual fact, it was Aliprandi Pieri who first interpreted the role at the Teatro Gerbino in Turin on 15 February 1889, the same actress who had also starred as Santuzza in the early 1880s. While Aliprandi's acting technique was well received by critics, the play generally was not. The *Gazzetta dei teatri* predicted (wrongly) that the play would not be performed for long in Italy, and the *Illustrazione Italiana* concluded that audiences in Turin did not share the same tastes as those in Copenhagen.[58] Similarly, the *Gazzetta piemontese* on 16–17 February comments that during the closing scene where Nora abandons her children, 'il pubblico ha fatto il viso arcigno' [the spectators looked askance].[59] *L'arte drammatica*, a few days later on 23 February 1889, states that

> Il lavoro si presterebbe alla più lunga ed intricata discussione, tanto che non credo che la sua rappresentazione vorrà essere tentata da altre attrici: certo è che la signora Aliprandi Pieri vi mise tutto il suo ingegno e ottenne un successo: ma puramente d'attrice ed in grazia del quale la commedia si è replicata tre volte.[60]

> [The work would lend itself to a longer and more intricate discussion, so much so that I do not believe that other actresses will want to attempt to perform it: certainly Mrs Aliprandi Pieri put all her genius into it and scored a success, but purely owing to her acting, thanks to which the play was repeated three times.]

What might have hindered the success of this early staging was the actual translation of the script *Nora o la casa della bambola* by Pietro Galletti,[61] based on a German translation of the play, *Nora oder ein Puppenheim*.[62] Indeed, the play was not retranslated in Italy until Luigi Capuana did so for the interpretation of Duse. As Francesca Simoncini puts it: 'Più probabilmente Eleonora Duse volle avvicinarsi alle opere del norvegese senza passare sotto il giogo di una manipolazione compiuta da altri' [More likely Eleonora Duse wanted to get closer to the work of the Norwegian author without having to suffer the manipulation of others].[63]

Capuana published his translation, simply entitled *Bambola* [*Doll*], as a serial in the Roman journal *Carro di Tespi* in 1891, and later in 1894 as a book, this time with a title closer to the original — *Casa di bambola* — following Duse's request to make the title more faithful to Ibsen.[64] Capuana came to work on the translation as a result of the contact between Ibsen's agent and translator in France, the Polish-Lithuanian count Moritz Prozor, on whose 1889 French translation Capuana based his own. Significantly, Prozor was initially encouraged to translate the play by Verga's own translator Édouard Rod in the summer of 1888.[65] After the publication of Prozor's translations, Rod produced an article on Ibsen for the popular newspaper *Le Temps* on 15 January 1889, where, despite his admiration for the Norwegian playwright, he ultimately considered Ibsen's characters 'si différents de nous' [so different from us].[66] This article re-appeared almost word-for-word in Rod's preface to *Les Revenants* and *La Maison de poupée*, published in Paris by Albert Savine a month later on 15 February 1889, suggesting possible paths by which Verga might have already been familiar with Ibsen's Nora long before Capuana's translation.

The first time Capuana's mentions his collaboration with Ibsen and Prozor on his translation of the play is in a letter of 19 September 1890 to the actor and director Cesare Rossi:

> The famous Norwegian playwright Enrico Ibsen and his French translator Count M. Prozor [...] have given me the privilege to translate and bring to the Italian stage the wonderful play *Bambola* (*Maison de poupée*). It is one of the most powerful and interesting plays of modern drama and I am enthusiastic about it. It has been very much applauded in Germany and I am sure it will be equally successful in Italy. Four great actors, two men and two women, would have a chance to show their best artistic qualities. In the current lack of new plays of adequate quality, *Bambola* ought to become part of the repertoire of every primary company.[67]

This letter is significant in a number of ways. First of all, Capuana comments on Italy's lack of 'new plays', a void which Verga was also trying to fill. Moreover, the extract implies that Capuana was willing to translate the play once it had been tried and tested in Germany and France. Indeed, by the time Capuana came to translate *A Doll's House*, the play had already become very popular, particularly following the reaction of the renowned Hedwig Niemann-Raabe. Only a year after the première in Copenhagen, the German actress was to open *Nora oder ein Puppenheim* in Flensborg and Berlin in 1880 but refused to interpret the lead role unless the ending was changed. Despite Ibsen's reluctance, he was forced to re-write the closing scene in the absence of any official treaty concerning authors' rights between Norway and Germany. Ibsen thus included an episode in which Nora, just before her departure, looks at her sleeping children for the last time, and the thought of leaving them motherless makes her change her mind.[68]

Interestingly, eleven years later, Capuana actually shared the actress's concerns. In *Carro di Tespi*, Capuana included an open letter to the editor, the Neapolitan Edoardo Boutet (who wrote under the pseudonym 'Caramba'), in which he noted that '[t]he unravelling of the story is without doubt slightly strange for us Italians and a test-scene is needed to allow us to determine whether or not also the theatrical effects of it appear weakened'.[69] Three years after that, in the preface to his book, Capuana continued to elaborate on the unusual aspect of the play:

> Per noi, il personaggio di Nora diviene un'eccezione molto strana quando si risolve ad abbandonare marito e figli, per tentare di farsi, con la propria esperienza, un'idea netta e precisa della vita e dei grandi problemi amari, senza badare a quel che dice la gente e a quel che ne predichino i libri [...]. In quel momento questa fantastica scandinaica ci sconvolge, ci turba, così troppo diversa da noi: ma forse, appunto per questo, ci fa pensare.[70]

> [For us, the character of Nora becomes a very strange exception when she decides to abandon her husband and children in order to attempt to form for herself, on the basis of her own experience, a clear and precise idea of life and of its great bitter problems, without paying attention to what people say and what is taught in books about such things [...]. At that moment this fantastic Scandinavian shocks us, she troubles us, too different is she from us: but perhaps, precisely because of this, she makes us think.]

As a result of his reservations, Capuana advised Ibsen, via Prozor, to add a 'happy ending' to the play. Ibsen was, once again, reluctant to do so. In a letter to Capuana of 23 January 1891, he responds:

> Most honoured sir! I hereby insist, that the original ending of my play must not be changed in the performance. The whole play is written to lead towards the ending. The Italian audience is highly intelligent and sensitive. The Italians will soon understand my intentions![71]

And again to Prozor on 23 January 1891, Ibsen writes:

> A suo tempo, quando *Casa di bambola* era nuova nuova, sono stato costretto a dare il mio consenso perché il finale fosse cambiato per la Niemann-Rabbe, che doveva fare la parte di Nora a Berlino. Ma allora non avevo nessuna scelta, anche perché in Germania non ero protetto e non potevo impedire niente. A questo si aggiunge che il dramma esisteva già nella forma originaria e dunque non alterata; era quindi disponibile per il pubblico tedesco nella prima edizione tedesca già stampata e in commercio. Con il finale alterato il dramma non ha resistito a lungo in repertorio, mentre il finale inalterato si continua a rappresentare.[72]

> [At the time, when *A Doll's House* was brand new, I was obliged to give my consent for the final scene to be changed for Niemann-Rabbe, who was to play the part of Nora in Berlin. But at that point I did not have a choice, also because in Germany I was not legally protected and I was not able to veto anything. Moreover, the drama already existed in its original and therefore unaltered form; it was therefore available for the German public in the first German edition which had already been published and was on the market. With the altered ending the play did not last long in repertory, while the unaltered ending continues to be performed.]

Nevertheless, Ibsen advised Prozor to send Capuana an alternative ending to the play, but, unfortunately, this alternative has since been lost.[73]

Significantly, though Capuana considered the play 'slightly strange' for an Italian audience, what is of note is how he included the original ending of the play in his translation published in the journal and his book, but wanted to omit it from his script. This suggests that Capuana felt that readers of the play, in contrast to the actual spectators, would, as Giuliano D'Amico puts it, 'be able to understand and accept the play in its original form',[74] issues which, as we saw previously, also concerned Verga as he started to write for a theatre audience. Indeed, the problem with this play — as with many of Verga's — was that it did not provide audiences with either the pleasure of a happy ending or the catharsis of tragic one, causing them to feel uncomfortable.

According to Laura Caretti, Capuana felt uneasy about the original ending because he was '[p]reso dal timore che in Italia, patria dell'amore materno, il pubblico non possa accettare quel finale' [[a]fraid that in Italy, the nation of maternal love, the audience would not accept that final scene].[75] However, if the ending sat uncomfortably with Italian audiences because of what Caretti calls Italy's 'amore materno' [maternal love], then how does this explain the reaction in countries like Germany? Surely the issue about the ending is more to do with the way in which theatre audiences in general were sceptical of this 'new' woman. What is more, if, to return to Capuana's words, Nora was 'così troppo diversa' [too different], almost echoing Rod's earlier commentary that Ibsen's characters are 'si différents de nous' [so different from us],[76] then how is it possible that, not so long after her entrance into late nineteenth-century Italy, another Nora-like figure emerged in Aleramo's *Una donna*?

With hindsight, the Italian literary tradition at this time was actually providing fertile ground for the development of this 'new' type of character. One of the seeds which enabled this growth was undoubtedly Duse. Indeed, while Capuana was reluctant to stage what he called this 'eccezione molto strana' [very strange exception], Duse was keen to take on the role. Despite the somewhat foreseeable critical response to Nora's departure, as well as the reservations expressed not just by Capuana but also by Boito,[77] Duse boldly performed the original ending at the première on 9 February 1891. As Olga Signorelli reports in her biography, when asked about her interpretation of the original ending, Duse would reply: 'Non so quel che fanno le altre, so soltanto che la mia *Nora* non può non andare' [I do not know what other actresses are doing. All I know is that my Nora cannot *not* leave].[78] However, according to the French director Aurélien Lugné-Poë, during Duse's international tours, she would perform both endings of the play: firstly, the original version when Nora abandons her family and then the alternative ending produced following the demands of Niemann-Raabe, in which Nora remains at home for the sake of her children.[79] Duse possibly performed the two versions in this order so as to leave the audience with a lasting impression of the issues.

Perhaps it was the anticipation of the opening night which led to a full house in the theatre. In fact, the première did not cause any scandal as it had done in Germany. The great admirer of Ibsen, Giovanni Pozza, reviewing the play in the *Corriere della sera* on 9–10 February 1891, wrote that 'il teatro non era affollato, ma affollatissimo' [the theatre was not just crowded, but extremely crowded],[80] and called the production a 'vero trionfo. Non un trionfo d'applausi, ma di intima commozione' [real triumph. Not a triumph in terms of applause, but in terms of strong emotion].[81] The triumph which Pozza indicated was not one which met with a roar of applause. Indeed, he later noted that the only scene which the audience 'applaudì con prolungata insistenza' [applauded with prolonged insistence] was when Nora was playing with her children.[82] The triumph which Pozza pointed to was the one achieved in the theatre. According to the critic, theatre is not about entertainment but about thought-provoking ideas which are meant to touch and move the audience. In Ibsen's play, these ideas emerge in the closing scene between husband and wife, just before their separation. Audiences were presented with a play which brought to life 'new' theories about the reality of love and marriage, and this, inevitably, caused a backlash among Italy's predominantly Catholic critics:

> La grande scena fra marito e moglie, dove l'autore ha condensato ed esplicato il concetto del suo lavoro, s'impose al pubblico colla imperiosità delle creazioni inaspettate e potenti. Si udirono tratto tratto mormorii di ribellione, ma l'alto pensiero del poeta dominava, sovrano invincibile, il teatro. Da quanto tempo non si udivano dalla scena parole tanto profonde esprimere pensieri tanto meditati, verità tanto audaci![83]

> [The great scene between husband and wife, where the writer has condensed and explained the concept of his work, imposed itself on the audience with all the authority of unexpected and powerful creations. One could hear from time to time murmurs of protest, but the author's lofty thoughts reigned supreme in the theatre. How long it is since we have heard such profound words in the theatre expressing such elaborate ideas, such bold truths!]

In Pozza's review of 12–13 February 1891, also in the *Corriere della sera*, he comments on Italy's nineteenth-century spectators, the type who would have also seen Verga's theatre. Pozza here suggests that the underlying concepts of the play were incorrectly interpreted:

> Le teorie intorno al matrimonio, alle donne incomprese, alle rivendicazioni dei diritti femminili, enunciate nella commedia dell'Ibsen, non hanno trovato, neppure fra le nostre signore, seguaci ed oppositori eccessivamente appassionati. Fino ad ora ci interessiamo poco a questioni di tale natura, ignari persino della importanza che esse hanno acquistato in Germania, in Inghilterra, in tutti i paesi nordici, ove si teorizza forse troppo, ove si studia tutto.[84]

> [The theories surrounding marriage, misunderstood women, and the claims of women's rights, expressed in Ibsen's play, did not find, even among our female spectators, excessively passionate followers or adversaries. We are still little interested in issues of this nature, ignorant even of the importance that they have acquired in Germany, England and in the Nordic countries, where they perhaps over-theorise and study everything.]

Pozza concludes that the reason the philosophical overtones were misunderstood was that audiences expected plays to entertain rather than teach, an element he considered to be wholly reserved for books, something which, once again, closely affected Verga:

Perciò della *Casa di Bambola* il contenuto filosofico non fu quasi avvertito. La critica generale non penetrò oltre la corteccia scenica del lavoro. Ibsen ha dato al suo studio sociale una forma drammatica, ed il pubblico gli ha detto: 'Non vogliamo da te che la forma. A teatro non vi sono che autori drammatici; pei moralisti, pei riformatori c'è il libro'.[85]

[And so the philosophical content in *A Doll's House* was barely perceived. The general critical response did not penetrate beyond the outer layer of the theatrical work. Ibsen gave his social enquiry a dramatic form, and the audience said to him: 'All we want from you is the exterior form. In the theatre there are only playwrights; for moralists and reformers, there are books'.]

An example of this misinterpretation is expressed by a certain Zampaldi writing in *La Perseveranza* on 10 February 1891. He felt that Nora was 'semplicemente delusa' [simply disappointed] by her husband and, because of his lack of love and respect for her, 'è *costretta* a lasciare la casa maritale. Questo *costringimento* è l'arditezza del dramma' [[is *obliged* to leave her marital home. This *obligation* is the audacity of the play],[86] a viewpoint which entirely overlooks the fact that it is Nora's independent choice to abandon her children — instead of feeling as if she has to leave, arguably Nora *wants* to leave.

Similarly, in Boutet's response to Capuana's open letter in *Carro di Tespi* cited earlier, he maintained that Ibsen's philosophical theatre 'non è il teatro. E, più esattamente, non è l'arte' [is not theatre. And, more accurately, it is not art].[87] Moreover, G. M. Scalinger considered Ibsen's play to be symbolic rather than realistic: 'In Ibsen il Simbolo [...] [n]on è nell'intero dramma, è in un personaggio, in quello prescelto per rappresentare un'idea e introdotto nell'opera unicamente per questo' [In Ibsen the Symbol [...] [i]s not embodied in the entire play, but in the character who has been designated to represent an idea and is introduced in the work for this sole purpose].[88] Scalinger therefore saw Nora as a symbol of a woman (not a real woman) capable of walking away from her young children, despite the fact that Ibsen was allegedly inspired to write the play by his close friend Laura Kieler, who suffered a similar ordeal as Nora.[89]

In order to prepare for the audience's foreseeable reaction to such an unusual and controversial play, Luigi Foris, in a hypothetical conversation between Doctor Veritas (a pseudonym of the journalist Leone Fortis who signed the article) and a bourgeois lady, published in the *Illustrazione italiana* on 1 February 1891, felt that the play resembled a theatrical treatise on philosophy.[90] He claimed that *Casa di bambola* had been 'performed in Turin without so much preventive publicity — and the public did not like it — so that the company's manager decided not to stage it any more, even though he had paid for the permit'.[91]

Others felt that the play was too far removed from reality. A review of Duse's performance was published in *L'arte drammatica*, edited by Icilio Polese Santarnecchi, on 11 February 1891, and featuring a portrait of Duse dressed as Harlequin on the front page. Significantly, an earlier review in this same journal on 23 February 1889 did not criticise the play when it was first performed by Pieri. However, now that *Duse's* Nora was attracting a considerable amount of press attention, the journal changed its views quite substantially:

> Ibsen è un grande autore, ma è norvegese, è nordico, egli mette in scena gente della sua razza, egli fa ragionare i suoi personaggi come in quei paesi si ragiona, non come tra noi meridionali, ecco quello che il pubblico milanese non parve capire [...] La traduzione non mi parve troppo felice, e troppi poi i tagli.[92]
>
> [Ibsen is a great writer, but he is Norwegian, Nordic. He places on stage people from his own race. He makes his characters think as those in Nordic countries think, not as we southerners do. This is what the Milanese audience seemed to misunderstand [...]. The translation did not seem to me to be particularly successful and the cuts too abundant.]

In fact, the only 'taglio' [cut] introduced into the drama was Duse's choice to omit the tarantella scene and to appear as a harlequin instead of a Neapolitan fisherwoman.[93] Further alterations could have been related to her own dramatic stamp on the role. The German dramatist, Hugo von Hofmannsthal, noticed Duse's mute pauses and commented on the alterations in her tone of voice, changing from infantile to severe, to cold and harsh at the end, with her lips tightening and her shoulders stiff and upright.[94] In the final confrontation with Nora's husband, Duse was said to have looked as though she had aged throughout the course of the play, and her speech was monosyllabic, uttered by someone 'chi ora sa la verità, e deve dirla' [who now knows the truth and has to say it], as Zorzi put it in *L'Italia del popolo* on 10–11 February 1891.[95]

Duse's success inspired her to include the role of Nora in her international repertoire, and she later returned to the theatre of Ibsen following her temporary retirement, performing plays such as *The Lady of the Sea* and *Ghosts* but not *A Doll's House*. Indeed, according to Lugné-Poë, on 25 May 1906, after having assisted Susanne Després in her interpretation of *A Doll's House* in Paris, Duse allegedly presented the actress with her costume as a gift, a symbolic act marking the end of her interpretation and, the following day, sent her a detailed note indicating how to carry out all of her costume changes.[96] Although the *grande attrice* never interpreted the role again, the impact she had on the reception of Ibsen in Italy marked a milestone in the development of this 'new' type of woman in Italy's theatrical tradition.[97] It might have been Capuana who re-translated Ibsen's play for the Italian stage, but it was Duse who occupied a key position in facilitating Nora's introduction to Italian and later foreign audiences. Moreover, it might have been Pieri who first performed the character of Nora in Italy, but it was Duse who captured considerable media attention for her rendition.

A New Image of Women

If Duse chose to perform characters with whom she could identify, making what Paolo Puppa calls 'a particular sort of female character acceptable on Italian stages [...], the type of restive, non-conformist woman in search of autonomy',[98] can the same be said about the roles of Santuzza and Màlia which she included in her early repertoire? Further, is it possible that Verga, just five years after Duse's opening performances in Ibsen's play, might have been inspired by rising 'donne nuove' debates when adapting the title role in *La Lupa*, one of the most sexually liberated characters to emerge from the Italian stage? In the same way as authors and audiences were critical of Nora because she was 'new' for her time, it could equally well be argued that the similar critical response to Verga's theatre, particularly to *La Lupa*, was a result of the fact that his newly vocalised female roles were just as radical. In order to demonstrate, then, how the women in the dramatic adaptations of Verga and later Pirandello were ahead of their time, the ensuing chapters will show how both authors moved away from what Teresa Labriola called earlier 'il vecchio tipo femminile' [the old female archetype],[99] and, in so doing, created 'new' women whose antecedent can be traced back to the role of Nora.

Notes to Chapter 2

1. My translations of 'new woman' are not to be confused with the term New Woman, which was generally used in a nineteenth-century Anglo-American cultural context to describe a financially independent woman 'seen typically as young, middle class and single on principle', who 'had probably been educated to a standard unknown to previous generations of women and was certainly a devotee of Ibsen'; see Viv Gardner, 'Introduction', in *The New Woman and her Sisters*, ed. by Viv Gardner and Susan Rutherford (Hemel Hempstead: Harvester Wheatsheaf, 1992), pp. 4–6 (p. 4).
2. Giacomo Debenedetti, *Verga e il naturalismo* (Milan: Garzanti, 1976), p. 168.
3. See Franca Pieroni Bortolotti, *Alle origini del movimento femminile in Italia 1848–1892* (Milan: Einaudi, 1963).
4. Perry Willson, *Women in Twentieth-Century Italy* (Basingstoke: Palgrave Macmillan, 2010), pp. 16–17.
5. Carmela Covato, *Un'identità divisa: diventare maestra in Italia fra Otto e Novecento* (Rome: Archivio Guido Izzi, 1996), pp. 53–54.
6. Willson, *Women in Twentieth-Century Italy*, p. 18.
7. See Maria-Antonietta Macciocchi, 'Female Sexuality in Fascist Ideology', *Feminist Review*, 1 (1979), 67–83 (p. 75).
8. See Antonia Arslan and Rita Verdirame, 'Giovanni Verga e Neera: un carteggio con due lettere di Eleonora Duse', *Quaderni di filologia e letterature siciliana*, 5 (1978), 27–42.
9. See Ursula Fanning, *Gender Meets Genre: Women as Subject in the Fictional Universe of Matilde Serao* (Dublin: Irish Academic Press, 2002).
10. See *Un idillio letterario inedito verghiano: lettere inedite di Maria Messina a Giovanni Verga*, ed. by Giovanni Garra Agosta, with an intro. by Concetta Greco Lanza (Catania: Greco, 1979).
11. Saveria Chemotti, 'La voce e le parole: Alcuni modelli della narrativa femminile italiana nel Novecento', in *La galassia sommera: suggestioni sulla scrittura femminile italiana*, ed. by Antonia Arslan and Saveria Chemotti (Padua: Il Poligrafo, 2008), pp. 15–44 (p. 15).
12. See Katharine Mitchell, *Italian Women Writers: Gender and Everyday Life in Fiction and Journalism, 1870–1910* (Toronto: Toronto University Press, 2014).
13. Ann Hallamore Caesar, 'Writing by Women in Post-Unification Literary Culture: The Case for De-Segregation', in *Women and Gender in Post-Unification Italy*, ed. by Katharine Mitchell and Helena Sanson (Bern: Peter Lang, 2013), pp. 225–45 (pp. 231–32).
14. Rebecca Meitlis, 'The Adjusted Woman', in *Violetta and her Sisters. The Lady of the Camellias: Responses to the Myth*, ed. by Nicholas John (London: Faber and Faber 1994), pp. 284–91 (p. 288). More recently, Helen Greenwald has examined the portrayal of death among other operatic heroines, including Mimì in Puccini's *La bohème* (1859) and Marguerite in Gounod's *Faust* (1859) who both die from tuberculosis, as well as Puccini's Butterfly and Tosca who take their own lives; see Helen Greenwald, 'Aris moriendi': Reflections on the Death of Mimì', in *The Arts of the Prima Donna in the Long Nineteenth Century*, ed. Rachel Cowgill and Hillary Porris (Oxford: Oxford University Press, 2012), pp 167–85.

15. Susan Rutherford, *The Prima Donna and Opera 1815–1930* (Cambridge: University of Cambridge Press, 2006), p. 11.
16. Ralph Locke, 'What Are These Women Doing in Opera?', in *En Traversti: Women, Gender, Subversion, Opera*, ed. by Corinne E. Blackmer and Patricia Juliana Smith (New York: Columbia University Press, 1995), pp. 59–98 (p. 66).
17. See Ann Caesar, 'Women and the Public/Private Divide: The Salotto, Home and Theatre in Late Nineteenth-Century Italy', in *Gender, Family and Sexuality: The Private Sphere in Italy 1860–1945*, ed. by Perry Willson (Basingstoke: Palgrave Macmillan, 2004), pp. 105–21. See also Katharine Mitchell, 'Evenings out: Female Spectators of Opera and Theatre in Late Nineteenth-Century Italy', in *The Formation of a National Audience: Readers and Spectators in Italy, 1750–1890*, ed. by Jennifer Burns and Gabriella Romani (Madison and Teaneck: Fairleigh Dickinson University Press, 2017), pp. 259–80.
18. Giacinto Battaglia, *Mosaico: saggi diversi di critica drammatica* (Milan: Guglielmini, 1845), 248–49.
19. Susan Rutherford, *Verdi, Opera, Women* (Cambridge: Cambridge University Press, 2013), p. 9.
20. See Max Beerbohm, *Around Theatres* (London: Rupert Hart-Davis, 1953), p. 80.
21. Paul Robinson, 'It's Not Over Till the Soprano Dies', *New York Times Book Review*, 1 January 1989.
22. Carolyn Abbate, *Unsung Voices: Opera and Musical Narrative in the Nineteenth Century* (Princeton: Princeton University Press, 1991), p. 258.
23. Robinson.
24. See Francesca Simoncini, *Eleonora Duse capocomica* (Rome: Le Lettere, 2011).
25. See Rutherford, *The Prima Donna and Opera 1815–1930*, p. 243.
26. See Elizabeth Robins, 'On Seeing Madame Bernhardt's *Hamlet*', *North American Review*, 171.529 (1900), 908–19, who felt that '[f]or a woman to play at being a man is, surely, a tremendous handicap in the attempt to produce a stage illusion' (p. 908).
27. See Cesare Molinari, *L'attrice divina: Eleonora Duse nel teatro italiano fra i due secoli* (Rome: Bulzoni, 1985), p. 78.
28. Lucia Re, 'Eleonora Duse and Women: Performing Desire, Power, and Knowledge', *The Diva in Modern Italian Culture. Italian Studies*, ed. by Katharine Mitchell and Clorinda Donato, 70.3 (2015), 347–63 (p. 349).
29. Michela De Giorgio, 'Dalla donna nuova alla donna della nuova Italia', in *La grande guerra: esperienza, memoria, immagini*, ed. by Diego Leoni and Camillo Zadra (Bologna: Il Mulino, 1986), pp. 307–29 (p. 311).
30. Annarita Buttafuoco, 'Vita esemplari: Donne nuove di primo Novecento', in *Svelamento Sibilla Aleramo: una biografia intellettuale*, ed. by Annarita Buttafuoco and Marina Zancan (Milan: Feltrinelli, 1988), pp. 139–63 (p. 143).
31. Ibid., p. 143.
32. Quoted in Enrica Cavina, 'La "crisi femminile" e le istanze dei movimenti emancipazionisti tra il 1870 e la Prima Guerra Mondiale', in: <http://www.gentesdeyilania.org/IT/Downloads/seminari/SibillaAleramo/SibillaAleramoApprofondimento.pdf> [accessed 21 September 2018], p. 3.
33. Quoted in Laura Mariani, *Il tempo delle attrici: emancipazione e teatro in Italia fra Ottocento e Novecento* (Bologna: Monogolfiera, 1991), pp. 40–41.
34. Eleonora Duse, *Lettere d'amore: Eleonora Duse, Arrigo Boito*, ed. by Raul Radice, 16 photographs (Milan: Il Saggiatore, 1979), p. 821 (original emphasis).
35. See Guido Noccioli, *Duse on Tour: Guido Noccioli's Diaries, 1906–07* (Manchester: Manchester University Press, 1982); and *Eleonora Duse: viaggio intorno al mondo*, ed. by Maria Ida Biggi (Milan: Skira, 2010).
36. Re, p. 349.
37. Ibid., p. 350.
38. Now in Mariani, *Tempo delle attrici*, pp. 135–62.
39. Anna Sica and Alison Wilson, *The Murray Edwards Duse Collection* (Milan: Mimesis, 2012).
40. Anna Laura Mariani, 'Sibilla Aleramo. Significato di tre incontri col teatro: il personaggio di Nora, Giacinta Pezzana, Eleonora Duse', *Teatro e Storia*, 2 (1987), 67–133 (p. 70).

41. For more on the portrayal of motherhood in a variety of Italian women writers, including Aleramo, see Ursula Fanning, 'Maternal Prescriptions and Descriptions in Post-Unification Italy', in *Women and Gender in Post-Unification Italy*, pp. 13–37.
42. See Ann Caesar, 'Italian Feminism and the Novel: Sibilla Aleramo's *A Woman*', *Feminist Review*, 5 (1980), 79–87 (p. 80).
43. Willson, *Women in Twentieth-Century Italy*, p. 40.
44. Annarita Buttafuoco, *Le mariuccine: storia di un'istituzione laica, l'Asilio Mariuccia* (Milan: Franco Angeli Libri, 1985), p. 179.
45. See *Sibilla Aleramo e il suo tempo: vita raccontata e illustrata*, ed. by Bruna Conti and Alba Morito (Milan: Feltrinelli, 1981).
46. Sibilla Aleramo, *Una donna*, preface by Maria Corti (Milan: Feltrinelli, 1995), p. 158.
47. Marina Zancan, '*Una donna* di Sibilla Aleramo', in *Letteratura italiana: le opere*, ed. by Alberto Asor Rosa, 4 vols (Turin: Einaudi, 1995), IV, *Il Novecento*, pp. 101–43 (p. 130).
48. Sibilla Aleramo, *Un amore insolito: diario 1940–1944*, ed. by Alba Morino (Milan: Feltrinelli, 1979), p. 14.
49. Willson, *Women in Twentieth-Century Italy*, p. 40.
50. Sibilla Aleramo, *Il passaggio*, ed. by Bruna Conti (Milano: Serra e Riva Editore, 1985), p. 24.
51. Zancan, '*Una donna* di Sibilla Aleramo', p. 106.
52. Alessandra Cenni, *Gli occhi eroici. Sibilla Aleramo, Eleonora Duse, Cordula Poletti: una storia d'amore nell'Italia della Belle Époque* (Milan: Mursia, 2011), p. 13.
53. Rina Pierangeli Faccio, 'Evoluzione femminile', *Italia femminile*, 45.19 (November 1899).
54. Paola Lombroso, *Caratteri della femminilità* (Turin: F.lli Bocca, 1909), p. ix.
55. Teresa Labriola, *La quistione feminista* (Rome: Loescher, 1910), p. 86.
56. Aleramo, *Un amore insolito*, p. 14.
57. Andrea Camilleri, 'Ibsen', in *Enciclopedia dello spettacolo*, 12 vols (Rome: Le maschere, 1959), VI, pp. 459–75 (p. 459).
58. See Margherita Giordano Lokrantz, 'Three Unpublished Letters by Henrik Ibsen about the First Performances of *Et dukkehjem* in Italy', *Ibsen Studies*, 2.1 (2002), 59–74 (p. 60).
59. Quoted in Simona Urso, 'Ibsen in Italia', in *Scene di fine ottocento: l'Italia fin de siècle a teatro*, ed. by Carlotta Sorba (Rome: Carocci editore, 2004), pp. 193–220 (p. 199).
60. Ibid., p. 199.
61. See Giordano Lokrantz, p. 62. The translation was meant to be produced by Alfredo Mazza but his text never materialised.
62. See Giuliano D'Amico, 'Marketing Ibsen: A Study of the First Italian Reception, 1883–1891', *Ibsen Studies*, 11.2 (2011), 145–75 (p. 154).
63. Francesca Simoncini, *Rosmersholm di Ibsen per Eleonora Duse* (Pisa: ETS, 2005), p. 10.
64. For a comparison between Capuana's translation and the original version in Norwegian, see Roberta Todoros, 'Casa di bambola tra Luigi Capuana ed Eleonora Duse', *Castello di Elsinore*, 21 (1994), 59–66.
65. Michael G. Lerner, 'Édouard Rod and the Introduction of Ibsen into France', *Revue de littérature comparée*, 1 (1969), 69–82 (p. 71).
66. Quoted in Henrik Ibsen, *Théâtre: Les Revenants, La maison de poupée*, trans. from the Norwegian by Moritz Prozor, with a preface by Édouard Rod, 3rd edn (Paris: Albert Savine, 1892), p. i. Now digitised by the Bibliothèque nationale de France: <http://gallica.bnf.fr/ark:/12148/bpt6k232030p/f3.zoom.langFR> [accessed 21 September 2018].
67. Quoted in English in D'Amico, 'Marketing Ibsen', p. 154.
68. For the alternative German ending, see Henrik Ibsen, *Four Major Plays: A Doll's House, Ghosts, Hedda Gabler, The Master Builder*, trans. by James McFarlane and Jens Arup, with an intro. by James McFarlane (Oxford: Oxford University Press, 2008), pp. 87–88. It is noteworthy that, after much public outrage at having distorted Ibsen's play, particularly at the Residenztheater in Berlin, Raabe eventually interpreted the original ending.
69. Quoted in English in Giordano Lokrantz, p. 64.
70. Luigi Capuana, 'Prefazione', in *Casa di bambola* (Milan: Kantorowicz, 1894), pp 7–9 (p. 8).
71. Quoted in English in Giordano Lokrantz, p. 72, n. 24.

72. Quoted in Laura Caretti, 'Capuana, Ibsen e la Duse', in *L'illusione della realtà: studi su Luigi Capuana*, ed. by Michelangelo Picone and Enrica Rossetti (Rome: Salerno, 1990), pp. 185–203 (p. 201).
73. Giuliano D'Amico, 'Six Points for a Comparative Ibsen Reception History', *Ibsen Studies*, 14.1 (2014), 4–37 (p. 24).
74. D'Amico, 'Marketing Ibsen', p. 154.
75. Caretti, 'Capuana, Ibsen e la Duse', p. 200.
76. Ibsen, *Théâtre*, p. i.
77. Arrigo Boito's (perhaps envious) remarks about Ibsen's success are suggested in his letter to Duse of 3 June 1890: 'Non è possibile che ti piaccia — ora fingono di goderselo a Parigi' [You can't possibly like him — now they are pretending to like him in Paris]; quoted in Duse, *Lettere d'amore*, pp. 705–06.
78. Olga Signorelli, *Eleonora Duse* (Rome: Signorelli, 1938), p. 121.
79. Aurélien Lugné-Poë, *Ibsen* (Paris: Les Editions Rieder, 1936), p. 10.
80. Giovanni Pozza, *Cronache teatrali di Giovanni Pozza (1886–1913)*, ed. by Gian Antonio Cibotto (Vicenza: Neri Pozza editore, 1971), p. 101.
81. Ibid., p. 100.
82. Ibid., p. 99.
83. Ibid., p. 100.
84. Ibid., p. 101.
85. Ibid., p. 102.
86. Quoted in Urso, p. 209.
87. Quoted in Giordano Lokrantz, p. 69.
88. G. M. Scalinger, *Ibsen* (Napoli: Edizione del priodico fortunio, 1895), p. 93.
89. Ibsen, *Four Major Plays*, p. viii.
90. Giordano Lokrantz, p. 69
91. D'Amico, 'Marketing Ibsen', p. 163.
92. Urso, p. 202.
93. See Laura Caretti, 'La tarantella di Nora', in *La didascalia nella letteratura teatrale scandinava: testo drammatico e sintesi scenica*, ed. by Merete Kjøller Ritzu (Rome: Bulzoni, 1987), pp. 37–49.
94. Hugo Von Hofmannsthal, *Gabriele D'Annunzio e Eleonora Duse* (Milan: Shakespeare and Company, 1983), pp. 96–97.
95. Quoted in Molinari, p. 144.
96. Aurélien Lugné-Poë, *La parade: sous les étoiles, souvenirs de théâtre (1902–1912)* (Paris: Gallimard, 1933), p. 125.
97. Though she never performed *A Doll's House* again, Duse, following her temporary retirement, returned to the role of a further mother who abandons her child — in this case her son — in *Cenere* (1916), the only film in which she starred. See *Eleonora Duse and 'Cenere' ('Ashes')*, ed. by Maria Pia Pagani and Paul Fryer (Jefferson, NC: McFarland and Co., Inc., 2017).
98. Paolo Puppa, 'The Theatre of United Italy', in *A History of Italian Theatre*, ed. by Joseph Farrell and Paolo Puppa (Cambridge: Cambridge University Press, 2006), pp. 223–34 (p. 226).
99. Labriola, p. 86.

CHAPTER 3

The Sicilian Voice

The Innocent Persecuted Heroine

Feminist critics have largely maintained that male-authored literature tends to place emphasis on women's subjugation and passivity in patriarchal society. According to Gayle Austin, first-stage images of women criticism 'points out patterns in writing by men in which, for example, the female characters suffer or die in order for the male characters to grow or continue on their life journeys'.[1] As Edgar Allan Poe famously put it in an 1846 essay, 'the death of a beautiful woman is, unquestionably, the most poetical topic in the world', a notion which associates women with what Beth Ann Bassein has called 'the most passive state occurring'.[2] So while women have been associated with *passivity*, men, by contrast, have been associated with *activity*. Indeed, Laura Mulvey has argued that, 'within the typical narrative, the male is the one who makes something happen (the typical hero), who forces a change in another through a battle of wills'.[3] It seems that the 'typical hero' makes an explicit appearance in popular folk- and fairy-tale tradition. Teresa de Lauretis has claimed that fairy tales depend on 'making something happen, forcing a change in another person, a battle of will and strength, victory / defeat, all occurring in a linear time with a beginning and end', concluding with the 'typical hero' finding his usually dormant and placid heroine 'at the end of *his* journey',[4] leaving her journey entirely ignored.

The present chapter demonstrates how Santuzza in both versions of Verga's *Cavalleria rusticana* (1880 and 1884), as well as Mommina in Pirandello's *Questa sera si recita a soggetto* (1928–29), taken from the short story '"Leonora, addio!"' (1910), are not passive spectators in their respective narratives and plays, each situated in Sicily. Though on the surface both women bear some resemblance to the innocent persecuted heroine trope, it is assured here that the pair are not typical damsels in distress. Santuzza and Mommina are seen as active heroines who force a change in other characters — namely in their lovers — and fight their own battle of wills, similar to Ibsen's Nora.

As one of Verga's most successful and popular works, *Cavalleria rusticana*, based on what the author allegedly witnessed outside his own home in Vizzini,[5] has inevitably received a considerable amount of critical attention.[6] The general consensus has been summarised (somewhat harshly) by Giorgio Bàrberi Squarotti: '*Cavalleria rusticana*, in effetti, sembra, nella versione teatrale, una sorta di involontaria parodia della novella, ridotta com'è a una semplice questione di adulterio e di vendetta' [*Cavalleria rusticana*, in effect, seems, in the theatrical version, to be a sort of involuntary parody of the *novella*, reduced as it is to a simple question of adultery and vendetta].[7] This chapter, however, does not favour one version over the other. Instead, it illuminates how Santuzza, in refusing to stay silent about her lover's affair and thereby rebelling against her traditional representation as passive victim, becomes a 'new' woman. In fact, while Franca Angelini has claimed that '[n]ella *Cavalleria* non c'è personaggio protagonista attorno a cui si organizza la coppia o il triangolo' [[i]n *Cavalleria* there is no main character around which the couple or triangle revolves],[8] it is suggested that Verga specifically designs his play to emphasise the role of Santuzza who dominates the plot structure, particularly following Duse's willingness to take on the lead part. The chapter thus adds to the perspective that, to use the words of Rita Verdirame, the '[n]ucleo e motore' [[n]ucleus and motive force] in Verga's fiction is none other than 'la donna' [the woman],[9] in line with Siro Ferrone's observation that 'l'uomo è quasi sempre il passivo strumento di opposte forze femminili' [the male character is almost always the passive instrument of opposing female forces].[10]

The second part then focuses on Pirandello's portrayal of Mommina.[11] In contrast to the argument that Pirandello's treatment of women is 'patriarchal in orientation',[12] and that the typical heroine is an 'estrema vittima' [extreme victim],[13] not forgetting Walter Starkie's early view that, in Pirandello, 'the Sicilian women, living in the keeping of traditionally jealous husbands, find it difficult to rebel',[14] this chapter draws attention to Mommina's insubordinate attitude and shows how she stimulates Verri's unbalanced mind, previously disturbed by his violent upbringing. Although he is portrayed as an intimidator who locks his wife and daughters in a Rapunzel-like tower because of his jealousy, it is arguable that beneath the surface the tormen*tor* is also the tormen*ted*, as Giovanni Macchia has proposed: 'È la rappresentazione di un sacrificio dolente e ineluttabile, come in certi misteri medievali, ove il carnefice diventa anche la vittima e il torturatore il torturato' [It is a play about a painful and inescapable sacrifice, like in certain mystery plays, where the executioner also becomes the victim and the torturer the tortured].[15] Despite the fact that Mommina does nothing to provoke him physically, she nonetheless triggers his madness. Her influence is psychological, alive in the memories he will never be able to erase. In fact, much here will reveal *how* Verri suffers as a result of his fixation with her past, rather than *what* Mommina does to torment him. Though Mommina does die at the end of '"Leonora, addio!"' and *Questa sera si recita a soggetto* — unlike *Cavalleria rusticana* where the male lead is killed — Pirandello conveys the implication that it is Verri who will never be able 'to grow or continue on his life journey', to use Austin's words above.

Furthermore, Pirandello continues to break with convention in the play by placing Mommina's death in the realm of the meta-theatre. Once the character Mommina dies, the actress playing her role faints, personifying what Pirandello considered the ideal fusion of fiction and non-fiction, which he initially saw in Duse and Abba. Consequently, the author poses yet another unusual challenge to the perceived association between women's passivity and death. It is proposed here that Pirandello's choice to embody his ideal relationship between art and reality in Mommina and the lead actress performing her role enables him to turn both women into his 'new' mouthpiece characters in his pioneering meta-theatre.

The Damsel in Distress

Aleksandr Isaakovich Nikiforov was one of the first writers to discuss the innocent persecuted heroine trope in 1927. He divides fairy tales into two traditions:

> Tales about winning (mainly of a groom, but with a completely different morphological composition of episodes than in the [male] fairy tale about winning); [and] Tales about the sufferings of the innocently persecuted (maiden or woman).[16]

Shortly afterwards, Antti Aarne and Stith Thompson offer a definition of this genre typology in their *The Types of the Folklore* (1929 and revised in 1961), a classification system separating the different fairy-tale characters into various categories with an AT number for each entry. The persecuted heroine is designated AT 510:

> *The persecuted heroine.* (a) The heroine is abused by her stepmother and stepsisters, and (a1) stays on the hearth or in the ashes, and (a2) is dressed in rough clothing — such as a cap of rushes, wooden cloak, and so on; (b) flees in disguise from her father who wants to marry her; or (c) is cast out by him because she has said that she loved him like salt, or (d) is to be killed by a servant.[17]

Several classic fairy-tale heroines fit this designation, including Cinderella, Sleeping Beauty, and Rapunzel. These tales can be traced back to Giambattista Basile's Neapolitan *Lo cunto de li cunti overo lo trattenemiento de peccerille* (1634–1636) in the form of 'La gatta cenerentola', 'Sole, luna e Talia', and 'Petrosinella'. This collection, known as the *Pentamerone* and reminiscent of Boccaccio's *Decameron* (1349–1350), is one of the earliest in Europe and consists of forty-nine tales framed by a fiftieth, each told over the course of five days. Though the three heroines have been adapted over the centuries, such as by the brothers Jacob and Wilhelm Grimm in their *Kinder-und Hausmärchen* (1812) and the popular cartoonist Walt Disney, ultimately they have remained persecuted victims in need of rescuing.

Even though the women in such tales are portrayed as persecuted *maidens*, their virginity is somewhat questionable, particularly in Maiden-in-the-Tower stories. In Basile's 'Petrosinella', for example, each night the protagonist would throw her braids over the window sill and pull the prince up into the tower. After further intimate encounters, the ogress guarding her hostage learns about their assignations and fears that Petrosinella will run away. After a series of events aimed at preventing her victim from escaping, she is killed by a hungry wolf and the lovers are safe. Other variations continue to point more explicitly to the lovers' sexual relationship. In the version by the seventeenth-century French writer Charlotte-Rose de La Force, Persinette is entirely unaware that she is expecting a baby and only the witch notices when her pregnancy starts to show. Moreover, in Grimms's version of 1857, Rapunzel is referred to as the prince's 'wife' and he learns about their children once they are re-united following the witch's death.[18]

Critical literature has pointed out the prevalence of this type of heroine in Italian tales, from both northern and southern Italy, especially the designation AT 510B where the character runs away from her paternal home.[19] Indeed, fleeing the family home was not a rare occurrence in Italy at a time when women largely had no say in their choice of spouse and were often treated as part of a financial transaction from father to husband — a transaction which Ibsen's Nora openly rejects in her final exchange with her husband: '[D]alle mani di papà son passata fra le tue' [[F]rom my father's hands I was passed into yours], as Capuana writes in his translation.[20] It is therefore unsurprising that the designation AT 510B also sits comfortably, at least on the surface, with Santuzza and Mommina who both leave their homes following their *own* choice of spouse.

According to Steven Swann Jones, persecuted heroines not only share common characteristics but are placed in similar plots, which he divides into acts:

> The tales of The Innocent Persecuted Heroine genre share not only related motifs and general episodes, but most importantly, they share a plot outline. This generic paradigm involves three major acts (so termed because they correspond roughly to the function of acts in drama). Act One concerns the heroine's initial family situation and her life at home, where she is frequently the victim of various jealous, ambitious, overprotective, or generally hostile family members. Act Two concerns the heroine's meeting and acquiring a mate. It dramatises various obstacles that interfere with the desired union and concludes with the heroine's marriage to her husband. And Act Three concerns the heroine's difficulties in her husband's home, where she is the victim of persecution, generally after giving birth to one or more children.[21]

This tripartite division, again on the surface, seems to correspond well with the works in question. In the dramatic version of *Cavalleria rusticana*, in what Swann Jones calls 'Act One', Verga turns Santuzza into a poor orphan and portrays her as a victim of her family who has left her home because she conceived out of wedlock. In 'Act Two', the obstacle Santuzza encounters is Lola, Compare Alfio's wife with whom Turiddu is involved. In 'Act Three', following Turiddu's death, Santuzza continues to be a victim, this time at the hands of her brothers now that she has been left an unmarried pregnant woman.[22] As for Mommina, she is also a victim of her family in Swann Jones's 'Act One', mainly because of the 'loose' reputation she has acquired through the operatic recitals held in her home. In 'Act Two', she meets her 'hero' Verri and leaves when they marry, despite her family's objections. But in 'Act Three', she continues to be persecuted at the hands of her husband. Because of the memories he suspects her of cherishing, Verri locks Mommina in a tall tower and forbids her from even mentioning her past involvement with the opera. Suffocated by her imprisonment, she collapses and dies.

Even though Aarne and Thompson's *The Types of the Folklore* is a useful means to identify female characters who face similar forms of persecution, the codification system has led to an inevitable feminist backlash. Torborg Lundell, for instance, points out the gender bias against women in the index, indicating a number of examples where powerful female characters are overlooked by the selective labelling system.[23] Many feminists in the twentieth century have thus challenged the representation of submissive women in traditional fairy tales, particularly those by the Grimm brothers. Indeed, most feminist literary criticism from as early as the 1960s grew from a condemnation of the restrictive social roles which perpetuate the idea of women's subordination in a male-dominated world, the wrong kind of role model for children.[24] Consequently, in recent years there has emerged a shift in critical interpretation and the passive female victim has come to be read more as a character with inner strength — an active heroine who counters the helpless female stereotypes in canonical tales. Kay Stone has, in fact, urged critics and scholars to offer new perceptions 'if we are to break the magic spell of gender stereotyping',[25] and, as a result, many have provided re-readings of these passive heroines.[26]

Significantly, the first published corpus of fairy tales by women authors, which can be traced to the French salons of the 1680s, seemed to have anticipated the emergence of the active heroine. Silenced from politics and denied the equal right to an education, several aristocratic authors, including Madame d'Aulnoy, Marie-Jane Lhéritier, Catherine Bernard, Charlotte-Rose de La Force and Henriette-Julie de Murat, reverted back to the world of children in their fairy tales, which they produced for an adult readership, as a means of mocking classical literature and contemporary society. The genre enabled the authors to delve into a make-believe world and create an ideal fictional world where they could engage in the political and intellectual discourse from which they were excluded:

> These writers conceived of worlds inhabited by extraordinarily majestic and powerful *female* fairies, a mirror of their own omnipotence within the salon as contrasted with the conditions of their real lives.[27]

Benedikte Naubert continued the tradition of storytelling for adults in the 1780s in Germany. She sought inspiration not in classical sources but in medieval Anglo-Saxon and German traditions, and, as with her French predecessors, was equally fascinated by powerful sorceresses. Topics in her fiction included women's rejection of marriage in favour of independence and the supernatural powers of magical wise-women.

Italy also fostered a rich female folklore tradition during Verga's and Pirandello's lifetimes. The *Oxford Companion to Fairy Tales* (2002) pays homage to Emma Perodi's *Le novelle della nonna* of 1892,[28] but there is an even earlier female author whose collection of tales made an extraordinary contribution: Laura Gonzenbach, born in Sicily in 1842 of Swiss descent. In 1868, the German historian Otto Hartwig commissioned her to send him a collection of fairy tales for a volume he was compiling on Sicilian history and she collated ninety-two tales from village communities in Catania and her native city of Messina, which she later published in her 1870 *Sicilianische Märchen*. Gonzenbach's collection became the only volume of Sicilian tales in the nineteenth century composed *by* a woman and *from* the perspective of local women storytellers.[29] Both the sheer quantity and content of the tales are particularly impressive. The stories cover a range of unusual topics, including rape, beatings, and murder, which are not developed in canonical tales. In addition, to use the words of Jack Zipes, almost all of the stories 'call for women to challenge the oppression they experienced in their daily lives and take power into their own hands'.[30] Even the Virgin Mary is portrayed in a different light: she is more 'omnipotent, clever, compassionate, and stern'.[31]

In the same way as Gonzenbach gave voice to female storytellers in rural Sicily, so did the physician-turned-folklorist, Giuseppe Pitrè. During the major cholera epidemic throughout Sicily in 1866 to 1867, Pitrè devoted himself to recording his patients' songs, proverbs, and tales, famously gaining a name for himself as the doctor who, after his visits, recorded their stories and wrote books on horseback. Pitrè compiled his twenty-five volume series, *Biblioteca delle tradizioni popolari siciliane*, from 1871 to 1913, three years before his death. Approximately sixty-six percent of Pitrè's collection consists of tales narrated by women. As Zipes puts it: 'Since women told most of these tales, they tend to be candid and stark depictions of extraordinary young women who cleverly shape their own destinies.'[32]

Here emerges a fascinating point of contact between Sicilian folklore tradition and the treatment of women in Verga and Pirandello. Though superficially Santuzza and Mommina fit in with the persecuted maiden trope, their voices remain strong, clever, and assertive. Just as various women are 'heard' in the tales of Gonzenbach and Pitrè, so are the two *active* heroines considered here, especially so in the stage adaptations, which go one step further in breaking what Stone called earlier 'the magic spell of gender stereotyping'.[33]

Cavalleria rusticana

The first short story that Verga adapted into a play was 'Cavalleria rusticana', which he initially published in the journal *Fanfulla della domenica* on 14 March 1880. Verga then included the story in the first edition of *Vita dei campi* later that year, finally republishing it in the Neapolitan journal *Fortunio: Cronaca illustrata della settimana* on 25 January 1891. 'Cavalleria rusticana' tells the tale of the triangular relationship involving husband (Compare Alfio), wife (Lola) and lover (Turiddu). Following Turiddu's return from military service, he finds his betrothed Lola married to the wealthy cart driver Alfio. He begins to court another woman — called Santa in the short story and the diminutive Santuzza on stage — and this makes Lola jealous. The two former lovers rekindle their relationship, leaving Santa / Santuzza enraged. She subsequently informs Alfio of the adultery and it is her revelation which ultimately leads Alfio to kill Turiddu in a climactic duel.[34]

Only three years after its publication in *Vita dei campi*, the narrative was turned into a play. The première took place at the Teatro Carignano in Turin on 14 January 1884 under the direction of Cesare Rossi and starring Italy's *grande attrice*, Eleonora Duse, as Santuzza. According to Federico De Roberto, Verga adapted the play towards the end of the summer of 1883 in a matter of days. De Roberto recounts the mostly negative response Verga received from his literary friends, namely the writers Arrigo Boito and Luigi Gualdo, as well as the publisher Emilio Treves, and the journalist Eugenio Torelli-Viollier. The only person truly to encourage him was the author Giuseppe Giacosa, to whom the drama was later dedicated.[35]

Perhaps it was the reaction from his contemporaries which led Verga, in a letter of 10 January 1884, days before the opening night, to confide his fears to his translator

Édouard Rod: 'La mia commedia (tentativo di commedia, chiamiamola meglio, in un genere arrischiatissimo e che fa pugni col gusto attuale del pubblico) passerà inosservata anche in Italia' [My play (or attempted play, to put it more accurately, in a very risky genre which challenges the current taste of the audience) will also pass unnoticed in Italy] (*Lt*, p. 80). Verga was so apprehensive about his first theatre production that he avoided the première altogether,[36] and understandably so. This was the first time he had placed his Sicilian village characters onto the typically bourgeois stage. As Giacosa stressed when announcing the première in the *Gazzetta piemontese*: 'La novità del Verga non consiste nel *fare di più*, ma, forse nel fare di meno, certo nel *fare diversamente*' [Verga's innovation does not consist in *doing more*, but perhaps in doing less, and certainly in *doing things differently*].[37]

Cavalleria rusticana was, in fact, a very different play. In just one act, with no spectacular scene changes and uncomplicated dialogue, Verga managed to convey Sicily's peculiar traditions to the recently united Italian public. In fact, despite his doubts, *Cavalleria rusticana* enjoyed phenomenal success, so much so that the composer Mascagni was inspired to transpose the same characters onto the operatic stage in 1890, leading Verga to gain worldwide recognition.[38] As Cesare Levi observes, the play 'era un nuovo soffio d'aria pura che spirava sul palcoscenico italiano, a spazzare gli ultimi residui del Romanticismo tragico e dal convenzionalismo della Commedia borghese' [was a new breath of fresh air that blew through the Italian stage, sweeping away the last residues of tragic Romanticism and the conventionalism of the bourgeois theatre] and, as a result, Verga offered the Italian stage 'il suo primo dramma realista' [its first Realist play].[39] Indeed, rather than elaborating on the characters' inner turmoil and including melodramatic dénouements as with his Romantic predecessors, particularly the historical writer Alessandro Manzoni whose novel *I promessi sposi* (1827) emerged during the romantic period,[40] the *veristi* broke away from this trend by concentrating on their characters' external actions — '[i]l semplice fatto umano' (*Tn* I, p. 191) [the plain simple facts (*CROS*, p. 93)] as Verga states in his prelude to 'L'amante di Gramigna' (1880) — to suggest their suffering; usually a logical train of actions which, ultimately, led to tragedy. The *veristi* thus strove to avoid this sort of 'crescendo', as Verga boldly puts it: '[S]acrifichiamo volentieri l'effetto della catastrofe' (*Tn*: I, 191) [We gladly sacrifice the narrative's climax and its psychological effect (*CROS*, 93)], a radical technique which he replicated in the theatre for the first time with his new Sicilian play.

Santuzza

One of the major alterations which Verga introduces into the dramatic version of *Cavalleria rusticana* is the development of the role of Santuzza following Duse's willingness to perform in the play. In the *novella*, Santa is simply one of many, a face amongst the crowd whose individual voice is effectively silenced as she becomes part of a 'whole'. Instead, the main narrative voice to emerge is the collective voice of the villagers, which tells the story of all of those affected by the triangular relationship in free indirect speech. Firstly, the multi-voiced narrator recounts how, following Turiddu's arrival from military service, still dressed in his new soldier's uniform, he discovers that his betrothed Lola is married to Compare Alfio from Licodia. In the midst of the villagers' voice, the readers detect Turiddu's more enraged voice:

> Dapprima Turiddu come lo seppe, santo diavolone! voleva trargli fuori le budella della pancia, voleva trargli, a quel di Licodia! Però non fece nulla, e si sfogò coll'andare a cantare tutte le canzoni di sdegno che sapeva sotto la finestra della bella. (*Tn* I, 179)
>
> [When Turiddu first got to know about it, Christ in Heaven! he wanted to tear the guts out of that chap from Licodia, he really did! But the only thing he did was to give vent to his feelings by going and singing all the abusive songs he could think of under the fair young woman's window.] (*CROS*, 27)

Indifferent to her former fiancé, Lola 'non si fece né bianca né rossa' (*Tn*, 179) [didn't turn a hair (*CROS*, 27)] and actually enjoyed standing on her balcony exhibiting the jewellery that her husband bought her to all the villagers, including Turiddu, who the sympathetic narrator — or the compassionate Verga — calls a 'poveraccio' (*Tn* I, 180) [poor wretch (*CROS*, 27]. In retaliation, Turiddu begins to court Santa. Standing outside her window, he charms her in front of the community. Their flirtatious exchange, reported by means of direct speech, alludes to a popular folktale in a kind of Sicilianised Italian:

> 'La volpe quando all'uva non ci poté arrivare...'
> 'Disse: come sei bella, *racinedda* mia!' (*Tn* I, 181)[41]
>
> ['When the fox couldn't get the grapes...'
> 'He said: what a lovely girl you are, my currant bun!'] (*CROS*, 29)

As soon as Lola learns about Turiddu's involvement with Santa, she suddenly becomes pale and red with envy and eventually lures him away: 'Turiddu tornò a salutarla così spesso che Santa se ne avvide, e gli batté la finestra al muso' (*Tn* I, 182) [Turiddu called to say hello to her so often that Santa took notice, and slammed her window in his face (*CROS*, 30)]. What is noteworthy about these opening passages is how they highlight not just the hustle and bustle of village life, but also how Turiddu fluctuates from one woman to the next; that is, from Lola to Santa and then back again to Lola, a final move which will ultimately lead him to his death.

The opening of the dramatic version differs considerably. While the reader of the play would acquire a substantial amount of description from the stage directions depicting 'la piazzetta' [the small piazza] (*Tt*, 31), the spectators of the performance simply see how the square has been set on stage. Furthermore, Verga chooses to open the play *after* the adultery has occurred, effectively depriving the audience of the 'drama' leading up to the triangle. As Roberto Bigazzi has explained, the narrative genre provided Verga with 'una possibilità di punti di vista e di prospettive mutevoli che il teatro non sapeva ancora offrire' [the possibility of conveying changing points of views and perspectives that the theatrical genre did not yet know how to offer].[42] In fact, the spectators do not gain any insight into Turiddu's sense of rejection following Lola's engagement to another man, nor do they see how the two former lovers reignite their affection. Instead, they acquire a background into the previous events through a series of dialogue exchanges, mainly between Santuzza and Turiddu's mother, Gnà Nunzia. However informative, the dialogue throws light *only* on Santuzza's point of view:

> SANTUZZA: Egli [Turiddu] si metteva a cantare sotto la mia finestra per far dispetto a lei che s'era maritata con un altro. Tanto è vero che l'amore antico non si scorda più. Io come lo sentivo cantare, quel cristiano, sembrava che il cuore mi scappasse via dal petto. Ero pazza, sì! Come potevo dir di no, quand'egli mi pregava: 'Apri, Santuzza, s'è vero che mi vuoi bene!' (*Tt*, 36)
>
> [SANTUZZA: He [Turiddu] would sing under my window to spite her who was married to another man. First love dies hard as they say. As I heard him singing, Turiddu, it seemed like my heart wanted to escape from my chest. I was out of my mind, I really was! How could I refuse when he would beg me: 'Open the window, Santuzza, if it's true that you love me!']

In contrast to the narrative, the role of Santuzza in the drama is singled out from the village people and positioned centre stage. As a result, despite relying predominantly on dialogue, the dramatic version ironically reduces all the different voices: the choral voice of the villagers in the narrative is now replaced by the presence of only four minor characters (Zio Brasi, his wife Compare Camilla, Zia Filomena and Pipuzza), and the main voice to emerge is that of Santuzza.

As well as becoming the play's central focus, Santuzza is transformed into what was called earlier an innocent persecuted heroine, or, as others have put it, an archetypal *'personnage sympathique'*,[43] a 'povera ragazzetta patetica' [poor pathetic young girl].[44] In the narrative she is the daughter of Massaro Cola, 'il quale era ricco come un maiale' (*Tn* I, 181) [who was said to be rich as a pig (*CROS*, 28)];[45] she has a 'dote' (*Tn* I, 181) [dowry (*CROS*, 29)]; and is known for being 'ricca' (*Tn* I, 181) [rich (*CROS*, 29)]. In the stage version, however, she is a poor orphan disowned by her brothers because she is an unmarried expectant mother: 'Ora che sono in questo stato... che i miei fratelli quando lo sapranno m'ammazzano colle sue mani stesse!' [Now that I am in this state... as soon as my brothers find out they will kill me with their own hands!] (*Tt*, 36). According to Giorgio Prosperi, Verga's overly sympathetic approach to Santuzza actually prevents the audience from responding to her in the same way as the reader of the *novella*:

> [L]a Santa del racconto [...] ha la simpatia irresistibile delle creature artisticamente vive [...]. Mentre la simpatia che suscita la povera Santuzza è un dato quasi tutto esterno, ed è fatto in gran parte di pietà per la vittima di un giuoco più grande di lei.[46]
>
> [The Santa of the narrative [...] commands an irresistible sympathy proper to lively artistic creations [...]. The sympathy which poor Santuzza arouses, however, is almost wholly external, and consists predominantly of pity for the victim of a game larger than herself.]

Indeed in the short story, the reader does not need to hear Santa lament her fate because the narrator reveals her emotions succinctly on her behalf. At first, when she falls in love, the reader is told that 'la nappa del berretto del bersagliere gli aveva fatto il solletico dentro il cuore, e le ballava sempre dinanzi gli occhi' (*Tn* I, 182) [the tassel on the sharpshooter's cap had begun to tickle her fancy, and kept on dancing up and down in front of her eyes (*CROS*, 29)]. Later, once she acknowledges his infidelity, the narrator reports, again concisely, that 'gli batté la finestra al muso' (*Tn* I, 182) [[she] slammed her window in his face (*CROS*, 30)]. In the play, on the other hand, Santuzza has to express her emotions for herself and does so quite extensively. Throughout the first five consecutive scenes she does nothing but talk about Turiddu: in the first scene she confides in Gnà Nunzia; in the second she confronts Turiddu about Lola; and in the fifth scene she discloses the truth about the affair to Compare Alfio. As a result, Verga places greater importance on *what* she says in order to show *how* she feels. While he was keen to move the events in the *novella* around the page (shifting the action from the village piazza to Lola's balcony, to outside Santa's window, and hence adding what Pietro Gibellini calls a kind of 'teatralità virtuale' [virtual theatre] to these opening passages),[47] on stage Verga focusses purely on Santuzza.

Not only does Santuzza in the play have to speak for herself, but she does so melodramatically. From her very first entrance on stage, frantically searching for Turiddu, she immediately uses religious terminology: 'Ah, gnà Nunzia, non mi vedete la faccia che ho? Fate come Gesù Cristo a Maria Maddalena... Ditemi dov'è vostro figlio Turiddu, per carità' [Oh Gnà Nunzia, can't you see the state I'm in? Do as Jesus did for Mary Magdalene... Tell me where your son Turiddu is, I beg you] (*Tt*, 32). Later, when Turiddu accuses her of putting his life at risk, she falls at his feet, '*cadendo ginocchioni a mani giunte*' [*falling to her knees with her hands joined together*] (*Tt*, 39). As the pair clash over Lola, she exclaims in despair: 'Ammazzami, non me ne importa, via!' [Kill me, I don't care, go ahead!] (*Tt*, 41). Even though Verga maintained in his 'L'amante di Gramigna' that his literary works would be composed of 'parole semplici' (*Tn* I, p. 191) [simple words], it appears that Santuzza's style of language contradicts his principles.

However, in placing Santuzza centre stage, Verga also gives her the freedom to confront Turiddu more directly. When Turiddu denies his whereabouts, she boldly challenges him: 'Non è vero. Ieri sera a due ore di notte eravate ancora qui' [That's not true. You were still here at two o'clock in the morning] (*Tt*, 38). In addition, Santuzza expresses her jealousy towards Lola to a much greater extent:

> SANTUZZA: Ma la gnà Lola, no, vedete! Quella lì mi vuol far dannare l'anima.
> TURIDDU: Lascia stare la gnà Lola, ch'è per casa sua.
> SANTUZZA: E lei perchè non mi lascia stare, me? Perchè mi vuol rubare voi, che non ho altro? (*Tt*, 39)
>
> [SANTUZZA: But not Gnà Lola, no, don't you see! That girl wants to damn my soul.
> TURIDDU: Leave Gnà Lola alone, she's devoted to her family.
> SANTUZZA: So why doesn't she leave me alone then? Why does she want to steal you from me, the only person I have left?]

As well as being given the chance to challenge Turiddu on stage, Santuzza also faces Lola more spontaneously. In the *novella* Santa meets Lola only once in church and barely confronts her rival:

'Ah!' mormorava Santa di massaro Cola, aspettando ginocchioni il suo turno dinanzi al confessionario dove Lola stava facendo il bucato dei suoi peccati. 'Sull'anima mia non voglio mandarti a Roma per la penitenza!' (*Tn* I, 183)

['Ah!' murmured Cola's daughter Santa as she waited her turn, kneeling in front of the confessional where Lola was laundering her sins. 'I swear I won't let you get away with it by crawling to Rome!'] (*CROS*, 30)

The reliance on dialogue in the stage version, instead, provides Santuzza with more scope to express her resentment. As Lola enters the stage looking for her husband, Santuzza is clearly disturbed by her presence: 'In chiesa ci ha da andare chi ha la coscienza netta, gnà Lola' [Those who go to church are those with a clear conscience, Gnà Lola] (*Tt*, 40), an exchange missing from the short story.

Although Verga portrays Santa / Santuzza's jealousy differently in the two versions, he nevertheless leads both the reader of the *novella* and the audience of the play to the same crucial point: her revenge. The crux of the plot is instigated by Santa / Santuzza as soon as she betrays Turiddu. As Bàrberi Squarotti underlines: 'Il tradimento di Santa mette in moto la tragedia' [Santa's betrayal sets the tragedy in motion].[48] This is the moment which, arguably, exposes Santa / Santuzza in a new light. Here she reveals herself as the antithesis of a passive victim, a woman who refuses to stay silent about her lover's infidelity. In both versions, she refers to the affair in a rhetorical and euphemistic way. Santa meets Alfio returning home from work, with a new dress for his wife, and she enlightens him about the truth: '"Avete ragione di portarle dei regali, gli disse la vicina Santa, perchè mentre girate il mondo a buscarvi il pane e a comprar dei regali per vostra moglie, essa vi adorna la casa!"' (*Tn* I, 183) ['You do well to bring her presents', his neighbour Santa told him, 'because while you're away your wife dresses up your home with a pair of horns!' (*CROS*, 30)], repeating the same words in the play.

According to Luigi Russo, in this exchange 'i motivi fondamentali sono le tre o quattro espressioni della *novella*, che l'artista ha parafrasato e diluito, per la necessità pratica teatrale' [the key themes are the three or four expressions in the *novella*, which the author has paraphrased and diluted for practical reasons connected to the theatre].[49] Russo fails to mention, however, that Santuzza is forced to develop her response on stage for the benefit of the audience: she criticises herself for having betrayed Turiddu by calling herself 'una scellerata' [a villain] (*Tt*, 43), a self-condemning term which is absent from the *novella*. Indeed, once Verga places Santuzza on stage, he gives her the chance to reflect on her own actions and, in so doing, adds depth to her personality. But instead of taking her reflections any further, Verga withdraws her from both the narrative and theatrical plots once she has disclosed the truth. Perhaps Verga cut this scene short because he was only just beginning to experiment with this more articulate side of his characters' personalities on stage. In fact, each of Verga's subsequent stage roles, in particular his female leads in *La Lupa* and *La caccia al lupo*, becomes increasingly self-aware as his theatre develops.

Despite Santuzza's physical absence, the consequences of her betrayal pervade the plots. After her betrayal, the last parts of the *novella* and play are devoted to portraying the inevitable duel. In the *novella*, Alfio meets Turiddu at the tavern to discuss 'quella cosa' (*Tn* I, 183) [the thing (*CROS*, 31)] and both men exchange a series of peculiar rituals: 'Turiddu da prima gli aveva presentato il bicchiere, ma compare Alfio lo scansò colla mano' (*Tn* I, 183) [Turiddu began by holding out a glass of wine to him, but Alfio brushed it aside with a sweep of his arm (*CROS*, 31)]. Once they have arranged to meet at sunrise, 'si scambiarono il bacio della sfida, Turiddu strinse fra i denti l'orecchio del carettiere, e così gli fece promessa solenne di non mancare' (*Tn* I, 184) [they exchanged the kiss of the challenge. Turiddu took the tip of the cart-driver's ear between his teeth and bit it, by way of a solemn promise to keep the appointment (*CROS*, 31)].[50]

In the theatrical version, soon after Santuzza's betrayal, instead of leading up to the dénouement, Verga interrupts the action by adding a scene between Turiddu and Lola. While in the narrative the impending tragedy is suggested by Lola's bad dream 'dell'uva nera' (*Tn* I, 182) [of black grapes],[51] on stage she is visibly concerned about her husband's return: 'Vado a casa perchè sono in pensiero per mio marito, che non l'ho visto in chiesa' [I'm going home because I'm worried about my husband whom I didn't see in church] (*Tt*, 44). What is noteworthy about this exchange is how the audience is finally able to see the lovers together. Whereas in the *novella* Verga conveys Turiddu and Lola's feelings for each other from the beginning, in the dramatic version, because the play has consistently been focused on Santuzza, it is only here, near the end of the plot, that Verga provides a scene for the pair. During their dialogue, Lola hints at her jealousy as she speculates about his behaviour with other women during his military service: 'Chi sa quante ne avete fatte di queste galanterie colle donne di laggiù, fuorivia, mentre eravate soldato! Si vede che ci avete pratica!' [Who knows how many women you courted down there, out of sight, while you were a soldier! We can see that you're good at it!] (*Tt*, 44). Turiddu responds to her provocation by suggesting his feeling of rejection following the discovery of her engagement:

> TURIDDU: Dite le donne, piuttosto! che prima vi fanno mille giuramenti; e poi, quando un povero diavolo se n'è andato lontano, che il cuore l'ha lasciato via, e la testa anche, e non mangia, e non dorme più, pensando sempre a una cosa, tutt'a un tratto gli arriva come una schioppettata la notizia: 'Sai? la tale si marita!' Come se vi pigliasse un accidente! (*Tt*, 45)
>
> [TURIDDU: What about you women, instead, who first make you a thousand promises, and then when a poor devil has gone far away, leaving his heart behind, and his head too, and he no longer eats or sleeps, thinking about one thing only, suddenly like a gunshot he hears the news: 'You know what? So-and-so is getting married?' As if you'd had a stroke!]

However, by opening the play once the adultery has taken place, Verga is unable to show how the lovers' feelings for each other developed. The audience of the play thus cannot respond to the characters as empathetically as the reader of the *novella*.

Following this, Alfio enters the stage and, just as he does in the narrative, refuses to drink the wine that Turiddu offers him. As a result, Turiddu throws the cup to the ground and seals the duel with a kiss and a bite to his rival's earlobe. But whereas the reader of the *novella* is then made to witness how Alfio, during the duel, dishonestly kills Turiddu — '[Alfio] acchiappò rapidamente una manata di polvere e la gettò negli occhi dell'avversario' (*Tn* I, 185) [he suddenly grabbed a handful of dust and hurled it into the eyes of his opponent (*CROS*, 32)] — the spectators of the play never see the two men actually fighting. All that is heard is one of the minor characters, Pipuzza, announcing: 'Hanno ammazzato compare Turiddu! Hanno ammazzato compare Turiddu!' [They've killed Compare Turiddu! They've killed Compare Turiddu!] (*Tt*, 48), and, unlike in the original version, two *carabinieri* run on stage at the news, reminding the audience of an official body sent from the recently united nation-state.

Many critics have tended to examine the socio-economic implications of the duel. Bàrberi Squarotti has argued that Turiddu is fighting a kind of futile social feud against the wealthier Alfio:

> La vendetta è contro tutti coloro che, per il denaro, possono comprare tutto, anche le donne, se sono uomini, come compare Alfio nei confronti di Lola, e anche gli uomini, come Santa pensa di poter fare nei confronti di Turiddu.[52]
>
> [The vendetta is against all those who, because of money, can buy anything they want, including women if they are men, as Compare Alfio does with Lola, and men if they are women, as Santa thinks she can do with Turiddu.]

Others have observed the fatalistic aspect of the duel. According to Franca Angelini, Turiddu's death on Easter day represents a sort of

> morte senza 'resurrezione', senza speranza di riscatto agli occhi del villaggio, poiché per il villaggio, le cui figure emblematiche sono Lola, Santa e compare Alfio, ciò che conta è salvare il codice della famiglia-roba contro il codice della famiglia-amore, posseduto e difeso da Turiddu.[53]
>
> [death without a 'resurrection', without hope of redemption in the eyes of the villagers, since for the village, whose emblematic figures are Lola, Santa and Compare Alfio, what counts is saving the family-wealth code against the code of family-love, possessed and defended by Turiddu.]

The interpretation of Turiddu's death proposed here takes into consideration the question of gender. Even though it is the men who do the fighting, it is the women, namely Santuzza, who dominate the plot structure and lead the men to their fate. But while Santuzza will continue with her 'life journey', to use Austin's words once more, Turiddu's life has come to a premature end. Consequently, it is arguable that Santuzza, in breaking away from the passive victim trope and becoming an active heroine, is turned into what Guido Nicastro has called one of the first 'prime donne' — or 'new' women — of the nineteenth-century stage:

> La donna è al centro della storia d'amore che si vuol rappresentare. E Santuzza, dopo Margherita Gautier, dopo Carmen e insieme alle eroine ibseniane, si inserisce, a buon diritto, nel catalogo delle prime donne del teatro ottocentesco.[54]
>
> [The woman is at the centre of the love story as it appears on stage. And Santuzza, after Marguerite Gautier, after Carmen and together with Ibsen's

heroines, takes her place, rightfully, in the catalogue of the *prime donne* of nineteenth-century theatre.]

The Overshadowed Women

Somewhat paradoxically, the emphasis on Santuzza overshadows the importance of other equally crucial women in the play, particularly Gnà Nunzia. From the very first line of the *novella*, Turiddu is portrayed as 'il figlio della gnà Nunzia' (*Tn* I, 179) [the son of Gnà Nunzia (*CROS*, 27)], while his father is not mentioned in either version. Although Gnà Nunzia in the tale never speaks about her son, her maternal love is underlined by the sympathetic voice of the narrator. Aware that he is involved with Compare Alfio's wife, 'La gnà Nunzia, *poveretta*, l'aspettava sin tardi ogni sera' (*Tn* I, 184) [*Poor* Gnà Nunzia had been waiting up for him till a late hour for nights on end (*CROS*, 31), my italics]. Here, the reader can sense Verga's own compassion for the elderly mother not only through the choice of affectionate words, but also through the descriptions of her actions.

Indeed, according to Verga in a letter to Felice Camerino on 19 March 1881, 'il lettore deve vedere il personaggio, per servirmi del gergo, l'*uomo* secondo me, qual è, dov'è, come pensa, come sente, da dieci parole e dal modo di soffiarsi il naso' [the reader has to see the character — to use the technical terminology — the *man*, in my view, as he is, where he is, how he thinks and feels, from ten words and by the way he blows his nose] (*Ls*, p. 109). This statement supports Verga's views in his interview with Ugo Ojetti several years later in 1894 where he maintained that 'un pensiero può essere scritto, in tanto quanto può essere descritto, cioè in tanto quanto giunge a un atto, a una parola esterna: esso deve essere *esternato*' [a thought can be written insofar as it can be described, that is to say insofar as it gives rise to an act, an external word: the thought needs to be *externalised*].[55]

This strong mother-and-son bond is reinforced in the *novella*, again through the physical descriptions provided by the narrator, on the day of the duel. Here Turiddu reveals why he will defend himself against his rival:

> Come è vero Iddio so che ho torto e mi lascierei ammazzare. Ma prima di venire qui ho visto la mia vecchia che si era alzata per vedermi partire, col pretesto di governare il pollaio, quasi il cuore le parlasse, e quant'è vero Iddio vi ammazzerò come un cane per non far piangere la mia vecchierella. (*Tn* I, 184)
>
> [[A]s God is my witness I know I did wrong and I'd be glad to let you kill me. But before coming to meet you I caught sight of my old mother, who had got up to see me leaving with the excuse of cleaning out the chicken run, looking as though her heart was breaking, and as God is my witness I'm going to kill you to stop my mother shedding any tears.] (*CROS*, 32)

By gaining an insight into Gnà Nunzia's external actions, mainly her excuse of cleaning out the chicken run in order to see her son off for the last time, the readers are offered an intimate understanding of their close relationship. This is further strengthened moments before Turiddu is knifed, when he calls out for her: '"Ah! mamma mia!"' (*Tn* I, 185)' (*CROS*, 33)],[56] bringing the plot full circle as his final line links back to his portrayal as a son in the opening line. Interestingly, the closing was later re-employed in the last aria of Mascagni's operatic adaptation, 'Mamma, quel vino è generoso' [Mamma, that wine is generous].

In the dramatic version, on the other hand, Gnà Nunzia's importance is predominantly reduced to a mere means of allowing Santuzza the possibility of informing the audience of the previous facts. In contrast to the narrative, Gnà Nunzia on stage barely interacts with her son and is sterner towards him:

> TURIDDU *(chiamando verso l'interno della bettola)*: O madre! Che ne avete ancora di quel buono?
> GNÀ NUNZIA: *(s'affaccia brontolando)*. Sì, di quel buono che dovevi portar oggi da Francoforte!...
> TURIDDU: Via, via, oggi ch'è Pasqua! Non mi fate il muso lungo anche voi. (*Tt*, 44)

> [TURIDDU *(calling inside the inn)*: Oh mother! Do you have any more of that fine wine?
> GNÀ NUNZIA: *(peering out grumbling)*. Yes, that fine wine you were supposed to bring from Frankfurt today!
> TURIDDU: Come now, today's Easter! Don't give me that look, you as well.]

Moreover, whereas in the *novella* the physical descriptions convey Gnà Nunzia's fear, particularly as Turiddu makes his way to the duel, on stage she is evidently more confused: 'Che c'è ancora?' [What now?] (*Tt*, 47), 'Ma dov'è andato mio figlio Turiddu? Ma che vuol dire tutto questo?' [But where's my son Turiddu gone? But what's this all about?] (*Tt*, 48). Soon after, she learns of her son's death '*colle mani nei capelli, fuori di sé*' [with her hands on her head, beside herself] (*Tt*, 48). Here, Verga is able to use the stage directions to shed light on her sheer desperation following the loss of her son. However, because the mother-and-son bond has been weakened on stage by the emphasis placed on Santuzza, the audience of the play is made to identify Turiddu more with a *lover* than a *son*. In fact, while in the *novella* Turiddu defends himself in the duel for the sake of his mother, on stage he defends himself, for the sake of Santuzza:

> TURIDDU: *(chiamando in disparte compare Alfio)*. Sentite, compare Alfio, come è vero Dio so che ho torto, e mi lascierei scannare da voi senza dir nulla. Ma ci ho un debito di coscienza con comare Santa, chè son io che l'ho fatta cadere nel precipizio; e quant'è vero Dio, vi ammazzerò come un cane, per non lasciare quella poveretta in mezzo alla strada. (*Tt*, 46)

> [TURIDDU: *(calling out to the side to Compare Alfio)*. Listen, Compare Alfio, as God is my witness I know I've done wrong, and I'd let you slaughter me without saying a word. But I have a debt to Comare Santuzza on my conscience. I'm the one who brought ruin on her, and, as God is my witness, I will kill you like a dog so as not to destroy that poor girl.]

A further character whose significance is undermined in the theatrical adaptation is Lola. In both versions, once Turiddu is challenged to a duel, she inevitably becomes anxious. In the *novella*, the storyteller provides an insight into her anxiety, reporting what she does in private for the benefit of the reader: as the two men make their way to the duel, she wonders where they are heading and, acknowledging the consequences of her actions, 'in camicia, pregava ai piedi del letto e si stringeva sulle labbra il rosario che le aveva portato fra Bernardino dai Luoghi Santi, e recitava tutte le avemarie che potevano capirvi' (*Tn* I, 184) [in her nightdress, knelt down to pray at the foot of the bed, pressing her lips to the rosary that Brother Bernardino had brought back for her from the Holy Land, and she recited as many Ave Marias as there were beads on it (*CROS*, 32)].

Similarly, in the stage version Lola appears worried as Turiddu and Alfio make their way to the duel: 'O Vergine Maria! Dove andate, compare Alfio?' [Oh Virgin Mary! Where are you going, Compare Alfio?] (*Tt*, 46); and 'O compare Turiddu! In questo stato mi lasciate anche voi?' [Oh Compare Turiddu! You're leaving me in this state as well?] (*Tt*, 47). However, the audience is not provided with a detailed account of her remorse. Although Lola is one of the main instigators of the plot, the '[p]unto di svolta fra commedia e tragedia è l'invito di Lola a Turiddu' [[t]urning point from comedy to tragedy occurs when Lola entices Turiddu],[57] she is never given the opportunity to convey her emotions because the focal point is Santuzza. The audience only ever sees her momentarily on stage, saying little to contribute to her personality.

So though the theatrical genre is a largely verbal form of art, which might explain why Verga adapted his dialogic narratives into plays, there is essentially a reduction in the number of individual voices in his first dramatic work. By prioritising the role of Santuzza in the play because of the influence of Duse, Verga (inadvertently perhaps) condenses the various narrative voices in the story, overshadows the importance of other key women, and risks making his heroine sound rhetorical. However, in strengthening Santuzza's voice at the expense of the above, Verga manages to introduce a different kind of woman into Italy's theatrical tradition; that is, an active heroine who, well aware of the fatal consequences of her actions, refuses to tolerate her lover's infidelity.

'"Leonora, addio!"' and *Questa sera si recita a soggetto*

In the aftermath of Verga's *Cavalleria rusticana*, Pirandello published his '"Leonora, addio!"' in the *Corriere della sera* on 6 November 1910. In the same way as *Cavalleria rusticana* was allegedly based on Verga's observations from his window in his younger years, it could be said that Pirandello based the jealous Verri on his own wife, Antonietta, who suffered from a severe form of paranoia and was eventually committed to an asylum. As Gaspare Giudice has pointed out, Antonietta was perhaps the first to introduce Pirandello to the notion that 'ognuno è, davanti a ogni altro, un altro da ciò che si crede' [everyone is, faced with everyone else, other than what one thinks one is].[58] However, according to Pirandello's son Stefano in an interview much later on 21 November 1961, Verri was, in fact, inspired by Antonietta's father whose jealousy prevented a doctor from examining his wife during her pregnancy and, as a result, she died in childbirth (*Mn* IV, 248).

'"Leonora, addio!"' brings to life an ambivalent triangular relationship. In spite of the fact that Pirandello completed the tale during the early phase in his career while he was still associated with the *veristi* writers, he had already begun to show signs of his gradual divergence from the realist literary movement. Whereas Verga's *Cavalleria rusticana* portrays the typical husband-wife-lover triangle, Pirandello's "'Leonora, addio!'" distorts the triangle by replacing the role of the lover with the memories Verri suspects his wife Mommina of cherishing. Verri cannot tolerate how Mommina and her sisters used to perform various operas for the entertainment of several air force officers. Agonised by the memory of her past, he eventually locks Mommina along with their daughters in a tall tower and forbids her from even speaking about the opera.

As well as distorting the typical triangular relationship and Maiden-in-the-Tower story, Pirandello also deforms the age-old device of portraying the early return home of the betrayed husband — a device which was employed in the *novella* tradition, such as in Boccaccio's *Decameron* that drew its source from Apuleius,[59] and exploited by the *veristi* in tales such as Verga's 'Jeli il pastore' and 'Pentolaccia', both in *Vita dei campi*. Towards the end of the plot, Mommina finds a leaflet advertising Giuseppe Verdi's *La forza del destino* in Verri's coat pocket and this prompts her to reminisce about the opera. In his absence, Mommina 'cheats' on her husband as she performs all the different roles in Verdi's *Il Trovatore*.[60] One evening, however, as Verri returns home early, he catches his wife 'in the act' as she is singing the part of Azucena. Overwhelmed by the opera, Mommina collapses and dies, leaving her bewildered children wondering whether it is her operatic character who has died or Mommina herself.

Perhaps it was this meta-literary aspect of the story which led Pirandello, almost three decades after its initial publication, to adapt the narrative into one of his last meta-theatrical plays. Following the success of *Sei personaggi in cerca d'autore* (1921) and *Enrico IV* (1922), Pirandello was, by now, an established playwright residing in Berlin, disheartened by his Italian contemporary critics. Macchia has described this period in the author's life as 'una sorta di volontario esilio' [a sort of voluntary exile] (*Mn* IV, 247). It was during this time that Pirandello completed *Questa sera si recita a soggetto*, as he wrote in a letter to Abba on 29 March 1929: '[L]'ho finita, l'ho finita in quattr'ore di fervidissimo lavoro' [I finished it, I finished it in four hours of feverish effort].[61]

With the title *Heute Abend wird aus dem Stegreif gespielt* and directed by Hans Carl Müller, the première took place in Königsberg (today's Kaliningrad) on 25 January 1930 and was received positively by German critics and audiences. In Italy, the play, under the direction of Guido Salvini, did not première until a few months later, on 14 April 1930 at the Teatro di Torino, while Pirandello was still in Germany. The Italian press continued to respond exceptionally well. The critic Eugenio Bertuetti in *La Gazzetta del Popolo* the day after the opening welcomed Pirandello back to the stage 'rinato e rinvigorito sulle torturate esperienze passate' [reborn and reinvigorated after his painful past experiences] and Francesco Bernardelli in *La stampa* a few days later on 27 April praised Pirandello's 'frutto della sua grande esperienza e passione di uomo di teatro' [fruit of his great experience and passion as a playwright] (*Mn* IV, 266).[62] Acknowledging the favourable response,

Pirandello, in a letter to the director of 20 April 1930, congratulated Salvini on their unprecedented success: 'Dunque, *Questa sera si recita a soggetto* è proprio andata come meglio non si poteva desiderare. Ne sono veramente contento, tanto per me, quanto per Lei' [So, *Tonight We Improvise* went as well as could be desired. I am very happy about it, for myself as well as for you] (*Mn* IV, 267).

In the meta-theatrical play, Pirandello uses his early '"Leonora, addio!"' to exemplify the most modern concept to emerge from his writing, his theatre-within-the-theatre. In the Preface to the first volume of his *Maschere nude* (1933), he states how *Sei personaggi in cerca d'autore*, *Ciascuno a modo suo* (1923), and *Questa sera si recita a soggetto*:

> formano come una trilogia del teatro nel teatro, non solo perché hanno espressamente azione sul palcoscenico e nella sala, in un palco o nei corridoi o nel ridotto d'un teatro, ma anche perché di tutto il complesso degli elementi d'un teatro, personaggi e attori, autore e direttore-capocomico o regista, critici drammatici e spettatori alieni o interessati, rappresentano ogni possibile conflitto.[63]

> [form a sort of theatre-within-the-theatre trilogy, not just because they explicitly include action on the stage and in the auditorium, in a theatre box or in the corridors or the foyer of the theatre, but also because from the whole complex of elements that make up the theatre — characters and actors, author and theatre manager or director, theatre critics and hostile or responsive spectators — they represent every possible conflict.]

Questa sera si recita a soggetto is based on what Pirandello called the conflict between 'Attori divenuti Personaggi e il loro Regista' [Actors who have become Characters and their Director].[64] The play is composed of various dimensions of reality: the characters in '"Leonora, addio!"' (characters / characters); the actors interpreting the characters (actors / characters); the 'real' actors (actors / actors); the fictional director Dottor Hinkfuss (director / character), allegedly inspired by Max Reinhardt to whom the 1930 German edition of the play was dedicated; the 'real' director (director / director); the pseudo audience (audience / characters); the genuine audience (audience / audience); and finally the actual playwright (playwright / playwright).[65] By merging fiction with non-fiction, Pirandello's meta-theatre draws attention to two fundamental layers of reality in the play: the inner layer of the play (directly drawn from '"Leonora, addio!"') and outer layer (how Pirandello uses drama to make observations about the theatre). In exploiting these layers, Pirandello is able to stress the fine line between art and reality and therefore to inspire the audience to question what a performance really is.

Significantly, Pirandello places Mommina at the heart of *both* inner and outer layers of the play. The inner story is based on the suffering she causes her husband by stimulating his previously damaged psychology. Macchia has defined this pair of texts as the '[t]ragedia della gelosia, nella forma più terribile: la gelosia del passato' [[t]ragedy of jealousy, in the most terrible form: the jealousy of the past] (*Mn* IV, 248), and, similarly, Silvio D'Amico has added that this form of jealousy '[è] della più tremenda, perchè irrimediabile' [[is] the most awful because the most irremediable].[66] Mommina might therefore superficially appear as an innocent maiden trapped in a tower, but the influence she has on Verri is essentially the most brutal as he will for evermore be unable to eradicate his 'rival'.

In terms of the outer layer, Pirandello chooses to embody his ideal fusion of art and reality in the lead actress performing the role of Mommina, the only actress able truly to embody her character. So while Emanuele Licastro has claimed that the relation between '"Leonora, addio!"' and *Questa sera si recita a soggetto* 'è del tutto superficiale' [is entirely superficial],[67] and Jørn Moestrup has suggested that 'the play would have gained if the story of the La Croce [sic] had been more impressive, if the new representation of reality, which is in itself revolutionary and not merely formal, had represented a more interesting reality',[68] a different angle is offered here.

Mommina

'"Leonora, addio!"' is centred on how Mommina's association with the opera deteriorates Verri's state of mind. By organising the events chronologically in the story, Pirandello is able to shed light on his gradual psychological deterioration: from the moment they meet to the time of her death. In free indirect speech, the popular narrator, reminiscent of the *veristi*, introduces the Sicilian Verri and his fellow aviation officers who, away from their duties, enjoy the company of four sisters. Encouraged by their exuberant mother from Naples, Signora Ignazia, also known as *La Generala*, the women perform various operas together with the officers in the family home and this inevitably creates a scandal:

> Con la scusa che in Continente 'si faceva così', quegli ufficiali tra lo scandalo e la maldicenza di tutte le altre famiglie del paese, erano riusciti a far commettere a quelle quattro figliuole le più audaci e ridicole matterie. (*Na* III, 374)

> [With the excuse that 'this is the way it is done on the Continent', the officers had been able to persuade the four girls to do the silliest, most reckless things, in spite of the malicious gossip of the other families in town.] (*TWI*, 115)

Through the voice of the narrator, Pirandello enables the reader to detect the Sicilian town's disapproval at the family's involvement with the theatrical form. The recurring motif, 'in Continente "si faceva così"' ['this was the way it is done on the Continent'], prepares the reader for the imminent tragedy. Indeed, as Verri begins to fall in love with Mommina, he causes chaos:

> Tutto andò bene finché Rico Verri, il quale s'accordava prima con donna Ignazia nell'odio per tutti i selvaggi dell'isola, a poco a poco, innamorandosi sul serio di Mommina, non cominciò a diventare un selvaggio anche lui. E che selvaggio! (*Na* III, 375)

> [Everything went well until Rico Verri, who had at first joined Donna Ignazia in her hatred for the savages of the island, little by little fell genuinely in love with Mommina. Then he too started to become a savage. And what a savage!] (*TWI*, 116)

From this moment on, Verri's passion for Mommina triggers him to fight off potential rivals in various duels, 'tre sfide, tre duelli. Ferì due avversarii e fu ferito dal terzo' (*Na* III, 376) [three challenges, three duels. He wounded two opponents and was wounded by the third (*TWI*, 116–17)], recalling the events in *Cavalleria rusticana*. Concerned about his aggressive behaviour, *La Generala* enquires into Verri's family background and learns that his father 'aveva fama in paese d'usurajo e d'uomo così geloso, che in pochi anni aveva fatto morir la moglie di crepacuore' (*Na* III, 377) [was well known in town as a money-lender, but he had such a jealous nature that his wife had died of a broken heart after only a few years of marriage (*TWI*, 117)]. While at first the reader may feel that history was repeating itself, the narrator confirms that his jealousy was 'la stessa gelosia del padre, anzi più feroce' (*Na* III, 378) [the same jealousy as his father, only more ferocious (*TWI*, 117)].

Despite Verri's violent tendencies, Mommina, 'buona, la più saggia tra le quattro sorelle, la sacrificata' (*Na* III, 376) [a good girl, the wisest of the four sisters, the one who sacrificed herself (*TWI*, 116)], agrees to marry him. Although she is portrayed as a sacrificial victim, beneath the surface she is strong-minded and independent, able to choose her own husband against her family's will. As the narrator outlines, the reason why she accepts Verri's marriage proposal is more to do with her *head* than her heart. Aware of her father's financial difficulties which would prevent him from providing her with a prosperous dowry, and of the 'loose' reputation which her family had acquired because of the recitals, she feels this might be her only chance to get married. In contrast to Santa / Santuzza who was instinctively attracted to Turiddu, Mommina is drawn to Verri by her logic:

> Mommina capiva tante cose: prima di tutto, che gli anni passavano; che il padre con quel disordine in casa non riusciva a mettere un soldo a parte; che nessuno del paese si sarebbe mai messo con lei, come nessuno di quegli ufficiali si sarebbe mai lasciato prendere da qualcuna di loro. (*Na* III, 376)

> [Mommina was conscious of so many things: first of all that the years were passing by; that her father, with all that disorder at home, hadn't been able to put anything aside; that no young man in town would ever marry her, nor would any of the officers ever let himself be caught by one of the sisters.] (*TWI*, 116)

Mommina is also attracted to Verri because of her love for melodrama. Flattered by his duels and in an attempt to recreate her passion for the opera, she agrees to marry her 'hero'. Here, again, Pirandello's experimentation with the meta-literary continues to emerge — Mommina, a fictional character in the narrative, wants to perform an operatic role in her own life:

> Mommina, oltre alle tante cose che capiva, aveva anche la passione dei melodrammi; e Rico Verri... Rico Verri aveva fatto tre duelli per lei; Raul, Ernani, don Alvaro... *né togliermi potrò l'immagin sua dal cor...* Fu irremovibile e lo sposò. (*Na* III, 377)

> [But Mommina, besides understanding so many things, had a passion for melodrama. And Rico Verri... Rico Verri had fought three duels for her. Raul, Ernani, Don Alvaro... *né togliermi potrò l'immagin sua da cor...* She held firm, and she married him.] (*TWI*, 117)

Just as Verga entirely avoids portraying Turiddu and Lola's 'love story', Pirandello overlooks how Verri and Mommina eventually marry. Instead, both authors divert the readers' attention to how the jealous husbands attempt to eliminate the triangular relationships in which they are involved. However, unlike in the case of Compare Alfio who kills his wife's lover in a duel, Verri will never be able to destroy the memory of Mommna's past, making the effect she has over him all the more potent:

> [P]er la sua gelosia non c'era salvezza: era del passato; il tradimento era lì, chiuso in quella carcere; era in sua moglie, vivo, perenne, indistruttibile; nei ricordi di lei, in quegli occhi che avevano veduto, in quelle labbra che avevano baciato. (*Na* III, 378)
>
> [[T]here was no remedy for his jealousy; it was jealousy of the past. The betrayal was right there, locked inside the prison — inside his wife, alive, everlasting, indestructible. It was in her memories, in those eyes that had seen, in those lips that had kissed.] (*TWI*, 118)

Incapable of distinguishing fiction from non-fiction, Verri cannot accept how Mommina performed various operas with his fellow officers, in the same way as Elj cannot accept Donata's acting profession in *Trovarsi* (1932). The reader in the extract above is explicitly told that for Verri 'non c'era salvezza' [there was no remedy]. The implication Pirandello thus conveys is that Verri will always be 'chiuso in quella carcere' [locked inside the prison].

Following her incarceration, the author depicts Mommina contemplating the outside world from the tower in a passage which Benvenuto Terracini has called a 'soliloquio di Mommina'.[69] By means of free indirect speech, Pirandello enables the reader to gain an insight into her intimate thoughts:

> Guardava le stelle; aveva sotto gli occhi tutto il paese; una strana vista: tra il chiarore che sfumava dai lumi delle strade anguste, brevi o lunghe, tortuose, in pendio, la moltitudine dei tetti delle case, come tanti dadi neri vaneggianti in quel chiarore; udiva nel silenzio profondo dalle viuzze più prossime qualche suono di passi; la voce di qualche donna che forse aspettava come lei; l'abbajare d'un cane e, con più angoscia, il suono dell'ora dal campanile della chiesa più vicina. Perché misurava il tempo quell'orologio? a chi segnava le ore? Tutto era morto e vano. (*Na* III, 380)
>
> [She looked at the stars. Below her she could see the whole town. A strange sight: there in the light that drifted up from the lamps in the narrow streets, short or long, winding, sloping, a crowd of roofs appeared, like so many shimmering black blocks. From the deep silence of nearby alleys she could hear the echo of footsteps; the voice of some woman who was perhaps waiting as she was; the barking of a dog, or even more sadly, the ringing of the hour from the bell tower of the nearest church. Why did that clock measure the time? For whom did it count the hours? All was death and vanity.] (*TWI*, 119)

This passage is reminiscent of the descriptions of Màlia's isolation in Verga's *In portineria*, considered in the next chapter. However, whereas Màlia does not question her feelings any further, Mommina clearly does: 'Perché misurava il tempo quell'orologio? a chi segnava le ore? Tutto era morto e vano' [Why did that clock measure the time? For whom did it count the hours? All was death and vanity].

Indeed, it is the very fact that Mommina has a mind of her own which torments her husband. Verri is convinced that she is reminiscing about the opera and it is precisely his inability to refrain her from thinking which drives his psychosis. As a result, Pirandello gives the intimation that the only way Verri can prevent Mommina from thinking is through death.

While the main focus in "'Leonora, addio!'" is consistently on the couple, in *Questa sera si recita a soggetto* the chronology of the narrative is disrupted throughout. Consequently, the two protagonists only confront each other directly in three key scenes: during the Intermezzo, the *Zingarella* scene, and the finale. By fragmenting the linear structure of the story in the play, Pirandello is unable to illustrate how Verri's obsession with Mommina's past develops. In contrast to the reader of the narrative, the spectators of the performance do not acquire a background into the main characters. They subsequently see signs of Verri's jealous rage before they realise the cause of his behaviour.

The first time the spectators are made aware of Verri's jealousy is during the Intermezzo. In this scene, the actors enact five improvised sketches without any interruption from Dottor Hinkfuss who, from the very beginning, has been distressing the lead actor by calling him by his 'real' name as opposed to his character's name. Indeed, all through the course of the play, Pirandello specifies in the stage directions whether the actors are in or out of character by referring to them either by their conventional roles in a travelling theatre company or by their characters' names. During the Intermezzo, the actors, firmly fixed in their roles, are referred to by their characters' names. It is here, in one of these uninterrupted sketches, that Pirandello offers the audience an insight into Verri's madness for the first time. Verri is infuriated at the mere presence of Mommina's sisters who are speaking with the officers: '[S]e stavo un altro po' nel palco, finiva che la facevo davvero la pazzia' (*Mn* IV, 339) [[I]f I stayed in that box a little longer I'd have ended up doing something foolish (*TWI*, 66)]. Mommina is also apprehensive about Verri's agitation: 'Sono arrivata al punto che non so più quasi muovermi né parlare' (*Mn* IV, 339) [I've got to the point where I hardly know how to move or speak (*TWI*, 66)]. Verri is troubled at how Mommina's sisters, together with the troops, are drawing attention to themselves, as though they were performing 'uno spettacolo' (*Mn* IV, 339) [a show (*TWI*, 66)], 'a spese della buona reputazione di tre ragazze perbene' (*Mn* IV, 340) [at the expense of three respectable girls (*TWI*, 66)]. What triggers Verri's agitation is the fact that Mommina, in her younger years, also took part in the entertainment, as he states: 'Lasciamo andare, lasciamo andare, per carità. Anche lei, anche lei prima, l'ha permesso!' (*Mn* IV, 340) [Oh, let's just forget about it, please let's just forget about it. But even you — you allowed it too... before (*TWI*, 67)]. Although at this point the spectators do not understand what it is about the sisters, above all Mommina, which distresses Verri, they are nonetheless made to suspect that his motivations are rooted in their involvement with the theatre.

Pirandello continues to offer the audience an insight into Verri's jealousy during the *Zingarella* scene. While Signora Ignazia is suffering from toothache, the family and aviation officers start to sing *La Zingarella* and this immediately troubles

Mommina, who refuses to join in: 'No, no, mammà, io non mi sento! no!' (*Mn* IV, 352) [No, no, Mama, I don't feel like it! No! (*TWI*, 76)]. As soon as Verri enters the stage, he is enraged to see Mommina amidst the singing, causing a fight: '*Poi, un parapiglia, col rialzarsi di Pomàrici che si avventa su Verri, mentre gli altri si fanno in mezzo, a dividerli e trattenerli, parlando tutti simultaneamente, in gran confusione*' (*Mn* IV, 356) [*Then an explosion: Pomàrici springs up and throws himself on Verri, while the others try to separate them and stop them. There is a great confusion, with everyone speaking at once* (*TWI*, 79)]. According to the officer Nardi, Verri had always been unable to distinguish art from reality during the operatic recitals, stating that 'da siciliano serio, non poteva più stare allo scherzo!' (*Mn* IV, 359) [as a true Sicilian, you're well past the point where you can take a joke! (*TWI*, 81)]. What is striking about these statements is how here, early on in the play, the two characters already know the tragic outcome Verri's prejudices will have for Mommina. Similarly, in the opening act, during the initial confrontation scene between the actors and the director, *L'attrice caratterista* makes reference to Verri's 'sanguaccio nero dei siciliani' (*Mn* IV, 319) [cursed Sicilian blood (*TWI*, 48)], condemning 'questi selvaggi dell'isola' (*Mn* IV, 319) [the savages of the island (*TWI*, 48)]. Such conflations of time are scattered throughout the plot hinting at the impending tragedy.

Eventually, Dottor Hinkfuss, who has continued to disturb the actors, is sacked from what he considers to be his own play. However, just before this, the director offers the audience some information about Mommina, revealing the antecedent facts directly drawn from the short story:

> Mommina è per lei [la prima attrice] la più saggia delle quattro sorelle, la sacrificata [...] e capisce tante cose, e prima di tutto che gli anni passano; e che il padre, con tutto quel disordine in casa, non ha potuto mettere nulla da parte; che nessun giovine del paese si prenderà mai in moglie qualcuna di loro. (*Mn* IV, 370)
>
> [For her Mommina is the wisest of the four sisters, the one who sacrifices herself [...]. And there are so many things she is conscious of: first of all, that the years are passing by; that her father, with all that disorder at home, hadn't been able to put anything aside; that there isn't a young man in town who'd marry any one of them.] (*TWI*, 89)

Interestingly, the actress's viewpoint of Mommina is different from his own: 'La mia eccellentissima Prima Attrice, signorina... *dirà il nome della Prima Attrice* non è veramente del mio parere' (*Mn* IV, 370) [Miss _____, my excellent leading lady, doesn't really agree with me (*TWI*, 89)], without explaining what his perception of Mommina is. Pirandello thus introduces various perspectives into the play which continue to break away from the *verista* trend of portraying one view of 'reality'.

Once the director is fired, 'Il vero teatro' (*Mn* IV, 375) [Real theatre (*TWI*, 93)] begins, and the audience is finally given the same chance as the readers of the narrative to see Mommina and Verri live out their 'drama'. It is here that the play essentially catches up with the tale and portrays Mommina's overwhelming effect on Verri's state of mind, only to a greater extent than in the original. To begin with, the spectators in the play see the lead actress physically transform herself into her role. In so doing, Pirandello is able to draw attention to the improvisational aspect of the scene. The women first help her to look as though she has aged before her time by undoing her hair, assisting her into her old clothes, removing her make-up and applying white powder on her face. The lead actress is then given a mirror, but because Verri has removed all the mirrors from the tower, she reveals that she is unable look at her reflection. Once in character, she curiously places her forehead on each of the three stage walls, demarcating Mommina's *'carcere'* (*Mn* IV, 379) [cell (*TWI*, 96)], and theatre space: 'Questo è muro! — Questo è muro! — Questo è muro!' (*Mn* IV, 379–80) [This is a wall! — This is a wall! — This is a wall! (*TWI*, 96)], actions which evidently do not occur in the short story.

As well as drawing the audience's attention to the improvisational nature of the play, Pirandello also illuminates the extent to which Mommina has severely damaged Verri's psychology. Though she is under lock and key, he prohibits her from even brushing her hair and looking at herself in the mirror. Indeed, in the story, the narrator explicitly states that Verri will never cease to see Mommina as the young woman he fell in love with. No matter how different she had become over the years, 'egli la vedeva *sempre* quale era stata tanti anni addietro, quando la chiamava Mommina, o anche Mummì' (*Na* III, 379) [he *always* saw her as she had been so many years before, when he used to call her 'Mommina', or 'Mummi' (*TWI*, 119), my italics]. So while he continues to see her as the young 'Mummi', others would notice how her physical appearance had drastically changed following her incarceration, as the narrator continues to confirm: '[L]e spalle non più sostenute dal erano quasi scivolate e, davanti, il ventre salito enormemente, quasi a sorreggere il grosso petto floscio' (*Na* III, 379) [[H]er shoulders had fallen forward, and her enormous belly had crept upward to support the huge flabby breasts (*TWI*, 119)]. Here emerge several more distinctions between Pirandello and his predecessor. Whereas Verga focuses largely on physical descriptions, Pirandello is keen to unravel what is concealed underneath, providing the reader of the narrative with an *inward-looking* perspective onto his characters. Further, while the characters in Verga's narratives are fixed (Santa / Santuzza is a betrayed lover throughout the plots), Pirandello in this early tale already brings to light his view of the multitude of different perspectives: Verri's warped view of Mommina is unlike any other individual view of her.

As soon as the actress is in character, the 'drama' starts. This part of the play begins with the episode in the narrative where Mommina is by the window contemplating the relevance of time. Because Mommina's so-called soliloquy cannot be transposed onto the stage, Pirandello introduces a prologue recited by *L'attrice caratterista*, who throws light on the antecedent facts and voices Mommina's contemplations as though she were telling a fairy tale:

> L'ATTRICE CARATTERISTA: 'Tutti quei tetti, come tanti dadi neri, le vaneggiavano sotto, nel chiarore che sfumava dai lumi delle strade anguste del paese in pendìo; udiva nel silenzio profondo delle viuzze più prossime qualche rumor di passi che facevano l'eco; la voce di qualche donna che forse aspettava come lei; l'abbajare d'un cane e, con più angoscia, il suono dell'ora dal campanile

della chiesa più vicina. Ma perché séguita a misurare il tempo quell'orologio? A chi segna le ore? Tutto è morto e vano'. (*Mn* IV, 380–81)

[THE CHARACTER ACTRESS: 'All the roofs of the town, aslant upon the hill, were like so many little black blocks shimmering below her, in the light drifting up from the lamps in the narrow streets. From the deep silence of nearby alleys she could hear the echo of footsteps, the voice of some woman who was, perhaps, waiting as she was, the barking of a dog, and even more sadly, the ringing of the hour from the bell tower of the nearest church. Why does that clock continue to measure time? For whom does it count the hours? All is death and vanity'.] (*TWI*, 97)

Following the prologue, the drama proceeds to depict what happens to Mommina in the Rapunzel-like tower, closely mirroring the events in the narrative. In this scene, Pirandello strengthens the use of dialogue. The exchanges which he introduces considerably develop Mommina's effect on Verri. While the storyteller is able to articulate Verri's suffering on his behalf, the added speech on stage allows the character the freedom to express his torture for himself. Pirandello thus transforms Verri from being essentially silent in the narrative to verbally aggressive in the play. For instance, during one of their final altercations, which is absent from the short story, Verri forces Mommina to tell him what she is thinking about, and the language that Pirandello adds to this extract is particularly violent. It is the spectators of the play who, by hearing Verri express his own pain in his own words, acquire a raw understanding into his obsession with Mommina:

VERRI: Anche se t'accecassi, ciò che i tuoi occhi hanno veduto, i ricordi, i ricordi che hai qua negli occhi, ti resterebbero nella mente; e se ti strappassi le labbra, queste labbra che hanno baciato, il piacere, il piacere, il sapore che hanno provato baciando, seguiteresti sempre a provarlo, dentro di te, ricordando, fino a morirne, fino a morirne di questo piacere! (*Mn* IV, 383)

[VERRI: Even if I blinded you, what your eyes have seen — your memories, your memories — you have them here in your eyes — they'd stay in your mind; and if I tore your lips — these lips that have kissed — the pleasures, the pleasures, what they've felt and tasted when they kissed, you'd still be able to feel it inside, remembering it, even to the point of dying of it!] (*TWI*, 99)

The emphasis of dialogue not only gives Verri the possibility to express his torment for himself, but also to expand on his troubled past. Indeed, while in the short story the narrator mentions Verri's abusive father in passing, once the role of the narrator is withdrawn on stage, Verri has to explain the effect of his violent childhood for himself:

VERRI: Basta un niente, una parola, un suono — la più piccola sensazione — guarda, in me, l'odore della salvia, e sono in campagna, d'agosto, ragazzo d'otto anni, dietro la casa del garzone [...] lo vedo tremare sul gambo quel fiore violentato, all'urto della voracità feroce di quella bestia che mi fa paura, e l'ho qua ancora, alle reni, questa paura, l'ho qua! (*Mn* IV, 387)

[VERRI: All it needs is the tiniest thing — a word, a sound — the smallest sensation — Listen: for me it's the smell of sage, and I see myself in the county, in August, a boy of eight, behind the servant's house [...]. I see the

> ravished flower, trembling on its stalk, under the savage, gluttonous assault of the beast — that terrifying beast! And I still feel the fear — here, in the pit of my stomach!] (*TWI*, 103)

Though Verri's neurosis is a result of his upbringing, it is Mommina who has set it alight. She is the catalyst who has opened up Verri's psychological wounds, particularly on stage where Pirandello is able to exploit the use of dialogue to shed light on the extent of her influence.

Significantly, according to Pirandello in an interview for the Parisian journal *Le Temps* on 20 July 1925, only three years before producing his meta-theatrical play, it was the war which inspired him to make his words 'explode' on stage.[70] As Pirandello expressed in *Quadrivio* in 1934: 'Il mio è stato un teatro di guerra. La guerra ha rivelato a me stesso il teatro' [Mine has been a theatre of war. War has revealed theatre to me].[71] This theatre of war here emerges above all in the crescendo to Mommina's death. Since the betrayal consists of Mommina's memories of the opera, the reader of the narrative and audience of the play acknowledge that the only way Verri will be able to prevent his wife from reminiscing is through death. But while the storyteller in the narrative only suggests Mommina's inescapable death, the explosive speech in the play enables Pirandello to strengthen his portrayal of the impending tragedy. For example, in a further episode on stage, which is also absent from the narrative, Mommina states to Verri: 'Tu morta mi vuoi; morta; che non pensi più; che non sogni più' (*Mn* IV, 382) [You want me dead — dead, so that I can't think any more, can't dream any more (*TWI*, 99)], to which he asks the rhetorical question: '[P]osso spaccarle la testa per vederle dentro, ciò che pensa?' (*Mn* IV, 383) [[C]an I crack her head open to see what's inside, what she thinks? (*TWI*, 99)].

Another illustration emerges when Verri asks Mommina to describe how she was kissed by one of the officers during a recital, a kiss which, as he re-enacts it, turns into a bite. In the narrative, this episode is reported by the empathetic narrator:

> [E] la baciava e la mordeva e le strappava i capelli, quei poveri capelli non più pettinati, perché egli non voleva che si pettinasse più, né che più tenesse il busto, né che si prendesse la minima cura della persona. (*Na* III, 378)

> [[A]nd he kissed her and bit her and tore her hair, that wretched hair that was never combed, because he didn't want her to look after it, nor to wear her corset, nor to take the least care of her body.] (*TWI*, 118)

On stage, the same episode comes to life through body language and speech. First of all, while Verri is imploring Mommina to inform him of the details of the kiss, he holds her arm so tightly that it causes her to scream: 'Per carità, lasciami! Io muojo!' (*Mn* IV, 388) [Please, let me go! I'm dying! (*TWI*, 103)]. Soon after his kiss turns into a bite, she calls for help: 'Ajuto! Ajuto!' (*Mn* IV, 388) [Help! Help! (*TWI*, 103)]. What eventually stops Verri from essentially attacking his wife is the sight of his daughters — a sight which makes Verri aware of the sheer extent of his madness: 'Impazzisco! Impazzisco! Impazzisco!' (*Mn* IV, 388) [I'm going mad! I'm going mad! I'm going mad! (*TWI*, 104)]. The repetition of 'Impazzisco' [I'm going mad] shows how, once transposed to the stage, Verri is able to express his self-awareness.

Interestingly, this part of his personality is left undeveloped in the narrative, in the same way as Verga earlier did not develop Santuzza's self-reflection.

Finally, the reliance on dialogue enables Pirandello to expose a different side to Mommina's personality — her rebellious side. In fact, while Verri in both versions forbids her from even mentioning the opera, this does not stop her from doing so, particularly after discovering a leaflet advertising Verdi's *La forza del destino* in her husband's overcoat. In the narrative, this episode is reported by the storyteller who continues to delve deep within her thoughts to express her reaction to the leaflet:

> Vedere quell'annunzio, leggere il titolo dell'opera, e rompere in un pianto disperato fu tutt'uno. Il sangue le aveva fatto un tuffo, le era piombato d'un tratto al cuore e d'un tratto risalito alla testa, fiammeggiandole innanzi agli occhi il teatro della sua città, il ricordo delle antiche serate, la gioja spensierata della sua giovinezza tra le sorelle. (*Na* III, 381)
>
> [It all happened in a moment — she saw the announcement, she read the title of the opera, she broke into a desperate cry. A sudden rush of blood to her head: the theatre of the town she grew up in flashed before her eyes, the memory of evenings past, the carefree joy of her youth with her sisters.] (*TWI*, 120)

Not only does the storyteller offer the reader an insight into her intimate thoughts, but Mommina herself is given the chance to express to her daughters her own reaction to her discovery in direct speech: '"Il teatro... il teatro [...]. Ah voi, piccoline mie, povere animucce mie, non sapete"' (*Na* III, 381) ['The theatre... the theatre... [...] You, my dear girls, my poor darlings, you don't know' (*TWI*, 120)]. As well as this, she is provided with the opportunity *to sing*, actions which reinforce her defiance of her husband:

> Si mise a cantarla [l'ultima aria] con tanta passione che, dopo i versi
> *Come il dì primo da tant'anni dura*
> *Profondo il mio soffrir,*
> non poté andare più avanti: scoppiò di nuovo in pianto. (*Na* III, 381–82)
>
> [She began to sing with such passion that after the verses,
> *Come il dì primo da tant'anni dura*
> *Profondo il mio soffrir,*
> she couldn't continue, but burst out crying again.] (*TWI*, 120)

While the narrative throws light on her emotional response to the leaflet, which has provoked her strong feeling of nostalgia for the opera, the meta-theatrical version continues to point to the improvisational aspects of the play. Firstly, before she discovers the leaflet, Mommina's mother and sisters unexpectedly arrive at the tower to inform her that Totina is performing the opera at the nearby theatre. Signora Ignazia then comes out of character to inform the lead actress to look inside Verri's coat pocket, explaining to the spectators in a side comment: '(Bisogna ajutarla a fare la scena, adesso; siamo alla fine!)' (*Mn* IV, 390) [(We must help her set the scene now; we're getting to the end!) (*TWI*, 105)]. As soon as she does, Pirandello in the stage version gives Mommina the freedom to express her passion for singing to a greater degree than in the *novella*. In her longest monologue, she enlightens her daughters as to her past:

> Vedete che so cantare anch'io? Sì, sì, anch'io, anch'io so cantare; cantavo sempre, io, prima, lo so tutto a memoria *Il Trovatore*; e ve lo canto io! [...]. Ma io, prima, avevo io prima la voce più bella, non la zia Totina; io, io, più bella assai [...]. Sì, era mia, era mia, la parte d'Azucena. (*Mn* IV, 391)
>
> [You see? I can sing too. Yes, yes, I can sing too, I can sing too! I used to sing all the time! I know *Il Trovatore* by heart — all of it; I'll sing it for you! [...] Back then before... I was the one with the prettiest voice — it wasn't aunt Totina, it was me — a much better voice [...] Yes, that was my part... — Azucena, it was mine.] (*TWI*, 107)

Although these final passages indicate Mommina's gradual physical deterioration, they also reveal the emergence of her insubordinate attitude, bold enough to break away from the identity which Verri (in vain) has attempted to impose on her. In fact, while the only role Verri thinks Mommina should have is that of a mother — as he points out when enquiring about their daughters' whereabouts: 'Te lo domando per richiamarti all'unico pensiero che dovresti avere: quello di loro' (*Mn* IV, 381) [I am simply asking you so as to remind you that they are the only thing you should be thinking about] (*TWI*, 98) — these extracts highlight how Mommina has something on her mind other than her children. Though her rebellion is restricted to a domestic setting rather than a public one, she nonetheless has the courage to bring her husband's 'rival' to the tower and perform the operas he has always prohibited under his own roof, hence doubling the 'offence'.

Both versions lead up to Mommina's inevitable death. In the narrative, her death is portrayed more callously than it is in the play. Noticing a change in his wife's behaviour, one evening Verri returns to the tower earlier than usual. To his horror, he catches Mommina in the midst of performing *Il Trovatore*:

> Si precipitò in casa; salì a balzi la scala; trovò in camera, dietro la cortina del letto, il corpo enorme della moglie buttato per terra con un cappellaccio piumato in capo, i baffetti sulle labbra fatti col sughero bruciato; e le due figliuole sedute su due seggioline accanto, immoboli, con le mani su le ginocchia, gli occhi spalancati e le boccucce aperte, in attesa che la rappresentazione della mamma seguitasse.
>
> Rico Verri con un urlo di rabbia s'avventò sopra il corpo caduto della moglie e lo rimosse con un piede.
>
> Era morta. (*Na* III, 383)
>
> [He hurried into the house and rushed up the stairs; in the bedroom, behind the curtain, he found the enormous body of his wife thrown on the floor, with a huge feathered hat on her head, a moustache of burnt cork on her lips, and the two girls seated beside her on their little chairs, motionless, with their hands on their knees, their eyes wide open and their little mouths open too, waiting for their mother's performance to continue.
>
> With a shout of rage Rico Verri rushed over to the fallen body of his wife. He rolled it over with his foot.
>
> She was dead.] (*TWI*, 121)

Verri checks to see if his wife is dead by moving her large corpse with his foot in front of his bewildered daughters. Unlike earlier in the tale where Pirandello offered ample accounts of the characters' thoughts, here he avoids giving any insight into how she was feeling just before her death, thus adding to the coldness of the ending. Yet, despite being cold, the final passages are far from empty of emotion, in contrast to Walter Starkie's point of view:

> [T]here are many morbid touches in this story, both in the description of the madly jealous Rico Verri and the pathetic lackadaisical wife. Not at any time do these characters assume mortal form; they are exaggerated caricatures, symbols of Pirandello's warped manner of looking at the world. He takes the characteristics of the Sicilian shown by Verga and exaggerates them till the characters becomes like the caricatures of Dickens. But he has not got the humanity, the pity that we find in the English writer; we always feel that he looks on these creatures with contempt, and for that reason he does not scruple to show us Rico Verri kicking the dead body of his wife.[72]

Starkie points to the inhumanity of Verri's actions, but overlooks the character's desperation disguised behind his aggressive exterior, as well as Pirandello's own compassion for the couple and their daughters who are left wondering whether it is their mother who has died or the character she was performing. There is no contempt on Pirandello's behalf in this final image of Verri but a strong sense of empathy evoked by a writer who recognises the complexities of the human mind.

Different from the narrative, Pirandello in the stage version takes Mommina's death into the meta-theatre. The lead actress is so immersed in her role that, as soon as the protagonist dies, she faints:

> *S'alza, disperata, e canta con tutta la voce:*
> 'Ah! che la morte ognora
> è tarda nel venir
> a chi desia
> a chi desia morir!
> Addio,
> Addio, Leonora, addio...'
> *Cade, di schianto, morta. Le due bambine, più che mai sbalordite, non ne hanno il minimo sospetto; credono che sia il teatro che la mamma sta loro rappresentando; e restano lì immobili sulle loro sedioline ad aspettare* (Mn IV, 394).
>
> [*She gets up, desperate, and sings in full voice:*
> 'Ah! che la morte ognora
> è tarda nel venir
> a chi desia
> a chi desia morir!
> Addio,
> Addio, Leonora, addio...'
> *Suddenly she falls dead. The two little girls, more bewildered than ever, did not have the least suspicion. They think it is the performance their mother is putting on for them, and they remain there, motionless in their little chairs, waiting.*] (*TWI*, 108)

Whereas in the narrative Verri races up the tower to find his wife 'in the act', in the dramatic version he simply re-enters the stage and is confused to hear all the singing:

VERRI: Canta: avete sentito? Era la sua voce...
LA SIGNORA IGNAZIA: Sì, come l'uccello in gabbia!
TOTINA: Mommina! Mommina!
DORINA: Eccoci, siamo qua con lui; s'è arreso...
NENÈ: Col trionfo di Totina... avessi inteso!... il paese in de...
Vuol dire 'in delirio', ma resta in tronco, esterrefatta con gli altri alla vista del corpo inerte lì per terra, e delle due bambine, che aspettano ancora, immobili. (Mn IV, 395)

[VERRI: Is she singing: did you hear? It was her voice...
SIGNORA IGNAZIA: Yes, like a bird in a cage!
TOTINA: Mommina! Mommina!
DORINA: Here we are! We're here with him! He gave in...
NENÈ: With Totina's triumph... You should have heard it!... The town in del...
She wants to say 'in delirium,' but she stops short, terrified with all the others at the sight of the lifeless body there on the floor, and of the two little girls, still waiting, motionless.] (*TWI*, 108)

While Mommina's inevitable death is the climax of the narrative, the crux of the play is the collapse of the lead actress. In fact, as she loses consciousness, she is referred to as *la prima attrice* in the stage directions and not as Mommina. Whereas the reader of the tale simply learns about Mommina's end, the spectator of the performance is made to think about the implications of the actress's fall:

L'ATTORE BRILLANTE: Ohé, non sarà morta per davvero?
Tutti si chinano premurosi su la prima attrice.
IL PRIMO ATTORE: *(chiamandola e scotendola)* Signorina... signorina...
L'ATTRICE CARATTERISTA: Si sente male davvero?
NENÈ: Oh Dio, è svenuta! Solleviamola!
LA PRIMA ATTRICE: *(sollevandosi da sé col solo busto)* No... grazie... È il cuore, davvero... Mi lascino, mi lascino respirare... (Mn IV, 396)

[THE COMIC ACTOR: Oh! I hope she's not really dead!
Everybody crowds solicitously around the Leading Actress.
THE LEADING ACTOR *(calling her and shaking her)*: Miss_____!
THE CHARACTER ACTRESS: Is she really feeling ill?
NENÈ: Oh, my God, she's fainted! Let's lift her up!
THE LEADING ACTRESS *(half raising herself)*: No... thank you. It really was my heart, though... Just let me, please, let me get my breath...] (*TWI*, 109)

According to Bàrberi Squarotti, this final part of the play represents

[la] dissoluzione del teatro, della finzione del teatro, dello spazio teatrale come luogo della finzione, e, contemporaneamente, alla fine del genere tragico e di ogni altro genere di teatro nell'irripetibilità e nella distruzione della ritualità della recitazione.[73]

[[the] dissolution of the theatre, the fiction of the theatre, of the theatrical space as a place of fiction, and, simultaneously, the end of the tragic genre and any other theatrical genre owing to the unrepeatability and the destruction of the ritual of acting.]

He explains how, once actors start to 'live' their performances, the theatre as an artistic form ceases to exist as it is transformed into a form of life. This transition from pretending to be a role and becoming the role symbolises the disintegration of the theatre, since on stage there is no longer any element of make-believe. However, Bàrberi Squarotti fails to indicate that Pirandello embodies this so-called dissolution of the theatre in the lead actress. The very instance Mommina falls to the ground as her operatic role dies, Verdi's opera ceases to exist and Pirandello subsequently merges the character Mommina (who is herself performing a fictional role) with the lead actress. Douglas Campbell and Leonardo Sbrocchi have observed that in the narrative, 'Mommina is not simply showing the story, she has *become* the story',[74] and the same applies to the meta-play: the point in which Mommina and the lead actress collapse together, they too *become* the play. Consequently, they embody Pirandello's ideal fusion of fiction and non-fiction, which he so admired in Duse and Abba.

In fact, throughout the play, Pirandello prioritises the lead actress, in the same way as Verga prioritised the role of Santuzza. For example, in an earlier comical but crucial scene, the actor performing the role of Sampognetta finds it almost impossible to perform his character's death. In this scene, he tries to protect a cabaret singer from her jealous lover and is stabbed as a result, a kind of parody of *Cavalleria rusticana*. As the actor states to the irritated director: '[N]on riesco a morire, signor Direttore; mi viene da ridere, vedendo come tutti son bravi, e non riesco a morire' (*Mn* IV, 365) [I can't die, Doctor Hinkfuss. When I see how well everybody is doing, I feel like laughing, and I can't die (*TWI*, 86)]. Eventually he is able to perform Sampognetta's death but what is interesting is that, from the entire cast, it is Mommina who is the first to shed real tears, '*si mette a piangere davvero*' (*Mn* IV, 368) [*And she bursts into tears* (*TW*, 87)], actions which are described in the stage directions as an '*impeto di vera commozione nella prima attrice*' (*Mn* IV, 368) [*outburst of true emotion on the part of the Leading Actress* (*TWI*, 87)]. Pirandello thus continues to distinguish the lead actress from the rest as she is the first performer to become her role.[75]

Instead of concluding the play following the collapse of the lead actress, Pirandello guides the audience's attention to his view of the importance of a script. In this sort of 'coda', the cast returns on stage along with Dottor Hinkfuss who stresses the need for scripted parts, an essential need which even takes precedence over the actual playwright: 'No, l'autore no! Le parti scritte, sì, se mai, perché riabbiano vita da noi, per un momento' (*Mn* IV, 396) [No, not an author, no! The written parts, maybe, yes, if you must, so that they can come to life for a moment through us (*TWI*, 109)].

In a letter of 10 March 1930 to the director Salvini, Pirandello explained why he added this coda: 'Gli attori non possono far questo ogni sera [...] devono avere una parte da recitare. E ci vuole il poeta che la dia loro' [Actors cannot do this every night [...] they must have a part to perform. And the author is needed to give them one] (*Mn* IV, 262). According to Pirandello, performers cannot be put through the kind of ordeal which the lead actress experiences at the end of the play and therefore the provision of a script is fundamental. Indeed, in spite of his admiration for the *Commedia dell'arte*, Pirandello was well aware of the limitations of improvised drama, as he confirms in his introduction to Silvio D'Amico's *Storia del teatro italiano* (1936): 'Basta conoscere un po' come si svolge il lavoro dell'attore sulle tavole del palcoscenico [...] per intendere che, ad attori, non poteva mai nascere l'idea di mettersi a recitare *all'improvviso*' [It is enough to know a little about how the job of the actor works on the stage [...] to understand that actors could never have come up with the idea of improvisation].[76] In the words of Richard Sogliuzzo, '*Questa sera* rappresenta la futilità del teatro improvvisato' [*Tonight We Improvise* represents the futility of improvised theatre].[77]

It is precisely the synthesis of art and reality which leads Pirandello to insist on the importance of the script, a fusion which once again fixes Mommina at the heart of the play. Though some have claimed that Dottor Hinkfuss represents Pirandello's mouthpiece character as he voices the author's underlying message,[78] it is Mommina and the lead actress who actually personify this message. By collapsing and therefore embodying the extent to which a written part would have avoided such an ordeal, the women animate the dangers of improvisation in a way Dottor Hinkfuss does not and, more importantly, could not.

So while Anthony Caputi has argued that *Questa sera si recita a soggetto* is 'loosely structured',[79] this chapter has shown how Pirandello carefully intertwines the events in the short story with the play to form an extremely controlled piece of drama, which fixes his female protagonist at the heart of both inner and outer layers of the plot. Moreover, Mommina's influence on her husband's psychology is strengthened on stage as soon as the characters rely on dialogue and the conventions of the metatheatre. Superficially, Mommina may appear as a Rapunzel-like heroine victimised by her ruthless husband, but beneath the surface she is a non-conformist character who indirectly torments her husband. As a result, Pirandello portrays Verri as just as much a victim as Mommina, perhaps even more so because of his inability ever to destroy her past.

A Different Story

As with their predecessor Nora, Santuzza and Mommina rebel against the innocent persecuted heroine trope: Santuzza is unafraid to disclose the truth about her lover's adultery and Mommina defies Verri's 'rules'. The women thus reveal themselves as the antitheses of the marginalised bystander in subjection to her husband and become active heroines who dominate the plot structure, which Pirandello then takes to another level in *Questa sera si recita a soggetto*. Although Mommina does die at the end of both versions, the lead actress and the 'actual' actress in the metatheatrical play clearly do not. As a result of this unusual death scene, Pirandello continues to pose an even stronger challenge to the association between women and death by using Mommina's end to personify his ideal union between fiction and non-fiction, as well as to emphasise the importance of a script. Consequently, Pirandello employs Mommina and the lead actress both to embody and express his groundbreaking metatheatre, which was about to change the course of modern drama, thus turning the pair into his most radical *female* mouthpiece characters to date.

Notes to Chapter 3

1. Gayle Austin, *Feminist Theory for Dramatic Criticism* (Michigan: The University of Michigan Press, 1990), p. 21.
2. Quoted in Elizabeth Bronfen, *Over her Dead Body: Death, Femininity and the Aesthetic* (Manchester: Manchester University Press, 1992), p. 59.
3. Laura Mulvey, 'Visual Pleasure and Narrative Cinema', *Screen*, 16.3 (Autumn 1975), 6–18 (p. 14).
4. Teresa De Lauretis, *Alice Doesn't: Feminism, Semiotics, Cinema* (Bloomington: Indiana University Press, 1984), pp. 132–33.
5. See Federico De Roberto, *Casa Verga e altri saggi verghiani*, ed. by Carlemo Musumarra (Florence: Le Monnier, 1964), p. 183.
6. See in particular Siro Ferrone, *Il teatro di Verga* (Rome: Bulzoni, 1972), pp. 95–154; and Anna Barsotti, *Verga drammaturgo* (Florence: La nuova Italia, 1974), pp. 37–68. For a comparison between the reworkings of *Cavalleria rusticana* and *La Lupa*, see Giorgio Prosperi, 'Teatro verghiano: due restauri', *Rivista italiana di drammaturgia*, 2 (1976), 3–24. See also Silvana Monti, 'Il teatro di Verga e la società della "Nuova Italia"', *Problemi*, 4–5 (1967), 174–86; Roberto Alonge, *Teatro e spettacolo nel secondo Ottocento* (Rome: Laterza, 1988), pp. 152–60; Gabriele Moroni, *Verga e il teatro del suo tempo: l'esperimento di Cavalleria rusticana* (Udine: Companotto, 1997); Francesca Malara, *Copioni e drammaturgie di fine ottocento* (Milan: Edizioni universitarie di Lettere Economia Diritto, 2000), pp. 107–60; and Guido Baldi, *Reietti e superuomini in scena* (Naples: Liguori, 2009), pp. 7–32.
7. Giorgio Bàrberi Squarotti, 'La realtà a teatro: Verga', in *La letteratura in scena: il teatro del Novecento*, ed. by Giorgio Bàrberi Squarotti (Turin: Editrice Tirenia stampatori, 1985), pp. 9–24 (p. 9).
8. Franca Angelini, 'Alla ricerca di una nuova drammaturgia', in *La letteratura italiana: storia e testi*, ed. by Carlo Muscetta, 9 vols (Bari: Laterza, 1975), VIII, *Il secondo ottocento: lo stato unitario e l'età del positivismo*, pp. 606–33 (p. 608).
9. Rita Verdirame, '*Femme Fatale* e Angelo del Focolare nel primo Verga', in *Famiglia e società nell'opera di G. Verga: atti del convegno nazionale (Perugia 25–26–27 ottobre 1989)*, ed. by Norberto Cacciaglia, Ada Neiger, and Renzo Pavese (Florence: Olschki, 1991), pp. 225–42 (p. 225).
10. Ferrone, p. 247.
11. For more critical literature, see *La Trilogia di Pirandello: atti del convegno internazionale sul teatro pirandelliano (Agrigento 6–10 dicembre 1976)*, ed. by Enzo Lauretta (Agrigento: Centro Nazionale Studi Pirandelliani, 1977); and Dorothea Stewens, *Pirandello scrittura e scena* (Agrigento: Centro Nazionale Studi Pirandelliani, 1983), pp. 57–66. I have offered an examination of Pirandello's portrayal of the female performer but without placing my argument in the context of the innocent persecuted maiden, or in comparison to Verga; see Enza De Francisci, 'Pirandello's Actress From Page to Meta-Theatrical Stage: "*Leonora, addio!*" to *Questa sera si recita a soggetto*', *L'anello che non tiene: Journal of Modern Italian Literature*, 24 (2014), 12–37.
12. Maggie Günsberg, *Patriarchal Representations: Gender and Discourse in Pirandello's Theatre* (Oxford: Berg, 1994), p. 192.
13. Umberto Mariani, *La donna in Pirandello: l'estrema vittima* (Caltanisetta-Rome: Salvatore Sciascia Editore, 2012), p. 139.
14. Walter Starkie, *Luigi Pirandello 1867–1936* (Berkeley and Los Angeles: University of California Press, 1965), pp. 260–61.
15. Giovanni Macchia, 'Il personaggio sequestrato', in *Omaggio a Pirandello*, ed. by Leonardo Sciascia (Milan: Bompiani, 1987), pp. 85–92 (p. 86).
16. Aleksandr Isaakovich Nikiforov, 'On the Morphological Study of Folklore', trans. with additional notes by Heda Jason, *Linguistica Biblica*, 27–28 (1973), 25–35 (p. 32).
17. Antti Aarne and Stith Thompson, *The Types of the Folktale: A Classification and a Bibliography*, 2nd edn (Helsinki: Suomalainen Tie-deakatemia, 1961), p. 175.
18. For other variations, see *The Oxford Companion to Fairy Tales*, ed. by Jack Zipes (Oxford: Oxford University Press, 2002).
19. For northern Italian tales, see Daniela Perco and Cristina Bacchilega, 'Female Initiation in

Northern Italian Versions of *Cinderella*', *Western Folklore: Perspectives on the Innocent Persecuted Heroine in Fairy Tales*, 52.1 (1993), 73–84. For southern tales, see Gianfranco D'Aronco, *Le fiabe di magia in Italia* (Udine: Arti grafiche friulane, 1957). For similar tropes in Italy, see *Tradizioni orali non cantate*, ed. by Alberto Mario Cirese and Liliana Serafini, with the collaboration of Aurora Milillo (Rome: Ministero per i beni culturali e ambientali, Discoteca di Stato, 1975); and Renato Aprile, *Indice delle fiabe popolari di magia* (Florence: Olschki, 2000).

20. Luigi Capuana, *Casa di bambola* (Milan: Kantorowicz, 1894), p. 109.
21. Steven Swann Jones, 'The Innocent Persecuted Heroine Genre: An Analysis of its Structure and Themes', *Western Folklore*, p. 16.
22. For more interpretations of Santuzza, see Katharine Mitchell, 'La Femme, Fatal or Fallen', *Opera Magazine*, October 2017, pp. 1271–76. See also Katharine Mitchell, 'Le traviate: Suffering Heroines and the Italian State between the Nineteenth and Twenty-First Centuries', in *Prostitution and Sex Work in Global Visual Media: New Takes on Fallen Women*, ed. by Danielle Hipkins and Kate Taylor (London: Palgrave Macmillan, 2017), pp. 195–217.
23. Torborg Lundell, 'Gender-Related Biases in the Type and Motif Indexes of Aarne and Thompson', in *Fairy Tales and Society: Illusion, Allusion, and Paradigm*, ed. by Ruth B. Bottigheimer (Philadelphia: University of Pennsylvania Press, 1986), pp. 149–63.
24. See Kay Stone, 'Things Walt Disney Never Told Us', *The Journal of American Folklore: Women and Folklore*, 88.347 (1975), 42–50.
25. Kay Stone, 'Feminist Approaches to the Interpretation of Fairy Tales', in *Fairy Tales and Society*, pp. 229–36 (p. 233).
26. See for instance Karen Rowe, 'To Spin a Yarn: The Female Voice in Folklore and Fairy Tale', in *The Classic Fairy Tales: Texts, Criticism*, ed. by Maria Tatar, 1st edn (New York: Norton, 1999), pp. 297–308; and Cristina Bacchilega, 'Cracking the Mirror: Three Re-Visions of *Snow White*', *Boundary 2*, 15. 3 (1988), 1–25.
27. *The Oxford Companion to Fairy Tales*, s. v. feminism and fairy tales, p. 187.
28. Ibid., p. 310.
29. See Laura Gonzenbach, *Beautiful Angiola: The Great Treasury of Sicilian Folk and Fairy Tales Collected by Laura Gonzenbach*, trans. with an intro. by Jack Zipes (New York: Routledge, 2004); and Laura Gonzenbach, *The Robber with a Witch's Head: More Stories from the Great Treasury of Sicilian Folk and Fairy Tales*, trans. and ed. by Jack Zipes (New York: Routledge, 2004).
30. Jack Zipes, *The Irresistible Fairy Tale: The Cultural and Social History of a Genre* (Princeton University Press, 2012), p. 102.
31. Ibid., p. 103.
32. Ibid., p. 128.
33. Stone, *Fairy Tales and Society*, p. 233.
34. Originally, the plot was intended as an episode in *I Malavoglia* (1881). It is said that the return of 'Ntoni from military service in *I Malavoglia* recalls Turiddu's return in *Cavalleria rusticana*: 'Ntoni proudly arrives at his hometown of Aci Trezza, admired by the village girls, but eventually discovers that his former lover Sara has married Menico. See Piero Nardi's introduction in Giovanni Verga, *I Malavoglia*, ed. by Piero Nardi (Milan: Edizioni Scolastiche Mondadori, 1973), pp. 5–34 (p. 10); Lina Perroni and Vito Perroni, 'Storia de *I Malavoglia*', *Nuova Antologia* (16 March 1940), 105–31, and (1 April 1940), 237–51; and Vito Perroni, 'Sulla genesi de *I Malavoglia*', *Le ragioni critiche*, 2.6 (October-December 1972), 471–526.
35. For more background, see De Roberto's chapter, 'Stato civile della Cavalleria rusticana', in his *Casa Verga*, pp. 180–213.
36. According to Duse's biographer William Weaver, the shy Verga eventually did make an appearance on stage, the night after the première, mainly because of the actress who forced him onto the stage, with the help of the director, accusing him of 'not condescending' to appear with the actors: the only curtain-call of Verga's lifetime; see William Weaver, *Duse: A Biography with 53 illustrations* (London: Thames and Hudson, 1984), p. 43.
37. Quoted in De Roberto, p. 206.
38. For more on Mascagni's opera, see Matteo Sansone, 'Verga and Mascagni: The Critics' Response to *Cavalleria rusticana*', *Music and Letters*, 71.2 (1 May 1990), 198–214; Bianca Maria Brumana, 'G.

Verga e P. Mascagni: continuità e innovazione nella tematica di *Cavalleria rusticana* in rapporto al melodramma italiano dell'Ottocento', in *Famiglia e società nell'opera di G. Verga*, pp. 429–36; and Franca Angelini, '*Cavalleria rusticana* di Giovanni Verga', in *Letteratura italiana: le opere*, ed. by Alberto Asor Rosa, 4 vols (Milan: Einaudi, 1995), III, *Dall'Ottocento al Novecento*, pp. 955–81.
39. Cesare Levi, 'Giovanni Verga', in *Autori drammatici italiani: Giovanni Verga, Roberto Bracco, Marco Praga, Sebatino Lopez* (Bologna: Zanichelli, 1921), pp. 3–16 (pp. 4–5).
40. See Verina R. Jones, 'Lucia and her Sisters: Women in Alessandro Manzoni's *I promessi sposi*', in *Women and Italy: Essays on Gender, Culture and History*, ed. by Zygmunt G. Barański, Shirley W. Vinall (London: Macmillan, 1991), pp. 209–23.
41. For more on the dialectal features in the *novella*, see Moroni, pp. 51–61; and Pietro Trifone, *Malalingua: L'italiano scorretto da Dante a oggi* (Bologna: Il Mulino, 2007), pp. 95–109.
42. Roberto Bigazzi, *Le risorse del romanzo: componenti di genere nella narrativa moderna* (Pisa: Nistri-Lischi, 1996), p. 196.
43. Moroni, p. 46.
44. Prosperi, p. 3.
45. Although *Cavalleria rusticana* is known as one of Verga's most typically Sicilian tales, it is worth mentioning that every time Santuzza's father is referred to in the narrative, instead of employing the word that would normally be used for father ('papà'), Verga adopts the typically Florentine term: 'babbo' (*Tn* I, 182), which in Sicilian means 'stupido, scemo' [stupid, fool]; see *Vocabolario siciliano*, ed. by Giorgio Piccitto, with the contribution of the Regione Sicilina and the Consiglio nazionale delle ricerche (Catania: Centro di studi filologici e linguistici siciliani, 1977), s. v. babbo. Verga employs this word also in several other short stories collected in *Vita dei campi*, such as in 'Jeli il pastore' (*Tn* I, 139) and 'Rosso Malpelo' (*Tn* I, 167).
46. Prosperi, p. 6.
47. Pietro Gibellini, 'Tre coltellate per compare Turiddu: lettura antropologica di Cavalleria rusticana', *Strumenti critici*, 8 (1993), 205–23 (p. 206).
48. Giorgio Bàrberi Squarotti, *Giovanni Verga: le finzioni dietro il verismo* (Palermo: S. F. Flaccovio, 1982), p. 85.
49. Luigi Russo, *Giovanni Verga* (Rome: Laterza, 1995), p. 204.
50. Essentially, the image that Verga portrayed of the Sicilian working classes at the close of both versions is that of a society which treated honour as a rigid code, a kind of law for the lawless, instead of what it really was, a very loose and flexible set of practices and norms — an image of Sicily which Pirandello himself came to ridicule in his *Questa sera si recita a soggetto*. In an anthropological study conducted much later by Jane and Peter Schneider of a community in the west of Sicily, Villamura, over the period of two years (1965–1967) and two summers (1968 and 1971), they noted that 'the only way for cuckolds to lose their horns was to kill the people who placed them there. "Only blood would wash blood"; hence, the legendary crime of honor'. However, later on in their fieldwork, they point out that, 'although rigorous in theory, the code of honor was flexible in fact. Most cuckolds were not murderers and therefore not disposed to follow the rule that "blood washes blood", especially if their predicaments were not widely known in the community'; see Jane Schneider and Peter Schneider, *Culture and Political Economy in Western Sicily* (New York: Academic Press, 1976), p. 90 and p. 94.
51. For more on the use of prolepsis in the short story 'Cavalleria rusticana', see Anna Laura Lepschy, *Narrativa e teatro fra due secoli: Verga, Invernizio, Svevo, Pirandello* (Florence: Leo S. Olschki, 1984), p. 29.
52. Bàrberi Squarotti, *Giovanni Verga*, p. 82.
53. Angelini, 'Alla ricerca di una nuova drammaturgia', p. 609.
54. Guido Nicastro, '*Cavalleria rusticana* ossia una tragedia siciliana', in *Giovanni Verga e il teatro: atti del convegno Catania, 13–15 aprile, Teatro Stabile di Catania* (Catania: Assessorato regionale ai beni culturali e P. I., 1986), pp. 69–79 (p. 73).
55. Ugo Ojetti, *Alla scoperta dei letterati*, postface by Nicola Merola (Milan: Fratelli Dumolard, 1895), p. 66.
56. Similar terminology is employed in Verga's short story 'Il Mistero' also in his *Novelle rusticane* (1882). As Mastro Cola dies, he shouts: '"Mamma mia! m'ammazzarono!"' ['Mamma mia!

They've killed me!'] (*Tn* I, 245). Moreover, the two *novelle* are set at Easter, which is referred to as '[la] mala Pasqua' [[a] bad Easter] by both Mastro Cola's mother and Lola.

57. Gibellini, p. 207.
58. Gaspare Giudice, *Luigi Pirandello* (Turin: UTET, 1963), p. 302.
59. See Shirley W. Vinall and Peter S. Noble, 'Shrewd and Wanton Women: Adultery in the Decameron and the Heptameron', in *Women and Italy*, pp. 141–72.
60. Verdi's Il Trovatore, which is based on the vengeful Gipsy woman Azucena, premièred at the Teatro Apollo in Rome on 19 January 1853. The libretto was written by Salvadore Cammarano and Leone Emanuele Bardare, and draws its action from Antonio García Gutiérrez's play, *El trovador* (1836). For more on the opera, see Susan Bassnett-McGuire, 'Art and life in Luigi Pirandello's *Questa sera si recita a soggetto*', in *Drama and Mimesis*, ed. by James Redmond, Themes in Drama, 2 (Cambridge: Cambridge University Press, 1980), pp. 81–102 (pp. 95–98); and Graziella Corsinovi, '*Questa sera si recita a soggetto*: il testo. Tra progettazione vitalistica e partitura musicale', in *Testo e messa in scena in Pirandello*, ed. by Enzo Lauretta (Urbino: La Nuova Scientifica, 1986), pp. 105–32.
61. Luigi Pirandello, *Lettere a Marta Abba*, ed. by Benito Ortolani (Milan: Mondadori, 1995), p. 98.
62. See also Alessandro Tinterri, 'Le prime messinscene di *Questa sera si recita a soggetto*', in *Testo e messa in scena in Pirandello*, ed. by Enzo Lauretta (Urbino: La Nuova Italia Scientifica, 1986), pp. 133–46.
63. Luigi Pirandello, 'Premessa', in *Tutto il teatro di Luigi Pirandello, Maschere Nude: Sei personaggi in cerca d'autore, Ciascuno a suo modo, Questa sera si recita a soggetto* (Milan: Mondadori, 1958), pp. xi-xii (p. xi).
64. Ibid., p. xi.
65. For more on Pirandello's ironic presence in stage directions, in particular in his depictions of Dottor Hinkfuss, see Steen Jansen, 'Struttura narrativa e struttura drammatica in *Questa sera si recita a soggetto*', *Rivista italiana di drammaturgia*, 2.6 (December 1977), 55–70 (pp. 55–58).
66. Silvio D'Amico, '*Questa sera si recita a soggetto* di Pirandello, al Quirino', in *Cronache del teatro*, ed. by Eugenio Ferdinando Palmieri and Sandro D'Amico, 2 vols (Bari: Laterza, 1963), I, pp. 90–96 (p. 93).
67. Emanuele Licastro, *Luigi Pirandello dalle novelle alle commedie* (Verona: Fiorini, 1974), p. 181.
68. Jørn Moestrup, *The Structural Patterns of Pirandello's Work*, Études romanes de l'Université d'Odense, 2 (Odense: Odense University Press, 1972), p. 236.
69. Benvenuto Terracini, *Analisi stilistica: teoria, storia, problemi* (Milan: Feltrinelli, 1975), pp. 366–67.
70. Luigi Pirandello, 'En confiance', trans. by Benjamin Crémieux, *Le Temps*, 20 July 1925.
71. Quoted in Giudice, p. 341.
72. Starkie, p. 79.
73. Giorgio Bàrberi Squarotti, 'La trilogia pirandelliana e il rinnovamento del teatro', in *La Trilogia di Pirandello*, pp. 7–36 (p. 33).
74. See J. Douglas Campbell and Leonardo G. Sbrocchi, 'Introduction', in Luigi Pirandello, *Tonight We Improvise and ' "Leonora, addio!" '*, trans. with an intro. and notes by J. Douglas Campbell and Leonardo G. Sbrocchi (Ottawa: The Canadian Society for Italian Studies, 1987), pp. 7–26 (p. 20, my emphasis).
75. For a comparison between the two death scenes, see Olga Ragusa, 'Tonight We Improvise: Spectacle and Tragedy', in *A Companion to Pirandello Studies*, ed. by John Louis DiGaetani, foreword by Eric Bentley (New York: Greenwood Press, 1991), pp. 245–58.
76. Luigi Pirandello, 'Introduzione al teatro italiano', in *Storia del teatro italiano*, ed. by Silvio D'Amico (Milan: Bompiani, 1936), pp. 3–29 (p. 20).
77. Richard Sogliuzzo, 'L'arte dell'attore: teoria e pratica', in *La Trilogia di Pirandello*, pp. 149–63 (p. 160). For a similar viewpoint, see also Anne Paolucci, *Pirandello's Theatre: The Recovery of The Modern Stage for Dramatic Art* (Delaware: Griffon House, 2002), p. 60.
78. See Adriano Tilgher, *Il problema centrale: cronache teatrali 1914–1926*, ed. by Alessandro D'Amico (Genova: Edizioni del teatro stabile, 1973), p. 389; Robert Brustein, *The Theatre of Revolt*

(Guildford and London: Billing & Sons, 1965), p. 305; and Jo Ann Cannon, 'The Question of the Frame in Pirandello's Metatheatrical Trilogy', *Modern Language Studies*, 16.3 (1986), 44–56 (pp. 52–53).
79. Anthony Caputi, *Pirandello and the Crisis of Modern Consciousness* (Urbana and Chicago: University of Illinois Press, 1988), p. 121.

CHAPTER 4

The Silent Voice

The Silent Obedient Wife

The period considered here, from 1880 to approximately 1929, was an especially crucial one in that women were beginning to make their voices heard in the public arena. In the Italian theatrical tradition, this voice was above all strengthened by the *grande attrice* Eleonora Duse who specifically chose to interpret radical roles, such as Ibsen's Nora. But if women really were finding their own voice, on and off stage, then why would Verga's second female stage role, also for the interpretation of Duse, be the silent Màlia in *In portineria* (1885)? What is more, why would his successor Pirandello also devote a considerable part of his theatre to developing silent female characters in the years leading up to women's right to suffrage in Italy in 1946?

Even though women have often been associated with silence, this does not necessarily mean that they have lacked a voice. Indeed, while feminist literary criticism has focussed predominantly on three areas (exposing women's silences in literature in the form of absence and passivity; re-reading the works by female authors which have been silenced by the male-dominated canon; and reconnecting with their use of silence in their fiction), this chapter sheds light on how the silent female voices in Verga and Pirandello are in fact 'loud' voices, especially when transposed to the stage.

In the case of Màlia in 'Il canarino del n. 15' (1883) and *In portineria*, while struggling to find her voice, she expresses herself more effectively in the play than in the short story where the (male) narrator speaks on her behalf. Despite her inability to verbalise her real feelings, she is forced to do so on stage for the benefit of the audience either through broken speech or through her non-verbal communication and, as a result, articulates her emotions more strongly.[1]

As for Pirandello, he developed his use of silence through his characterisation of Signora Ponza. Whilst being physically absent in 'La Signora Frola e il Signor Ponza, suo genero' (1917) and only making an appearance at the end of *Così è (se vi pare)* (1917), she manages to rival the logic that Pirandello's male mouthpiece character, Laudisi, has been unable to put into words. In contrast to Laudisi, who rationalises all through the plot only to arrive at the conclusion that there is no conclusion, Signora Ponza, in both versions, crystallises the essence of the drama in no more than a few lines.[2] Pirandello further consolidated his treatment of silence through his portrayal of the late Silvia in both versions of *Tutto per bene* (1919 and 1920).[3] It is argued here that Silvia reveals more about herself in the play than she does in the short story where she is physically present for the most part, functioning as a silent voice capable of changing her husband's identity for evermore, even from beyond the grave.

Louder than Words

The pairing of women and silence is a particularly intriguing one. From as early as the Ancient Greeks, a wide range of writers have associated women with silence and men with words. To cite a few illustrations, according to Torquato Tasso in his *Discorso della virtù femminile e donnesca* (1582), 'il silenzio è virtù della donna, come l'eloquenza dell'huomo' [silence is the virtue of women, like eloquence is the virtue of men],[4] and, similarly, Ben Jonson in his *Epicoene* (or *The Silent Woman*) (1609) states that '[s]ilence in woman, is like speech in man' (2.3.111). But while speech for men has been considered a sign of intellectual superiority, it connotes something very different when applied to women. The traditional Virgin / Whore dichotomy, for example, associates sinners with speech and saints with silence, a notion which can equally be applied to the representation of women in fairy tales, where the persecuted maiden maintains silence and the witch uses her tongue to cast her spells.[5] Indeed, it is through the spoken word that Eve entices Adam to eat the forbidden fruit while the Virgin Mary does not utter a word in the Bible.[6]

Possibly owing to this historical tradition, silence during the Renaissance became viewed as a female virtue and was even imposed on women by many etiquette books. As Helena Sanson has pointed out: 'Il silenzio ha dunque molteplici valori per la bambina così come per la donna adulta: esso è innanzitutto ubbidienza, prima al padre e ai genitori in generale, poi al marito' [Silence has, therefore, multiple values for the young girl as it does for the adult woman: it is, above all, obedience, firstly towards her father and elders in general, then to her husband],[7] the kind of obedience which Nora rebels against in *A Doll's House*. Lesley Ferris has called this type of obedient and speechless heroine 'the patriarchal ideal of the silent woman',[8] an ideal which comes to life in a variety of early literary works. For instance, Jonson's *Epicoene* focuses on a wealthy gentleman who enjoys peace and tranquillity until he is driven to despair by his overly talkative wife. A further example can be traced in Colley Cibber's *The Careless Husband* (1709), which depicts how an adulterous husband is exposed by his docile wife as she catches him fast asleep with the housemaid without his wig on, leading her to put her handkerchief over his head to keep him warm — an act that inspires her husband to change his ways.

Ellen Moers's *Literary Women* (1976) is one of the first groundbreaking texts in terms of uncovering silences imposed on international female fiction- and non-fiction writers. These include, among others, George Eliot, Madame de Staël, Florence Nightingale, Beatrix Potter, and Mary Shelley, whose *Frankenstein* (1818) Moers considered to be a representation of the author's repressed fear of childbirth, as she states in her article on Gothic women writers, initially published in *The New York Review of Books* (1974).[9]

Tillie Olsen's *Silences* (1978) is another study to interrogate what she calls unnatural silences; that is, silences imposed onto those marginalised by class, race, and gender as a result of a lack of education. Olsen draws attention to the women writers who she feels have been excluded from the literary canon. One illustration is the fictional character Judith Shakespeare who features in Virginia Woolf's critical essay, 'A Room of One's Own' (1929). As Woolf shows, house-bound Judith is denied the same opportunities as her brother William and is therefore unable to develop her passion for literature. Whereas William goes on to become one of the world's greatest playwrights, Judith is forced into marriage. However, in refusing to marry her betrothed, she is disgraced by her father and this causes her to commit suicide. It is therefore Judith's lack of a voice which ultimately leads to tragedy.[10]

Lori Chamberlain has reminded us of a further (non-fictional) woman who has been silenced: Clara Schumann. While Robert Schumann is recognised as one of the most established violinists and composers of the nineteenth century, his wife — an equally talented musician — has generally been overlooked by music historians, despite the significant influence she had on her husband's compositions.[11]

Instead of associating women's silences with oppression or even censorship, the feminist critic Patricia Laurence adopts a different approach. She interprets the silence inherent in many of the literary works by Charlotte Brontë, Jane Austen, and Virginia Woolf as a kind of 'enlightened presence'.[12] With regards to Brontë's *Jane Eyre* (1847), written in first-person narrative, and Fanny Price in Austen's *Mansfield Park* (1884), composed in free indirect speech, Laurence demonstrates how both female narrators enable the heroines to express their viewpoints by articulating their silent thoughts and observations on their behalf.[13] The women might not speak out loud but their positions are nevertheless strongly conveyed by the narrators. Laurence compares this type of 'muteness' with Woolf's use of what she calls 'discourse of interiority',[14] or 'psycho-narration',[15] which delves even deeper into the characters' psyche, typical in *Mrs Dalloway* (1925). Even though some of Woolf's heroines may remain silent from a strictly verbal point of view, they are very much 'present' in her narratives by means of free indirect speech.

Laurence also takes into consideration the importance of what she calls 'resistant silence' in Woolf.[16] As Woolf writes in her *Three Guineas* (1938): 'To absent yourself — that is easier than to speak aloud [...]. It is worth watching very carefully to see what effects the experiment of absenting oneself has had — if any'.[17] Laurence thus concludes that

> [t]his literary development from indirectness and evasiveness to overt and resistant silence moves further the feminist discourse on the narration and cultural and literary interpretation of silence. In a new turn in feminist criticism, the preservation of these female silences by female authors is noted, and in a reversal of the traditional notion of women's complicity with oppressive circumstances of cultural exclusion, such silences are viewed as a difference of view, an alternative code of 'truth' or, sometimes, an expression of anger — the only kind that would be socially tolerated. Women's silence, that is to say, may be read as a strategy of resistance and choice — a ritual of both.[18]

Rather than associating silence with absence, Laurence considers the women's silences 'as a presence, and as a text waiting to be read'.[19] Just because the female characters do not speak, this does not necessarily mean that they cannot speak. Indeed, it could be said that they do not speak simply because they do not *want* to: their way of resisting the canon.

In the theatre, a key figure who stands her ground through her *intentional* silence is Cordelia in Shakespeare's *King Lear* (1606), who both Verga and Pirandello would have been aware of since the Elizabethan author had predominantly gained momentum in Italy in the nineteenth century owing largely to early performances of the great *mattatore* actors.[20] Unlike other Shakespearean characters, such as Lavinia in *Titus Andronicus* (1593) whose tongue is cut off after she is raped to stop her from revealing the truth about the assault, Cordelia's silence is arguably more a symbol of strength than a symbol of female oppression.[21] When Lear invites his daughter to flatter him in order to claim her share of his 'bounty' (I. i. 52), she remains silent:

> LEAR: [W]hat can you say to draw
> a third more opulent than your sisters? Speak.
> CORDELIA: Nothing my lord.
> LEAR: Nothing?
> CORDELIA: Nothing.
> LEAR: Nothing will come of nothing. Speak again. (I. I. 90)

Ferris concludes that 'Cordelia's refusal to enter into Lear's love market, although undoubtedly an heroic act, is intrinsically linked to her female-ness'.[22] However, what is especially fascinating about Cordelia is her verbal silence; that is, how she articulates her response through her silent voice. As Brian Rotman argues: 'Her "nothing", her failed attempt to remain silent, to stay outside the language of commodities set up by Lear, becomes for him an answer'.[23] It is this kind of voice which adds to Cordelia's strength of character, one of the most enlightened voices in the play. So while traditional feminist criticism has focussed on unveiling women's silences, the rest of this chapter will elucidate how silent female characters in Verga and Pirandello can also be equated with what Laurence calls a presence to be read — or rather a silent voice to be *heard* on stage.

'Il canarino del n. 15' and *In portineria*

Following the unprecedented success of *Cavalleria rusticana*, Verga felt both pressured and tempted to produce a new play. As he confessed in a letter to his friend Salvatore Paolo Verdura on 17 January 1885:

> Ora mi sento grave sulle spalle il fardello del poco che ho fatto e del molto che s'aspettano. [...] [N]on saprei più vivere adesso senza questa febbre e questa tortura, e una volta messo il piede su questa via bisogna andare avanti finché non ci si rompe il collo [...]. Basta, lavoriamo e avanti. Io sto scrivendo un drammettino in due atti che mi sembra di qualche effetto; e calcolatamente ho voluto che non sia d'argomento siciliano. (*Ls*, pp. 169–70)

[Now I feel heavy upon my shoulders the burden made up of the little I have achieved and the much that is expected of me. [...] I would not know how to live now without this fever and torture, and once you have placed a foot on this path you need to go on until you break your neck [...]. Enough, let us work and carry on. I am writing a little drama in two acts which seems to me of some consequence; and it has been my calculated desire that the topic be not Sicilian.]

This 'drammettino' [little drama] no longer 'd'argomento siciliano' [[of a] Sicilian topic] is *In portineria*, first performed on 16 May 1885 at the Teatro Manzoni in Milan, only a year after the première of *Cavalleria rusticana*, and staged by the Compagnia Nazionale. *In portineria* is based on 'Il canarino del n. 15', which was originally published in the journal *La Domenica letteraria* on 12 May 1882 and later included in Verga's collection of short stories *Per le vie* (1883), three years after the publication of *Vita dei campi*. But while *Cavalleria rusticana* had introduced a Sicilian village community to the bourgeois stage, *In portineria* now presented a new set of characters with different customs and values: an urban working-class Milanese family. Subsequently, what made Verga initially stand apart from other playwrights was now put to one side.[24] As Gianni Oliva explains:

> Dalla Sicilia ci si trasferiva nella grigia atmosfera di una portineria milanese, in cui si svolgeva la vicenda di due sorelle assai diverse tra loro e di un giovane operaio invaghito della più estroversa e segretamente amato dalla più debole e mite delle due, la quale finirà per morire. L'andamento stilistico del racconto, quella sorta di esasperante cantilena in cui era narrato l'ambiente della periferia, generava la condizione intima del dramma in cui scorreva la vita minore della Milano popolare di fine Ottocento: piccoli artigiani, portinai, giornalai, con i loro pettegolezzi, le superstizioni, i dialoghi veloci, quasi sincopati; il loro andirivieni sempre uguale significava il moto circolare dell'umanità scandito dall'alternarsi silenzioso delle stagioni.[25]

> [From Sicily we move to the grey atmosphere of a Milanese caretaker's lodge, where the story unfolds of two very different sisters and a young worker who has taken an interest in the outgoing sister and is secretly loved by the more fragile and gentler of the two, who ends up dying. The stylistic treatment of the short story, the sort of exasperating monotone in which the suburban atmosphere is recounted, generates the intimate nature of the play, in which the daily life of the late nineteenth-century Milanese working classes is portrayed: small artisans, caretakers, newsagents, with their gossiping, superstitions, and fast, almost syncopated exchanges; their ever-constant coming and going which echoes the circular motion of humanity punctuated by the silent passage of the seasons.]

But why would Verga choose to base his second play outside Sicily? It would appear that, through *In portineria*, Verga purposely aimed at distancing himself from *Cavalleria rusticana*. Indeed, what is curious is how, following the success of his Sicilian drama, Verga nurtured a distaste for the reaction caused by his climactic duel. In a letter of 7 July 1885, cited previously, he described his ideal audience to Capuana as 'un pubblico scelto e intelligente, non numeroso, non guastato dalle coltellate della *Cavalleria rusticana* e che non è venuto in teatro per vedere mordere l'orecchio a compare Alfio' [a select and intelligent audience, not great in number, not tainted by the terrible stabbing in *Cavalleria rusticana* and that has not come to the theatre to see Compare Alfio's ear being bitten] (CVC, 242). Verga here seemed to condemn the average spectator who attended his own play and effectively contributed to his only success in the theatre. In fact, Verga never quite 'digested' the praise he gained for his Sicilian play. In a letter to Sabatino Lopez of 16 January 1896, he referred to his success as 'il successo morboso della *Cavalleria*, che mi è rimasto sullo stomaco' [the morbid success of *Cavalleria* which is still sitting heavy on my stomach] (Ls, 308). Verga's unusual statement suggests that he felt as though his drama was valued for the wrong reasons.

This might explain why Verga composed the antithesis of *Cavalleria rusticana*, but why would he specifically chose to fix such a silent heroine at the heart of his new play? Presumably the reason for this was once again Duse, who was by now well known for her treatment of mime and gestures. In fact, in the same way as Verga composed the role of Santuzza for Duse's interpretation, so was the case with *In portineria*. In a letter to his contemporary Gegè Primoli of 8 March 1885 cited earlier, Verga writes: 'Figurati se vorrei dare alla Duse il mio lavoro [*In portineria*]! L'ho avuta sempre dinanzi agli occhi, nello scriverla' [Of course I would like Duse to interpret my work [*In portineria*]! I had her before my eyes the whole time I was writing it] (Ls, p. 174). And no wonder. Audiences responded well to Màlia *only* when the actress was able to make the protagonist's 'silent' voice heard through her body language, as we saw earlier.

Màlia

'Il canarino del n. 15' and *In portineria* are centred on Màlia who suffers from rickets in the *novella* and is in a wheelchair in the play. In both narrative and theatrical plots, she is fond of the local worker Carlini who visits her throughout her illness but, in reality, he calls on her to see her more ambitious sister, Gilda. Gilda, however, has her sights set on a wealthy gentleman and eventually elopes with him. Carlini confides his sense of rejection to Màlia as she continues to hide her true feelings for him. Following Gilda's flight, Màlia's health deteriorates. Unexpectedly, however, Gilda returns home and although this lifts Màlia's spirits for a while, she quietly passes away.

In both texts, Verga stresses the *unsaid*, particularly where Màlia's feelings for Carlini are concerned. Despite Verga's principle that in his literature 'la mano dell'artista rimarrà assolutamente invisibile' [the hand of the artist will remain completely invisible (CROS, p. 94)] and 'l'opera d'arte sembrerà *essersi fatta da sé*' (*Tn* I, p. 192) [the work of art will seem to have created itself (CROS, 94)], 'Il canarino del n. 15' is not as impartial as is seems. The narrator both exposes Màlia's hidden feelings on her behalf, and clearly empathises with her, especially when Carlini stops taking an interest: 'Ella pure ci aveva badato: tanto nessuno la guardava mai!' [And yet she did care: since no one ever laid their eyes on her!] (*Tn* I, 355).

Moreover, whereas Verga engineers his early Sicilian *novelle* so that he places emphasis on his characters' physical actions, in 'Il canarino del n. 15' his narrative largely focusses on Màlia's inner feelings. As Roberto Bigazzi puts it: 'Gran parte del racconto risulta da ciò che vede, ode e sente Màlia' [A large part of the tale is a result of what Màlia sees, hears and feels].[26] One of the episodes in the short story, missing from the stage version, which places importance of this more introspective narrator is the episode when Màlia is suddenly kissed by Carlini. Following Gilda's departure, Carlini, now part of the family, sees his former lover in Màlia, 'somigliava tutta a sua sorella' [the spitting image of her sister] (*Tn* I, 360), so much so that 'una volta che era stato all'osteria, e si sentiva una gran confusione dalla tenerezza, le diede anche un bacio' [once while he was at the tavern, greatly confused by her tenderness, he even gave her a kiss] (*Tn* I, 360). The kiss takes Màlia by surprise and 'la poveretta si sentiva sempre quel bacio sulla bocca, col fiato acre di lui, e vi aveva pensato tutta la notte' [the poor girl could always feel that kiss on her mouth, the bitter taste of his breath, and thought about it all night] (*Tn* I, 360). This is most probably the only kind of intimacy Màlia had ever experienced in her life and it is this unexpected sign of affection which gradually sends her ill health into further decline: 'Màlia cominciò a struggersi e a consumarsi a poco a poco' [little by little Màlia started to melt and burn up] (*Tn* I, 360). By means of free indirect speech, the narrator delves deep within Màlia's psyche to report her thoughts at the time of the kiss. Whereas Verga initially employed this narrative device in 'Cavalleria rusticana' to describe the characters' *external* behaviour, he now exploits the same device only this time to shed light on Màlia's *internal* turmoil. As Bigazzi continues to point out:

> Il discorso indiretto libero, che, escludendo l'autore, era stato mezzo per rappresentare gesti e parole del personaggio, risolto così in una totale visibilità 'popolare', suscita ora il monologo interiore fino alle soglie del flusso di coscienza. Si tratta infatti non di un monologo sintatticamente razionale (in quanto raccontato dallo scrittore col proprio linguaggio), ma di un monologo che conserva, grazie all'indiretto libero, le inflessioni e quindi il carattere del personaggio, con le sue libere associazioni (quasi correlativi oggetti) tra moti psicologici, eventi, cose.[27]
>
> [The use of free indirect speech, which, in excluding the role of the author, had been a way to convey the character's gestures and words, resulting in making a 'popular' character totally visible, now creates an interior monologue bordering on a stream of consciousness. Indeed, this is not a syntactically rational monologue (as it is recounted in the author's own words), but a monologue which preserves, thanks to free indirect speech, the nuances and therefore the personality of the character, with its free associations (almost objective correlatives) between psychological motives, events and things.]

Bigazzi here explains that Verga was more inclined to convey his characters' psychology in his later narratives, such as in *Mastro don Gesualdo* (1888) and *Per le vie*, the collection on tales which contains 'Il canarino del n. 15'. As Verga matured as a writer, he no longer employed free indirect speech to describe the characters' gestures or to reproduce their idiomatic register as he did in *Vita dei campi*, but he used the device as a kind of interior monologue, a technique inherent in the fiction of the aforementioned women writers as well as in Pirandello. But unlike these characters, above all in Pirandello, Màlia does not question her thoughts, perhaps because of her inexperience. As Guido Baldi suggests:

> Il racconto è dato in focalizzazione interna, cioè passa attraverso il filtro della prospettiva di Màlia stessa, ma i processi psicologici profondi non vengono portati esplicitamente alla superficie perché il soggetto, nella sua totale ingenuità e inesperienza di povero essere relegato fuori della vita, non è consapevole del senso di ciò che sta provando: per cui il filtro lascia passare solo sensazioni, percezioni fisiche, nelle quali però sono impliciti i sentimenti.[28]

> [The story is told from an internal focal point; it is filtered through the perspective of Màlia herself, but the profound psychological processes are not explicitly brought to the surface because the subject, in her total naivety and inexperience, a poor creature cut off from the world, is not aware of the meaning of what she is feeling. As a result, the filter only allows access to sensations, physical perceptions, in which, however, her emotions are implicit.]

Once the interior narrator is withdrawn from *In portineria*, Màlia needs to express her emotions for herself. One of the reasons that Verga introduces into the play the role of the housemaid Assunta, whom he later removes once she has served her purpose, is to provoke Màlia into admitting the truth about Carlini. When the curious Assunta asks how she would feel if Carlini were to marry her sister, the stage directions and suspension marks in her response underline her anxiety:

> MÀLIA: *(quasi le mancasse il fiato)*. Il sor Carlini, mamma? [...] *(premendosi il petto colle mani, balbettando dall'angoscia)*. Ma cosa devo dire io? [...]. Io... sì... s'è contento lui... e anche la Gilda... *(vacillando, e scostandola colle mani tremanti)*. Oh, mamma!... *Siede sullo scalino, pallidissima*. (*Tt*, 60)

> [MÀLIA: *(as though she was gasping for breath)*. Carlini, mother? [...] *(pressing her chest with her hands, stammering in distress)*. But what am I supposed to say? [...]. I... yes... If he is happy... and so is Gilda... *(staggering and pushing her away with her trembling hands)*. Oh, mother!... *She sits on the step, very pale.*]

Verga continues to include different scenes in the play so as to offer Màlia the possibility of expressing herself, such as a private scene with her sister. Her broken speech and long pauses again throw light on the difficulties she experiences:

> MÀLIA: *(abbracciandola tutta tremante)*. No, Gilda, no!... *Chinando il viso*. Ti dirò tutto!... come se fossi in punto di morte... Sai che sono stata in punto di morte!... Lui non mi ha detto una parola... una parola sola... mai!... Veniva a vedermi perchè ero ammalata... E nient'altro, ti giuro!... ti giuro!... Gli facevo soltanto compassione, ecco... Mentre io, sciocca... *Scoppia a piangere col viso tra le mani*. (*Tt*, 65)

> [MÀLIA: *(embracing her trembling all over)*. No, Gilda, no!... *Lowering her face*. I'll tell you everything!... As though I was on my deathbed... You know I was on the verge of dying!... He didn't say a word... Not even a word... never!... He used to come here to see me because I was unwell... And nothing else, I swear!... I swear!... He only felt sorry for me, that's all... Whilst I, stupid fool... *She bursts out crying holding her face in her hands.*]

Further, Verga gives Màlia the chance to release her emotions by developing her confession to the priest. While in the story Verga does not reveal to the readers what exactly she confessed other than Carlini's kiss — 'si confessò col prete, anche il bacio del Carlini' [she confessed to the priest, confessing also Carlini's kiss] (*Tn* I, 362) — on stage he gives Màlia the opportunity of developing her confession further. The hesitations, silences, and stage directions, however, continue to illuminate the difficulties she experiences when speaking about the 'giovane [a cui] volevo bene' [young man [whom] I used to love] (*Tt*, 75):

> MÀLIA: Egli lavorava nel magazzino, qui in corte... E così, vedendolo ogni giorno... Poi quando m'ammalai la prima volta, prese a venire anche la sera... Lì dov'è adesso vossignoria... *Tace un istante, sopraffatta dalla commozione.* (*Tt*, 75)
>
> [MÀLIA: He worked in the shop, here in the courtyard... And so, seeing him every day... Then when I got ill for the first time, he took to coming to see me even in the evening... There, where you are standing.... *She falls silent for a moment, overwhelmed by her emotions.*]

By adding and developing these different scenes so that the audience is given an insight into Màlia's psychology, Verga alludes to sensitive issues which are overlooked in the *novella*. As Màlia's confession on stage reveals, the play further develops the shame and guilt she experiences for having feelings for a man previously involved with her sister: 'Il Signore mi perdonerà, è vero, se non ho potuto rassegnarmi subito a fare il suo volere... se non ho potuto togliermelo dal capo, quel giovane?' [It is true, the Lord will forgive me if I was unable to immediately do His will... If I was unable to take him off my mind, that young man] (*Tt*, 76). As a result, Verga in the stage version is able to stress the reasons which contribute to the character's slow but gradual deterioration.

The last part of the short story and play is devoted to Malia's inevitable death. A doctor is introduced at the end of both plots to inform the family 'chiaro e tondo che poco le restava da penare, povera ragazza' [plain and simply that there was not much time left for her suffering, poor girl] (*Tn* I, 361), causing her parents suddenly to resolve their differences about Battista's heavy drinking and Gilda to make an unexpected return. Despite Màlia's short-lived joy, she suddenly passes away. Significantly, her death is conveyed unromantically in the two versions. In the short story, the family wait for the priest to give Màlia the Last Rites while Gilda and Carlini continue to quarrel about their past. At that moment, 'la poveretta passò senza che se ne accorgessero, e i vicini dissero che era morta proprio come un canarino' [the poor girl passed away without anybody noticing, and the neighbours said that she had died just like a canary] (*Tn* I, 362). Whereas in the first half of the *novella* Verga reports Màlia's moods and dispositions on her behalf, in the final part he does not offer any psychological introspection and mentions her death in passing, possibly in order to indicate how her quick death went unnoticed by her family. Even the description of her parent's grief remains undeveloped. The reader is told only that her father 'pianse come un vitello' [cried like a calf] (*Tn* I, 362) and her mother shouts out: 'Povero angelo! Ha finito di penare! Ma eravamo abituati a vederla là, a quella finestra, come un canarino' [My poor angel! She is no longer in pain! But we were used to seeing here there, by the window, like a canary] (*Tn* I, 362).

Luigi Russo has summarised the 'unromantic' portrayal of Màlia's death in the *novella*:

> La chiusa potrebbe parere romantica, e non è; l'amore silenzioso della Malia non è mai colorito sentimentalmente, ma ha, anzi, dei riflessi tristemente umoristici per l'incomprensione bonaria del Carlini, che parla affettuosamente alla vittima senza sapere che male le faccia; per le scene gustose tra la sora Giuseppina, ingenuamente bramosa di dar marito alle figliuole, e il sor Battista, bevitore, spaccamontagne, lettore del *Secolo*, il quale poi piange come un vitello quando la disgrazia gli è sopra. Il piccolo mondo di portineria è ritratto bene: grossolanità di tipi e cordialità di affetti, e miseria grigia su tutto [...]. Il metodo dei *Malavoglia*, dove le pene gemono il loro pianto sommesso in mezzo a un coro di pettegolezzi, è perseguito anche qui, con fedeltà. La pena di Màlia è in sordina: il romanticismo è stato rinnegato o travolto nel realismo.[29]

> [The ending could seem romantic, but it is not; Màlia's silent love is never coloured with sentimentality. However, it is given flecks of sad humour: the good-natured lack of awareness shown by Carlini, who speaks affectionately to the victim without knowing what harm he does to her; the pleasant scenes between Giuseppina, naively eager to marry off her daughters, and the heavy-drinker and braggart Battista, a reader of the *Secolo*, who then cries like a calf when disaster strikes. The small world of the caretaker's lodge is depicted well: simple 'types', warm affections, and an all-pervading wretchedness [...]. The narrative technique adopted in *I Malavoglia*, where suffering and sorrow are buried in the midst of a gossiping chorus, is also closely followed here. Màlia's suffering is silent: the play's romanticism has been denied or crushed by Realism.]

Interestingly, the protagonists' death scenes in *I Malavoglia* (1881) and *Mastro don Gesualdo* are also reported simply like in 'Il canarino del n. 15': Padron 'Ntoni 'aveva fatto quel viaggio lontano, più lontano di Trieste e d'Alessandria d'Egitto, dal quale non si ritorna più' [had travelled far away, further than Trieste and Alexandria in Egypt, from which there was no return] (*I Mala.*, 267), and Mastro don Gesualdo '[a] un tratto s'irrigidì e si chetò del tutto' [suddenly became stiff and kept silent for evermore] (*MDG*, 355). What differs is how the reader is made to react. From the start of *I Malavoglia*, the reader instantly recognises how important it is for Padron 'Ntoni to die in his own home: 'Beato chi muore nel proprio letto' [Blessed is he who dies in his own bed] (*I Mala.*, 161). Instead, he passes away in a hospital, far from his home town. As for Mastro don Gesualdo, he also dies alone but what touches the reader is how the servants judge him by looking at his hands. After a lifetime of working to secure a better life for Isabella (whom he believes to be his biological daughter), he continues to be considered as a manual labourer even on his deathbed: '"Si vede com'era nato..." osservò gravemente il cocchiere maggiore. "Guardate che mani!"' ['You can see where he was born...' observed the head coachman gravely. 'Just look at what hands!'] (*MDG*, 356). Although these scenes are narrated concisely, the deaths of the two men are nevertheless conveyed more compassionately than Màlia's death, supporting the notion that the portrayal of her death is far from romantic.

The play mirrors Màlia's death in the short story but without the role of the priest. While Gilda and Carlini argue, Màlia dies unobserved by her family:

> CARLINI: Penso a quei bei tempi che si era tutti qui, felici e contenti... Lei non se ne rammenta neppure forse...
> GILDA: Oh!... a che giova ormai?...
> CARLINI: Ecco! Non vuol nemmeno sentirne parlare!...
> GILDA: Basta, sor Carlini!... Vede, quella poveretta!...*Volgendosi alla Màlia che si scompone sempre più in viso, ed è rimasta immobile col capo chino sul petto.* Màlia! Màlia! (*Tt*, 87)

> [CARLINI: I am thinking about the good old days when we were all here, happy and content... You perhaps don't even remember...
> GILDA: Oh!... What's the point now anyway?....
> CARLINI: See! She doesn't even want to hear it spoken of!...
> GILDA: Enough, Carlini!... Look at that poor thing!... *Turning to Màlia whose face is increasingly dishevelled, and remains motionless with her head on her chest.* Màlia! Màlia!]

Although Verga designs the two versions to lead up to this critical point, the presentation of the death itself is conveyed without any drama. In fact, as soon as Màlia dies, both plots simply come to an end. This anticlimactic closing reinforces Verga's determination to produce an entirely different play from *Cavalleria rusticana*. While his Sicilian play is structured to build up to the dénouement, *In portineria* is stripped of a similar *coup de théâtre* and it is this novelty in Verga's theatre which gives the impression that he really was introducing a new kind of 'silent' heroine. Natalino Sapegno has praised Verga's style of writing:

> Forse il risultato più schietto, e non a caso, è raggiunto nel bozzetto *In portineria* dove proprio il Verga non ha più da fare i conti con la sua lingua poetica e personale e si affida a quella sorta di gergo indifferenziato e scialbo.[30]

> [Perhaps the clearest result, and not by chance, is achieved in the dramatic sketch *In portineria* where Verga himself no longer has to deal with his poetic and personal style and relies on that sort of unvariegated and colourless language.]

In fact, though Màlia in these scenes finds it difficult to speak about Carlini, she nonetheless manages to articulate her repressed feelings though her non-verbal communication. She is the only character able to go beyond the spoken word and reveal what is really at the heart of her suffering, capable of *voicing the un-voiceable*. Instead of resigning herself, Màlia perseveres to the point that she succeeds in expressing herself more 'loudly' in the play than in the short story where the narrator can actually speak on her behalf. Whether or not this can be traced to the influence of Nora who also was making her 'new' voice known, it is nonetheless intriguing that the second female character which Verga transposes to the stage should find her 'silent' voice on stage at the time when women were breaking their imposed silences off stage.

'La Signora Frola e il Signor Ponza, suo genero' and *Così è (se vi pare)*

Just as Verga was experimenting with the treatment of silence in his theatre, so was Pirandello in *Così è (se vi pare)* (1917), a play allegedly inspired by the 1915 earthquake that destroyed Marsica in the region of Abruzzo.[31] The drama is based on the *novella* 'La Signora Frola e il Signor Ponza, suo genero', which was initially written in 1915 and later published by Treves in the collection of short stories, *E domani, lunedì* (1917). On 3 April 1917, Pirandello first mentioned his almost completed play in a letter to his son Stefano: 'Ho quasi finito la commedia in tre atti (parabola, veramente, più che commedia): *Così è (se vi pare)*' [I have almost finished my three-act play (a parable, really, more than a play): *Right You Are (If You Think So)*].[32] But why would Pirandello call his play a parable? According to the critic Roger Oliver:

> While the term 'parable' does not suggest the *contrario*, or oppositeness, that is crucial to *umorismo*, it does point in the important direction of the movement beneath the surface. Although the characters and actions of a parable need not be seen totally as symbols, there is a larger, more generalized concept that is to be seen beneath the surface reality. There is also an educative purpose behind a parable, whereby a lesson with a general applicability can be deduced from the specific example of the incident. Pirandello is working in a similar way here, but in adapting the parable idea to his purposes, he adds the techniques of *umorismo*, so that not only is the 'truth' of his play to be deduced beneath its surface, but that 'truth' may be the opposite of what the surface might at first suggest.[33]

As Oliver indicates, a parable is intrinsically linked to the notion of relativism: what is portrayed on the outside does not necessarily correspond to what is concealed beneath. In fact, it is through *Così è (se vi pare)* that Pirandello, for the first time in his career, moved away from portraying the Sicilian community and started to concentrate mainly on the Italian bourgeoisie, which seemed to offer him the possibility of developing the intellectual and relativistic dimension in his plays. As Anthony Caputi puts it:

> Altogether, *Right You Are* provides a brilliant illustration of this crucial moment in Pirandello's career, when his increased attention to relativity as a cardinal principle in consciousness and self-consciousness and his increased use of drama began to determine the direction of his work.[34]

Indeed, as Pirandello was finishing *Così è (se vi pare)*, which is said to have only taken him six days to complete,[35] he was also having difficulties drafting one of his most relativistic novels, *Uno, nessuno e centomila*. Even though the novel was not published until 1925–1926, letters to Stefano reveal that he was nonetheless attempting to write it while finalising *All'uscita* (1916) and *Così è (se vi pare)*. According to Gigi Livio, *All'uscita* and *Così è (se vi pare)* are theatrical transpositions of the eventual novel.[36] Traces of the main theme, largely the fragmentation of different personalities, can be found in them, as well as in the short story 'La Signora Frola e il Signor Ponza, il suo genero', which was composed only a year before the première of *All'uscita*. Essentially, it is through these two plays that Pirandello really made his mark as a relativistic writer. Arcangelo Leone De Castris has called the pair 'parabole fondatrici' [pioneering parables],[37] and, in terms of *Così è (se vi pare)*, this foremost parable is personified in the mysterious character of Signora Ponza.

Signora Ponza

The *novella* and play depict the turmoil experienced by a town (called Valdana in the narrative but *'un capoluogo di provincia'* [*a provincial county town*] in the stage directions of the play (*Mn* I, 436)) following the arrival of three newcomers. The townspeople cannot understand why the new prefect's secretary (Signor Ponza), his wife (Signora Ponza), and mother-in-law (Signora Frola), who have moved from their earthquake-ridden hometown, form two separate households with the elderly Signora Frola living by herself. After probing into their private lives, they learn that this is caused by the mysterious identity of the enigmatic woman, Signora Ponza: Signora Frola believes that she is her daughter (Signor Ponza's first and only wife) while Signor Ponza believes that she is his second wife and that Signora Frola is a grieving mother who sees her late daughter (his first wife) in his new wife. While the narrative ends with the townspeople bemused by the mystery, different strategies are discussed to uncover the truth in the play. It is suggested by Pirandello's mouthpiece character, Laudisi, that Signora Ponza herself should reveal the truth about her identity. Covered in a veil, Signora Ponza enters the stage and reveals that she is both Signora Frola's daughter (Giulia) as well as Signor Ponza's second wife (Lina). Pirandello thus places Signora Ponza's inexplicable identity at the heart of the two versions. Even after Signora Frola and Signor Ponza have put forward their equally convincing yet contradictory arguments, the community is still confused by the mystery she represents.

What is striking about the voice of the narrator in this short story is its philosophical tone. It inspires the reader to distinguish fact from fiction, a viewpoint which becomes increasingly insightful and perhaps more sceptical as the narrative develops. Indeed, at the end of the plot, the narrator declares that '[la gente] non riesce ancora in nessun modo a comprendere quale sia il pazzo dei due, dove sia il fantasma, dove la realtà' (*Na* III, 781) [they still can't — it doesn't matter how hard they try — they still can't fathom which of the two is the mad one; in which of them sanity is a reality, in which of them it is merely fantasy (*SS*, 151)]. While in the short story the men generally side with Signor Ponza and the women with Signora Frola, the narrator takes more of an impartial outlook. One of the reasons the women believe Signora Frola's side of the story is that she possesses the letters she has exchanged with her daughter. But instead of expanding on what type of written evidence she owns, the narrative voice, different from the fickle attitude of the townspeople, focuses on how Signor Ponza refutes her written proof:

> Questa, difatti, viene premurosa a mostrar loro le letterine affettuose che le cala giù col panierino la figliuola, e anche tant'altri privati documenti, a cui però il signor Ponza toglie ogni credito, dicendo che le sono stati rilasciati per confortare il pietoso inganno. (*Na* III, 781)

> [She, in fact, comes along with great eagerness to show them the affectionate little notes that her daughter lets down to her in the little basket and, over and

above these, lots and lots of other private documents. Signor Ponza, however, destroys their value as evidence by saying that they've been issued to her to lend colour to the pitiful deception.] (*SS*, 151)

Ulrich Leo identifies the spokesperson in the *novella*, what he considers to be a 'dramatic narrative monologue',[38] as the eventual Laudisi in the play:

> By listening more carefully we still find something in the 'monologue' that cannot be so unquestionably attributed to a naïve member of the 'People say...' impersonal group. The speaker at some points seems to be half conscious of what will be the basic thesis of Laudisi in the play: that truth is defined just by its being unknowable. This naturally would never occur to any really harmless member of the 'Tutti' busybodies.[39]

Laudisi is most definitely 'il centro intellettuale dell'opera' [the intellectual centre of the play].[40] He becomes increasingly intellectual as the dramatic action proceeds, closing each act with a burst of laughter, and mocking the minor characters on Pirandello's behalf: 'Vi guardate tutti negli occhi? Eh! La verità? *Scoppierà a ridere forte:* Ah! Ah! Ah! Ah!' (*Mn* I, 466) [There you are, staring at each other with nothing to say! What price the truth now? *(Laughing loudly.)* Ha! ha! ha! ha! (*CP* I, 111)]. He effectively takes over the philosophical voice of the narrative by expanding on the theory of illusion and reality, as well as the notion of the unreliability of documents, particularly in the second act, during his soliloquy in front of the mirror: '[P]erché per me la realtà non consiste in essi, ma nell'animo di quei due' (*Mn* I, 468) [For me, reality is to be found not in pieces of paper, but in the minds of those two people (*CP* I, 113)]. At the end, he summarises the crux of the drama by identifying Signora Ponza as either '[i]l fantasma d'una seconda moglie, se ha ragione lei, la signora Frola. O il fantasma della figliuola, se ha ragione lui, il signor Ponza' (*Mn* I, 493) [[t]he ghost of a second wife, if Signora Frola is right; the ghost of Signora Frola's daughter, if we are to believe Signor Ponza (*CP* I, 136)], assuming the role of a sort of teacher who speaks on Pirandello's behalf. As mentioned above, Pirandello called this play a parable and, according to Oliver, '[t]here is also an educative purpose behind a parable, whereby a lesson with a general applicability can be deduced from the specific example of the incident',[41] a lesson here which, at least superficially, appears to be taught by Laudisi.

Although the narrator in the short story and Laudisi in the play are portrayed as the most rational figures in both versions, they essentially remain part of the inquisitive community. Towards the end of the narrative, the townspeople are just as confused as they were at the start: 'Dico, non vi sembra che a Valdana ci sia proprio da restare a bocca aperta, a guarda*rci* tutti negli occhi, come insensati?' (*Na* III, 780) [I ask you! Don't you think that those of *us* who live in Valdana have got good reason to stand about gaping at one another, staring into one another's eyes like half-wits? (*SS*, 150, my italics)]. The use of the first person plural reinforces the hypothesis that the narrator is from Valdana. Meanwhile in the play, Laudisi is just as intrusive as the minor characters when he suggests the idea of summoning Signora Ponza and forcing her to testify: 'Il signor Ponza ha "una" in casa con sé! La moglie' (*Mn* I, 492) [Signor Ponza has a wife living with him! His wife (*CP* I, 135)].

In fact, whereas these two most intellectual figures only go so far as guiding the reader of the *novella* and the audience of the play to question who the mysterious woman really is, it is Signora Ponza who offers a solution. In the *novella*, it is her silence which paradoxically voices the underlying 'truth'. By being continuously spoken about by the other characters, her absence is turned into a sort of metaphorical presence, and it is this powerful metaphor which confirms that she is *both* Signora Frola's daughter and Signor Ponza's second wife. Moreover, in the play, Pirandello introduces her physical presence, bringing the metaphor to life.[42] As soon as she enters the stage '*col volto nascosto da un fitto velo nero, impenetrabile*' (*Mn* I, 507) [*with her face hidden by a thick impenetrable black veil* (*CP* I, 149)], Signora Frola screams with joy: 'Lina... Lina... Lina...', embracing her '*con l'arsura d'una madre che da anni e anni non abbraccia più la sua figliuola*' [*with all the passion of a mother who has not embraced her daughter for years*], while Signor Ponza calls her 'Giulia!... Giulia! ... Giulia!' (*Mn* I, 508). Unlike the townspeople in the narrative, the minor characters on stage are given the possibility of seeing the mysterious woman for themselves, and yet the conclusion they are presented offers them no resolution. Indeed, as the pair make their way off stage, Signora Ponza is finally given the chance to reveal the 'truth': '*(con un parlare lento e spiccato)*: che cosa? la verità? è solo questa: che io sono, sì, la figlia della signora Frola [...] e la seconda moglie del signor Ponza' (*Mn* I, 509) [*(speaking slowly and very clearly)*: What do you want from me? The truth? The truth is this, and this alone: I am the daughter, yes, the daughter of Signora Frola [...] and I'm the second wife of Signor Ponza (*CP* I, 150)]. Although Signor Ponza and Signora Frola are content to live with their illusions, and Signora Ponza is only too happy to play both the role of Signora Frola's daughter and Signor Ponza's second wife,[43] behind the black veil, she recognises that she will never have an identity: '[i]o sono colei che mi si crede' (*Mn* I, 509) [I am what others believe me to be (*CP* I, 151)].

The ending of the play therefore represents a kind of epilogue, or as Licastro puts it, '*un'aggiunta conclusiva alla trama della novella*' [a conclusive addition to the narrative plot],[44] which completes the *novella* by following on from the suggestion made by the narrator to allow Signora Ponza to reveal the truth in her own words. Realising how both Signor Ponza and Signora Frola impose their views on her, she has become aware that she does not have an identity of her own. Although this perspective is conveyed in the *novella*, it is the play which further develops the human consequences.

So even though in the drama Pirandello chooses to express his theories in a man, he assigns the task of personifying them to a woman. As Daniela Bini argues, although Pirandello's male *raisonneurs*, such as Mattia Pascal, Lamberto Laudisi, Leone Gala, Baldovino, Serafino Gubbio, Enrico IV and Vitangelo Moscarda, appear to be intellectually superior to the rest, in reality their reasoning is self-defeating:

> What do these *raisonneurs* accomplish? What do they finally understand through the use and abuse of reason? That life is a '*flusso incandescente*'; that it is chaos; that there is neither order nor logic in it. In his sad attempt to rationalize chaos,

to find reasons where there are none, man stops and dissects life, thus killing it. Man's privileged, rational place is thus undermined by its tragic paradox: reason tries to make sense out of life that has none.[45]

In contrast to Laudisi, Signora Ponza hardly speaks on stage. The succinctness of her speech, combined with her striking appearance, conveys the same message that Laudisi has endlessly tried to articulate, but in a more effective way. Not only is there intellectual depth in what she says, there is also emotional substance. While Laudisi is the one who questions and inspires others to question, it is Signora Ponza who offers a reply through her recognition of 'the defeat of logical discourse'.[46] In fact, with regard to the male *raisonneurs* in *Uno, nessuno e centomila*, Maria Antonietta Grignani points out how '[n]ell'erma bifronte pirandelliana il paradigma del silenzio è l'altra faccia della coazione a parlare' [in the Pirandellian two-faced herm, the paradigm of silence is the opposing face of the compulsion to speak].[47] What is particularly revealing in 'La Signora Frola e il Signor Ponza, suo genero' and *Così è (se vi pare)* is how the use of silence (represented by Signora Ponza) eclipses the importance of words (represented by Laudisi), making an interesting challenge to the man-words and women-silence dichotomies.

Following this, Pirandello's contemporary critic, Adriano Tilgher, has associated Signora Ponza with a different type of *raisonneur*, the solitary philosopher Cosmo Laurentano in *I vecchi e i giovani* (1913) who, like Signora Ponza, 'si spoglia di ogni attaccamento alla sua forma individuale, e, annientato in sé il principio d'individuazione, radice dell'egosimo e del peccato, viva tutto e solo per gli altri, e per sé non sia nulla' [strips himself of every attachment to his own individual form, and, in annulling within himself the principle of individualisation, the root of all egoism and sin, lives entirely and only for other people, and for himself he does not exist].[48] However, unlike Laurentano, what is unique about Signora Ponza is how she actually rivals other *raisonneurs*, particularly Laudisi, through her silence in the narrative and the few words she utters on stage.

Though Silvio D'Amico initially praised the play in *L'idea nazionale* on 16 November 1918 ('Questa commedia è, come tale, perfetta' [This play is, as such, perfect]),[49] he later argued in his *Teatro dei fantocci* (1920) that

> le parole della donna velata son povere e secche, e per di più, insolitamente letterarie. Gli spettatori non sentono bene il gusto della deliziosa presa in giro; nè, tanto meno, intendono il singhiozzo sulla vanità delle illusioni umane. Restano disorientati e inappagati.[50]
>
> [the words of the veiled woman are poor and arid, and moreover, unusually literary. The spectators cannot really taste the flavour of the delicious joke, let alone understand the lament for the vanity of human illusion. They remain disorientated and unfulfilled.]

However, as Bini clarifies, in Signora Ponza's words Pirandello stresses the *unsaid*:

> There is an appeal to that sphere of emotional impulses, of the unsaid and inexpressible; there is an appeal to those empty spaces which must be respected for what they are, spaces that cannot be violated by being filled with external meaning.[51]

Similarly, Giorgio Pullini, referring to one of Signora Ponza's opening lines — '[la] sventura [...] deve restar nascosta, perché solo così può valere il rimedio che la pietà le ha prestato' [the tragedy [...] must remain concealed, because only in this way can the remedy granted by compassion take effect] (*Mn* I, 508) — suggests that these few words '[s]ono parole di pietà umana' [[a]re words of human compassion].[52] This again strengthens the extent to which Pirandello merges the emotional with the intellectual through the presence of the mysterious woman.

Although Pirandello was concerned with finding the right word for the right character, as he put it in his critical essay 'L'azione parlata' (1899), it would seem that as he developed as a writer, he began to add value to the unspoken. As Vitangelo Moscarda in *Uno, nessuno e centomila* points out in the final section of the novel, 'Non conclude': 'Non volendo più nulla, sapevo di non poter più parlare. E stavo zitto' [[N]ot desiring anything else, I knew that I could no longer speak. And so I remained quiet] (*Tr* II, 899). In the words of Corrado Donati: 'Tutto il linguaggio pirandelliano in ultima analisi, tende al silenzio come estrema rinuncia di fronte ad un dissidio insormontabile, e nello stesso tempo, come culmine espressivo' [The whole of Pirandello's language, in the final analysis, tends towards silence as an ultimate renunciation before an insurmountable disagreement, and, at the same time, as an acme of expression].[53] Indeed, at the end, Laudisi himself seems to be reduced to a form of non-verbal communication: he closes the play with a burst of laughter, recalling the breakdown of words in the form of La Demente's repetition of 'Le-na' at the end of *Come tu mi vuoi* (1929).[54]

Overall, there have been many interpretations of Signora Ponza's final appearance on stage. Antonio Gramsci has argued that her presence represents '[u]no sgambetto logico semplicemente' [simply a logical decoy].[55] Paolo Puppa has offered a religious interpretation of her appearance: '[L]a loro apparizione, agli occhi stuporosi del salotto del borghese profano, presenta i caratteri del "*sensus numinis*", del "*mysterium tremendum*"' [[H]er appearance, to the wide-eyed profane bourgeoisie in the salon, has the characteristics of a '*sensus numinis*', of a '*mysterium tremendum*'].[56] Lucienne Kroha has provided a Freudian perspective,[57] and Maggie Günsberg has suggested that the character represents a kind of 'insoluble mystery, and therefore threat, of female identity'.[58] It has been proposed here that Signora Ponza's silence symbolises more of an emblem of reality in *both* narrative and dramatic versions, capable of reducing Laudisi to (verbal) silence. As Pirandello himself confirmed about the closing scene in a letter of 3 May 1917 to the director Virgilio Talli, these were 'parole messe in bocca a una donna dal volto nascosto da un velo impenetrabile: *vivissima* donna, nel dramma, e pur simbolo di verità' [words placed in the mouth of a woman whose face is concealed by an impenetrable veil: *an extremely alive woman, in the drama, and the pure symbol of truth*] (*Mn* I, 421). No matter how much the philosophical voice of the narrator and Laudisi attempt to put the 'truth' into words, it is the metaphor of Signora Ponza in the *novella*, along with her brief appearance in the stage version, which silently articulates this '*simbolo di verità*' [symbol of truth].

Tutto per bene

Pirandello continues to experiment with the use of silence in *Tutto per bene*. Both narrative and theatrical versions develop the characterisation of the archetypal unknowingly betrayed husband, another popular topic among the *veristi* writers. Indeed, the original story was produced in 1906 when Pirandello was also still closely associated with the *veristi*. Almost two decades later, Pirandello adapted the *novella* into a play,[59] with Ruggero Ruggeri in mind for the lead role, as he revealed in a letter to the actor of 7 December 1919: 'Caro Amico, sì, è vero, ho pensato per Lei una commedia in tre atti, che ha per titolo *Tutto per bene*' [Dear Friend, yes, it's true, I have thought of a three-act play for you, which has as its title *All for the Best*].[60] Ruggeri starred as Martino Lori in the première on 2 March 1920 at the Quirino in Rome and audiences generally responded well to his performance, with the exception of Marco Praga in the *Illustrazione Italiana* on 10 March 1920: 'Ruggero Ruggeri in Martino Lori non mi ha convinto' [Ruggero Ruuggeri as Martino Lori did not convince me].[61]

Although the story was composed during the early stage of Pirandello's career, it nonetheless showed signs of its divergence from the *veristi*. While Verga's triangular relationships usually consist of the traditional husband, wife and lover, Pirandello continues to distort the triangle by adding problematic figures. In *Tutto per bene*, the triangular relationship involves husband (Lori), *late* wife (Silvia) and lover (Verona in the *novella* and Manfroni in the play).

Though the original version of 'Tutto per bene' is one of Pirandello's first *novelle*, traces of the story can be found in two even earlier narratives: 'Creditor galante' (1897) and 'La paura' (1897), which is based on the play *L'epilogo* (1892) and later renamed *La morsa: Epilogo in un atto* (1910). Elio Providenti observes that in 'Creditor galante' (as in 'Tutto per bene') 'la situazione è già quella dell'antefatto del dramma: una donna che riscopre in sé l'amore per il coniuge dopo averlo disprezzato e tradito' [the situation centres on the antecedent events of the play: a woman who rediscovers her love for her husband after having despised and betrayed him].[62] The two lovers, Maurizio Gueli and Fulvia Corsani (whose parts are merely sketched in 'come didascalie di una commedia' [like stage directions in a play]),[63] discuss their past relationship through uninterrupted dialogue. Their exchange reveals that fifteen years earlier, Fulvia, like Silvia, fell pregnant by her lover and gave birth to a girl. However, while in *Tutto per bene* the audience learns that Silvia's return to her husband is imposed on her by her lover, it is Fulvia's own decision to go back to hers, who happens to be Gueli's cousin Aldo, a gambling addict.

'La paura' is also presented as a form of dialogue between another pair of lovers, Antonio Serra and Lillina Fabris. In their exchange, Antonio is afraid that Lillina's husband, Andrea, is aware of their relationship. After much debate, Lillina decides to end their affair. As with Fulvia, it is Lillina's sense of remorse which leads her back to her husband. The theatrical re-visioning *L'epilogo* / *La morsa*, on the other hand, ends very differently. The adulterous wife is tricked into admitting her affair, after which she is forced to leave her children, and, as a result, shoots herself.

Alessandro D'Amico relates *L'epilogo* / *La morsa* to Verga's *La caccia al lupo*, 'che tuttavia, stando alle date, risulterebbe posteriore all'*Epilogo*, poiché la novella verghiana è del 1897 e l'atto unico fu rappresentato nel 1901' [which nonetheless, according to the dates, seems to be published after *Epilogo*, since Verga's story was published in 1897 and the one-act play was performed in 1901] (*Mn* I, 6, n. 4). Arnaldo Bruni also briefly compares *La morsa* with *La caccia al lupo*, showing how the term 'paura' [fear] is scattered throughout both plays.[64] Indeed, it is quite striking that Mariangela in Verga's play also turns to her husband at the end but in this case she does so to save herself from his metaphorical hunt.

All of these works therefore exemplify what D'Amico calls '[i]l tema dell'adultera che torna all'affetto del marito' [[t]he theme of the adulterous woman who returns to her husband's affection] (*Mn* I, 7, n. 1). Each woman not only commits adultery but eventually abandons her role as lover in order to resume her role as wife. What differentiates 'Tutto per bene', however, is how the narrator silences what happens between Silvia and her lover just before she goes back to her husband, unlike in the play where Pirandello enlightens the audience as to the real cause of her return and reveals the truth of her infidelity only after her death.

Silvia

One of the major alterations that take place in the dramatic version is related to the treatment of time and structure. In the *novella* Silvia dies towards the end of the plot, while at the start of the stage version she has already been dead for sixteen years. Even though Silvia has passed away, the effect she has on all the characters is still much in evidence. Lori only realises that he has been caught up in the triangle after her death, and it is at this moment that he becomes aware that his close friend Verona / Manfroni is the biological father of the daughter whom he considered to be his own (Ginetta in the short story and Palma on stage).

In contrast to the narrative which provides a linear overview of Silvia's life, guiding the reader from the start of her relationship with her husband and lover to the time of her death, the play is entirely set after Silvia's death. In inverting the linear plot of the *novella*, this 'backward-looking' structure provides Pirandello with the opportunity of portraying Silvia's effect on the protagonists more conspicuously on stage — the closer the spectators of the play come to the end, the more they are able to understand the events that preceded in her life. As the dramatic action unfolds, the audience is thus inspired to piece together the episodes leading up to her adultery. As John Humphreys Whitfield concludes: 'La novella è come un sigillo di cui la commedia si presenta come matrice, che noi dobbiamo appunto leggere a rovescio' [The short story is like a wax stamp, of which the play presents itself as the matrix, which we accordingly have to read in reverse].[65]

By entirely removing Silvia's physical presence from the drama and starting the action almost two decades after her death, Pirandello is able to convey the strength of her influence over all of the characters, especially Lori. As with Signora Ponza in 'La Signora Frola e il Signor Ponza, suo genero' and for the most part of *Così è (se vi pare)*, Silvia's physical absence from the drama is transformed into a re-created presence by Lori whose present-day is determined by his memory of her. As Licastro notes:

> Pirandello, eliminando la rappresentazione cronologica degli avvenimenti, non solo riesce a far convergere l'attenzione sulla psiche del protagonista, ma riesce anche a far dimenticare gli avvenimenti passati *per sé*, e a farli vedere solo attraverso la mente del protagonista, quasi *fossero una sua costruzione*.[66]
>
> [Pirandello, in eliminating the chronological representation of the events, not only succeeds in focusing attention on the protagonist's psyche, but also succeeds in eradicating the past events *per se*, and in conveying them only through the protagonist's mind, almost *as though they were his own construction*.]

Indeed, even after Silvia's death, the consequences of her adultery have a profound effect on the course of the action. Following her death, the short story emphasises how Verona introduces Ginetta to her future husband, the Marchese Flavio Gualdi. The wedding is needed here in order to put Lori's position as her father into perspective. Now that Ginetta / Palma is part of her husband's family, she is under no obligation to rely on Lori or to continue the pretence as his daughter. In fact, the last chapter of the story shows how, soon after the wedding ceremony, 'Lori s'era sentito se non propriamente respinto, quasi allontanato' [Lori had felt not exactly rejected, but as if distanced] (*Na* I, 377). The narrator points out that Verona, now treated as Gualdi's father-in-law, 'non era più venuto, neanche una volta per isbaglio' [no longer came round, not even once by mistake] (*Na* I, 378).

The play, on the other hand, opens with Palma's wedding and so the spectators immediately notice how Lori is shunned by all of the characters. Palma's hostility towards Lori is even described in the stage directions: '*Ha diciott'anni. È bellissima. Tratta il padre con mal dissimulata freddezza*' (*Mn* II, 430) [*She is eighteen, and very beautiful. She treats her father with barely-concealed coldness* (*CP* II, 83)]. Indeed, one of the reasons why Silvia's mother, La Barbetti, is introduced into the play is to comment on what the other characters no longer notice. She perceives Palma's coldness towards Lori, stating: 'Ma in casa di vostra figlia, tra me e voi, sarò accolta meglio io che voi' (*Mn* II, 447) [Between you and me, I'll be more welcome in your daughter's house than *you* ever will be (*CP* II, 96)]. Moreover, the audience actually witnesses how Manfroni and Gualdi ignore Lori. Whereas in the *novella* '[s]olo Ginetta gli rivolgeva qualche parola, di tanto in tanto' [[o]nly Ginetta would utter the odd word to him, now and then] (*Na* I, 378), the stage version re-enacts this description. As Lori tries to approach his new son-in-law, Gualdi responds: 'Scusi, non ho tempo' (*Mn* II, 441) [Sorry, I haven't the time (*CP* II, 91)]. Even though the spectators do not see how Manfroni facilitates the wedding between Palma and Gualdi, they nevertheless notice how he is being treated as the father of the bride. In fact, it is Manfroni who accompanies the newlyweds to the station. Through the use of stage directions, Pirandello is also able to stress Lori's sense of rejection as the three protagonists exit the stage without him: '*Il Lori resta assorto per lungo tratto nella sua gelida delusione*' (*Mn* II, 446) [*Lori stands for a time, absorbed in his icy disappointment* (*CP* II, 95)].

It is Lori's sense of rejection that leads him to acknowledge the truth about the adultery in both *novella* and play. In this part of the plot, both versions effectively catch up with each other and convey the events in the same way. In the *novella*, one evening, after an entire week of being left on his own, Lori recalls the moment he caught Verona weeping beside Silvia's death bed, and this memory triggers him to reminisce even further back in time to the moment when he first met Silvia. He evokes an image of her and speaks to her as if she were present: '"Possibile? Possibile?"' ['Possible? Possible?'] (*Na* I, 379), '"Tu? tu?"' ['You? You?'] (*Na* I, 379), giving the impression of a type of interior monologue, or, as Marziano Guglielminetti puts it, a soliloquy 'dal timbro drammatico' [of a dramatic stamp].[67] The narrator then proceeds to express Lori's discovery through free indirect speech, composed as a sort of stream of consciousness: 'Il Verona, no... Il Verona, no... Costui gli veniva in casa, là, come un padrone' [Verona, no... Verona, no... He used to come here as though he were the man of the house] (*Na* I, 379). This narrative technique is reminiscent of that employed in Verga's 'Il canarino del n. 15' and in the works of the aforementioned women writers. However, whereas Màlia does not develop her thoughts any further, Lori scrutinises every detail.

In the play, Lori discovers the truth about the adultery when Palma mistakes him for Manfroni at the end of the second act:

> PALMA: *(dirigendosi alla poltrona e sporgendo di sulla spalliera le mani per cingerle al mento di chi sta seduto, dice piano, teneramente)* Papà...
> LORI: *(subito, con slancio, commosso di riconoscenza)* Figlia mia!
> PALMA: *(nello stupore di non trovar lì Salvo Manfroni non riuscendo a frenare un grido, tra di ribrezzo e di paura, ritraendosi)* Ah!... Tu? E come?
> LORI: *(allibito nella certezza che quell'appellativo non era rivolto a lui)* Io... Ma dunque, sei arrivata anche a chiamarlo così, da sola a solo?
> PALMA: *(esasperata e spinta dallo sdegno per il suo stesso errore a un'estrema risolutezza)* Oh, finiamola! Io lo chiamo così, perché debbo chiamarlo così. (*Mn* II, 468)
>
> [PALMA *(softly and tenderly)*: Daddy...
> LORI *(at once, impulsively, overcome by gratitude)*: Oh, my own dear Palma!
> PALMA *(in surprise at not discovering Salvo Manfroni there, cannot restrain a cry of mingled revulsion and fright, as she draws back)*: Oh! It's you? Why are you here?
> LORI *(paling at the realisation that the word 'daddy' has not been meant for him)*: I... Do you mean you actually call him that when you're alone together?
> PALMA *(exasperated and driven by anger at her own mistake to an extreme boldness)*: Oh, can't we stop all this nonsense? I call him that because it's my duty to call him that!] (*CP* II, 113)

While Lori in the narrative engages in a kind of soliloquy after the discovery, in the play he expresses his reaction through speech, which becomes more explosive as the action proceeds. The audience is thus made to acknowledge his raw sense of recognition more directly and watch his shock come to life through the leading actor's interpretation of Pirandello's careful stage directions:

> No? Come no? Se ti disse che sei sua figlia! Vero o non vero questo, se poté dirtelo, è certo che lei... Oh Dio... oh Dio... Possibile? Possibile?... Lei... Non

è possibile! [...]. Lei?... Lei?... Lei?... *Dirà questi tre 'lei' con tre diversi toni, pieni dell'orrore di tre diverse visioni; e alla fine cascherà, come schiantato, a sedere, rompendo in un pianto convulso.* (*Mn* II, 469–70)

[No? What do you mean by no? If he said you were his daughter? Whether that's true or not, if he could say that to you, it shows she much have been... Oh God, oh God... Can it be? Can it be? She! Silvia! No! He was lying, lying! [...]. Silvia! Silvia! Silvia! *(The thrice-repeated name seems to reflect three different visions of horror: he collapses into the armchair, and bursts into convulsive weeping.]* (*CP* II, 114–15)

In the same way as the narrator in the short story employs metaphors drawn from theatre to express Lori's turmoil — 'Aveva rappresentato la parte del marito, poi quella del padre' (*Na* I, 380) [He had performed the role of the husband, then that of the father] — so does the theatrical adaptation:

> PALMA: Ma no! Via! Finiamo una buona volta questa commedia! Io ne sono stufa!
> LORI: Commedia? Che dici?
> PALMA: Commedia! Commedia! (*Mn* II, 468)

> [PALMA: No! Don't be ridiculous! Can't we put an end to this idiotic play-acting once and for all? I'm sick of it!
> LORI: Play-acting? What do you mean?
> PALMA: Yes, play-acting!] (*CP* II, 113–14)

In fact, throughout the concluding act, Lori continues to employ such metaphorical expressions, giving the impression that the play is a sort of play-within-a-play. Even in the stage directions Pirandello emphasises how dismayed Lori feels '*della commedia che s'ostina a rappresentare*' [*of the play he has continued to perform*] (*Mn* II, 489). Tilgher has described Lori as '[v]ile e inabile, perché ciò che per lui era sentimento sincero per gli altri era commedia ch'egli rappresentava, e rappresentava male: male, perché il disgraziato non sapeva di rappresentarla' [[c]owardly and inept because for him what was a sincere feeling, for others was a show he was performing, and performing badly: badly, because the poor wretch did not know he was even performing it].[68] Indeed, Lori was completely unaware of his 'play-acting':

> LORI: Sfido! Me le avete fatte rappresentare a mia insaputa, tutte: quella del marito gabbato e contento; quella dell'amico; del vedovo; del padre; del suocero. E le ho rappresentate male! Sfido! Non sapevo di rappresentarle! (*Mn* II, 488–89)

> [LORI: You made me play the various parts without knowing what I was supposed to be doing, all of them: the complaisant deceived husband; the friend; the widower; the father; the father-in-law. I played them all badly! Yes! I didn't know how they ought to be played, did I?] (*CP* II, 128–29)

Following his discovery of the affair, Lori attempts to piece together the time Silvia first fell in love with Manfroni. Silvia's immediate attraction for Verona is only suggested in the first part of the *novella* when the pair meet again in Rome years after the time when he used to visit her father as a student: 'E lui, l'onorevole Verona, quanti poteva averne? Venti, ventuno al più' [And he, the most honorable

Verona, how old could he be? Twenty, twenty-one at the most] (*Na* I, 359). In the play, meanwhile, it is Lori who is left with the task of informing the audience of this crucial moment in Silvia's life:

> LORI: S'innamorò subito, s'innamorò subito, venuta da Perugia alla morte del padre, s'innamorò subito del giovane deputato... Eh, perciò tutta accesa, quando venne con lui da me al Ministero per farsi presentare e raccomandare da lui. Era stato allievo del padre; era ora il deputato... S'innamorò subito di lui — e sposò me! (*Mn* II, 470–71)
>
> [LORI: She fell in love with him at first sight, when she came from Perugia after her father died; she fell in love at first sight with her young Member of Parliament... Yes, that must have been the reason she was blushing when she came with him into my office at the Ministry, to be introduced and recommended by him. He'd been her father's pupil; now he was in Parliament. She fell in love with him at first sight... and she married *me*!] (*CP* II, 115)

The audience subsequently acquires an insight into Silvia retrospectively through Lori's eyes. As Dante Della Terza explains:

> While there is no need to justify Lori's mistaken assumptions, there is the theatrical need to explain, through Lori to the public, without unnecessary ambiguities, what kind of person Silvia must truly have been, what kind of responsibilities she had in Lori's drama. In other words, the playwright undertakes the difficult task of tracing the borderline between good faith and moral responsibility in order to reconstruct on behalf of the reader a totally honest portrait of Silvia.[69]

Indeed, while the audience in *Così è (se vi pare)* gains an understanding of Signora Ponza through what other characters say about her, as well as what she reveals about herself (a viewpoint the reader in 'La signora Frola e il signor Ponza, suo genero' can only infer as Signora Ponza never makes a physical appearance in the *novella*), the audience in *Tutto per bene* is able to construct a portrait of Silvia in retrospect through the perspectives of a variety of characters. La Barbetti and her son Carletto, for instance, are introduced into the drama to inform the audience about earlier events, which are directly drawn from the narrative, yet, as soon as they have served their purpose, Pirandello withdraws them from the plot.[70]

As a result, the audience of the play gains an intimate portrait of Silvia through a pluralistic and subjective lens, which essentially offers more information about the character than the storyteller does in the original version, particularly during the scene when Lori confronts Manfroni about the affair, a confrontation which is missing from the short story. For instance, whereas the reader of the *novella* is left to infer why Silvia returned to her husband, the audience of the play discovers that Manfroni actually forced her to do so because he wanted to concentrate on his career:

> LORI: Voleva fare come la madre. Andarsene. Venirsene con te. Eh, ma tu avevi la tua carriera politica...
> SALVO: Smetti, ti prego!
> LORI: E persuadesti la pecorella a ritornare all'ovile! (*Mn* II, 486)

[LORI: She wanted to do what her mother had done. She wanted to go away. To come away with you. Ah, but you had your political career to think of!
SALVO: Stop it, please stop!
LORI: And so you persuaded the wandering lamb to return to the fold!] (*CP* II, 126)

The play continues to reveal more about Silvia when her reaction to motherhood is discussed. In the short story, Silvia is depicted as fervently embracing her newborn baby daughter: '[N]el vedere di quale gratitudine, di qual devozione per lui e di quali sacrifizii per la figliuola la maternità avesse reso capace quella donna, tant'altre cose comprese e si spiegò' [[I]n seeing what gratitude, what devotion for him and what sacrifices for her little girl motherhood had made that woman capable of, he understood and made sense of many other things] (*Na* I, 368–69). Yet although this passage conveys her maternal instinct, it is one offered from Lori's perspective. Indeed, Silvia might be physically present for much of the action but her actual voice is silenced. Most of the story is, in fact, recounted from Lori's point of view; he is the main focal lens of the narrative. Moreover, is this maternal role played successfully by Silvia so as to make Lori believe he is the father of the child? While in the short story Silvia is portrayed as *both* a lover and a mother — '[a Lori] gli pareva così piena, ora, la vita e così solidamente fondata, con quella donna accanto, sua, tutta sua, tutta per la casa *e per la figliuola*' [[t]o him [Lori] life appeared so complete, so firmly founded, with that woman next to him, all his, his, completely devoted to the home *and to their little daughter*] (*Na* I, 371, my italics) — on stage she is portrayed as less of a mother, leaving Manfroni to raise Palma, and more as Lori's lover. This viewpoint is confirmed in the drama by Lori as he confronts Manfroni: '[O]diò in sé il frutto del tuo amore. Non voleva esser madre, non lo voleva, lo so. Fu la mia amante, più che la madre di quella lì' (*Mn* II, 486) [[S]he hated the fruit of your love, inside her, too. She never wanted to be a mother, she never wanted to, I know. She was my mistress, far more than she was ever Palma's mother (*CP* II, 127)]. Whereas the narrator underlines how Silvia 'voleva esser madre' [wanted to be a mother] (repeated in *Na* I, 368–69), in the play it is explicitly stated that she rejects motherhood because her daughter is the result of her adultery. Consequently, the changes introduced into the play lead Pirandello to reveal *more* about Silvia than in the narrative where she is present for the most part. As Jørn Moestrup sums up: 'Il dramma migliora l'antefatto e la figura della donna, elabora tutto meglio' [The play enhances the antecedents and the figure of the woman; it develops everything better].[71]

Once the truth about the adultery is revealed, both the reader of the *novella* and audience of the play encounter a bolder Lori. In the short story, his thoughts in the latter part of the text are expressed more assertively in comparison with the first part. Although the reader is unsure of what he says to Silvia when he visits her grave, it is nevertheless made clear that the Lori making his way to the cemetery is a new, more forceful one: 'E Martino Lori riprese la via per il cimitero. Aveva qualche cosa di nuovo da dire alla morta, quella sera' [And Martino Lori once again made his way to the cemetery. He had something new to say to the deceased, that night] (*Na* I, 380).

Similarly, Lori's dialogue and body language on stage are also more confident. Whereas in the first act, set in Lori's house, he is depicted in the stage directions as '*turbato e concitato [...] remissivo e soprattutto credulo*' (*Mn* II, 429) [agitated and angry [...] submissive, and above all credulous (*CP* II, 81–82)], in the last act, this time set in Manfroni's house, '[*ha*] *una faccia da morto; gli occhi fissi e come insensati*' (*Mn* II, 477) [*his face is like a dead man's; the eyes fixed, and as though unseeing* (*CP* II, 121)]. His speech is now unbroken by suspension marks:

> LORI: Intendiamoci prima noi due. Voglio sapere quando fu!
> SALVO: Ma lascia!
> LORI: No. Rispondi. Subito dopo il matrimonio? (*Salvo scrolla le spalle*). Rispondi. Perché già v'eravate accordati, fin dal suo arrivo da Perugia?
> SALVO: Ma no! Io non ci pensai neppure, allora!
> LORI: Ma forse ci pensò lei?
> SALVO: No, no! (*Attenuando:*) Almeno io non so. Non credo. (*Mn* II, 485)

> [LORI: You and I shall talk first. I want to know when it was!
> SALVO: Be quiet!
> LORI: No. Answer me. Immediately after we were married? (*Salvo shrugs his shoulders*). Answer me. Had you already fixed it up, as soon as she came from Perugia?
> SALVO: No! I never even thought of it, then!
> LORI: Perhaps *she* thought of it?
> SALVO: No, no! *(More mildly.)* At least, I don't know. I don't think so.] (*CP* II, 126)

While the *novella* ends as this 'new' Lori confronts his wife's gravestone, the play completes the short story by showing exactly what Lori does after the sudden discovery. Just as Signora Ponza's presence in the final act of *Così è (se vi pare)* has been considered a coda to the play, Jean Spizzo has called the ending 'un indispensable épilogue, intimement commandé par les derniers développements de la nouvelle' [an indispensable epilogue, intimately controlled by the final developments of the short story].[72] In fact, Manfroni is so surprised at the sudden change of character that he admits to Lori: 'Io non ti riconosco più!' (*Mn* II, 481) [Why... I can hardly recognise you, Martino (*CP* II, 123)].[73] The purpose of the coda here is to illustrate exactly what Lori does once he discovers the truth. Palma persuades him not to cause a scandal by promising to convince the members of their community that she has accepted him as her real father. Lori can subsequently continue his existence in the same way as Signora Frola and Signor Ponza are content to live with their illusions in 'La Signora Frola e il Signor Ponza, suo genero' and *Così è (se vi pare)*, only Lori is now aware that he is living an illusion. What is more, Palma accepts Lori as her father (paradoxically) *after* the revelation that he is not her biological parent, in the same way as Marta Ajala's husband in *L'Esclusa* (1901) accepts her as his wife only after she has committed adultery.

Pirandello once described *Tutto per bene* in a letter of 7 December 1919 to the lead actor Ruggeri as a 'commedia [...] veduta dalla parte degli altri' [play [...] seen from the perspective of others].[74] The spectators thus see the reflection of the protagonist through the minor characters' eyes. As for the way Lori sees himself, he discovers that throughout his life he has been looking into a distorted mirror. Significantly, in an interview for the *Corriere della sera* on 28 February 1920, Pirandello defined his theatre as 'il teatro dello specchio' [the theatre of the mirror]:

> Quando uno vive, vive e non si vede. Orbene, fate che si veda, nell'atto di vivere, in preda alle sue passioni, ponendogli uno specchio davanti: o resta attonito e sbalordito del suo stesso aspetto, o torce gli occhi per non vedersi, o sdegnato tira uno sputo alla sua immagine, o irato avventa un pugno per infrangerla; e se piangeva, non può più piangere; e se rideva, non può più ridere, e che so io. Insomma, nasce un *guaio* per forza. *Questo guaio è il mio teatro.*[75]
>
> [When one lives, one lives and does not see oneself. Well then, imagine that one can see oneself, in the act of living, prey to one's passions, by putting a mirror in front of oneself. One will either remain dumbfounded and flabbergasted by one's appearance, or avert one's eyes away so as not to see oneself, or, indignant, spit on one's image, or, angered, hurl a punch to smash it. And if one was crying, one would no longer be able to cry. And if one was laughing, one would no longer be able to laugh — and so on. In short, *chaos* inevitably emerges. *This chaos is my theatre.*]

Tilgher later applied the concept of the metaphorical mirror to the character of Lori. Tilgher stated that 'lo specchio che gli è stato messo sotto gli occhi gli proietta l'immagine del turpissimo essere che egli è stato per lunghi anni agli occhi degli altri, onde ne rabbrividisce di orrore e di nausea' [the mirror which had been placed before his eyes projects the image of the extremely repugnant being that he had been for many long years in the eyes of others, making him shiver with horror and nausea].[76] Although it is in the play that the audience sees how Lori goes about readjusting his image and how the other characters are made to change their own views of him, Pirandello's 'teatro dello specchio' [theatre of the mirror] can equally well be applied to the *novella* — Lori in the short story acknowledges that he has been playing the wrong roles and ultimately is able to alter these reflections.

Likewise, Pirandello's concept of *vedersi vivere* [*seeing oneself live*] can be associated with another important passage in 'L'umorismo' centred on the notion of what he calls interior silence: 'In certi momenti di silenzio interiore, in cui l'anima nostra si spoglia di tutte le finzioni abituali, e gli occhi nostri diventano più acuti e più penetranti, noi vediamo noi stessi nella vita' [In certain moments of inner silence, in which our souls strip themselves of our usual fictions, and our eyes become more acute and penetrating, we see ourselves in our own lives] (*Spsv*, p. 152). As Pirandello explains, during these moments of what he calls interior silence, we begin to see ourselves more clearly. Such moments of clarity have been linked with the notion of epiphany, a term used in Christian writing to refer to the appearance of Christ. Literary epiphanies, as found in Romantic lyric poetry and later in modern literature, are descriptions of sudden realisation. As Catherine O'Rawe has pointed out: 'It was Joyce who codified modernist epiphany as a moment of illumination arising from a disproportionately trivial incident or object'.[77]

In relation to Lori, the one person to lead him to his 'epiphany' is none other than his late wife Silvia. Though she is physically absent in the last part of the narrative and throughout the course of the play, the effect she has on all the characters, predominantly Lori, permeates the entire plot. On stage, she indirectly reveals why she returned to her husband after their separation, and why she left Manfroni to raise their daughter. Pirandello might have therefore removed Silvia from the play but he makes her silent voice even 'louder' than it ever was in the narrative where her side of the story is silenced.

While it has been concluded by Walter Starkie that 'Pirandello's women are creatures of instinct, neurasthenic and ever hovering between madness and hysteria' and hence 'it is to man that the duty of analysis falls' (citing Laudisi as an example),[78] it is interesting to note how the various perceptions of women's silences have developed over the last forty years or so: Signora Ponza's silence effectively rivals the logic of Laudisi, and Silvia's silent voice is strong enough to give her husband a new identity even after her death.

Breaking the Silence

Despite the fact that Verga and Pirandello *do* associate their female characters with silence and their male characters with speech, especially Pirandello who even employs male mouthpiece characters, the 'silent' women nonetheless have 'loud' voices — similar to the protagonists in a number of early male- and female-authored works. Just as Laurence interprets the silences inherent in Brontë, Austen, and Woolf as a kind of presence rather than absence,[79] reversing the feminist view that silence equates to oppression, we have seen just how present these alleged speechless heroines are in the narratives and plays, a far cry from what Ferris called earlier 'the patriarchal ideal of the silent woman'.[80] In revealing the 'crescendo' of the different silent voices, with each of the women's silences amplified in the theatrical revisionings, this chapter has drawn attention to the sheer volume of their voices and offered a new way of 'hearing' their silences on stage.

Notes to Chapter 4

1. For more on Verga's 'silent' approach, see Baldo Curato, *Sessant'anni di teatro in Italia: da Giovanni Verga a Ugo Betti* (Milan: Denti, 1947), pp. 31–56 (p. 38); Siro Ferrone, *Il teatro di Verga* (Rome: Bulzoni, 1972), pp. 155–90 (p. 170); and Roberto Bigazzi, *Le risorse del romanzo: componenti di genere nella narrativa moderna* (Pisa: Nistri-Lischi, 1996), p. 202. In a previous article, I have discussed how Verga's collaboration with Duse anticipated the Symbolist Theatre of Silence; see Enza De Francisci, 'Verga and Duse Transposing Silence in "Il canarino del n. 15" and *In portineria*: A prelude to Symbolism?', *The Italianist*, 34.1 (2014), 73–87.
2. The question of Signora Ponza's identity has been a popular area of enquiry among scholars and critics. To name but a few, see Emanuele Licastro, *Luigi Pirandello dalle novelle alle commedie* (Verona: Fiorini, 1974), pp. 123–26; Jørn Moestrup, 'Gli atti unici', in *Gli atti unici di Pirandello (tra narrativa e teatro)*, ed. by Stefano Milioto (Agrigento: Centro Nazionale Studi Pirandelliani, 1978), pp. 337–50; Domenico Maceri, *Dalla novella alla commedia pirandelliana* (New York: Peter Lang Publishing, 1991), pp. 99–154; Daniela Bini, 'Enacting the Dissolution of the Self: Woman as One, No One, and One Hundred Thousand', in *Luigi Pirandello: Contemporary Perspectives*, ed. by Gian-Paolo Biasin and Manuela Gieri (Toronto: University of Toronto, 1999), pp. 163–88; and Roberto Alonge, 'La Signora Frola e il Signor Ponza, suo genero — Così è (se vi pare)', in *La novella di Pirandello: dramma, film, musica, fumetto*, ed. by Enzo Lauretta (Pesaro: Metauro edizioni, 2007), pp. 77–89.

3. Among the many to examine this work, see above all John Humphreys Whitfield, 'La metamorfosi della novella', in *Atti del congresso internazionale di studi pirandelliani, Venezia 2–5 ottobre 1961* (Florence: Le Monnier, 1967), pp. 735–42; Jean Spizzo, 'Répétition et reformulation du texte pirandellien *Tutto per bene*: de la forme narrative à la forme dramatique', *Revue des études italiennes*, 20 (1974), 74–104; and Dante Della Terza, 'Pirandello from Tale to Play: The Case of *Tutto per bene*', *Modern Language Notes*, Italian Issue, 92.1 (January 1977), 63–78. I have shown how Pirandello develops Silvia's portrait on stage but without comparing his techniques with Verga's; see Enza De Francisci, 'Silvia's Silent Voice in *Tutto per bene*', *Pirandello Studies*, 34 (2014), 33–43.
4. Cited in Torquato Tasso, *Le prose diverse di Torquato Tasso*, ed. by Cesare Guasti (Florence: Le Monnier, 1875), p. 206.
5. Ruth B. Bottigheimer, 'Silenced Women in the Grimms' Tales: The "Fit" Between Fairy Tales and Society in Their Historical Context', in *Fairy Tales and Society: Illusion, Allusion, and Paradigm*, ed. by Ruth B. Bottigheimer (Philadelphia: University of Pennsylvania, 1986), pp. 115–31.
6. See Marina Warner, *Alone of All Her Sex: The Myth and Cult of The Virgin Mary*, new edn (London: Vintage, 2000).
7. Helena Sanson, *Donne, precettistica e lingua nell'Italia del cinquecento: un contributo alla storia del pensiero linguistico* (Florence: Accademia dell Crusca, 2007), p. 73.
8. Lesley Ferris, *Acting Women: Images of Women in Theatre* (Basingstoke: Macmillan, 1999), p. xiii.
9. See Ellen Moers, *Literary Women* (London: W. H. Allen, 1977).
10. Tillie Olsen, *Silences* (London: Virago, 1980).
11. Lori Chamberlaine, 'Gender and the Metaphorics of Translation', in *The Translation Reader*, ed. by Laurence Venuti (London, New York: Routledge, 2000), pp. 314–29 (p. 314).
12. Patricia Laurence, 'Women's Silence as a Ritual of Truth: A Study of Literary Expressions in Austen, Brontë and Woolf', in *Listening to Silences: New Essays in Feminist Criticism*, ed. by Elaine Hedges and Shelley Fisher Fishkin (Oxford: Oxford University Press, 1994), pp. 156–67 (p. 156).
13. Although there were no Italian translations of Brontë and Austen available while Verga was composing his narratives, early French translations circulated widely (Brontë's *Jane Eyre o Le memorie d'un'istitutrice*, translated into Italian anonymously, was first published by Treves in 1904, and Austen's *Orgoglio e prevenzione*, translated by Giulio Caprin, was published by Mondadori much later in 1932). This could provide a possible route by which Verga might have become aware of the so-called 'discourse of interiority'. However, it seems more likely that he would have been familiar with this narrative form through his immediate Italian and French contemporaries, in particular Flaubert, who adopts this technique in his *Madame Bovary* (1857), and Italy's nineteenth-century women writers, such as La Marchesa Colombi, Neera, and Serao. For more on the translation and early circulation of *Jane Eyre*, see Inga-Stina Ewbank, 'Reading the Brontës Abroad: A Study in the Transmission of Victorian Novels in Continental Europe', in *Reconstructing the Book: Literary Texts in Transmission*, ed. by Maureen Bell et al. (Burlington: Ashgate, 1953), pp. 84–99.
14. Laurence, p. 156.
15. Ibid., p. 162.
16. Ibid., p. 156.
17. Virginia Woolf, *Three Guineas* (New York: Harcourt Brace Jovanovich, 1938), p. 135.
18. Laurence, pp. 156–57.
19. Ibid., pp. 157–58.
20. See *Shakespeare, Italy, and Transnational Exchange: The Early Modern Period to the Present*, ed. by Enza De Francisci and Chris Stamatakis (New York-London: Routledge, 2017).
21. For more on Shakespeare's treatment of silence and gender, see Christina Luckyj, *'A moving rhetoricke': Gender and Silence in Early Modern England* (Manchester: Manchester University Press, 2002).
22. Ferris, p. 103.

23. Brian Rorman, *Signifying Nothing: The Semiotics of Zero* (London: Macmillan, 1987), p. 81.
24. Verga was well aware of how the local colour of the play could not have been any further removed from the Sicilian *Cavalleria rusticana*. In a letter to Salvatore Di Giacomo of 31 December 1918, Verga declined Di Giacomo's offer to translate the drama into Neapolitan because, in his words, 'In portineria ha un carattere così spiccatamente locale — milanese — che poco mi sembrerebbe adatto a un'interpretazione diversa' [*In portineria* is so distinctly local — Milanese — which seems to me to be little suited to a different interpretation] (*Ls*, p. 414).
25. Gianni Oliva, *La scena del vero: letteratura e teatro da Verga a Pirandello* (Rome: Bulzoni, 1992), pp. 23–24.
26. Roberto Bigazzi, *Su Verga novelliere* (Pisa: Nistri-Lischi editore, 1975), p. 99.
27. Bigazzi, *Le risorse del romanzo*, p. 202.
28. Guido Baldi, *Reietti e superuomini in scena* (Naples: Liguori, 2009), p. 38.
29. Luigi Russo, *Giovanni Verga* (Rome: Laterza, 1995), pp. 206–07.
30. Natalino Sapegno, *Ritratto di Manzoni* (Bari: Laterza, 1961), p. 276.
31. See Eric Bentley, *Pirandello: Plays* (Evanston, Illinois: Northwest University Press, 1998), p. 56.
32. Luigi Pirandello, *Il figlio prigioniero: carteggio tra Luigi e Stefano Pirandello durante la guerra 1915–1918*, ed. by Andrea Pirandello (Milan: Mondadori, 2005), p. 188.
33. Roger W. Oliver, *Dreams of Passion: The Theatre of Luigi Pirandello* (New York: New York University Press, 1979), p. 26.
34. Anthony Caputi, *Pirandello and the Crisis of Modern Consciousness* (Urbana and Chicago: University of Illinois Press, 1988), p. 93.
35. Walter Starkie, *Luigi Pirandello 1867–1936* (Berkeley and Los Angeles: University of California Press, 1965), p. 128.
36. See Gigi Livio, *Il teatro in rivolta: futurismo, grottesco, Pirandello e pirandellismo* (Milan: Mursia, 1976), p. 98.
37. Arcangelo Leone De Castris, *Storia di Pirandello* (Bari: Laterza, 1971), p. 137.
38. Ulrich Leo, 'Luigi Pirandello zwischen zwei literarischen Gattungen', *Romanistisches Jahrbuch*, 14 (1963), 133–69, partially translated into English in Ulrich Leo, 'Pirandello between Fiction and Drama', in *Pirandello: A Collection of Critical Essays*, ed. by Glauco Cambon (New Jersey: Prentice-Hall, Inc., Englewood Cliffs, 1967), pp. 83–90 (p. 90). I am quoting from the translation.
39. Ibid., p. 85.
40. Maceri, p. 130.
41. Oliver, p. 26.
42. I have argued elsewhere that, by introducing Signora Ponza's physical presence at the end of the drama, Pirandello essentially turns the *unresolved question* in the narrative (a question that is not resolved) into an *irresolvable* question on stage (a question that can never be resolved); see Enza De Francisci, 'Pirandello's Women: From Page to Stage', *Pirandello Studies*, 28 (2008), 89–99 (pp. 90–91).
43. All through the theatrical plot, Signora Frola repeatedly stresses: 'Siamo contente, contentissime, tanto io, quanto la mia figliuola' (*Mn* I, 454) [Both I and my daughter are perfectly happy (*CP* I, 99)]. Signor Ponza also underlines how his mother-in-law is 'contenta' (*Mn* I, 459) [happy (*CP* I, 104)] to communicate with his wife from afar. At the end of the play, Signora Frola concludes: 'Siamo contente di vivere così; la mia figliuola è contenta' (*Mn* I, 507) [My daughter and I are quite content to live like this — yes, my daughter too! (*CP* I, 149)].
44. Licastro, p. 61.
45. Bini, p. 166.
46. Ibid., p. 168.
47. Maria Antonietta Grignani, *Retoriche pirandelliane* (Naples: Liguori, 1993), p. 99.
48. Adriano Tilgher, *Studi sul teatro contemporaneo* (Rome: Libreria di Scienze e Lettere, 1928), p. 196.
49. Silvio D'Amico, *Cronache del teatro*, ed. by Eugenio Ferdinando Palmieri and Silvio D'Amico, 2 vols (Bari: Laterza, 1963), I, p. 105.
50. Silvio D'Amico, *Il Teatro dei fantocci* (Florence: Vallecchi, 1920), p. 108.
51. Daniela Bini, *Luigi Pirandello: Contemporary Perspectives*, pp. 168–69.
52. Giorgio Pullini, '*Così è (se vi pare)*: dalla novella al dramma', in *Saggi di linguistica e di letteratura in*

memoria di Paolo Zolli, ed. by Giampaolo Borghello et al. (Padua: Antenore, 1991) pp. 619–28 (p. 627).

53. Corrado Donati, *Luigi Pirandello nella storia della critica* (Pesaro: Metauro edizioni, 1998), p. 140.
54. See Franca Angelini, 'Il resto è silenzio', in *Pirandello e la parola*, ed. by Enzo Lauretta (Agrigento: Centro Nazionale Studi Pirandelliani, 2000), pp. 93–100 (pp. 96–97).
55. Quoted in Antonio Gramsci, *Letteratura e vita nazionale* (Rome: Editori Riuniti, 1991), p. 362.
56. Paolo Puppa, *Fantasmi contro giganti: scena e immaginario in Pirandello* (Bologna: Pàtron editore, 1978), p. 62.
57. Lucienne Kroha, 'Behind the Veil: A Freudian Reading of Pirandello's *Così è (se vi pare)*', *The Yearbook of the Society for Pirandello Studies*, 12 (1992), 1–21.
58. Maggie Günsberg, *Patriarchal Representations: Gender and Discourse in Pirandello's Theatre* (Oxford: Berg, 1994), p. 54.
59. The play was further adapted into a Sicilian drama, *Ccu 'i nguanti gialli* in 1921. For more on the Sicilian adaptation and Musco's successful interpretation, see Sarah Zappulla Muscarà, *Pirandello in guanti gialli* (Caltanisetta — Rome: Salvatore Sciascia, 1988).
60. Luigi Pirandello, *Carteggio Pirandello — Ruggeri: appunti per uno studio del rapporto fra autore e interprete*, ed. by Leonardo Bragaglia (Fano: Biblioteca comunale federiciana, 1987), p. 35.
61. See Marco Praga, *Cronache teatrali* (Milan: Treves, 1920), p. 111.
62. Elio Providenti, 'Note di bibliografia sulle opere giovanili di Luigi Pirandello', *Belfagor*, 23.6 (30 November 1968), 721–40 (p. 732).
63. Ibid., p. 732.
64. Arnaldo Bruni, 'Modelli e interferenze nell'esordio di Pirandello drammaturgo: *La morsa*', *Cuadernos de filología italiana*, 5 (1998), 175–87 (pp. 184–86).
65. Whitfield, p. 742.
66. Licastro, p. 125.
67. Marziano Guglielminetti, *Struttura e sintassi del romanzo italiano del primo novecento* (Milan: Silva, 1964), p. 71. Although Guglielminetti here examines Pirandello's narrative voice in *L'Esclusa*, published only five years prior to *Tutto per bene*, his views can equally be applied to this short story.
68. Tilgher, *Studi sul teatro contemporaneo*, p. 216.
69. Della Terza, p. 75.
70. See Anna Laura Lepschy, 'The Treatment of Antefact in Pirandello's Theatre', *Yearbook of the Society for Pirandello Studies*, 11 (1991), 68–90.
71. Jørn Moestrup, 'La diversa funzione di novella e dramma nell'opera di Luigi Pirandello', *Analecta Romana Instituti Danici*, 5 (1969), 199–239 (p. 215).
72. Spizzo, p. 103.
73. Manfroni's shock at Lori's change of character is reminiscent of Verga's 'Pentolaccia' in *Vita dei Campi* (1880). Don Liborio is so surprised by the complaisant Pentaloccia's unexpected change of attitude to his wife's affair that he thinks the character is speaking gibberish when he suddenly becomes jealous: 'Don Liborio lo guardò negli occhi, quasi parlasse turco' [Don Loborio looked at him in the eyes; it was as if he was speaking double Dutch] (*Tn* I, 211).
74. Pirandello, *Carteggio Pirandello — Ruggeri*, p. 35.
75. Quoted in Adriano Tilgher, *Voci del tempo: profili di letterati e filosofi contemporanei* (Rome: Libreria di scienze e lettere, 1921), p. 78.
76. Ibid., p. 81.
77. Catherine O'Rawe, *Authorial Echoes: Textuality and Self-Plagiarism in the Narrative of Luigi Pirandello* (Oxford: Legenda, 2005), pp. 49–50. For more on *Tutto per bene*, see pp. 63–65.
78. Starkie, pp. 45–46.
79. Laurence, pp. 157–58.
80. Ferris, p. xiii.

CHAPTER 5

The Sexual Voice

The Adulteress

Overall, Verga's women can be seen as falling into two categories: 'madre' or 'distruttrice' [mother or destroyer].[1] From this, it comes as no surprise that the Sicilian she-wolf, Gnà Pina in both versions of *La Lupa* (1880 and 1896), should be comfortably placed in the latter group. This chapter, however, sets out to illustrate how the eponymous character disrupts the 'distruttrice' [destroyer] label. It is argued here that the newly vocalised 'Lupa' on stage expresses the aspirations not of a destructive woman but of a 'new' woman whose roots can be found in *A Doll's House*. In the same way as Nora resents being treated as a voiceless doll in patriarchal society, so does Gnà Pina who is caught up in her own struggle for existence in rural Sicily. Indeed, given that Capuana had translated Ibsen's play for the interpretation of Duse in 1891, Verga was well aware of Nora's Italian reception when placing one of his most transgressive heroines centre-stage only five years later.[2]

The last work that Verga adapted into a play, *La caccia al lupo* (1901), taken from the homonymous *novella* (1897), is also situated in Sicily.[3] It is suggested that, in line with Nora and Gnà Pina, Mariangela frees herself from the role of a subservient sexual object. Using her brain rather than her gender, she ensures her survival from the metaphorical wolf hunt by deliberately putting on a variety of 'performances', thus turning the work into a kind of play-within-a-play.[4]

The chapter concludes by considering one of the 'loudest' female voices to emerge from Pirandello's oeuvre, that of Cristina / Silia in 'Quando si è capito il giuoco' (1913) and *Il giuoco delle parti* (1918).[5] This part examines the extent to which the portrayal of Silia's liberal attitude to her sexuality fits in with developments in the years leading up to women's suffrage in Italy in 1946.[6] It will illuminate how Pirandello exploits various theatrical devices in the stage version to go beyond her sexual exterior, emphasising the depth of her personality and sense of awareness which even silences her logical husband at the end — not the typical embodiment of 'l'istinto' (*Mn* II, 677) [instinct (*CP* II, 7)] as the director in *Sei personaggi in cerca d'autore* would like to think.

The Sexual Monster

The trope of the female 'hysteric' has been a prominent feature in nineteenth- and twentieth- century literature, exploited by both male and female author: for example, Verga's contemporary Flaubert, in his *Madame Bovary* (1857), and many Italian women writers, such as Neera and La Marchesa Colombi.[7] According to Sandra Gilbert and Susan Gubar in their acclaimed *The Madwoman in the Attic* (1979), 'women are warned that if they do not behave like angels they must be monsters'.[8] As a result of this prevailing cultural tendency, they argue that many female authors have employed the double motif of the angel in the house and the mad sexual monster as a strategic means of deflecting criticism through their exploration of the monster and, simultaneously, asserting 'good' conduct through their characterisation of the angelic protagonist.[9]

Among the list of works which exemply this duality, Gilbert and Gubar include several of Jane Austen's works, such as *Mansfield Park* (1814), with the conservative Fanny placed in direct opposition to the vibrant Mary Crawford, and Charlotte Brontë's *Jane Eyre* (1847), with Jane opposite Bertha Mason Rochester — the woman locked in an attic who bears a subtle resemblance to the 'evil' sister in Elizabeth Barrett Browning's poem *Bertha in the Lane* (1844). Gilbert and Gubar claim that these 'madwomen' not only share a similar name, but also a 'demonic sexuality', which is juxtaposed to prevailing notions of feminine delicacy and compliance: '[A]ll Berthas seem to be symbols of powerful female sexuality.'[10]

Gilbert and Gubar maintain that the representation of the sexual madwoman enacts women writers' 'own, covert authorial anger' towards the patriarchal system',[11] an authorial anger which arguably comes to life in its most grotesque form in Mary Shelley's *Frankenstein* (1818). As Lizbeth Goodman, Helen Small and Mary Jacobus have put it:

> The attraction of the madwoman for all these writers is obvious: as a figure of rage, without power to alleviate her suffering or to express it in terms that make sense to society, she sums up virtually everything feminism might wish to say about the suppression of women's speech.[12]

The association between the sexual madwoman and her speechlessness reappears in several other late nineteenth-century literary works by women. In Mary Elizabeth Coleridge's poem, for example, *The Other Side of the Mirror* (1896), the protagonist looks at a mirror and sees a 'wild' and silent woman: 'No sigh relieved her speechless woe, | She had no voice to speak her dread'. As the poem progresses, she begins to recognise her own split personality in the reflection: 'I am she!'[13] Similarly, in the short story *The Yellow Wallpaper* (1892) by the American author Charlotte Perkins Gilman, composed in the first person, the protagonist, herself a writer, describes her painful experience with a severe case of postnatal depression and postpartum psychosis. Both her physician husband and therapist confine the narrator to a large room and prohibit her from developing her passion for writing until she has recovered, causing her to go 'mad' as she is prevented from using creative writing as her form of self-expression.[14] The protagonist's experience echoes the accounts in Zelda Fitzgerald and Sylvia Plath's own lives, both of whom were committed to psychiatric wards. According to Phyllis Chesler, these two writers threatened the supremacy of men by virtue of their creative talent and therefore tried to escape patriarchal society by 'going crazy'.[15]

In effect, women who deviated from dominant ideologies risked being sectioned. In the case of turn-of-the-century Italy, those who did not conform to social and above all sexual conventions were committed to asylums. As David Forgacs has pointed out:

> Women's transgressions could take the form of inappropriate manifestations of sexuality — same-sex desire, masturbation, promiscuity, erotic display in the wrong place or time — or of becoming aggressive, confrontational or violent towards a man.[16]

This viewpoint emerges primarily in Giuliana Morandini's ... *E allora mi hanno rinchiusa: Testimonianze dal manicomio femminile* (1977). The book compiled the oral histories of forty-seven female patients confined to four different psychiatric hospitals in Italy from 1975 to 1976 and many were sectioned for the above reasons.[17]

Gilbert and Gubar stress that 'patriarchal socialization literally makes women sick, both physically and mentally',[18] triggering disorders typically associated with the female gender, such as anorexia and agoraphobia. In line with this, it could be said that the psychological distress that characters like Gnà Pina and Silia endure are the result of 'patriarchal socialization'. Gnà Pina has to defend herself physically as well as verbally from the hostility she faces because of her sexual deviance. As for Silia, just like the protagonist in Coleridge's poem, she also feels detached from her mirror image and trapped in her own body.

Despite the similarities, one aspect which differs is the issue of women's voicelessness. While Goodman, Small and Jacobus argue that it is the suppression of women's speech which leads to madness, it would seem that, when transferred to the stage, the seductresses in Verga and Pirandello become more expressive and this enables them to distance themselves from the archetypal 'madwoman'. Whereas Gnà Pina in 'La Lupa' and Mariangela in 'La caccia al lupo' may seem like silent she-wolves, blinded by their uncontrollable passion, on stage their dialogues throw light on their not-so-'mad' capacity to articulate their thoughts for themselves. In the case of Silia, she might appear as a hysterical woman in the narrative version but on stage she is transformed into a somewhat philosophical protagonist who even rivals Pirandello's traditional male mouthpiece characters, in particular her logical husband Leone.

La Lupa

'La Lupa' was originally published as a short story on 15 February 1880 in the Neapolitan journal *Rivista nuova di scienze, lettere ed arti* and then added to the first edition of *Vita dei campi* in 1880. Verga initially mentioned the completion of the stage adaptation in his interview with Ugo Ojetti much later in August 1894: 'A Catania ho terminato una commedia, *La Lupa*, che è tolta da una mia novella' [In Catania I finished my play, *The She-Wolf*, which is taken from a short story of mine].[19] It is a *novella* which, over a decade earlier, had been described by Verga in a letter to Édouard Rod of 18 April 1881 as 'la più accentuata delle *novelle* di *Vita dei campi*' [the most accentuated of my *novelle* in *Vita dei campi*] (*Lt*, pp. 29–30). The play premièred at the Gerbino Theatre in Turin on 26 January 1896, the same year in which Verga's complete theatrical works were first collected and published by Emilio Treves.[20] Although the opening took place in the city where *Cavalleria rusticana* had also debuted, it lacked the star actress of Eleonora Duse who never returned to the theatre of Verga after performing in *In portineria*. Instead, *La Lupa* was staged by the theatre company Andò-Leigheb, directed by Paolo Ferrari, and with Flavio Andò as Nanni and Virginia Reiter in the lead roles. The composer Giacomo Puccini had hoped to transform the play into an opera using the libretto by Federico De Roberto with the help of Verga but his intention was never realised. Pier Antonio Tasca later turned the libretto into an opera but it was only ever performed once, in 1933.[21]

Both narrative and theatrical versions are based on a woman whom Capuana had encountered. As he revealed in the *Corriere della sera* in September 1880: 'Quella lupa io l'ho conosciuta. Tre mesi fa, tra le colline di S. Margherita, su quel di Mineo, passavo pel luogo dov'era una volta il pagliaio di lei' [I met that she-wolf. Three months ago, in the hills of St. Margaret, on that of Mineo, I was passing by the place where once she had a barn].[22] Verga confirmed this when paying tribute to to his *compaesano* in the *Giornale dell'isola* on 30 November 1915:

> Così a me venne *La Lupa*, la tragica avventura di una contadina sua vicina a Santa Margherita. In quel podere che gli era tanto caro, quasi vi sentisse le radici più salde dell'arte sua, egli mi fece vedere la capanna della 'gnà Pina' la sciagurata madre adultera.[23]

> [This is how I got the idea of *The She-Wolf*, the tragic story of a village woman, one of his neighbours in St. Margaret. It was in that land, which was so dear to him, as if he could feel the sturdiest roots of his art, that he showed me the shack where 'Gnà Pina' lived, the poor unfortunate adulterous mother.]

The triangular relationship in *La Lupa* is perhaps one of Verga's most unconventional, involving husband (Nanni), wife (Maricchia in the *novella* and Mara in the play) and mother-in-law (Gnà Pina, known as La Lupa). La Lupa is infatuated with the young Nanni but he expresses the desire to marry Maricchia/Mara. She then forces her daughter to marry Nanni and eventually they raise a family together. In both versions, however, La Lupa cannot resist her son-in-law and continues to seduce him right until he ends her life. As Carlo Alberto Madrignani puts it: 'È la vicenda di una donna, costretta ad essere madre invece che amante' [It is the story of a woman who is obliged to be a mother instead of a lover].[24]

But why would Verga choose to adapt this particular narrative for the stage? Owing to the poor reception of *In portineria*, perhaps Verga felt the need to situate his theatre back among the Sicilian village community. However, as Natale Tedesco explains, the literary climate, after the success of *Cavalleria rusticana*, had now changed:

> Il clima peraltro era sempre meno favorevole al rilancio del teatro verghiano:

> il pubblico e la critica, che, pur con alcune evidenti incomprensioni e contra-ddizioni avevano decretato, nel 1884, il successo clamoroso di *Cavalleria rusticana*, ora si mostravano insofferenti o, peggio, freddi nell'accogliere l'ultima prova teatrale del maestro catanese. (*Tt*, 14)
>
> [The climate, moreover, was increasingly less favourable to the return of Verga's theatre: the audience and critics, who, albeit with some evident mis-understandings and contradictions, had determined the resounding success of *Cavalleria rusticana* in 1884, now were intolerant or, worse still, cold in their reception of the latest theatrical attempt of the maestro from Catania.]

Indeed, by the time *La Lupa* was first performed, over a decade after the première of *Cavalleria rusticana*, situating a play in Sicily was not considered a challenging innovation — Realism was no longer attractive. As Ferrone observes: '[L]a borghesia esigeva un dramma che, come prima era stato testimone della sua fortuna sociale, fosse ora elusivo di una realtà segnata dal suo fallimento come classe sociale dirigente' [[J]ust as previously the middle classes had demanded a drama which reflected their social success, they now required it to ignore a reality marked by their failure as a leading social class].[25] Moreover, 'si polemizzava sulla rappresentazione di maniera (fatta di vendette rusticane e di passioni bestiali) che gli autori siciliani avevano dato della loro terra, in teatro come in letteratura' [there were arguments over the stereotypical representation (rustic vendettas and bestial passions) which the Sicilian authors had conferred on their motherland, in their theatre as in their narrative prose].[26]

However, it seems to me that something else had changed at this time. By the 1890s, Ibsen's Nora had already attracted notable attention in Italy, particularly after Duse's opening performance in 1891. Perhaps, then, by placing one of his most subversive heroines on stage, Verga was making his own contribution to this 'new' kind of woman on stage: a woman no longer from Scandinavia but homegrown in his native Sicily — a radical move which might explain why he did not achieve quite the same success as he did with *Cavalleria rusticana*.

Gnà Pina

In the original version, the popular narrator tells the story of the so-called 'Lupa', from the moment she first catches sight of the young Nanni to the time of her death. Through the eyes of the villagers, the reader is told that she was 'alta, magra; aveva soltanto un seno fermo e vigoroso da bruna e pure non era più giovane' (*Tn* I, 186) [dark-haired, tall and lean, with firm, well-rounded breasts, though she was no longer young (*CROS*, 34)]. From the first line, she is conveyed as a true she-wolf, ready to prey on other women's husbands and to even corrupt the local priest: 'Al villaggio la chiamavano *la Lupa* perchè non era sazia giammai — di nulla' (*Tn* I, 186) [In the village they called her the She-Wolf because, no matter what she had, she was never satisfied (*CROS*, 34)].

On stage, the characterisation of the protagonist differs considerably. To begin with, in contrast to the reader of the *novella* who gains an understanding of La Lupa through the eyes of the villagers, the reader of the play is offered merely a short physical description of her character in the stage directions: 'La Gnà Pina, detta La Lupa, ancora bella e provocante, malgrado i suoi trentacinque anni suonati, col seno fermo da vergine, gli occhi luminosi' (Tt, 90) [Gnà Pina, known as La Lupa, was still beautiful and alluring, despite being well into her thirties, with firm breasts like that of a virgin, luminous eyes]. Moreover, the stage version delays her entrance into the drama by opening with an episode somewhat unrelated to the plot. The villagers here discuss a popular myth about a sorceress, similarly to the way In portineria starts with a conversation about a painter who left the inn without paying his rent. Instead of building up the impending tragedy, the first few scenes are devoted to contextualising the drama with popular folk songs and proverbs. According to Giorgio Prosperi, 'certo come introduzione è debole, incerta, e, per chi non conosce o non ricorda la novella, distraente' [certainly as an introduction it is weak, vague and, for those who do not know or remember the short story, distracting].[27] By waiting for the protagonist's arrival later on in Act One, the audience subsequently gains an insight into Gnà Pina's personality through the various dialogues, just as they learn about Turiddu through Santuzza's initial exchange with Gnà Nunzia in Cavalleria rusticana and find out about Gilda from the early discussion in In portineria.

Whereas in the *novella* the choral voice of the villagers is expressed through the role of the narrator, on stage the villagers come to life in the form of several minor characters, as was the case previously with Cavalleria rusticana. Once all the music and singing commences, Gnà Pina is called out for the first time by the villager Malerba, whom Verga (not so objectively) describes in the stage directions as having a '*faccia di scimmia, dal ghigno malizioso*' [a monkey's face, with a malicious sneer] (Tt, 90): 'O venite qua, gnà Pina bella!' [Oh come over here, beautiful Gnà Pina] (Tt, 93). While the reader of the *novella* is informed that Gnà Pina worked in the fields 'proprio come un uomo' (Tn I, 188) [just like a man (CROS, 36)], the audience instantly notices that she is not participating in the festivities because she is busy harvesting the wheat. Besides this, in this extract she is referred to by her actual name, Gnà Pina, as opposed to her nickname La Lupa, which turns her into more of an individual in the play. In fact, in the aforementioned stage directions, she is simply referred to as Pina.

Further, whereas La Lupa is portrayed as an isolated figure in the *novella* — 'la gnà Pina era la sola anima viva che si vedesse errare per la campagna' (Tn I, 188) [Pina was the only living soul you could see out and about (CROS, 36] — in the play she is integrated within the community. In the opening scenes, she sings and dances along with the villagers and later exits the stage '*colle altre donne*' [*with the other women*] (Tt, 96). In fact, in the dramatic version it is no longer the masses actively hostile to Gnà Pina but mainly Malerba who provokes her: 'O gnà Pina! ... benedetta! gioia mia! ... cuore mio! ... Venite qua che vogliamo fare un terremoto!' [Hey Gnà Pina!... blessed Gnà Pina... My joy! ... My love! ... Come over here, let's make an earthquake] (Tt, 94–95). Though Gnà Pina in the narrative does not respond to the prejudices expressed against her, in the stage version she vehemently defends herself against him: '*(irritata)*. Voi che c'entrate nei fatti miei?' [*(irritated)*.

What have you got to do with my business?] (*Tt*, 99); and '*(minacciosa). Se ce l'avete con me, e cercate di attaccar briga, guardate che li ho i denti per mordere!*' [*(in a threatening tone). If you have a problem with me, and you are trying to start a fight, watch out, I have teeth that bite!*] (*Tt*, 99). At one point, she even attacks Malerba: '*(alzandosi infuriata e buttandogli in faccia una scodella). Te! senti questa, tu!*' [*(rising up infuriated and throwing a bowl in his face). Here! Take that, you!* (*Tt*, 101)]. As a result of these changes, the 'new' Pina on stage is no longer the stoic character wandering alone in the countryside, but a resilient woman who is more than capable of fighting her own corner.

What also differs about the play is Verga's portrayal of her 'mad' desire. In the narrative, the storyteller gives the impression that La Lupa is addicted to Naomi. The repetition of certain terms, such as 'manipoli' [sheaf] and 'covoni' [bundle], as well as the chant-like proverb which runs throughout the narrative ('*In quell'ora fra vespero e nona, in cui non ne va in volta femmina buona*' (*Tn* I, 188) [In hours that run from dusk till dawn goes no good woman ever born (*CROS*, 36)]),[28] suggest that she is spellbound by the 'incantesimo' (*Tn* I, 190) [spell (*CROS*, 38)]:

> Nei campi immensi, dove scoppiettava soltanto il volo dei grilli, quando il sole batteva a piombo, *la Lupa* affastellava manipoli su manipoli, e covoni su covoni, senza stancarsi mai, senza rizzarsi un momento sulla vita, senza accostare le labbra al fiasco, pur di stare sempre alle calcagna di Nanni. (*Tn* I, 187)

> [In the vast expanse of the fields, where all you could hear was the chirping of the crickets as they leapt, with the sun beating straight down, the She-Wolf tied up sheaf after sheaf, bundle after bundle, showing no signs of fatigue, never looking up for an instant, never putting her lips to the flask, just as long as she could be there behind Nanni.] (*CROS*, 35)

Eventually, La Lupa finds her 'prey' and seduces him. This pivotal point in the tale, recounted in both direct and indirect speech, resembles an extract from a folk tale:

> 'Svegliati!' disse *la Lupa* a Nanni che dormiva nel fosso, accanto alla siepe polverosa col capo fra le braccia [...].
> 'No! non ne va in volta femmina buona nell'ora fra vespero e nona!' singhiozzava Nanni, ricacciando la faccia contro l'erba secca del fossato, in fondo in fondo, colle unghie nei capelli. 'Andatevene! Andatevene! non ci venite più nell'aia!' (*Tn* I, 188)

> ['Wake up!' said the She-Wolf to Nanni, who was lying asleep in the ditch under the dust-laden hedgerow, head resting in his arms [...].
> 'No! No good woman's abroad from dusk till dawn!' bewailed Nanni, pressing his face down again into the dry grass of the ditch as hard as he could, with his fingernails tearing at his hair. 'Go away! Go away! Keep away from the barn!'] (*CROS*, 36)

The narrator then hints at the sexual act when La Lupa is seen making her way from her lover '*riannodando le treccie superbe*' (*Tn* I, 188) [tying up her splendid tresses (*CROS*, 36)]. Although Nanni instructs La Lupa to keep her distance, eventually he finds it difficult to keep away and even waits for her when she is late:

Ma nell'aia ci tornò delle altre volte, e Nanni non le disse nulla; e quando tardava a venire, nell'ora fra vespero e nona, egli andava ad aspettarla in cima alla viottola bianca e deserta, col sudore sulla fronte. (*Tn* I, 188)

[But she kept going back to the barn, and Nanni said nothing. In fact, whenever she was late arriving, in the hours which run from dusk till dawn, he would go and wait for her at the top of the ashen-white, deserted lane, beads of sweat on his forehead.] (*CROS*, 36)

After a further encounter, the narrator reflects Nanni's despair through his actions: '[E] *dopo* si cacciava le mani nei capelli, e le ripeteva ogni volta: "Andatevene! andatevene!"' (*Tn* I, 188–89) [*And afterwards*, he would thrust his hands through his hair and repeat every time, 'Go away! Go away! Don't come back to the barn!' (*CROS*, 36–37), my italics]. Interestingly, Nanni here reacts in the same way as La Lupa will do later when she also thrusts 'le mani nei capelli' (*Tn* I, 187) [her hands into her hair (*CROS*, 35)] after hearing him express his intention to marry her daughter — a gesture which recalls Verga's interview with Ugo Ojetti in 1894 where he described how thoughts can be externalised.[29]

Whereas the narrator in the *novella* gives the impression that the protagonist is bewitched by her lust, in the dramatic version this impression is weakened. In the same way as Verga opens *Cavalleria rusticana* and *In portineria* once the love affairs have already taken place, presumably to avoid portraying their physical relationships on stage, he starts this play *after* the suggestion that Gnà Pina and Nanni have been associated with each other. Early on in the plot, Cardillo approaches Nanni about La Lupa's pursuit: 'No. È lei [Gnà Pina] che ti corre dietro le calcagna!' [No. It is she [Gnà Pina] who is chasing after you!] (*Tt*, 93). As a result, Verga is unable to portray how her fascination with Nanni grows. Unlike the reader of the *novella* who immediately sees the protagonist in a trance-like state, hypnotised by her passion in the heat of the day, the audience of the play only hears about her actions as Nanni discusses her behaviour with one of the minor characters later in the second act:

NANNI: E quando viene a ronzarmi intorno poi? sul colle e sul piano... Non sapete ch'è peggio! Gira e rigira... col pretesto di cogliere erbe selvatiche... come una vera lupa! (*Tt*, 126)

[NANNI: And what about when she comes buzzing around me here then? On the hilltops and in the fields... You have no idea which is worse! She comes around and around again... with the excuse of collecting wild herbs... like a real she-wolf!]

In addition, rather than *seeing* Gnà Pina pursue the object of her desire, the spectators are made to *listen* to her articulate her desire. Whereas the physical descriptions provided by the narrator convey her infatuation with him, on stage she expresses her feelings for herself. As soon as Gnà Pina is invited to join the festivities in the opening act, her first line is: 'No... Voglio ballare con compare Nanni' [No... I want to dance with Nanni (*Tt*, 95). When he refuses, she tries to make him jealous by dancing with another man. Not only does Gnà Pina reveal her passion for Nanni through her exchanges and flirtatious dancing, but also through folk songs. She even serenades him, reversing the traditional male / female roles:

'"*O voi che avete occhi e non vedete, allora di quegli occhi che ne fate?*"' ['*You who have eyes and cannot see, then what is the point of having them?*'] (*Tt*, 95).

The actual seduction scene in the play does not occur until the end of the first act, after Gnà Pina has forced Mara to marry Nanni. Once again, in contrast to the narrative, this scene continues to be built up through dialogue. Before the sexual encounter, Gnà Pina confronts Nanni about the upheaval his marriage proposal has caused and he expresses his regret, which he does not in the original version:

> NANNI: Non lo sapevo! Non voglio farvi fare le cose per forza, no!
> PINA: *(fissando cogli occhi ardenti e lagrimosi)*. Lo vedete almeno se vi ho voluto bene? (*Tt*, 109)
>
> [NANNI: I didn't know! I don't want to force you to do anything, that's not what I want!
> PINA: *(staring at him with her ardent and teary eyes)*. Can you at least see then how much I love you?]

At this point, instead of gaining an insight into how La Lupa seduces him, the audience simply watches the lovers exit the stage: '*Scompaiono dalla sinistra, in fondo. Silenzio*' [*They disappear to the left, at the far end. Silence* (*Tt*, 111)]. According to Tedesco, the reduced sense of passion between the lovers compromises the artistic value of the work:

> *La Lupa* perde nella redazione drammatica quella stringatezza che è il segno stilistico della coesione fantastica avuta dal Verga nell'inventare lo straordinario personaggio di questa donna tormentata fino all'inverosimile nei sensi, il cui chiuso dramma interiore, appena colorito dalla descrizione viva ma castigata del suo aspetto fisico, dovette costringersi alla espansione scenica, dove quell'aspetto è tratteggiato con più di un segno di golosa e compiaciuta sensualità nel pretestuoso scivolare verso il gusto del pubblico delle platee.[30]
>
> [*The She-Wolf* loses in the dramatic version that succinctness which is the stylistic stamp of the superb cohesion achieved by Verga in inventing the extraordinary character of this woman whose senses are tormented to an unlikely degree. Her closed interior drama, only slightly affected by the vivid but measured description of her physical appearance, was forced to be developed on stage, where her appearance includes more than one sign of an avid and self-satisfying sensuality, as a result of the spurious inclination to conform to the tastes of the audience.]

Although the reliance on dialogue in the play weakens the stylistic and poetic qualities of the *novella* and causes Gnà Pina to become less of a seductive figure, it nonetheless enables her to express her thoughts for herself. As a result, she breaks away from her portrayal as the stereotypical she-wolf who *feels* rather than *thinks*.

This more articulate side to her personality continues to surface in the episode where Nanni reveals his wish to marry Maricchia / Mara '"*che è zitella*"' (*Tn* I, 187) ['that unmarried daughter of yours' (*CROS*, 35)], or 'carne fresca' [fresh meat] (*Tt*, 105) as she is referred to on stage. When Nanni enlightens Gnà Pina on his wish to marry her daughter, her reaction in the narrative is expressed through her body language: '*La Lupa* si cacciò le mani nei capelli, grattandosi le tempie senza dir parola, e se ne andò, né più comparve nell'aia' (*Tn* I, 187) [The She-Wolf thrust her hands into her hair, tearing at the sides of her head without uttering a word, then strode off and stayed away from the barn (*CROS*, 35)], actions which relate again to Verga's interview with Ojetti.

Whereas La Lupa's response to Nanni's proposal is externalised in the narrative, and therefore essentially silenced, in the play she openly declares her reaction: 'Ah, compare Nanni!... Come vorrei vedervi piangere coi miei occhi!' [Ah, compare Nanni!... How I long to see you cry with my own eyes!] (*Tt*, 105); and 'Perché vi divertite a calpestarmi coi piedi sulla faccia? Sono la lupa è vero... Sono una cosa vile...' [Why do you enjoy trampling on my face with your feet? I am a she-wolf that is true... I am a vile thing...] (*Tt*, 105). The silent she-wolf thus continues to be turned into an articulate character on stage who even expresses her reluctance to involve her daughter in the triangle, as she exclaims in depair: 'Mettete il coltello in mano alla mia figlia stessa, anche?' [Are you putting the knife into my own daughter's hands as well?]. Indeed, the words added to the script confirm that she feels a strong degree of sorrow for Maricchia who will now be left holding what she calls 'il coltello' [the knife].

Consequently, although Susan Amatangelo has argued that in this *novella* 'Verga portrays the quintessential bad mother',[31] here we see how Gnà Pina is not a selfish mother ready to renounce her daughter in order to satisfy her lust, but a Phèdre-like character who is powerless against her all-consuming passion: she would like to stop herself from forcing her daughter to marry Nanni but she cannot resist his demands. Following the narrator's descriptions of her inability to distance herself from the object of her desire, the reader of the *novella* is made to feel as though she cannot but succumb to Nanni's wish. As for the play, through the words included about the metaphorical knife, Verga underlines how patently difficult she finds the decision to hand over her daughter.

In both versions, Gnà Pina eventually forces her daughter to marry Nanni. In the *novella*, the narrator confirms in a short line: 'Maricchia non lo voleva a nessun patto; ma sua madre l'afferrò pe' capelli, davanti al focolare, e le disse co' denti stretti: "Se non lo pigli ti ammazzo!"' (*Tn* I, 187) [Maricchia wanted nothing whatever to do with him, but when they got home her mother grabbed her by the hair and said to her through clenched teeth: 'If you don't take him, I'll kill you!' (*CROS*, 35)]. To show that Nanni has succeeded in marrying Maricchia, Verga refers to him as La Lupa's 'genero' (*Tn* I, 188) [son-in-law (*CROS*, 36)], just as the author uses the term 'innamorata' [the woman in love] (*Tn* I, 357) in 'Il canarino del n. 15' to imply that Gilda has fallen in love with Carlini: an anti-Romantic style which is used in order to avoid having to go into detail about the protagonists' relationships, as Verga confirmed in the preface to 'L'amante di Gramigna': '[S]acrifichiamo volentieri l'effetto della catastrofe' (*Tn*: I, 191) [We gladly sacrifice the narrative's climax and its psychological effect (*CROS*, 93)].[32]

Whereas the storyteller reflects the clash between mother and daughter through succinct sentences, in the theatrical version their emotions are conveyed in extended dialogues, which continue to show Gnà Pina behaving aggressively:

PINA: *(torva, quasi minacciosa)*. Non lo vuoi? Perchè non lo vuoi?
MARA: *(tutta tremante, fuori di sè dallo sbigottimento)*. Perchè non può essere... *(fissandola con gli occhi in cui balena il sospetto atroce)*. Sapete bene che non può essere! [...].
PINA: *(afferrandola per le treccie e guardandola torva, viso contro viso)*. Che dici? Parla! Parla chiaro!
MARA: *(strillando)*. Mamma! mamma mia! (*Tt*, 108)

[PINA: *(frowning, almost threatening)*. You don't want to marry him? Why not?
MARA: *(trembling all over, out of her mind with distress)*. Because it's not possible... *(staring at her, her eyes gleaming with the atrocious suspicion)*. You know well why it's not possible! [...].
PINA: *(grabbing her by her plaits and looking at her resentfully, face to face)*. What are you saying? Speak! Speak clearly!
MARA: *(shrieking)*. Mother! Mother!]

What was originally a brief episode in the short story is now turned into a long and drawn-out struggle between the two women. Moreover, by starting the play with the suggestion that Gnà Pina and Nanni have already been linked with each other, Verga (again inadvertently perhaps) adds more of an incestuous emphasis to the triangular relationship. La Lupa in the stage version is therefore forcing her daughter to marry the man *she has already seduced*. In fact, Mara's horror at Nanni's 'indecent proposal' emerges not just in her dialogue but also in the stage directions above.

The women continue to clash over Nanni when Maricchia / Mara begins to feel jealous of her mother after she has fallen in love with her husband. As the storyteller indicates, 'adesso l'amava anche lei quel marito' (*Tn* I, 189) [she too loved the husband they had forced upon her (*CROS*, 37)]. Although most of the narrative is composed in free indirect speech, important exchanges, such as when Maricchia confronts her mother about the adultery, are reported in direct speech:

'Scellerata! le diceva. Mamma scellerata!'
'Taci!'
'Ladra! Ladra!'
'Taci!'
'Andrò dal brigadiere, andrò!'
'Vacci!' (*Tn* I, 189).

['You wicked slut!' she cried. 'You wicked slut of a mother!'
'Shut up!'
'I'll tell the police sergeant, that's what I'll do!'
'Go ahead and tell him!'] (*CROS*, 37)

In the stage version, Mara challenges her mother in the same way as she does here, but Verga adds a few extra exchanges which are not included in the original, such as when Gnà Pina confronts Nanni about the family he has raised with Mara: '... e dà la poppa alla tua creatura! ... dinanzi a me! ... *Con voce sorda*. Vi ho fatto il letto colle mie mani, la prima notte...' [... and she is breastfeeding your baby! ... In front of me! ... *In a monotonous tone*. I prepared your wedding bed with my own hands, on your wedding night...] (*Tt*, 119).

Casting Gnà Pina in an aggressive light, Verga also makes her daughter Mara appear antagonistic during these confrontations. Once Mara is given the chance to expand on her suffering, she also becomes more hostile: 'La lingua vi dovrebbero legare! Vi dovrebbero legare per i capelli, sulla pubblica piazza!' [They should tie your tongue! They should tie you up by the hair in the public square! (*Tt*, 123)]. By making the audience of the play actually witness the scratching and biting between mother and daughter, Verga inevitably caused some degree of uneasiness. As the unconvinced Giovanni Pozza put it:

> Che Nanni, dopo di avere ceduto una prima volta ai desideri amorosi di costei, non sappia più reggere ai fascini ed alle violenze di lei, si capisce perchè è naturale e comune; ma si capisce anche che il pubblico ieri abbia trovato difettosa la preparazione della catastrofe.[33]
>
> [We can understand the fact that Nanni, after having ceded for the first time to the amorous desires of the She-Wolf, does not know how to resist her charms and violence, since it is natural and commonplace. But we can understand why the audience yesterday saw shortcomings leading up to the catastrophe.]

Adolfo Orvieto's review in *Il Marzocco* on 17 May 1896 confirms the same reaction to the concluding second act:

> [D]obbiamo assistere a scene disgustose e rivoltanti di gelosia fra madre e figlia: lo scandalo impera: al dialogo sottentra la violenza: ecco i graffi, i pugni, colpi di scure in ultimo (proprio i colpi di scure [...] sulla scena!), dopo i quali, la bestia umana essendo soppressa e giustizia fatta, il dramma finisce.[34]
>
> [[W]e are forced to witness unsavoury and repulsive scenes of jealousy between mother and daughter. Scandal dominates: dialogue succumbs to violence — we see scratches, punches, even blows from an axe (blows from an axe [...] on stage!), after which, the human beast having been overcome and justice established, the play finishes.]

The general consensus amongst Verga's contemporary critics is that audiences enjoyed the first act but were uneasy with the second where mother and daughter — and later Gnà Pina and Nanni — violently clash. As Orvieto stresses: 'Due atti di valore assai diverso: uno (il primo) quasi bello, l'altro quasi... brutto' [Two very different acts: one (the first) almost beautiful, the other almost... ugly].[35]

Despite these limitations in terms of both content and style, Gnà Pina on stage never loses her self-awareness. Soon after the seduction, she enters '*timidamente e sorridendo umilmente, come a farsi perdonare la sua venuta*' [timidly and smiling humbly, as if to excuse her arrival] (*Tt*, 116) and later condemns her behaviour: 'Le madri come me andrebbero bruciate vive!' [Mothers like me ought to be burnt at the stake!] (*Tt*, 128). As a result, it would seem that the mythical 'Lupa' in the narrative has been replaced on stage by a woman able to judge her own actions, a woman 'che pensa a chiedere compassione più che imporre la sua selvaggia passione' [who thinks about asking for compassion rather than imposing her wild passion],[36] and is 'a volte smarrita e pensosa' [sometimes lost and contemplative].[37]

Anna Barsotti provides a practical justification for this new side to Gnà Pina's personality:

> Nella traduzione teatrale della tragica vicenda, Verga aveva sentito il bisogno (forse pratico) di umanizzare, psicanalizzare il personaggio, spiegandone i modi e le azioni con argomenti normali e quotidiani, riducendolo, si vedrà, anche sul piano della resa poetica.[38]
>
> [In the theatrical translation of the tragic story, Verga felt the (perhaps practical) need to humanise, to psychoanalyse the main character, to explain her ways and actions by means of normal, everyday arguments, reducing the character, as will be evident, also in terms of poetic force.]

Similarly, according to Romano Luperini:

> [[L]o sforzo di introspezione psicologica è rivolto soprattutto a cogliere l'elemento irresistibilmente morboso della passione incestuosa di cui la *Lupa* ha piena e dolorosa consapevolezza [...] confermando quel nuovo interesse per la psicologia.[39]
>
> [Verga's emphasis on psychological introspection is above all directed to seizing the irresistibly pathological element of the incestuous passion which the *She-Wolf* is fully and painfully aware of [...] confirming Verga's new interest in psychology.]

It seems that Verga's new interest in providing his characters with more psychological introspection has been stimulated by the theatrical genre. With the removal of the role of the narrator, the characters now need to explain for themselves why they behave in a particular way. In fact, *all* of Verga's stage women undergo a similar transformation: Santuzza has to justify her betrayal in *Cavalleria rusticana* and in *In portineria* extra scenes are added so that Màlia can expand on her suffering.

The last part of both versions focusses on Gnà Pina's inevitable death. As the narrative progresses, her passion intensifies until it reaches its climax. Nanni himself calls in the *brigadiere* and implores him to put an end to her temptation: '"Per carità, signor brigadiere, levatemi da questo inferno! fatemi ammazzare, mandatemi in prigione; non me la lasciate veder più, mai! mai!"' (*Tn* I, 189) ['For pity's sake, sergeant, take me out of this hell on earth! Have me killed, send me to prison, never let me set eyes on her again, ever!' (*CROS*, 37)]. Although at first she refuses to leave — '"La casa è mia. Non voglio andarmene!"' (*Tn* I, 189) ['The house is mine. I don't intend to leave it!' (*CROS*, 37)] — when Nanni is kicked in the chest by a mule, she distances herself for his benefit, an episode in the play only referred to in passing by Mara. However, as the narrator reveals, it is not long before she returns: 'E meglio sarebbe stato per lui che fosse morto in quel tempo, prima che il diavolo tornasse a tentarlo e a ficcarglisi nell'anima e nel corpo quando fu guarito' (*Tn* I, 189) [And it would have been better for him if he had died then and there, before the Devil returned to tempt him and to take over body and soul as soon as he recovered (*CROS*, 37)]. Nanni then seeks help from the church — 'andò a confessarsi, e fece pubblicamente sei palmi di lingua, in penitenza' (*Tn* I, 190) [he went to confession, and did penance in public by crawling on his belly for six feet over the cobblestones in front of the church (*CROS*, 38)] — but, despite his efforts, she returns. As La Lupa refuses to keep her distance, Nanni threatens to kill her. She responds: '"Ammazzami", rispose *la Lupa*, "ché non me ne importa; ma senza di te non voglio starci"' (*Tn* I, 190) ['Go ahead and kill me', replied the She-Wolf. 'It doesn't worry me. I can't live without you' (*CROS*, 38)].

Verga, here, gives the impression that La Lupa acknowledges that the only way to end her passion is through death. In fact, it could be said that she sacrifices herself in order to protect her family from further suffering. Russo has, indeed, identified her as 'una martire fermissima del suo peccare' [a martyr unrelenting in her sin],[40] indicating that in the narrative 'il desiderio sensuale splende d'una luce tragica, il desiderio è una sofferenza, un'agonia' [the sensual desire shines with a tragic light, the desire is a form of suffering, an agony].[41] As Verga himself stressed in a letter to Rod on 29 January 1908:

> Non è più la passione cieca, carnale, brutale anche se volete, ma quasi fatale della Lupa, che dà la figlia a Nanni non per turpe mercimonio, ma perchè egli la vuole, ed essa non sa resistere alla sua volontà, carne della sua carne, che arde e si consuma e soffre della sua passione, e si pente del suo peccato, sinceramente, ma non può divellersene, e torna a lui, e lo avvince così nel suo spasimo che egli ne è vinto pure, e sempre, e per sottrarsene non sa far altro che ucciderla. (*Lt*, p. 245)

> [It is no longer a blind, carnal or even, if you like, brutal passion, but rather an almost fatal one, the She-Wolf's, who hands her daughter to Nanni not through some sordid dealing, but because he wants her, and the She-Wolf cannot resist his will, flesh of her flesh, that burns and consumes itself and suffers because of her passion. And she truly repents of her sin, but she cannot wrest herself from it, and she returns to him. She so enfolds him in her torment that he too is conquered by it, for evermore, and in order to save himself from it, he does not know what else to do than to kill her.]

In the play, however, the reliance on speech continues to expose Gnà Pina's fighting spirit, especially in her final confrontation with Nanni which is inevitably conveyed more physically on stage. When Nanni pleads with her to leave him alone, she is openly defiant: '*(rivoltandosi, colla bocca amara)*. Che non ne sapete altra canzone?' [*(turning to him, with bitter words)*. Can you not change the tune?] (*Tt*, 127–28). Even as Nanni is about to kill her, she challenges him: 'E tu pure che mi tieni nell'inferno! [...]. Il diavolo ci ha legati insieme!' [You, too, keep me in this hell! [...]. The devil has tied us together!] (*Tt*, 128); and finally: '*(voltandosi verso di lui, col petto nudo, come a sfidarlo)*. Finiscila! Via! colle tue mani!' [*(turning towards him, bare breasted, as if to challenge him)*. Finish it! Come on! With your own hands!] (*Tt*, 128). While the reader of the story is encouraged to pity La Lupa as she essentially sacrifices herself in order to relieve Nanni and Maricchia from her destructive desire, the spectators of the performance are left feeling as if they are watching a resilient character caught up in her own struggle for existence.

Francesca Malara has concluded that, although it is La Lupa who perishes in the end, 'la vera vincitrice sembra essere La Lupa. La gnà Pina infatti, pervasa da una forza primeva, incurante della morte, va incontro al suo giustiziere che è pallido, stralunato e balbettante' [the real winner seems to be the She-Wolf. Gnà Pina, in fact, pervaded by a primitive force, unconcerned with death, goes towards her pale, wide-eyed and stammering executioner].[42] Whether Gnà Pina can be read as a winner or not, what remains the case is that Verga produces a very different 'Lupa' in the dramatic version. On stage, she is transformed from a silently tormented victim into an articulate and self-critical individual who is more than capable of fighting her own battles. The audience by no means meets a sexual she-wolf always 'alle calcagna di Nanni' (*Tn* I, 187) [in pursuit of Nanni (*CROS*, 35)] (literally at his heels) but rather a bold and nonconformist character, fully aware of her sexual deviance.

By giving Gnà Pina a voice of her own on stage, Verga reveals how she is no longer a 'mad' she-wolf whose sole thought is to seduce Nanni, but rather a complex character capable of expressing herself and reflecting upon her behaviour. Although the alterations introduced in the dramatic version cause Gnà Pina to appear more aggressive in the play than she does in the short story, they nonetheless shed new light on a stronger side to her personality. Gnà Pina appears on stage as a rounded character who feels remorse as she painfully yields to Nanni's demands and, in so doing, sacrifices Mara who is now left holding the metaphorical knife — not the actions of the typically callous 'distruttrice' [destroyer].[43] Consequently, it is arguable that, in intentionally staging such an unorthodox character only a few years after the turmoil Ibsen's Nora caused in Italian theatres, Verga was introducing Italian audiences to a 'home-grown' version of Ibsen's Scandinavian herione.

La caccia al lupo

In *La caccia al lupo*, Verga continues to employ the motif of the wolf but while it was used to symbolise animal passion in *La Lupa*, this time the (male) wolf is of a predatory and violent nature.[44] The story was initially published in Catania in the journal *Le Grazie* on 1 January 1897, and republished in *Siciliana* in 1923. Now it is part of Verga's collection of short stories, *Novelle sparse*. The homonymous play premièred at the Teatro Manzoni in Milan on 15 November 1901 and was staged by the theatre company belonging to Virginia Reiter and Francesco Pasta, with Reiter as Mariangela, Luigi Carini as Lollo, and Cesare Dondini as Bellamà. The play was performed together with *La caccia alla volpe* starring the actors above but in different roles (Reiter as Donna Livia, Carini as Artale, and Dondini as Di Fleri). The same evening, both plays were staged, again simultaneously, at the Teatro Alfieri in Turin, this time produced and performed by Tina Di Lorenzo and Flavio Andò.[45]

Verga first mentioned these two plays in a letter to his friend Dina Pallanza on 26 September 1901:

> Io ho lavorato molto e bene, tutto il santo giorno, dalla mattina alla sera [...]. Presto avrai la *Caccia al lupo* stampata, da Treves, e in seguito anche l'altra commediola [...]. Ho rifatto quasi per intero la *Caccia al lupo*, vedrai, e sto rifacendo l'altra, e ne son contento. Da un pezzo, non lavoravo così di lena come in questo mese.[46]

> [I have worked hard and well, the whole blessed day, from dawn to dusk [...]. Soon you will have the copy of *The Wolf Hunt* published by Treves, with the other play following on [...]. I have almost completely re-written *The Wolf Hunt*, as you will see, and I am rewriting the other play, and I am satisfied with it. It has been a while since I worked with such vigour as I have done this month.]

In a further letter a couple of days later, on 28 September 1901, this time to another friend, Giselda Fojanesi-Rapisardi, Verga revealed: 'Ho quasi rifatto di pianta la *Caccia al lupo*, che ora è perfetta! La vedrai presto e me ne dirai il tuo avviso. Sto rifacendo adesso l'altra commedia, che voglio riesca il *meglio possibile*' [I have almost completely rewritten *The Wolf Hunt*, and now it is perfect! You will see it soon and give me your opinion. I am currently also rewriting the other play, which I hope will turn out in the *best possible way*].[47]

In contrast to *Cavalleria rusticana* and *La Lupa*, which are situated in a Sicilian village community, both versions of *La caccia al lupo* are set behind closed doors in the protagonists' home, as was the case with 'Il canarino del n. 15' and *In portineria*. The triangular relationship is more traditional in character, involving husband (Lollo), wife (who remains nameless in the *novella* but is called Mariangela in the play) and lover (Michelangelo in the *novella* and Bellamà in the play). The two versions progress in a similar way, opening with Lollo's wife's agitation at her husband's unexpected return home. Lollo explains how he has returned early in order to prepare for a wolf hunt. In his dialogue, full of double meanings, the wolf is turned into a euphemism for his wife's lover and the lamb is used to represent her. This triangle is subsequently turned into a metaphorical one involving hunter, lamb and wolf.[48] Lollo then leaves for the hunt and locks his wife indoors. At this point, Michelangelo / Bellamà comes out of hiding and confronts her about their entrapment. Both are well aware that in the Sicilian unwritten code of honour, it is allegedly the husband's role to kill the wife's lover, as portrayed in *Cavalleria rusticana*. Whereas the *novella* closes during their confrontation, the play ends as Lollo re-enters the house, accompanied by two men, and catches his wife with her lover.

Mariangela

Although Lollo's wife appears as the most defenceless character in both versions, as the plots develop, she reveals herself as one of the strongest. To build up to this moment, Verga chooses to portray her as a vulnerable woman at the outset so that the contrast is more startling at the end, particularly in the drama. To begin with, the reader of the *novella* and the audience of the play are inspired to pity her. All through the narrative, she is referred to as a 'poveretta' [poor little thing] (*Tn* II, 451 and *Tn* II, 455), 'la povera donna' [the poor woman] (*Tn* II, 452 and *Tn* II, 455), and 'la povera moglie' [the poor wife] (repeated twice in *Tn* II, 454). Verga also describes her as 'la povera donna' [the poor woman] (*Tt*, 131) in the stage directions of the play, though he refers to her in this way only this one time, here at the beginning. This not only highlights his own presence in the text but also his reduced sympathy for her. Cesare Levi has maintained that '[i]l maggior merito di Verga come autore drammatico è l'impersonalità delle sue creature teatrali: e cioè l'assenza di ogni influsso personale sul carattere dei personaggi' [Verga's greatest merit as a playwright is the fact that his theatrical creations are impersonal: that is to say, the personalities of his characters are not at all influenced by the personality of the author].[49] Yet Verga's influence does emerge in his portrayal of Mariangela, particularly when compared to the *novella*, in the same way as his presence can be identified in the stage directions describing Malerba in *La Lupa*.

In both narrative and play, Lollo's wife is also referred to as bait. As for Lollo, despite being described as a '[u]omo di poche parole' [[m]an of few words] (*Tn* II, 451) in the short story and a '[u]omo di poche chiacchiere' [[m]an with little chitchat] (*Tt*, 131) in the play, he nevertheless elaborates in considerable detail on how he plans to capture the wolf, directly comparing his wife to a lamb. In the narrative, Lollo's description of the hunt is reported through direct speech, perhaps in preparation for its eventual transposition to the stage: '"Vuoi sapere come si fa? ... Ecco: gli si prepara il suo bravo trabocchetto [...] l'agnella legata là sopra... che lo tira la carne fresca, il mariolo!"' (*Tn* II, 453) ['Do you want to know how to do it?... Like this: you prepare a nice trap for him [...] the lamb tied up there... ah, how the fresh meat tempts him, the scoundrel!'], repeating virtually the same words in the play (*Tt*, 136).

Realising how she is the bait in the metaphorical hunt, Lollo's wife starts to look for ways to escape the trap: 'Essa lo guardava fisso fisso, per indovinare quel che covasse sotto quel ghigno; gli si strusciava adosso, proprio come una gatta, col seno palpitante, e il sorriso pallido in bocca' [She fixed her gaze on him, trying to guess what was going on beneath that malign grin; she brushed up against him, just like a cat, her heart pounding and a pale smile on her lips] (*Tn* II, 454). Her cunning, feline-like nature is also transposed to the play and described in the stage directions:

> *Mariangela seguita a fissarlo in viso, per indovinare che ci covi sotto quel ghigno; gli si struscia addosso, proprio come una gatta, col seno palpitante, e il sorriso pallido in bocca.* (*Tt*, 135)
>
> [*Mariangela continues to stare at him in the face, trying to discern what he is concealing beneath that malign smirk; she brushes up against him just like a cat, her heart pounding, and a pale smile on her lips.*]

Mariangela's animalistic behaviour has led Barsotti to associate her with Gnà Pina. Barsotti argues that, while the latter is enigmatic and contradictory, the former remains a one-dimensional character:

> Mariangela è vicina alla Lupa, ma senza la grandezza enigmatica di quella della novella, né l'umanità trepidante e contraddittoria di quella teatrale: è semplicemente, e sempre, una donna animalesca.[50]
>
> [Mariangela is close to the She-Wolf, but without the same enigmatic greatness as the She-Wolf of the short story, or the anxious and contradictory humanity of the theatrical counterpart: she is simply, and constantly, an animalistic woman.]

In contrast to this view, it seems that, in the dramatic adaptation, Verga is keen to exploit the theatrical genre in order to further develop different aspects of Mariangela's character, which are neither present in the *novella* nor limited to her animalistic nature. Failing to tempt Lollo into telling her the truth about the hunt through her feline-like performance, she interprets a further role missing from the short story — that of a vulnerable wife: '*(stringendosi a lui, carezzevole).* Non mi lasciate!... Non mi lasciate così!... Ho paura!... Venite a letto piuttosto... con questo freddo!... sentite?...' [*(embracing him, endearingly).* Don't leave me!... Don't leave me like this!... I'm frightened!... Come to bed instead... with this cold!... Are you listening?...] (*Tt*, 137). When her performance is unsuccessful, she takes on another role which is also overlooked in the original — that of the servant wife: '*(timidamente).* Voi siete il padrone... *Accennando col capo.* Il mio padrone siete!...' [*(timidly).* You are the master... *Nodding her head.* You are my master!...] (*Tt*, 135). As a result of these changes, it would appear that the varying sides to her personality, left undeveloped in the story, reveal Mariangela to be a woman capable of *thinking* her way out of the 'hunt'.

Verga continues to throw light on Mariangela's play-acting in the dramatic version, when she is eventually locked in the house. Before Lollo exits to prepare for the hunt, it is explicitly stated in the stage directions that Mariangela actively puts on a performance: '*fingendo di stare a vedere attentamente per nascondere la sua inquietudine*' [*pretending to be looking at him attentively in order to disguise her anxiety*] (*Tt*, 134), turning the play into a kind of 'play-within-a-play'. This was the first time Verga started to use stage directions to allude to the duplicity of drama: how Mariangela behaves on the surface and her true intentions hidden underneath. In *Cavalleria rusticana*, Verga hardly ever employed stage directions other than to describe Santuzza's external actions, mainly her physical interaction with Turiddu. In *In portineria*, the more frequent stage directions depict Màlia's repressed feelings for Carlini. In *La Lupa*, Verga specifies both Gnà Pina's physical response and her remorse after the adultery. In *La caccia al lupo*, however, Verga began to exploit stage directions in order to strengthen the different layers of Mariangela's 'performances'.

In addition, Verga introduces certain exchanges into the play to further develop the multiple sides to her character. For instance, in contrast to the narrative, as soon as her lover Bellamà comes out of hiding following her husband's exit, she is initially portrayed as being playful and affectionate towards him (whose first name is Mariano), '*(abbracciandolo, piangendo).* Mariano! Mariano mio! Non ho che te al mondo!' [*(embracing him, in tears).* Mariano! My Mariano! I have no one in this world but you!] (*Tt*, 140), almost echoing the same words she uttered previously to her husband when distracting him from the hunt ('che non ho altro al mondo!' [I don't have anyone else in the world!] (*Tt*, 135)) — further evidence of her manipulative nature.

Immediately after her 'performance' as the affectionate lover, Mariangela interprets the role of the jealous lover. Even though in the original version she reproaches Michelangelo for all the trouble their affair has caused — '"Doveva cogliermi un accidente, quando mi siete venuto fra i piedi! [...] Doveva cogliermi una febbre maligna!"' ['I should have been struck down the moment you came into my life! [...] I should have been struck down by the plague!'] (*Tn* II, 456) — in the dramatic version Verga introduces additional dialogues which give Mariangela further motivation for anger. Before Lollo locks her in the house, he enlightens her in detail as to who will be accompanying him in the hunt. In the narrative, he simply leaves his home to meet the other hunters, informing his wife: '"Ho già avvisato Zango e Buonocore"' ['I've already told Zango and Buonocore'] (*Tn* II, 453), without clarifying who exactly these two men are and, more importantly, why '[c]i hanno il loro interesse pure' ['[t]hey have their own reasons as well'] (*Tn* II, 453). On stage, however, the men become Musarra and his son Neli, and just before his exit, Lollo reveals the reason that they are so eager to assist him with the hunt:

> LOLLO: Mi aspettano i Musarra, padre e figlio qui accanto... Sai, il figlio Musarra, che chiamano il matto perchè sua moglie gli è fuggita con Bellamà, quello che fa il gallo colle donne altrui (*Tt*, 137)
>
> [LOLLO: The Musarras, father and son, are waiting for me here nearby... You know, Musarra's son, they call him the crazy one because his wife ran off with Bellamà, the guy who shows off in front of married women.]

During this exchange, Lollo elaborates on the antecedent events: 'Bellamà piantò la moglie di Musarra in mezzo alla strada, povera e pazza davvero, lei!... chè suo marito almeno, quando si sarà lavata la faccia nel sangue di quell'altro...' [Bellamà abandoned Musarra's wife, in a sorry state indeed!... Her husband, at the very least, once he has washed his face in that man's blood...] (*Tt*, 137). By introducing his involvement with Compare Neli's wife, Verga gives Mariangela more reason to be enraged with her lover. In fact, when Bellamà comes out of hiding, she reveals that her husband is in the company of Compare Neli and Musarra and this inevitably makes him fear for his life: '*(facendo sforzi disperati per arrivare al tetto)*. Si è messo d'accordo coi Musarra perchè ce l'hanno con me anche loro!' [*(desperately trying to climb up to the roof)*. He's got together with the Musarras because they've also got it in for me!] (*Tt*, 140). She then berates him about his involvement with Compare Neli's wife: 'Lo so! A causa della moglie di compare Neli Musarra...' [I know! Because of Nelli Musarra's wife...] (*Tt*, 140–41), which leads to a confrontation:

> MARIANGELA: M'avete rovinata come la moglie di Musarra, scellerato!
> BELLAMÀ: Adesso mi rinfacci la moglie di Musarra? Quando mi correvi dietro per farmela lasciare, no! (*Tt*, 141)
>
> [MARIANGELA: You've ruined me like Musarra's wife, you wretch!
> BELLAMÀ: Now you're throwing Musarra's wife back in my face? While you were chasing after me to make me leave her, weren't you!]

This exchange suggests that Mariangela pursued Bellamà despite knowing about his affair. Earlier on in the theatrical plot, Lollo also implies that Mariangela was already aware of Bellamà's involvement with Compare Neli's wife: '[L]o sai anche tu' [[Y]ou also know why] (*Tt*, 137). She, however, denies the accusation, leaving the spectators to make up their own minds.

Mariangela's performances climax at the end when she exploits her play-acting to avoid the trap. As she tries to escape from with her lover, initially this episode is portrayed in an identical way in both versions. In the narrative, the storyteller describes their reactions which are echoed in the stage directions of the play:

> Poi, tutt'a un tratto, fosse il naturale suo proprio che lo vincesse, o il nervoso che gli metteva addosso il va e vieni di lei che pareva proprio una bestia presa in gabbia, scappò a correre anche lui all'impazzata. (*Tn* II, 455)
>
> [Then, all of a sudden, perhaps his nature got the better of him, or perhaps it was the nervousness caused by her toing and froing like a trapped beast in a cage, he also started to run around like a madman.]

What differs is how the characters' altercations are developed on stage once they realise that there is no way out. These extended scenes offer the audience of the play a better insight into their relationship:

> MARIANGELA: *(eccitata anche lei).* Pensi solo alla tua pelle tu!...
> BELLAMÀ: *(furioso).* Alla mia pelle!... Sissignora!... M'hai fatto cadere in trappola!...
> MARIANGELA: *(tirandolo per una gamba).* E mi lasci sola... colla morte sul collo!...
> BELLAMÀ: *(dandole un calcio).* Lasciami andare, maledetta!
> MARIANGELA: *(esasperata, facendolo cadere giù dalla scranna).* Maledetto tu! Tutto maledetto, che mi hai rovinata!
> BELLAMÀ: *(brandendo la scranna furioso sul capo di lei).* Ti faccio la festa! Com'è vero Dio, ti faccio la festa, prima di tuo marito! (*Tt.* 141)
>
> [MARIANGELA: *(also agitated).* You only care about saving your own skin!...
> BELLAMÀ: *(furious).* My own skin!... Yes Ma'am!... You've made me fall into this trap!...
> MARIANGELA: *(pulling him by the leg).* And you're leaving me all on my own?... with death at the door! ...
> BELLAMÀ: *(giving her a kick).* Let me go, you damn wretch!
> MARIANGELA: *(exasperated, making him fall from the chair).* Damn you! Damn you, you've ruined me!
> BELLAMÀ: *(furious, wielding the chair above her head).* I'm going to kill you! As God is my witness, I'm going to kill you before your husband does!]

The lovers' confrontations are reminiscent of the violent clashes between Gnà Pina and Nanni in the dramatic version of *La Lupa*. Both men threaten to kill their lovers and the women fight back:

> MARIANGELA: *(udendo aprir l'uscio scappa a rifugiarsi nello stanzino in fondo, imprecando).* Aiuto! Aiuto!
> BELLAMÀ: *(afferrandola alla gola).* Taci, maledetta!... Ti strozzo!...
> MARIANGELA: *(dibattendosi, mordendogli le mani).* Aiuto!... Cristiani! (*Tt*, 141)
>
> [MARIANGELA: *(hearing the door opening runs to take shelter in the small room at the back, cursing).* Help! Help!
> BELLAMÀ: *(grabbing her by the throat).* Shut up or I'll throttle you!...
> MARIANGELA: *(thrashing about, biting his hands).* Somebody help me!]

Even though the course of events develops in the same way in both texts, it is the ending which sets them apart. The narrative concludes with Michelangelo blaming his lover for putting their lives at risk, so the reader does not see Lollo return home once he has locked up his wife. The play, by contrast, reveals how Lollo comes back to the house accompanied by none other than the angry Musarra and Compare Neli. The appearance of these men inevitably makes the ending of the play more gripping for the audience of the performance.

Moreover, what is striking about the last scene is Mariangela's reaction to her husband's return. As she is caught with her lover, she pretends that Bellamà has broken into the house while she was undressing herself:

> MARIANGELA: (*al marito che appare sulla soglia, guardingo, e col fucile spianato*). Aiuto! C'è un uomo! Lì dentro!... Mentre stavo spogliandomi!...
> LOLLO: (*chiamando i Musarra di fuori*). Musarra! Compare Neli!... È qui quello che andate cercando...
>
> TELA. (*Tt*, 141)
>
> [MARIANGELA: *(to her husband who is opening the door, warily, taking aim with his rifle)*. Help! There's a man! Inside!... Just as I was getting undressed!...
> LOLLO: *(calling the Musarras outside)*. Musarra! Compare Neli!... He's here the one you've been looking for...
>
> END.]

The closing scene here resembles the ending in the dramatic adaptations of *Cavalleria rusticana* and *La Lupa*, with each of the murder scenes occurring off-stage. What differentiates the murder in the narrative version of 'La caccia al lupo' from these previous two Sicilian short stories, however, is that Verga does not show how Michelangelo is killed. Whereas the reader of the *novella* is left wondering what will happen to the lovers when Lollo returns, the audience of the play *knows* that Mariangela will exploit her play-acting in order to try to save her life. Throughout the drama Verga has exposed various aspects of Mariangela's personality and it is this very final act which encapsulates the essence of her character. As Marianne Fallon underlines: 'Il suo discorso si modifica per diventare, nel dramma, più pensato, costruito, più distante grazie al suo mascherarsi, che finalmente promette una via d'uscita fuori della trappola' [Her dialogue changes, in the drama, to become more calculated, constructed, and more distant owing to her play-acting, which ultimately promises a way out from the trap].[51]

Although Mariangela's survival is a possibility and not a certainty, she is nonetheless bold enough to protect herself by manipulating the circumstances to her benefit. Mariangela effectively takes advantage of Lollo's rage by inciting him to kill Bellamà, ultimately turning Lollo into a means of obtaining *her* ends. Even though in both versions she has been compared to the lamb in the allegorical triangle, here it is the lamb using the hunter as a means of destroying her potential predator. Essentially, in this triangular relationship, it is no longer the husband who takes revenge on his wife's lover, but the wife who attempts to take vengeance on her lover by manipulating her husband.

Further, Mariangela appears indifferent to the suffering she inflicts on Bellamà. In contrast to Santuzza, Màlia, Lola, and Gnà Pina who are deeply moved by the way in which they have affected the lives of those close to them, Mariangela shows no signs of remorse, thus fitting more neatly in the 'distruttrice' [destroyer] category.[52] As Luperini puts it: 'Nel bozzetto scenico [...] il personaggio, appena abbozzato nel racconto, ha maggior rilievo e ne sono accentuati gli aspetti negativi' [In the dramatic sketch [...] the main character, barely sketched in the narrative, is further developed and her negative aspects are given greater importance].[53]

Natalino Sapegno stresses the apathetic mood of the play:

> [R]ispetto alla *Cavalleria* e alla *Lupa*, troviamo nella *Caccia al lupo* [...] una partecipazione più intensa dello scrittore all'amarezza della vicenda e alla chiusa psicologica dei personaggi, e cioè un più genuino impulso drammatico, meno documentario e più appassionato; ma anche vi si fa più scoperta via via la visione pessimistica e sterile dell'autore, quei suoi modi di distacco fra il sarcastico e il desolato, quella gelida osservazione da cui è aliena ogni fiducia positiva e perfino l'ombra della speranza.[54]
>
> [[C]ompared with *Cavalleria* and the *She-Wolf*, we find in *The Wolf Hunt* [...] the writer's more intense participation in the bitter action and the characters' closed psychology, and, that is to say, a more genuine dramatic impulse, less documentary and more passionate. However, what is increasingly evident is the writer's pessimistic and sterile vision, his detached ways located somewhere between the sarcastic and the desolate, that icy observation to which any sign of faith and even a glimmer of hope is foreign.]

Perhaps it is the cold aspect of the texts which has led Gaetano Ragonese to conclude that 'l'accento del Verga nel rappresentare il tema della vendetta rusticana ha perduto la sua freschezza' [Verga's emphasis in portraying the theme of the rustic vendetta has lost its freshness].[55] This may also account for why it was received less favourably than *Cavalleria rusticana* and *La Lupa*.[56] Essentially, *La caccia al lupo* is a very different 'rustic' play, centring on a very different lead character. What makes Mariangela stand apart from Verga's other characters (regardless of their gender) is how she helps to facilitate the end of the triangular relationship through her ability *to think*. Nanni in *La Lupa*, for instance, ends the triangle in which he is involved through instinct, killing Gnà Pina in a passionate rage, just as Compare Alfio in 'Cavalleria rusticana' throws dust in Turiddu's eyes a result of impulse. Mariangela's attempt at survival, on the other hand, is devised through her thought. She calculates a way out of the trap by purposely putting on a pretence in front of her husband before leaving her lover to perish. In fact, by the time Verga came to write *La caccia al lupo*, it seems as if he had gone beyond portraying the rudimentary nature of human relationships. As Russo has maintained, in this play 'sono intellettualmente tipizzate le passioni del mondo rusticano' [the passions of the rustic world are intellectually typified].[57]

Indeed, this is the first time in Verga's career that both the reader of the *novella* and the audience of the play are presented with a more complex triangular relationship. Unlike in Verga's previous works, all three protagonists in both versions are trying to deceive each other: Lollo's vengeance has been disguised by what appears to be a wolf hunt; Mariangela pretends not to understand the implications of the hunt when in reality she is very much aware of the truth; and her lover seems to have no intention of being faithful to her, particularly on stage where his involvement with other women is revealed.

This element of play-acting within the drama has led many like Paolo Mario Sipala to the conclusion that 'i personaggi sono partecipi di una finzione; recitano due volte, tra loro e per il pubblico. Se non temessimo di scomodare una formula pirandelliana, potremo dire che fanno *Teatro nel teatro*' [the characters are participants in a piece of make-believe: they perform twice, between themselves and for the audience. Were we unafraid of abusing a Pirandellian formula, we could say that they perform a *play-within-a-play*.[58] Several others have associated the characters' play-acting with the theme of the mask. Luperini has claimed that 'i personaggi del triangolo amoroso hanno perso ormai ogni dignità umana, recitano tutti una parte, portano tutti una maschera o si sforzano sino all'ultimo di portarla' [the characters of the love-triangle have by now lost every form of human dignity; they each perform a role, wear a mask, or force themselves to the very last moment to wear one].[59] Equally, in Gino Tellini's words, 'i tre personaggi del classico triangolo si attengono ognuno ad un falso repertorio di gesti e di parole: dietro non è dato intravedere che i segni di una medesima ferina disumanità' [the three characters in the classic triangle abide by a false repertoire of gestures and words: behind which there is nothing to see apart from the traces of a single ferocious inhumanity].[60]

However valid, each observation ignores how Mariangela is the only character with the greatest number of 'masks'. She is exposed as the most talented game-player in the triangle. Although this aspect is conveyed in the story through the role of the narrator, the dramatic version draws attention to the multiple sides of her personality. Mariangela alters her masks from the rhetorical-sounding woman (reminiscent of Santuzza), to the sexual lover (La Lupa), and lastly to the cold avenger. It is her final mask which continues to distinguish her from the other women in Verga's work. Whereas the women analysed thus far are consistent throughout the narrative and theatrical plots (Santa / Santuzza is a jealous woman; Màlia remains 'silent' in both plots; and La Lupa cannot resist Nanni), Mariangela has several personas and callously exploits her last mask in an attempt to ensure her survival. This final mask challenges Malara's view that '[l]'infedeltà della donna [...] è la risposta — giusta o sbagliata che sia — a una condizione femminile sentita come schiavitù' [[t]he woman's infidelity [...] is the response — be it right or wrong — to a feminine condition experienced as slavery],[61] and contradicts Levi's argument:

> [S]i chiami Santuzza o Pina, Lola o Mariangela, è sempre la donna della Sicilia, che striscia, che si fa umile, che si fa schiava dell'uomo, il quale abbia parlato ai suoi sensi, dell'uomo che ella considera come il suo padrone, al quale non sa, non può rinunziare, poichè nelle sue carni ha ancora l'impronta dei suoi baci, e le arde il sangue il ricordo del recente amplesso.[62]

> [[W]hether she is called Santuzza or Pina, Lola or Mariangela, she is always the same Sicilian woman, who creeps around, who humbles herself and enslaves herself to her man; he has spoken to her senses; she considers him to be her master, she does not know how and is not able to relinquish him, because beneath her skin she still has the imprints of his kisses, and the memory of his recent embrace which still burns her blood.]

However, as proposed here, Verga's female stage roles are by no means slaves to their lovers: Santuzza adamantly refuses to be the submissive lover who tolerates his infidelity; Gnà Pina on stage is not the typical she-wolf; and Mariangela knows exactly which strings to pull, ultimately becoming the puppet master of the play who manipulates her marionettes in order to manoeuvre her way out of the trap at the expense of her lover's life, a side of her character which disrupts the view that 'Lollo domina la scena perché padrone della situazione' [Lollo dominates the scene because he is the master of the situation].[63] Moreover, it is not until Verga produces *La caccia al lupo* that he starts to exploit the theatrical genre to reveal a 'new' woman on stage, capable of using her *head* over her heart, and to illuminate two levels of reality on stage: the way characters respond on the surface and their true intentions disguised beneath, a 'meta-theatricality' embodied above all in Mariangela, the most talented 'actress'. Consequently, it would appear that towards the end of his career as a playwright, Verga began to experiment with a different form of drama, which seemed to be treading on the very grounds that would later be developed by his successor.

'Quando si è capito il giuoco' and *Il giuoco delle parti*

'Quando si è capito il giuoco' was initially published in the *Corriere della Sera* on 10 April 1913. The theatrical adaptation, with its original title from the *novella*, was first mentioned by Pirandello in a letter of 22 March 1918 to the actor Ruggero Ruggeri who would later play the lead role: 'Potrò dargliela certamente da leggere qua a Roma in settembre, o anche prima, se Lei volesse. La commedia avrà per titolo: *Quando si è capito il giuoco* e sarà in tre atti' [I could certainly give it to you to read here in Rome in September, or even before, if you want. The play will have as its title: *When the Game is Understood* and it will be in three acts].[64] That same year, on 4 August, Pirandello sent the actor the first draft of the play, adding how he had changed the title, which now focussed on the notion of role playing: 'Le ho cambiato il titolo: invece di *Quando si è capito il giuoco* la chiamerò *Il giuoco delle parti*. Mi sembra più bello e più proprio' [I have changed the title: instead of *When the Game is Understood* I will call it *The Rules of the Game*. It seems to me to be better and more appropriate].[65] The rehearsals started in November, at the Teatro Quirino in Rome, with the assistance of Pirandello. In a letter to his son Stefano on 29 November 1918, Pirandello commented on the actor's 'mirabilissima' [extremely admirable] interpretation and called the play 'il mio più bel lavoro di teatro' [my best theatrical work] (*Mn* II, 120). The play premièred on 6 December 1918 at the Quirino and audiences generally responded well to Ruggeri. A few days later, on 8 December, the *Giornale d'Italia* states: 'Magnifico interprete, e, direi, prezioso *collaboratore* del Pirandello fu ieri sera il Ruggeri, rivelatosi ancora una volta artista sommo' [Last night Ruggeri was a magnificent interpreter and, I would say, a precious *collaborator* of Pirandello, distinguishing himself yet again as a great artist].[66]

Ruggeri interpreted a very different husband compared with the jealous Signor Ponza and Rico Verri. Both versions feature an apparently complaisant husband (Memmo in the short story and Leone Gala in the stage version). In a startling *coup de théâtre*, he foils the attempt of his unfaithful wife (Cristina in the *novella* and Silia in the stage version) to manipulate him into participating in a potentially fatal duel by logically arguing, in a challenge to contemporary notions of social roles, that the defence of her 'honour' should be the responsibility of the man who, in effect, is her 'husband': that is, her lover (Gigi in the narrative and Guido in the stage adaptation).

Silia

One of the major changes which occurs in the passage from 'Quando si è capito il giuoco' to *Il giuoco delle parti* is the development of the lead female character. In the same way as Gnà Pina and Mariangela hardly ever utter a word in their respective narrative plots, Cristina in 'Quando si è capito il giuoco' barely speaks. Instead, the story concentrates almost entirely on the perspective of Memmo. By seeing the events through Memmo's eyes, the reader of the narrative is never given the chance to hear his wife's side of the story. For instance, the sympathetic storyteller simply confirms that Cristina, 'per quante gliene facesse sotto gli occhi, di tutti i colori' [no matter what different kinds of things she got up to, right under his nose] (*Na* III, 710), forced 'povero Memmo' [poor Memmo] (repeated twice, *Na* III, 710) out of their home, and yet it is never explained what exactly she did. As a result, by leaving such questions unanswered, Pirandello prevents the reader from understanding why she would want to separate from her husband and later devise such a violent scheme to end his life.

Whereas the *novella* prioritises the role of Memmo, the play begins with a scene between Silia and Guido, one missing from the narrative, which finally gives the protagonist the chance to have her say. Here, Silia reveals her alienation: 'Fuori, sì! fuori fuori!' [Outside, yes! Outside, outside!] (*Mn* II, 136). Her sense of detachment even causes her to feel separate from her reflection, as she informs Guido: 'Non t'è mai avvenuto di scoprirti improvvisamente in uno specchio, mentre stai vivendo senza pensarti, che la tua stessa immagine ti sembra quella di un estraneo' (*Mn* II, 139) [Have you ever caught yourself in a mirror, at a time when you have been living without thinking about yourself? And it seems that the reflected image belongs to someone else, a stranger (*CP* III, 6)]. What is striking about Silia's dialogue is how it is reminiscent of one of Lamberto Laudisi's key soliloquies in *Così è (se vi pare)*. Speaking to his own mirror image, Pirandello's mouthpiece character states: 'Il guaio è che, come ti vedo io, non ti vedono gli altri! E allora, caro mio, che diventi tu! [...] Un fantasma, caro, un fantasma!' (*Mn* I, 472–73) [The trouble is that other people won't see you as I see you. So what's to become of you, my poor friend [...] For them, you're a ghost, my dear fellow — nothing more but a ghost! (*CP* I, 116–17)]. But whereas Laudisi rationalises about how each person sees a different image in the reflection of a mirror, Silia further develops this relativistic argument by revealing the imprisonment she feels as a result of all the different and changing perceptions of her:

> SILIA: Ma sono, in una carcere!
> GUIDO: E chi ti ci tiene?
> SILIA: Tu... tutti... io stessa... questo mio corpo, quando mi dimentico che è di donna... (*Mn* II, 138)

[SILIA: I am in a prison!
GUIDO: Oh? And who's keeping you there?
SILIA: You, and everyone else! Even my own body, because I can never forget that it's a woman's.] (*CP* III, 5)

Much in the same way as Signora Ponza's silent voice rivals Laudisi in *Così è (se vi pare)*, so do Silia's spoken words. As soon as Silia is given the possibility of articulating her feelings freely, she becomes more critical, similar to Gnà Pina in the stage version of *La Lupa*. However, whereas Gnà Pina reveals herself capable of reflecting upon her actions, Silia shows the capacity to take her reasoning further and to express the frustration experienced by women at the time in a similar situation.

Roberto Alonge has argued that Silia's sense of detachment from her body stems from the fact that she feels trapped by the conditions of her gender:

> Riscontriamo una volta di più l'ideologia tutta e solo macho di Guido, che trova normale che Silia abbia invece a felicitarsi di essere una bella donna, un corpo piacevole, e come tale, quindi, meta dei flussi desideranti dei maschi che la circondano. C'è invece in Silia la capacità di sorpassare tutto questo, di andare al di là del puro fenomeno fisico. La donna è soltanto carne, estensione corporale per il piacere del maschio, e Silia arriva a provare una vera e propria ripugnanza per il proprio corpo.[67]

> [We see once more Guido's completely macho ideology, which considers it normal that Silia should by contrast congratulate herself on being a beautiful woman, an attractive body, and as such, therefore, the object of the desires of the men who surround her. Instead, there is in Silia the ability to go beyond all this, to go beyond the purely physical phenomenon. Woman is mere flesh, a corporeal extension for male pleasure, and Silia therefore begins to develop an outright resentment towards her own body.]

As Alonge illustrates, Silia resents being seen as a mere sexual object of male desire and thereby develops revulsion towards her own body. The emphasis on dialogue in the theatrical version continues to reinforce how trapped Silia feels in her body as well as in her unhappy marriage. In fact, the play was composed years before the legalisation of divorce in Italy, which, after a long campaign, was only passed in 1974, and thus Silia in this dialogue seems to anticipate the kind of problems which will later become crucial among female emancipationists, such as the objectification of women's bodies and the right to an autonomous life. Her sense of incarceration stems from the fact that she lacks independence, a side of her personality which continues to be silenced in the narrative. As suggested by Maggie Günsberg, 'Silia's financial dependency and resulting lack of self-determination mean that she has no power in the relationship with her husband'.[68] Silia's alienation therefore results from the fact that she is 'ricca... padrona di me... libera...' (*Mn* II, 141) [rich... my own mistress... free!] (*CP*, 7) but in effect she is dependent on Leone:

> SILIA: Io vedo sempre lui che me l'ha data, questa libertà, come una cosa da nulla, andandosene a vivere per conto suo, e dopo avermi dimostrato tre anni, che non esiste, questa famosa libertà, perché, comunque possa avvalermene, sarò sempre schiava... (*Mn* II, 141)

> [SILIA: Throwing this precious freedom at me like an old show, and going

off to live by himself — after spending three years proving to me that this wonderful freedom has no real existence. No matter what use I try to make of it, I shall always be his slave!] (*CP* III, 8)

Silia believes that, by paradoxically trapping her through her freedom and even allowing her to take up with a lover, Leone is punishing her for their separation, which she calls his 'vendetta' (*Mn* II, 141) [revenge] (*CP* III, 7). As a result, she cannot enjoy the liberty he has given her because his ghost is ever present. Despite her freedom, he visits her 'ogni sera, per mezz'ora. Ogni sera!' (*Mn* II, 142) [half an hour every evening (*CP* III, 8)] in their apartment, '*bizzarramente addobbato*' (*Mn* II, 135) [*bizarrely decorated*] where even the furniture reminds her of him, details missing from the short story. In desperation, she declares to Guido: 'Io ho l'incubo di quest'uomo' (*Mn* II, 142) [That man haunts me (*CP* III, 8)], 'M'ha paralizzata, quest'uomo' (*Mn* II, 143) [That man has paralised me! (*CP* III, 9)], and, moreover, 'Ah Dio, morisse!' (*Mn* II, 142) [Dear God, I wish he were dead (*CP* III, 8)].

Silia might sound hysterical here, but beneath the superficial exterior lies an acute sense of self. Although Adriano Tilgher has described her as a 'pazza depravata sensuale, istinto bruto e irragionevole' [mad, depraved sensualist, [with a] brute and irrational instinct],[69] he nevertheless classified her among the raisonneurs, such as Moscarda in *Uno, nessuno e centomila* (1926), who are fully aware of their distorted mirror image and the incarceration that their reflection imposes on them, an awareness which male characters like Lori in *Tutto per bene* effectively lacked:

> Se uno specchio gli rimanda la sua immagine, gli sembra quella di un estraneo che si diverta a contraffarne i gesti e le mosse, e (come Silia in *Il giuoco delle parti*, Fulvia in *Come prima, meglio di prima*, Lando Laurentano ne *I vecchi e i giovani*, Vitangelo Moscarda in *Uno, nessuno e centomila*...), stupore e sgomento lo coglie che il suo corpo debba essere proprio fatto così e non altrimenti, con queste e queste particolarità fisiche, e finisce per provarne sdegno e nausea come di una infrangibile prigione.[70]

> [If a mirror reflects his image, it seems as though it is a reflection of a stranger who takes pleasure in mimicking his own gestures and movements, and (like Silia in *The Rules of the Game*, Fulvia in *As Before, Better Than Before*, Lando Laurentanto in *Old and Young*, Vitangelo Moscarda in *One, No One, One Hundred Thousand*...), he is struck by shock and horror that his body should be made in this particular way and not otherwise, with such and such physical peculiarities. As a result, he ends up feeling disdain and nausea for them, as though they were an unbreakable prison.]

Though Silia is associated with 'l'istinto' (*Mn* II, 677) [instinct (*CP* II, 7)] by the director of *Sei personaggi in cerca d'autore*, as the scenes unfold Pirandello continues to develop sides of her character demonstrating she is not *incapable* of rational thought. In fact, the director is not the most enlightened character in the metatheatrical play and therefore his view of Silia can be taken with a pinch of salt. In her opening dialogue with Guido, Pirandello stresses just how aware she is of the oppressive conditions of her gender and therefore it could be argued that she goes to such extreme lengths to free herself from her incarceration because of her awareness of these very conditions.

One of the ways in which Cristina / Silia attempts to free herself from her husband is to perform a number of roles where she is able to manipulate those around her as a means to *her* ends, much in the same way as Mariangela in *La caccia al lupo*. In the *novella*, however, Cristina's play-acting is not developed to the same extent. Without any warning, the narrator simply explains how Memmo is suddenly woken up by her to the news that he has been challenged to a duel. Through this exchange and Cristina's outline of the challenge, the narrator suggests that she has no idea what the duel involves:

> 'Sfidato... non so bene: o sei sfidato o devi sfidare. Non so di queste cose... so che ho qua il biglietto di quel mascalzone. Lavati, vestiti, spicciati, non mi star davanti con codest'aria di mammalucco intronato!' (*Na* III, 711)

> ['You've been challenged to a duel... I really don't know: either you've been challenged or you have to challenge him. I don't know anything about such things... All I know is that I have a note here from that crook. Get washed, get dressed, make it quick, don't just stand there like a dazed idiot!']

She then uses her body to manipulate him into participating in the duel:

> 'Che?' Gli gridò la moglie, avventandoglisi di nuovo addosso, quasi con le mani in faccia. 'Sono stata vigliaccamente, sanguinosamente insultata in casa mia, per causa tua... perché sono rimasta sola, senza difesa, capisci?... Insultata... oltraggiata... Mi hanno messo le mani addosso, capisci? a frugarmi, qua, in petto, capisci? Perché hanno sospettato ch'io fossi...' (*Na* III, 711)

> ['What?' shouted his wife, going for him once more, almost with her hands in his face. 'I have been insulted in a cowardly and brutal manner in my own home, because of you... because I was alone, defenceless, do you see?... Insulted... offended... They put their hands all over my body, see? Molested me, my breasts, see? Because they suspected I was...']

Subsequently the narrator, in free indirect speech, mimics the way in which she informs her husband of the alleged assault. In this description there is nothing to suggest that she has fabricated the scenario other than her hyperbolised account of events. But, by omitting Cristina's motivations at the start of the *novella* and not showing how the assault actually takes place, Pirandello ultimately leaves the reader to decide whether her actions are the result of malice or instinct.

The stage version, on the other hand, fills in the gaps which are left open in the *novella*. First of all, by the time the spectators are led up to the assault, they have already gained an insight into the cause of Silia's rage from the opening scene. Although they cannot condone her scheme to avenge Leone's 'imperdonabile, inqualificabile indifferenza' (*Mn* II, 141) [insufferable, limitless apathy! (*CP* III, 42)], they have nevertheless been placed in the position to understand why a woman with a strong temperament might go to such extreme lengths to end her suffocation. The spectators are then invited to see exactly how Silia pursues her revenge scheme by playing a number of roles. By watching her cleverly manipulate the drunken men, they acknowledge that there is nothing evil or premeditated in her actions. In her childlike manner, she simply sees a way out of her torment and seizes it without considering the consequences. As Alonge has noted: 'Il tentativo di assassinio perde così la gratuità del gesto di pazzia di una donnetta isterica, come poteva essere nella novella, e assurge a cosciente atto di difesa' [The attempted murder loses the gratuity of an act of madness appropriate to a hysterical woman, as the case could have been in the short story, and becomes a conscious act of self-defence].[71]

One of the first roles Silia performs during the assault scene is that of the frigid lover. Before this scene begins, Guido tries to make advances towards her but she shuns him: 'Ti dico di no...' (*Mn* II, 156) [No. I tell you (*CP* III, 20)], 'Ma no... per carità... lasciami...' (*Mn* II, 156) [No, please! Leave me! (*CP* III, 20)], 'Sai che qui non voglio... C'è la donna...' (*Mn* II, 156) [Not in the flat! I shouldn't like the maid to... (*CP* III, 20)]. Immediately after she attracts the attention of the drunken men, she locks Guido away and interprets a very different role, that of a prostitute, a further role not developed in the *novella*. This 'performance' starts as she spontaneously throws an egg shell out of the window and accidentally hits one of the four men who are looking for the prostitute Pepita. Once she has attracted their attention, Pirandello indicates Silia's thoughts in the stage directions, emphasising his own explicit presence and giving the reader of the play a privileged insight: '*Poi, con una luce sinistra negli occhi, come se le fosse balenata una diabolica idea*' (*Mn* II, 157) [*Then a sinister light comes into her eyes, as though a diabolical idea has come into her head* (*CP* III, 21)]. This is not dissimilar to how Verga, in *La caccia al lupo*, states in the stage directions that Mariangela was putting on a pretence. Impersonating Pepita, Silia entices the men to her apartment, sending the housemaid Clara to find help and locking Guido away. She then coaxes Miglioritti to give her their visitor passes and lures them into her scheme by proposing to dance naked for them in the piazza: 'Ma sì! C'è la luna... Non passa nessuno... C'è solo la statua del re a cavallo...' (*Mn* II, 160) [Of course! Why not? It's the ideal place. The moon is shining — there won't be anybody about... just the statue of the king on horseback (*CP* III, 24)].

Following this, Silia attracts the attention of the neighbours by acting the part of the offended wife, the part which Cristina initially performed in the *novella*: 'Aggredita! aggredita in casa, signori! Hanno forzato la porta, mi sono saltati addosso, mi hanno strappato, come lor signori vedono, e insultato in tutti i modi, vigliaccamente!' (*Mn* II, 161) [I've been assaulted! Assaulted in my own home! They forced their way in, knocked me down, and pulled me about, as you can see. They've molested me and insulted me in every possible way, the cowards! (*CP* III, 24)]. Once the neighbours become involved, Miglioriti pleads for forgiveness, as he does in the short story, but she adamantly refuses to accept his apology and the duel is arranged. Soon after, she frees Guido and goes back to playing his lover, but this time more passionately: '*(reclinando la testa indietro, gli solletica coi capelli il volto)* Voglio essere la tua bambina folle' (*Mn* II, 165) [*(leaning her head back and tickling his face with her hair.)* Guido... do you remember calling me a wayward child? *(Seductively)* I want to be your wayward child (*CP* III, 28)], further episodes missing from the narrative.

In witnessing Silia coordinate her scheme to her advantage, the audience continues to gain multiple perspectives of her personality which in essence Guido and Leone lack, both of whom are absent from this key scene. The continuing exposure of all the various sides of Silia's character challenges Silvio D'Amico's viewpoint in *Il teatro dei fantocci* that 'la psicologia di Silvia [sic] rimane in gran parte inesplicata' [Silia's psychology remains for the most part unexplained],[72] as well as Jørn Moestrup's take that '[t]he figure of Silia is not complex enough to make her contradictory actions plausible; we are told how she is supposed to be, but she does not exist like that'.[73] Instead, the changes introduced into the drama support Dorothea Stewens's argument that '[a] livello dei personaggi Silia è solo nel dramma un vero personaggio (nella novella no), e perciò la sua presenza significa già un cambiamento rispetto alla novella' [Silia is only a real character in the play (she is not in the *novella*) and for this reason her very presence heralds a development with respect to the *novella*].[74]

All these many different masks have led Gigi Livio to conclude that 'Silia è dei tre, l'unico personaggio che risulta "umoristica" fin dall'inizio e per tutto lo svolgimento del dramma' [Silia is, out of the three, the only character who is 'humoristic' from the beginning and through the course of the drama].[75] He explains that

> Silia, come la vita (almeno come la vede Pirandello), va verso la sofferenza con un insieme di ribellione e di voluttà; Silia la sofferenza la cerca perché questa risulta un suo modo di essere viva, perché la vita fa male.[76]
>
> [Silia, like life (at least like Pirandello sees it), goes towards suffering with a mixture of rebellion and pleasure; Silia searches for suffering because this is her way of life, because life hurts.]

Further, Franca Angelini has suggested that Silia's varying faces transform the play into 'un dramma metateatrale, di teatro nel teatro' [a metatheatrical drama, a play-within-a-play],[77] and Paolo Puppa has associated Silia's play-acting with 'l'infinita molteplicità di ruoli insita nella donna attrice' [the infinite multiplicity of roles inherent in the role of the actress].[78] Similarly, as Alonge has pointed out:

> Silia dichiara di *essere* Pepita, entra nella pelle della prostituta. In realtà — esattamente come avviene all'attore stanislavskjiano quando si *cala nel personaggio* — anche Silia non può che far ricorso a impulsi e ad accenti che sono *suoi*, e che meglio le permettono di impersonare il personaggio.[79]
>
> [Silia claims *to be* Pepita, she gets into the skin of the prostitute. In reality — exactly as in the case of the Stanislavskian actor, when he *immerses himself in the character* — Silia can only fall back on impulses and accents that belong to *her*, and which better enable her to impersonate the character.]

What is unusual about Silia's different masks is the conflict between her frigidity and sexuality. Although she is portrayed as a provocative woman, the scene starts with her physically rejecting her lover and locking him away. Alonge interprets Silia's frigidity as a refusal to accept the objectification of women. While earlier Alonge had maintained that Silia's detachment from her body was the result of her rejecting patriarchal society, here he suggests that her frigidity represents her rejection of all men:

> La frigidità finisce per assumere in Silia un significato leggermente diverso: è il modo a lei proprio di sottrarsi all'universo maschile tutto piattamente fondato sul valore del piacere, egoisticamente restio all'impegno della generazione.

> Forse c'è una avversione sorda e tenace di Silia *contro tutti gli uomini*, contro Leone che non le ha saputo dare dei figli, e contro l'amante, Guido, che non vuole che usarla per il suo meschino e privato godimento. Negarsi alla dimensione orgasmatica è, per Silia, la sola maniera di rifiutare l'integrazione nel cosmo maschile e maschiloide; è la sua unica possibilità di costruirsi in una *marginalità* che è *diversità*, che è garanzia di una identità differente, financo di una supremazia morale.[80]

> [Silia's frigidity ends up taking on a slightly different meaning: it is her own way of removing herself from the masculine world, wholly and squarely based on the value of pleasure, selfishly reluctant to obey the dictates of her generation. Perhaps it is an unvoiced and determined aversion on the part of Silia *to all men*: to Leone who was unable to give her children, and to her lover, Guido, who only wants to use her for his petty and private enjoyment. Denying the orgasmic dimension is, for Silia, the only way she can avoid being subsumed in the masculine and masculoid universe; it is the only way possible for her to fashion herself in a *marginality* which is *diversity*: a guarantee of a different identity and even of a moral supremacy.]

However, it would seem that during the alleged assault, Silia does not dismiss men in general. She treats the drunken men as her *own* (sexual) objects, cleverly manipulating them as though they were her marionettes by objectifying her own body. The assault scene is thus crucial in revealing how Silia uses her wits to get what she wants, similar to Mariangela in *La caccia al lupo*.

Moreover, whereas most of Verga's women are instinctively attracted to their lovers (perhaps with the exception of Mariangela), Silia consciously uses her sexuality to facilitate her revenge, in the same way as both Tuzza and Mita in *Liolà* purposely seduce Liolà in order to seek vengeance. Firstly, Silia entices the drunken men by pretending to be a prostitute and proposes the idea of dancing naked for them in public. Secondly, she seduces Guido once the duel has been arranged, possibly as a way of distracting him from the implications of her actions. Finally, she tries to manipulate Leone in the second act when she informs him of the attack by employing sexually explicit language. Just as she does in the narrative, Silia intrudes on Leone's 'strana sala' (*Mn* II, 166) [*unusual room* (*CP*, 28)] and declares 'Tu sei sfidato!' (*Mn* II, 172–73) [You've been challenged (*CP* III, 34)], again, unaware of the formalities governing the issuing of the challenge. It is at this point that she uses her body in an attempt to lure him into her scheme, as she does in the *novella*, only this time in a more extended way:

> SILIA: Perché sono stata insultata, oltraggiata, vigliaccamente, sanguinosamente, capisci? in casa mia, per causa tua... perché sola, senza difesa... insultata, oltraggiata... con le mani addosso, qua... a frugarmi... qua, in petto... capisci?... perché hanno sospettato ch'io fossi... ah! (*Si copre il volto con le mani, e rompe in un pianto stridulo, convulso, d'onta, di rabbia*). (*Mn* II, 173–74)

> [SILIA: Because I've been insulted, and outraged and indecently assaulted — in my own home, too! And all through you — because I was alone and defenceless! Grossly insulted! They put their hands on me, and mauled me — *(touching her breast)* here, do you understand? Because they thought I was... Oh! *(She covers her face with her hands and breaks out in harsh, convulsive sobs of shame and rage.)*] (*CP* III, 34–35)

As soon as Leone grows suspicious of Guido's whereabouts during the assault (asking Guido: 'Non t'ha chiamato in difesa, mentr'era aggredita da quei quattro' (*Mn* II, 175) [So she didn't call you to her aid, though she was being attacked by four dangerous drunks! (*CP* III, 36)]), Silia tries to distract him once more by exploiting her body: '*(subito, quasi infantilmente)* — che mi stavano addosso, sai? tutti con le mani addosso... per strapparmi la veste' (*Mn* II, 175) [*(quickly, almost childishly)* — They were crowding round me, all of them, clutching at me and trying to tear my clothes off (*CP* III, 36)].

Significantly, Guido's absence during the assault scene was not received well. In a telegram on 9 May 1919, the lead actor, Ruggeri, reporting on a performance in Milan, sheds light on the audience's unease with the opening act: 'primo atto silenzio' [silence in the first act] (*Mn* II, 126). Likewise, Renato Simoni, in the *Corriere della Sera* on 10 May 1919, confirmed the reaction in Milan to this act: 'Il primo atto non piacque' [The first act was disliked].[81] In *L'idea nazionale*, Silvio D'Amico attributed the problem with this act to 'l'assenza di Guido' [Guido's absence] (*Mn* II, 121). Audiences felt uncomfortable with Guido not rescuing Silia from the drunken men. It would seem that by staying out of harm's way during the assault, he not only looked like a voyeur but an accomplice of the four drunken men. Simoni condemns Guido for not defending her, 'pur non essendo ancora mezzanotte, quando è ancora lecito alle signore trattenere in casa delle visite' [even though it is not yet midnight, when it is still legitimate for women to have visitors in the home].[82]

While contemporary audiences responded harshly to Guido's absence, it could equally well be argued that critics felt uneasy with the characterisation of Silia, the woman who caused his absence. Indeed, the time in which Pirandello staged this play was particularly important with regards to the 'woman question'. As Perry Willson has explained:

> Although legal reforms of considerable importance were passed in the ferment of 1919, they excluded the most important one — the vote. The perception of change was, however, great. Some women had stepped into men's shoes and proved that they could manage. For many men, this was disturbing.[83]

Perhaps, then, what was 'disturbing' about the drama was not just the fact that Guido stayed out of the way, but that Silia forced him to do so, especially given the historical context. Indeed, *Il giuoco delle parti* premièred in the immediate aftermath of the First World War when many women had proved to have been more than capable of being part of the male-dominated workforce, a time which served as a precursor to female suffrage.

Finally, there are two aspects of Silia's personality which continue to be overlooked in the closing of the original *novella* but developed in the play: her growing self-awareness and strength of power over her husband. These aspects are once again silenced in the narrative where Cristina's reaction to the duel is not explored. It is only when her character is transposed to the stage that Pirandello reveals how she reacts to her scheme backfiring. Towards the end of the plot, Silia is brought back on stage as Guido makes his way to the duel and, in contrast to the reader of the short story, the audience of the play is able to witness her response to her flawed plan:

> SILIA: Oh Dio! Intanto... Ah Dio, che cosa... È orribile... Si batte qua sotto? A quelle condizioni... E le ha volute lui!... Ah, è perfetto!... E lui, *indica il marito*, gli dava ragione... Sfido! Non ci si doveva battere lui... Tu sei il demonio! Tu sei il demonio! Dov'è andato a battersi? dov'è andato a battersi? Qua sotto? *Cerca una finestra.* (*Mn* III, 205)

> [SILIA: God, what can be happening to him? It's horrible. Is he down there fighting? Fighting on *those* terms! [...] Oh, it's perfect, perfect! And you let him have his way. I swear he never intended to fight, not he! You are the devil! The devil incarnate! Where are they fighting? Tell me! Down there? In the orchard? *(She looks for a window.)* (*CP* III, 58)]

Further, Silia is also made to face how she is the underlying cause of her husband's brutal revenge. As Leone declares to her and Guido moments before the duel: 'Ah! Avete creduto di giocarvi me, la mia vita? Avete fallito il colpo, cari miei! Io ho giocato voi' (*Mn* III, 202) [You thought you'd have a little game with me, didn't you? You thought between you, you could win my life from me? Well, you've lost the game, my friends. I have outplayed you (*CP* III, 56)]; 'Io vi ho puniti' (*Mn* III, 204) [I have punished you both! (*CP* III, 58)]; and stating directly to Silia: '[L]a mia vergogna sei tu!' (*Mn* III, 205) [You are my dishonour! (*CP* III, 58)]. These extracts confirm that his revenge is specifically aimed at Silia, or as Alonge puts it, his 'grande nemica, la portatrice di pazzia e di sventura, *la donna*, in una parola' [his great enemy, the bringer of madness and misfortune, *the woman* in a word].[84] So while the readers of the *novella* are left to deduce this for themselves, the audience is led deeper into the drama.

According to Livio, although Silia is punished at the end by her husband, equally she punishes him by revealing what truly lies beneath his indifferent exterior:

> [A]l di là della vergogna dell'essere 'squalificato' come duellante indegno si legge ben altro: la vergogna dell'istinto che smaschera la ragione, che la riduce in frantumi, che le fa gettare la maschera di 'indifferenza' per rivelare che 'indifferente' non può essere.[85]

> [[B]eyond the shame of being 'disqualified' as an unworthy duellist lies something very different: the shame of instinct which unmasks reason, which shatters it into fragments, which forces it to jettison the mask of 'indifference' and reveal that it cannot be 'indifferent'.]

Livio concludes that Leone, 'nel proferire la battuta "Io vi ho puniti" si rivela per quello che è, un uomo che soffre, altro che machiavellico organizzatore d'eventi' [in uttering the line 'I have punished you' shows him for what he is, a man who suffers, by no means a Machiavellian organiser of events].[86] Again, it is Silia who removes her husband's mask to reveal his suffering, a sense of suffering which Pirandello extends in the play where the audience is made aware of Leone's response:

> LEONE: *(resta assorto in una cupa gravità, e non si muove). Lunga pausa.*
> FILIPPO: *(entra dall'uscio a sinistra col vassojo della colazione e va a deporlo su la tavola apparecchiata. Poi, nel silenzio tragico, lo chiama con voce cupa)* Oh!

> *Come Leone si volta appena, gl'indica con un gesto incerto la colazione:* È ora.
> *Leone, come se non udisse, non si muove.*
> *Tela.* (*Mn* III, 206)
>
> [LEONE: *(remains motionless, absorbed in deep, serious thought. A long pause.*
> *Philip enters, left, with the breakfast tray and puts it down on the table.*
> PHILIP *(calling in a hollow voice)*: Hey! (*Leone barely turns his head. Philip indicates the*
>   *breakfast with a vague gesture.)* Breakfast time!
> *Leone, as though he has not heard, does not move.*
> *Curtain.*] (*CP* III, 59)

Leone's silent reaction here is juxtaposed with the coldness of Filippo who continues to fulfil his duties despite the fact that Guido has been killed, making the closing more acid than the short story. So while Verga portrays the duel in *Cavalleria rusticana* as a means to re-establish order, Pirandello in *Il giuoco delle parti* reveals the harsh reality caused by such challenges. Whereas Verga's play ends once Compare Alfio has 'triumphed', Pirandello exposes the psychological effects of Leone's empty and shallow victory. As Joseph Farrell has observed: 'This duel thus portrayed is no longer a chivalric rite but an absurdity and an indulgence in unalloyed violence stripped of all aristocratic demeanour.'[87]

Even though Silia is cruelly outwitted by her husband, arguably the logic he uses to destroy her lover is a false one. The chaos in the characters' lives will continue to prevail, perhaps even more so following the fatal outcome, further evidence supporting the notion Leone that Pirandello's male *raisonneurs* (or, as De Castris calls Leone and Baldovino, 'questi superuomini del razionalismo, questi mostri della logica'] [these supermen of reason, these monsters of logic])[88] are self-defeating as they 'attempt to rationalise chaos, to find reasons where there are none', to return to Bini's words.[89] As the aftermath of the death scene here confirms, Leone's logic has led to nowhere. In fact, while Leone has reasoned all through the play, here at the end, he is reduced to silence. His reaction to the death is expressed through his body language, just as Màlia's suffering was expressed through her silence in *In portineria*. Although it is not known what Leone is thinking, his reaction nonetheless closely resembles the responses of Laudisi in *Così è (se vi pare)* and to some extent Lori in *Tutto per bene*. Both Laudisi and Leone at the end of their respective plays make heavy use of words only to be reduced to silence, and, likewise, aspects of Lori's personality are eventually silenced when he realises he has been performing the wrong roles. What is more, each of the men has been silenced by a woman: Signora Ponza reduces Laudisi to verbal silence when he closes *Così è (se vi pare)* with a burst of laughter; the late Silvia silences the roles Lori was unaware of performing in *Tutto per bene*; and here in *Il giuoco delle parti* Leone is silenced at the end by Silia, the true cause of his punishment.[90]

By watching Silia co-ordinate the assault scene, therefore, it is the audience of the play who is made to recognise the sheer lengths she goes to in her attempt to free herself from her unhappy marriage. Silia may be associated with instinct but through the considerable amount of attention Pirandello devotes in the play to showing the extent of her awareness of the oppressive conditions of her gender and illustrating the complexity of her intricately designed 'performances', he manages to show just how strong-minded she actually is, similar to Verga's earlier heroines only with a 'louder' voice. Furthermore, in placing Silia at the heart of Leone's revenge, Pirandello draws attention to the strength of power she has over her logical husband as she reduces his reasoning to silence at the end.

The Un-Sexed Voice

In the passage from narrative to play, Gnà Pina, Mariangela, and Silia appear somewhat 'unsexed' as both Verga and Pirandello emphasise the women's ability to *speak* rather than *seduce*. It is the new voice which the women acquire on stage that enables them to rebel against their portrayals as mere sexual objects driven to madness by their hysteria. While feminist literary critics have associated the sexual madwoman with her lack of self-expression, it would appear that this association can be applied to the characters considered here *only* in their narrative forms. Indeed, the three plays span a crucial time in women's history: *La Lupa* and *La caccia al lupo* premièred when post-unification Italy saw the upheaval caused by Nora's feminist voice in Ibsen's *A Doll's House*, and Pirandello's *Il giuoco delle parti* opened after the First World War, when women were proving themselves more than capable of assuming a role in the instustrial workplace. It is therefore especially revealing that, in amplifying the characters' articulate voices on stage, both Verga and Pirandello should offer these alleged sexual predators a platform of their own during such critical times for women.

Notes to Chapter 5

1. Nicolò Mineo, 'Famiglia e società nel primo Verga', in *Famiglia e società nell'opera di G. Verga: atti del convegno nazionale (Perugia 25–26–27 ottobre 1989)*, ed. by Norberto Cacciaglia, Ada Neiger and Renzo Pavese (Florence: Olschki, 1991), pp. 3–23 (p. 6). For more critical literature, see Siro Ferrone *Il teatro di Verga* (Rome: Bulzoni, 1972), pp. 191–252; Anna Barsotti, *Verga drammaturgo* (Florenza: La Nuova Italia, 1974), pp. 101–38; Giorgio Prosperi, 'Teatro verghiano: due restauri', *Rivista italiana di drammaturgia*, 2 (1976), 3–24; Francesca Malara, *Copioni e drammaturgie di fine ottocento* (Milan: Edizioni universitarie di Lettere Economia Diritto, 2000), pp. 107–60; Anna Barsotti, 'L'indicibile delle passioni nel teatro da Verga a d'Annunzio (*La Lupa* e *La figlia di Iorio*)', *Il Castello di Elsinore*, 22 (2009), 31–61; Giuseppina Scognamiglio, '*La Lupa* di Giovanni Verga dalla novella alla scena', *Rivista di letteratura teatrale*, 1 (2008), 73–91; and Guido Baldi, *Reietti e superuomini in scena* (Naples: Liguori, 2009), pp. 51–82.
2. Elsewhere I have considered the portrayal of La Lupa; see Enza De Francisci, 'Giovanni Verga's "New Woman" in *La Lupa*', *Modern Language Review*, 110.1 (2015), 149–65. However, I did not compare La Lupa towards Matiangela or Pirandello's Silia.
3. See Ferrone, pp. 253–306; Barsotti, *Verga drammaturgo*, pp. 139–48; Malara, pp. 107–60; and Marianne Fallon, '*La caccia al lupo* di Verga fra novella e teatro: letture di una dinamica di riscrittura', *Rassegna europea di letteratura italiana*, 20 (2002), 81–98.
4. I have examined how Verga adapts the role of Mariangela for the stage but without placing her within the typology of the mad sexual adulteress, or comparing her with the feminist voice to emerge in the work of Pirandello; see Enza De Francisci, 'Mariangela in Verga's *La caccia al lupo*: From Page to Stage', *Between: Rivista dell'Associazione del Teoria e Storia Comparata della Letteratura*, 2.4 (2012).
5. Roberto Alonge has written extensively on this work. See Roberto Alonge, '*Il giuoco delle parti*, Pirandello dalla narrativa al teatro', *Comunità*, 22, 153 (July-August 1968), 113–21; Roberto Alonge, 'Madri, puttane, schiave sessuali e uomini soli', in *Studi pirandelliani: dal testo al sottotesto*,

ed. by Roberto Alonge et al. (Bologna: Pitagora, 1986), pp. 91–110; Roberto Alonge, '*Il giuoco delle parti*, atto primo: un atto tabù', in *Pirandello fra penombre e porte socchiuse: la tradizione scenica del 'Giuoco delle parti'*, essays by Roberto Alonge et al. (Turin: Rosenberg & Sellier, 1991), pp. 7–60; Roberto Alonge, *Madri, baldracche, amanti: la figura femminile nel teatro di Pirandello* (Milan: Costa & Nolan, 1997); and Roberto Alonge, *Pirandello tra realismo e mistificazione* (Rome: Bonanno, 2009).
6. In a previous article, I have examined the role of Silia; see Enza De Francisci, 'The Female Voice: From "Quando si è capito il giuoco" to *Il giuoco delle parti*', *Pirandello Studies*, 33 (2013), 79–90. This article, however, does not consider how the character fits in with the context of the adulteress when compared with the women in Verga's works.
7. See Katharine Mitchell, 'Neera's Refiguing of Hysteria as *nervosismo* in *Teresa* and *L'indomani*', *Rethinking Neera. Supplement to The Italianist*, ed. by Katherine Mitchell and Catherine Ramsay-Portolano, 30 (2010), 101–22. See also Katharine Mitchell, *Italian Women Writers: Gender and Everyday Life in Fiction and Journalism, 1870–1910* (Toronto: Toronto University Press, 2014).
8. Sandra M. Gilbert and Susan Gubar, *The Madwoman in the Attic: The Woman Writer and the Nineteenth-Century Literary Imagination*, 2nd edn (New Haven and London: Yale University Press, 2000), p. 59.
9. This duality has also come to light in Matilde Serao's narrative prose; see Ursula Fanning, 'Angel vs. Monster: Serao's Use of the Female Double', *The Italianist*, 7.1 (1987), 63–87. See also Ursula Fanning, *Gender Meets Genre: Women as Subject in the Fictional Universe of Matilde Serao* (Dublin: Irish Academic Press, 2002).
10. Gilbert and Gubar, p. 463.
11. Ibid., p. 77.
12. Lizbeth Goodman, Helen Small and Mary Jacobus, 'Madwomen and Attics: Themes and Issues in Women's Fiction', in *Literature and Gender*, ed. by Lizabeth Goodman (New York: Routledge, 1996), pp. 109–44 (p. 116).
13. Mary Elizabeth Coleridge, *Selected Poems of Mary Elizabeth Coleridge*, selected and ed. by Simon Avery (Exeter: Shearsman Books, 2010), p. 33.
14. Gilbert and Gubar, p. 89.
15. Phyllis Chesler, *Women and Madness* (London: Allen Lane, 1974), p. 14.
16. David Forgacs, *Italy's Margins: Social Exclusion and Nation Formation since 1861* (Cambridge: Cambridge University Press, 2014), p. 227.
17. Giuliana Morandini, *… E allora mi hanno rinchiusa: testimonianze dal manicomio femminile*, 2nd edn (Milan: Bompiani, 1977).
18. Gilbert and Gubar, p. 59.
19. Ugo Ojetti, *Alla scoperta dei letterati*, postface by Nicola Merola (Milan: Fratelli Dumolard, 1895), p. 70.
20. See Gianni Oliva, *La scena del vero: letteratura e teatro da Verga a Pirandello* (Rome: Bulzoni, 1992), pp. 29–30.
21. See Matteo Sansone, 'Verga, Puccini and La Lupa', *Italian Studies*, 44 (1989), 63–76.
22. Now in Luigi Capuana, *Studi sulla letteratura contemporanea*, ed. by Paola Azzolini (Naples: Liguori, 1988), pp. 75–76.
23. Quoted in Giovanni Verga, *Le novelle*, ed. by Gino Tellini, p. 123.
24. Carlo Alberto Madrignani, *Effetto Sicilia: genesi del romanzo moderno* (Macerata: Quodlibet Studio, 2007), p. 67. For more on Verga's portrayal of motherhood, see Ada Neiger, 'La maternità trasgressiva nell'opera verghiana', in *Famiglia e società nell'opera di G. Verga*, pp. 163–73.
25. Ferrone, p. 238.
26. Ibid., p. 239.
27. Prosperi, p. 19.
28. For more on the use of this proverb, see Giovanni Cecchetti, *Il Verga maggiore: sette studi* (Florence: La nuova Italia, 1968), pp. 43–44; and Anna Laura Lepschy, *Narrativa e teatro fra due secoli: Verga, Invernizio, Svevo, Pirandello* (Florence: Leo S. Olschki, 1984), p. 29, n. 2.
29. See Ojetti, p. 66.
30. Natale Tedesco, *Il cielo di carta: teatro siciliano da Verga a Joppolo* (Palermo: S. F. Flaccovio editore, 1989), p. 46.

31. Susan Amatangelo, *Figuring Women: A Thematic Study of Giovanni Verga's Female Characters* (Massachusetts: Rosemary Publishing & Printing Corp, 2004), p. 73.
32. Similarly, in 'L'amante di Gramigna' the narrator does not go into detail about Peppa's sexual relationship with Gramigna but nevertheless explicitly mentions that the two have become lovers by referring to Gramigna as Peppa's 'amante' [lover] (Tn I, 196).
33. Giovanni Pozza, *Cronache teatrali di Giovanni Pozza (1886–1913)*, ed. by Gian Antonio Cibotto (Vicenza: Neri Pozza editore, 1971), p. 230.
34. Quoted in Tedesco, p. 36.
35. Ibid., p. 37. For more critical reviews, see Ferrone, pp. 195–96.
36. Ferrone, p. 202.
37. Gaetano Mariani, 'Giovanni Verga', in *Letteratura italiana: i maggiori*, ed. by Carlo Marzorati, 2 vols (Milan: Marzorati, 1956), II, pp. 1203–74 (p. 1252).
38. Barsotti, *Verga drammaturgo*, p. 107.
39. Romano Luperini, *L'orgoglio e la disperata rassegnazione: natura e società, maschera e realtà nell'ultimo Verga* (Rome: Savelli, 1974), p. 121.
40. Luigi Russo, *Giovanni Verga* (Rome: Laterza, 1995), p. 95.
41. Ibid., p. 95.
42. Malara, p. 128.
43. Mineo, p. 6.
44. See Paolo Mario Sipala, 'Il lupo e la volpe', in *Giovanni Verga e il teatro: atti del convegno Catania, 13–15 aprile, Teatro Stabile di Catania* (Catania: Assessorato regionale ai beni culturali e P. I, 1986), pp. 37–45.
45. See the Appendix in Ferrone, p. 310.
46. Giovanni Verga, *Lettere a Dina*, ed. by Gino Raya, 1st edn (Rome: Ciranna, 1962), pp. 83–84.
47. Quoted in Giulio Cattaneo, *Giovanni Verga* (Turin: UTET, 1963), p. 302.
48. This work has been labelled an apologue (a moral fable especially with animals as characters) in Mario Apollonio, *Storia del teatro italiano*, 2 vols (Milan: Rizzoli, 2003), II, p. 714.
49. Cesare Levi, 'Il teatro di Giovanni Verga', *Nuova Antologia di lettere, scienze ed arti*, 6th series (July-August 1920), 141–47 (p. 146).
50. Barsotti, *Verga drammaturgo*, p. 140.
51. Fallon, p. 93.
52. Mineo, p. 6.
53. Luperini, p. 117.
54. Natale Sapegno, *Ritratto di Manzoni e altri saggi* (Bari: Laterza, 1961), p. 275.
55. Gaetano Ragonese, *Interpretazione del Verga: saggi e ricerche*, 2nd edn (Rome: Bulzoni, 1977), p. 198.
56. For more reviews, see Ferrone, pp. 280–81.
57. Russo, p. 190.
58. Sipala, p. 45.
59. Luperini, p. 115.
60. Quoted in Verga, *Le novelle*, p. 488.
61. Malara, p. 145.
62. Levi, p. 143.
63. Gianni Oliva, *La scena del vero: letteratura e teatro da Verga a Pirandello* (Rome: Bulzoni, 1992), p. 36.
64. Luigi Pirandello, *Carteggio Pirandello — Ruggeri: appunti per uno studio del rapporto fra autore e interprete*, ed. by Leonardo Bragaglia (Fano: Biblioteca comunale federiciana, 1987), p. 26.
65. Ibid., p. 27.
66. Ibid., p. 28.
67. Alonge, *Madri, baldracche, amanti*, p. 47.
68. Maggie Günsberg, *Patriarchal Representations: Gender and Discourse in Pirandello's Theatre* (Oxford: Berg, 1994), p. 130.
69. Adriano Tilgher, *Studi sul teatro contemporaneo*, 3rd edn (Rome: Libreria di scienze e lettere, 1928), p. 222.

70. Ibid, p. 197.
71. Alonge, 'Il giuoco delle parti, Pirandello dalla narrativa al teatro', p. 117.
72. Silvio D'Amico, *Il teatro dei fantocci* (Florence: Vallecchi, 1920), p. 99.
73. Jørn Moestrup, *The Structural Patterns of Pirandello's Work*, Études romanes de l'Université d'Odense, 2 (Odense: Odense University Press, 1972), p. 166.
74. Dorothea Stewens, *Pirandello, scrittura e scena* (Agrigento: Centro Nazionale Studi Pirandelliani, 1983), p. 44.
75. Gigi Livio, 'Il giuoco delle parti e il grottesco', *Il Castello di Elsinore*, 1 (1988), 49–68 (p. 64).
76. Ibid., p. 64.
77. Franca Angelini, 'Il teatro del Novecento. Dal grottesco a Dario Fo', in *La Letteratura italiana: storia e testi*, ed. by Carlo Muscetta, 9 vols (Bari: Laterza, 1976), IX, *Il Novecento: dal decadentismo alla crisi dei modelli*, pp. 355–441 (p. 397).
78. Paolo Puppa, 'Prefazione', in Luigi Pirandello, *Così è (se vi pare), Il giuoco delle parti, Come tu mi vuoi* (Milan: Garzanti, 1995), pp. lvi-lxxii (p. lxvi).
79. Alonge, *Madri, baldracche, amanti*, p. 50.
80. Ibid., p. 48.
81. Quoted in Alonge, *Pirandello fra penombre e porte socchiuse*, p. 8.
82. Ibid., p. 9.
83. Perry Willson, *Women in Twentieth-Century Italy* (Basingstoke, Palgrave Macmillan, 2010), p. 61.
84. Alonge, *Studi pirandelliani*, p. 92.
85. Livio, p. 67.
86. Ibid., p. 67.
87. Joseph Farrell, 'The Duel and the Code of Honour for Pirandello', *Pirandello Studies*, 28 (2008), 100–10 (p. 102).
88. Arcangelo Leone De Castris, *Storia di Pirandello* (Bari: Laterza, 1971), p. 155.
89. Daniela Bini, 'Enacting the Dissolution of the Self: Woman as One, No One, and One Hundred Thousand', in *Luigi Pirandello: Contemporary Perspectives*, ed. by Gian-Paolo Biasin and Manuela Gieri (Toronto: University of Toronto, 1999), pp. 163–88 (p. 166).
90. For more on the portrayal of Leone, see Enza De Francisci, 'A Different Leone in Il giuoco delle parti', *The Journal of The Pirandello Society of America*, 26 (2013), 33–48.

CONCLUSION

Visibility and Voice

Central to this book has been an investigation into the emergence of newly vocalised female figures in Verga's and Pirandello's theatre translations against the background of debates on women and the 'donna nuova'. New parameters can now be set in terms of the *questione della donna*. First of all, just as many heroines at the end of the nineteenth century were being placed centre stage throughout the peninsula in both opera and theatre, at a time when women were beginning to gain a political voice of their own, the female characters considered here also acquire a voice when transposed to the stage. In so doing, the characters reveal themselves as women who are able to articulate their thoughts, as well as to reflect on their actions, and it is their capacity for articulation which enables them to break away from their traditional identification with emotion. Though the texts analysed here remain male-authored, the process they undergo in the shift from narrative to play both envoices and empowers the characters, transforming them into heretofore unseen 'new' women stage roles whose antecedent can be found in Ibsen's *A Doll's House*.

As the foregoing analysis has demonstrated, the female characters on stage predominantly rebel against three popular images of women typically found in both male- and female-authored works: the innocent persecuted heroine, the silent obedient wife, and the mad sexual adulteress. Chapter 3 has highlighted how Santuzza in *Cavalleria rusticana* and Mommina in *Questa sera si recita a soggetto* are far from being two damsels in distress: Santuzza refuses to tolerate the infidelity of her lover and Mommina defies her husband as she performs the operas he has always forbidden. Chapter 4 has shown how, despite the verbal silences of Màlia in *In portineria*, Signora Ponza in *Così è (se vi pare)* and the late Silvia in *Tutto per bene*, they nevertheless have strong silent voices, like the classical Muse and Siren.[1] Lastly, Chapter 5 has illustrated that, while 'mad' sexual desire in the works of nineteenth-century female authors have been intrinsically linked to their lack of self-expression by feminist critics, the development of the women's speech in *La Lupa*, *La caccia al lupo* and *Il giuoco delle parti* enables the heroines to reveal the depth of their personalities and thus to distance themselves from their typical representation as seductress.

Hence, though Verga and Pirandello cannot be considered feminist authors, with previous scholarship asserting that 'non c'è posto per l'autonomia femminile' [there is no space for female autonomy] in the work of Verga,[2] and that the representation of gender relations in Pirandello is 'patriarchal in orientation',[3] there is nonetheless a curious exchange between the Sicilian writers and feminist critical thought. If, according to Gayle Austin, a 'feminist approach to anything means paying attention to women' by 'making some "invisible" mechanisms visible',[4] then, as the volume has shown, the two authors *do* pay attention to women and make women's voices heard when transposing their narratives for the stage, albeit with a silent voice. Consequently, while readers are made to identify with the traditional male subject and thus 'taught to think as men',[5] a viewpoint which rings true in terms of the short stories analysed here, what is noteworthy is that, when adapted for the theatre, the stage versions invert this viewpoint as the *female* subject takes centre stage, owing initially to the influence of Duse and later Abba.

By emphasising the female perspective on stage, the two authors inevitably tread on ground similar to that explored by the Italian women writers of the turn of the twentieth century. Although Verga and Pirandello had different concerns from contemporary female writers, both nevertheless show a strong interest in exploring the role of women in *fin-de-siècle* society, in particular the tension between the radical 'new' woman and the conservative New Italy. Each of the women considered here attempts to overcome barriers and push the boundaries existing within patriarchal society predominantly by rebelling against their traditional social roles. Even two of the most seemingly subordinated characters strive to rise above their repression: Màlia attempts to release her concealed desire for a man formerly involved with her sister Gilda, and Mommina resists her husband's efforts to suppress her passion for the opera, not quite the 'estrema vittima' [extreme victim].[6]

Similarly to how many Italian and English nineteenth-century women writers — transmitted to Italy via early French intermediary translations — composed their narratives in the first person to express their heroine's thoughts, the two authors in question are also keen to immerse themselves in their characters' psyche. Both thus reveal a strong sense of identification with their female characters, rooted, perhaps, in the same kind of empathy that Flaubert felt for his heroine when he notoriously declared: 'Madame Bovary c'est moi.' This empathetic side in Verga can be traced above all in the narratives where he employs free indirect speech in order to see the action through his characters' eyes and express their emotions in their own words. In fact, despite claiming to be impartial in his work, he is by no means dispassionate. Though disguised amongst a variety of narrative voices, Verga's own sympathetic voice does indeed emerge. Affectionate terms such as 'poveretta' [poor thing] or 'povera madre' [poor mother] reveal the artful presence of 'la mano dell'artista' (*Tn* I, 192) [the hand of the artist (*CROS*, p. 94)]. As for Pirandello, though his intellectual approach may have caused him to be considered a somewhat clinical writer, he never loses sight of the emotional. Silia's feminist speech in *Il giuoco delle parti*, for instance, sheds light on Pirandello's acute awareness of the restrictive condition of the female gender, in much the same way as Ibsen recognised the difficulties women experienced in being deprived of the right to a legal and political voice.

One of the concerns of the female authors of the 1880s was to break traditional stereotypes of women writers, contesting the common view that they were portraying themselves in their literary works. Chapter 5 showed how writers such as the Brontë sisters and Shelley employed the angel-monster dichotomy to avoid criticism and censorship. As male authors, Verga and Pirandello inevitably did not have to deal with such prejudices. Instead, Pirandello, in particular, fought hard against the preconception that female performers could not separate themselves from their art, perhaps as a result of the influence of Abba. In '"Leonora, addio!"' and *Questa sera si recita a soggetto*, Pirandello is committed to opposing the belief that on stage 'actresses merely *play themselves*'.[7] Pirandello takes this perception one step further in the dramatic version by not only drawing attention to the dangers it causes, but also by employing this *backward-looking* perspective to take it into the *forward-looking* dimensions of the meta-theatre: choosing to personify the ideal relationship between art and reality in a *female* actor — a choice he later expands through the portrayal of Donata Genzi in *Trovarsi*. The moment the lead actress becomes her character as she falls to the ground, she embodies the very epitome of the ideal fusion between fiction and non-fiction: a fusion which he had initially witnessed in Duse and Abba.

Given the affinities between feminist thought and the aforementioned women writers, could Verga have been influenced by the emerging debates about the 'donna nuova' when creating his 'new' women on stage? Admittedly, Verga's heroines do not encompass the key characteristics of Nora and later Aleramo's heroine who both abandon their children. Yet it is intriguing that at around the same time as Nora was making her entrance onto the late nineteenth-century stage, while Italy's early emancipationists and contemporary female writers were refashioning their sense of 'io' [self],[8] Verga, inspired by the 'new' woman actress Duse, should also be refashioning his female characters for the stage. Instead of creating his characters *ab ovo*, Verga transposed his roles from the narrative genre into the theatrical, and it is the new voice in his stage adaptations which enables his female characters to express their new sense of self.

What is more, Verga's 'new' women had never before been placed on the Italian national stage, arguably becoming home-grown versions of Ibsen's Scandinavian heroine. The first woman Verga sets centre stage is the rebellious Santuzza in *Cavalleria rusticana* who, together with Nora, refuses to sit pretty and do as she is told. Following this non-conformist woman is the silent Màlia in *In portineria*. Despite her physical disability and apparent fragility, Màlia is portrayed as a woman with a deep and complex psychology, not the mere 'canarino' imprisoned by her illness. Shortly after Duse's interpretation of Nora in 1891, Verga staged the most provocative women to emerge from his theatre: Gnà Pina in *La Lupa* and Mariangela in *La caccia al lupo*. These two women explicitly reject unwritten rules governing female sexuality in patriarchal and Catholic Sicily, ironically through their 'unsexed' portrayals in the plays, by putting up a strong fight. In the case of Gnà Pina, it was suggested that the additional words included in the script throw a more compassionate light on the character, challenging the accepted scholarly view that the women in Verga can be classified into two main groups: the 'madre / distruttrice' [mother / destroyer].[9]

The evolution of Verga's new female stage roles thus illuminates a different side to the author's contribution to the Italian theatrical tradition. Indeed, a new perspective has surfaced here in contrast to the views maintained by critics, including Luigi Russo (a fond admirer of Verga) who has concluded that '[i]l Verga, in fondo, non è scrittore da teatro' [Verga, fundamentally, is not a playwright];[10] Paolo Mario Sipala who has forcefully stated that 'i suoi critici sono pressocché unanimi nel sancire l'inferiorità dei risultati del suo teatro, rispetto alla vena narrativa' [his critics are more or less unanimous in confirming the inferiority of his theatrical works, compared with his narrative creativity];[11] and Sicilian author Leonardo Sciascia who stressed that '*Cavalleria rusticana* e *La Lupa* preferiremmo Verga non le avesse mai trasportate sulle scene' [[w]e would have preferred Verga never to have adapted *Cavalleria rusticana* and *La Lupa* for the stage].[12] In fact, while mid-nineteenth century Italy might not have been generating the same calibre of plays as the French tradition, Verga's theatrical production flourished during this very period: *Cavalleria rusticana* gained phenomenal success at the time of its première owing predominantly to Duse's interpretation of Santuzza; *In portineria* arguably anticipated what would later become the theatre of silence, owing once again to Duse's interpretation of Màlia;[13] Gnà Pina was one of Italy's most sexually liberated women on stage; and Mariangela's performances in *La caccia al lupo* turns the drama into a kind of meta-theatrical play, veering towards grounds which Pirandello would later develop to make significant innovations in the theatre, above all in *Questa sera si recita a soggetto*.

Moreover, the development of Verga's new female stage roles reinforced the centrality of Duse in his theatre. Verga's theatre essentially belonged to an era which placed importance on the actor, and Duse proved that, if performed with the kind of empathy that she shared with her roles, his plays could enable audiences to identify with the women she interpreted. Indeed, both Verga and Duse were united in their naturalistic approach to art. Just as Verga aimed to see the characters' drama through their eyes and convey their feelings in their own words, here was an actress who did precisely that, only this time through her acting. Significantly, Pirandello, in his tribute to Duse in *The Century Magazine*, was dismayed at how the actress's 'real tragedy has been this, that her age did not succeed in supplying her with her author',[14] but to judge from the powerful effect she had on Verga's theatre, perhaps she did potentially find her author in the *verista* writer, however short their collaboration.

So to what extent was the treatment of women in Verga and Pirandello different from that of their contemporary *male* authors in the late nineteenth century? As Ann Caesar points out:

> As distinct from many nineteenth-century writers such as Hawthorne or Tolstoy, Flaubert or Fontane, he [Pirandello] is not interested in a psychological study of the figure of the adulteress herself (even in *L'Esclusa*, an early novel he wrote in 1893, but which was published *a puntate* in 1901, the actual act of adultery comes at the very end of the novel) but in the potential it gives him to explore yet another mutation in family life.[15]

Whereas writers such as Flaubert were largely concerned with developing the emotional and psychological reasons which led to their heroines' infidelity, the two authors, especially Pirandello, go beyond this typical portrayal of adultery. Traditionally, female characters have been essential if the writer is concerned with exploring topics such as romantic or sexual love, but what is unique about Verga and Pirandello is how each of the narratives and plays analysed here is not based on a *love story* and yet the women characters remain crucial to the action.

With regard to Verga, he is predominantly interested in investigating how Sicilian country women were caught up in their own version of the 'survival of the fittest'. Both readers and audiences gain a strong sense of the kind of struggle Sicily faced shortly after political unification, at a time when the island, to some extent, governed itself. Although Verga shows how the men in his fiction are left to create their own sense of justice, equally the women are also left to fight their own battles, unafraid to extend their conventional social roles still further. Santa / Santuzza protects herself by refusing to tolerate her lover's infidelity. Despite the alienation and persecution which her sexual deviance causes her, Gnà Pina reveals herself to be bold enough to break the unwritten rules governing women's sexuality, and Mariangela attempts to save herself through the shrewd performances she puts on in the play. Interestingly, what distinguishes Màlia from the rest of Verga's women is how she fights an internal battle: she is not struggling for existence like the Sicilian women, or attempting to climb the social ladder like her ambitious sister, she is struggling against herself — preventing herself from revealing her repressed desire for Carlini.

As for Pirandello, he uses the dramatic form to develop the human consequences inherent in his oeuvre. In the same way as the *umorista* deconstructs what is portrayed on the surface so as to reveal what is concealed beneath, 'egli *scompone il carattere nei suoi elementi*' [he *disassembles* the characteristics of the individual into its elemental parts] (*Spsv*, p. 158), audiences of his plays are led to delve deeper than the readers of his short stories, in order to see beyond the superficial exterior. Indeed, Pirandello employs the theatre to explore the depths of his characters' inner drama, stripping away even further 'ogni finzione ideale' [every ideal fiction] (*Spsv*, p. 146) so that he can reveal his characters' *naked masks*. Significantly, once all the different masks are effectively peeled off and we reach the heart of his works, what we find is the ever-present role of the woman. What affects Verri's previously disturbed mind in '"Leonora, addio!"' and *Questa sera si recita a soggetto* is the 'passive' Mommina. Beneath the drama in 'La Signora Frola e il Signor Ponza, suo genero' and *Così è (se vi pare)* lies the inexplicable identity of Signora Ponza. The person who places a metaphorical mirror in front of Lori in *Tutto per bene* is Silvia. And the main cause of the duel at the end of 'Quando si è capito il giuoco' and *Il giuoco delle parti* is Cristina / Silia.

How, then, does this book add to our understanding of the way in which Pirandello spans the transition from *verismo* to *umorismo*? If it is Pirandello's *umorismo* which mainly causes his divergence from his predecessor, we can also conclude that his representation of women is one of the key factors which contribute to this move, particularly in his theatre where he is able to develop the heroines' characterisations as well as the impact they have on those close to them. In fact, what is most striking about Pirandello's theories, which constitute a challenge to *verismo*, is how each is based on a woman: the fine line between illusion and reality (embodied in Signora Ponza) and between fiction and non-fiction (fused in Mommina and the *prima attrice*); the relativity of truth (personified in Signora Ponza); and the multiplicity of these constantly changing 'truths' (crystallised in the 'performers' Silia and Silvia).

By revealing the evolution of the female voice in Pirandello, and the added enrichment of this voice as a result of its transposition to the dramatic genre, this volume illuminates just how increasingly intellectual his dramatic approach became. Not only does his treatment of women become more complex on stage but Pirandello begins to use the theatre to expand on the ideas which he initially sketches in the *novelle*. In *Così è (se vi pare)*, he adapts the structure of the *novella* by introducing the physical presence of Signora Ponza in order to enhance the mystery of her identity and to personify what Daniela Bini calls 'the defeat of logical discourse'.[16] In *Tutto per bene*, what makes the portrait of Silvia all the more striking in the play is her physical absence. In *Il giuoco delle parti*, not only does the reliance on dialogue give Silia the freedom to express her suffering, but it also enables Leone to elaborate on his reasoning and to reveal his secret feelings for his wife. Perhaps the best example of how Pirandello incorporates one of his earliest Sicilian *novelle* into one of the most modernist concepts to emerge from his oeuvre is *Questa sera si recita a soggetto* which brings to light the meta-theatre, exemplified by the fusion between Mommina and the lead actress.

Besides providing an indication of how Pirandello exploits the theatre in order to go one step further than he does in the narrative, this volume has also shown how Pirandello's drama in no way eclipses his *novelle* in terms of artistic achievement. In fact, without the narrative springboards from which the majority of his plays emerge, his dramatic works might never have developed in the way they did, strengthening the notion that in Pirandello 'il narratore e il commediografo coesistono' [the narrator and playwright co-exist].[17] In these four stories alone, he alters his narrative technique, from the meta-literary tale '"Leonora, addio!"' to the more introspective 'Tutto per bene', to the intellectual mystery in 'La Signora Frola e il Signor Ponza, suo genero', and finally to the rapid 'Quando si è capito il giuoco'.

To conclude, just as feminist critical literature seeks 'to make women visible, to find their voice, to recover the works that the dominant history suppressed' and consequently 'to create new ways to read a play, to view a production and to deconstruct the canon of dramatic criticism',[18] I have sought to uncover the visibility and the (silent) voices of the women which take centre stage as soon as the two authors shift their narratives to the dramatic genre. Further, my book has drawn attention to the 'real' women who are instrumental in the passage from page to stage. Without the presence of leading actresses, above all Duse, early characters like Nora might not have able to make their voices heard in auditoriums around the world. These voices would eventually give rise to many later feminist roles in a variety of works by both male and female writers, including Aleramo who epitomised 'donne nuove' debates with her *Una donna*. Indeed, just as Aleramo admitted in a diary entry that without the influence of Nora, she might not have become the 'new' woman she came to represent, who knows how Verga's and later Pirandello's newly vocalised female figures would have developed, had it not been for what Aleramo called Nora's 'voce "ottocentesca"'.[19]

Notes to the Conclusion

1. See Adriana Cavarero, *For More Than One Voice: Towards a Philosophy of Vocal Expression*, trans. with an intro. by Paul A. Kottman (Stanford: Stanford University Press, 2005).
2. Carlo Alberto Madrignani, *Effetto Sicilia* (Rome: Grafica editrice romana, 2007), p. 69.
3. Maggie Günsberg, *Patriarchal Representations: Gender and Discourse in Pirandello's Theatre* (Oxford: Berg, 1994), p. 192.
4. Gayle Austin, *Feminist Theory for Dramatic Criticism* (Michigan: University of Michigan Press, 1990), p. 1.
5. Judith Fetterley, *The Resisting Reader: A Feminist Approach to American Fiction* (Bloomington and London: Indiana University Press, 1978), p. xx.
6. Umberto Mariani, *La donna in Pirandello: l'estrema vittima* (Caltanisetta-Rome: Salvatore Sciascia Editore, 2012), p. 139.
7. Lesley Ferris, *Acting Women: Images of Women in Theatre* (Basingstoke: Macmillan, 1990), p. xi.
8. Paola Lombroso, *Caratteri della femminilità* (Turin: F.lli Bocca, 1909), p. ix.
9. Nicolò Mineo, 'Famiglia e società nel primo Verga', in *Famiglia e società nell'opera di G. Verga: atti del convegno nazionale (Perugia 25–26–27 ottobre 1989)*, ed. by Norberto Cacciaglia, Ada Neiger and Renzo Pavese (Florence: Olschki, 1991), pp. 3–23 (p. 6).
10. Luigi Russo, *Giovanni Verga* (Rome: Laterza, 1995), p. 200.
11. Paolo Mario Sipala, 'Due note sul teatro di Verga', *Misure critiche*, 15.55–56 (1985), 43–55 (p. 51).
12. Leonardo Sciascia, *Pirandello e il pirandellismo: con lettere inedite di Pirandello a Tilgher* (Palermo: Cappugli e figli, 1953), pp. 59–60.
13. Enza De Francisci, 'Verga and Duse Transposing Silence in "Il canarino del n. 15" and *In portineria*: A prelude to Symbolism?', *The Italianist*, 34.1 (2014), 73–87.
14. Luigi Pirandello, 'Eleonora Duse: Actress Supreme', *The Century Magazine*, June 1924, pp. 244–51 (p. 249).
15. Ann Caesar, 'The Branding of Women: Family, Theatre and Female Identity in Pirandello', *Italian Studies*, 45 (1990), 48–63 (p. 49).
16. Daniela Bini, *Luigi Pirandello: Contemporary Perspectives* (Toronto: University of Toronto, 1999), p. 168.
17. Nino De Bella, *Narrativa e teatro nell'arte di Luigi Pirandello* (Messina-Florence: G. D'Anna, 1962), p. 120.
18. Sue-Ellen Case, *Feminism and Theatre* (London: Macmillan, 1988), p. 113.
19. Sibilla Aleramo, *Un amore insolito: diario1940–1944*, ed. by Alba Morino (Milan: Feltrinelli, 1979), p. 14.

BIBLIOGRAPHY

Primary Sources

VERGA, GIOVANNI, *Carteggio Verga-Capuana*, ed. by Gino Raya (Rome: Edizioni dell'Ateneo, 1984)
—— *Cavalleria rusticana and Other Stories*, trans. with an intro. by G. H. McWilliam (Harmondsworth: Penguin, 1999)
—— *Dal mio al tuo* (Milan: Treves, 1906)
—— *Drammi intimi*, ed. by Gabriella Alfieri (Florence: Le Monnier, 1987 [1884])
—— *Lettere a Dina*, ed. by Gino Raya, 1st edn (Rome: Ciranna, 1962)
—— *Lettere a Luigi Capuana*, ed. by Gino Raya (Florence: Le Monnier, 1975)
—— *Lettere a Paolina*, ed. by Gino Raya (Rome: Fermenti, 1980)
—— *Lettere sparse*, ed. by Giovanna Finocchiaro Chimirri (Rome: Bulzoni, 1980)
—— *Lettere al suo traduttore*, ed. by Fredi Chiapelli (Florence: Le Monnier, 1954)
—— *La Lupa: novella, dramma, tragedia lirica*, ed. by Sarah Zappulla Muscarà (Palermo: Novecento, 1991)
—— *I Malavoglia* (Milan: Mondadori, 1998 [1881])
—— *I Malavoglia*, ed. by Pietro Nardi (Milan: Edizioni Scolastiche Mondadori, 1973 [1881])
—— *Mastro don Gesualdo* (Milan: Mondadori, 2000 [1889])
—— *Le novelle*, ed. by Gino Tellini, 2 vols (Rome: Salerno Editrice, 1980)
—— *Tutte le novelle*, 2 vols (Milan: Mondadori, 1983)
—— *Tutto il teatro* (Milan: Mondadori, 1980)
—— *Verga-De Roberto-Capuana*, ed. by Angela Ciavarella (Catania: Gianotta, 1955)
PIRANDELLO, LUIGI, *Carteggio Pirandello — Ruggeri: appunti per uno studio del rapporto fra autore e interprete*, ed. by Leonardo Bragaglia (Fano: Biblioteca comunale federiciana, 1987)
—— *Così è (se vi pare), Il giuoco delle parti, Come tu mi vuoi*, intro. by Nino Borsellino, preface and note by Paolo Puppa (Milan: Garzanti, 1995)
—— *Dalle novelle al teatro*, ed. Paolo Briganti (Milan: Edizioni Scholastiche Bruno Mondadori, 2000)
—— 'Eleonora Duse: Actress Supreme', *The Century Magazine*, June 1924, pp. 244–51
—— 'En confiance', trans. by Benjamin Crémieux, *Le Temps*, 20 July 1925
—— 'Fede e bellezza', *Roma letteraria*, 6.22 (1898), 518–22, 542–47
—— *Il figlio prigioniero: carteggio tra Luigi e Stefano Pirandello durante la guerra 1915–1918*, ed. by Andrea Pirandello (Milan: Mondadori, 2005)
—— 'Introduzione al teatro italiano', in *Storia del teatro italiano*, ed. by Silvio D'Amico (Milan: Bompiani, 1936), pp. 3–29
—— 'Lettere al figlio Stefano di Luigi Pirandello', in *Almanacco letterario Bompiani* (Milan: Bompiani, 1937), pp. 32–44
—— *Lettere a Marta Abba*, ed. by Benito Ortolani (Milan: Mondadori, 1995)
—— 'Lettere di Pirandello a Ruggeri', *Il dramma* (August-September 1955), 59–70
—— *Maschere nude*, ed. by Alessandro D'Amico, 4 vols (Milan: Mondadori, 1986–2007)

—— *Novelle per un anno*, ed. by Manilo Costanzo, 3 vols (Milan: Mondadori, 1985–1990)
—— 'Pirandello e lo specchio', *Corriere della sera*, 28 February 1920
—— 'Premessa', in *Tutto il teatro di Luigi Pirandello, Maschere Nude: Sei personaggi in cerca d'autore, Ciascuno a suo modo, Questa sera si recita a soggetto* (Milan: Mondadori, 1958), pp. xi-xii
—— 'Romanzo, racconto, novella', *Le Grazie*, 16 February 1897, now in *Allegoria*, 3.8 (1991), 158–60
—— *Saggi, poesie, scritti vari*, ed. by Manilo Lo Vecchio Musti (Milan: Mondadori, 1960)
—— *Saggi e interventi*, ed. and with an intro. by Ferdinando Taviani, and with a testimony by Andrea Pirandello (Milan: Mondadori, 2006)
—— *Tonight We Improvise* and *"Leonora, addio!"*, trans. with an intro. and notes by J. Douglas Campbell and Leonard G. Sbrocchi (Ottawa: The Canadian Society for Italian Studies, 1987)
—— *Tutti i romanzi*, ed. by Giovanni Macchia and Manilo Costanzo, 2 vols (Milan: Mondadori, 1973)

Secondary Sources

AARNE, ANTTI and S. THOMPSON, *The Types of the Folktale: A Classification and a Bibliography*, 2nd edn (Helsinki: Suomalainen Tie-deakatemia, 1961)
ABBA, MARTA, *Caro Maestro... Lettere a Luigi Pirandello 1926–1936*, ed. by Pietro Frassica (Milan: Mursia, 1994)
ABBATE, CAROLYN, *Unsung Voices: Opera and Musical Narrative in the Nineteenth Century* (Princeton: Princeton University Press, 1991)
ALERAMO, SIBILLA, *Un amore insolito: diario 1940–1944*, ed. by Alba Morino (Milan: Feltrinelli, 1979)
—— *Una donna*, preface by Maria Corti (Milan: Feltrinelli, 1995 [1906])
—— *Il passaggio*, ed. by Bruna Conti (Milan: Serra e Riva Editore, 1985 [1919])
ALEXANDER, ALFRED, *Giovanni Verga: A Great Writer and his World* (London: Grant and Cutler, 1972)
ALFIERI, GABRIELLA, 'Ethnos rusticano ed etichetta mondana: La gestualità nel narrato verghiano', in *Annali della Fondazione Verga* (Catania: Fondazione Verga, 1987), pp. 7–77
ALONGE, ROBERTO, 'Il giuoco delle parti, atto primo: un atto tabù', in *Pirandello fra penombre e porte socchiuse: la tradizione scenica del 'Giuoco delle parti'*, essays by Roberto Alonge et al. (Turin: Rosenberg & Sellier, 1991), pp. 7–60
—— 'Il giuoco delle parti, Pirandello dalla narrativa al teatro', *Comunità*, 22.153 (July-August 1968), 113–21
—— 'La Signora Frola e il Signor Ponza, suo genero — Così è (se vi pare)', in *La novella di Pirandello: dramma, film, musica, fumetto*, ed. by Enzo Lauretta (Pesaro: Metauro, 2007), pp. 77–89
—— *Madri, baldracche, amanti: la figura femminile nel teatro di Pirandello* (Milan: Costa & Nolan, 1997)
—— 'Madri, puttane, schiave sessuali e uomini soli', in *Studi pirandelliani: dal testo al sottotesto*, ed. by Roberto Alonge et al. (Bologna: Pitagora, 1986), pp. 91–110
—— *Pirandello tra realismo e mistificazione* (Rome: Bonanno, 2009)
—— *Il teatro di Massimo Castri* (Rome: Bulzoni, 2003)
—— *Teatro e spettacolo nel secondo Ottocento* (Rome: Laterza, 1988)
ALTIERI BIAGI, MARIA LUISA, 'La lingua in scene: dalle novelle agli atti unici', in *Gli atti unici di Pirandello (tra narrativa e teatro)*, ed. by Stefano Milioto (Agrigento: Centro Nazionale Studi Pirandelliani, 1979), pp. 259–315

AMATANGELO, SUSAN, *Figuring Women: A Thematic Study of Giovanni Verga's Female Characters* (Massachusetts: Rosemary Publishing & Printing Corp, 2004)

ANDERSSON, GÖSTA, 'Articoli di critica del 1897: *Romanzo, racconto, novella*', in *Arte e teoria: studi sulla poetica del giovane Luigi Pirandello* (Stockholm: Almqvist & Wiksell, 1966), pp. 123–25

ANGELINI, FRANCA, 'Alla ricerca di una nuova drammaturgia', in *La letteratura italiana: storia e testi*, ed. by Carlo Muscetta, 9 vols (Bari: Laterza, 1975), VIII, *Il secondo ottocento: lo stato unitario e l'età del positivismo*, pp. 606–33

—— '*Cavalleria rusticana* di Giovanni Verga', in *Letteratura italiana: Le opere*, ed. by Alberto Asor Rosa, 4 vols (Milan: Einaudi, 1995), III, *Dall'Ottocento al Novecento*, pp. 955–80

—— 'Il resto è silenzio', in *Pirandello e la parola*, ed. by Enzo Lauretta (Agrigento: Centro Nazionale Studi Pirandelliani, 2000), pp. 93–100

—— 'Il teatro del Novecento: dal grottesco a Dario Fo', in *La Letteratura italiana: storia e testi*, ed. by Carlo Muscetta, 9 vols (Bari: Laterza, 1976), IX, *Il Novecento: dal decadentismo alla crisi dei modelli*, pp. 355–441

APRILE, RENATO, *Indice delle fiabe popolari di magia* (Florence: Olschki, 2000)

APOLLONIO, MARIO, *Storia del teatro italiano*, 2 vols (Milan: Rizzoli, 2003)

ARCHER, WILLIAM, *The Theatrical 'World' of 1894*, with an intro. by George Bernard Shaw, and a synopsis of playbills of the year by Henry George Hibert (London: Walter Scott, LTD, 1895)

ARSLAN, A., and R. VERDIRAME, 'Giovanni Verga e Neera: un carteggio con due lettere di Eleonora Duse', *Quaderni di Filologia e Letterature Siciliana*, 5 (1978), 27–42

AUSTIN, GAYLE, *Feminist Theory for Dramatic Criticism* (Michigan: University of Michigan Press, 1990)

BACCHILEGA, CRISTINA, 'Cracking the Mirror: Three Re-Visions of *Snow White*', *Boundary 2*, 15.3 (1988), 1–25

BALDI, GUIDO, '*Cavalleria rusticana* dal linguaggio narrativo alla scrittura drammatica', *Il Castello di Elsinore*, 14.43 (2001), 17–38

—— *Reietti e superuomini in scena* (Naples: Liguori, 2009)

BANG, HERMAN, 'Menschen und Masken', in *Eleonora Duse, Bildnisse und Worte*, ed. by Bianca Segantini and Francesco von Mendelssohn (Berlin: Kaemmerer, 1926)

BÀRBERI SQUAROTTI, GIORGIO, *Giovanni Verga: le finzioni dietro il verismo* (Palermo, S. F. Flaccovio, 1982)

—— 'La realtà a teatro: Verga', in *La letteratura in scena: il teatro del Novecento*, ed. by Giorgio Bàrberi Squarotti (Turin: Editrice Tirenia stampatori, 1985), pp. 9–24.

—— 'La trilogia pirandelliana e il rinnovamento del teatro', in *La Trilogia di Pirandello: atti del convegno internazionale sul teatro pirandelliano (Agrigento 6–10 dicembre 1976)*, ed by Enzo Lauretta (Agrigento: Centro Nazionale Studi Pirandelliani, 1977), pp. 7–36

BARBIERA, RAFFAELLLO, *Polvere di palcoscenico: note drammatiche*, 2 vols (Catania: N. Giannotta, 1908)

BARSOTTI, ANNA, 'L'indicibile delle passioni nel teatro da Verga a d'Annunzio (*La Lupa* e *La figlia di Iorio*)', *Il Castello di Elsinore*, 22 (2009), 31–61

—— *Verga drammaturgo* (Florenza: La Nuova Italia, 1974)

BASSNETT, SUSAN, 'Art and life in Luigi Pirandello's *Questa sera si recita a soggetto*', in *Drama and Mimesis*, ed. by James Redmond, Themes in Drama, 2 (Cambridge: Cambridge University Press, 1980), pp. 81–102

—— 'Eleonora Duse', in *Bernhardt, Terry, Duse: The Actress in her Time*, ed. by John Stokes, Michael R. Booth and Susan Bassnett (Cambridge: Cambridge University Press, 1988), pp. 119–70

—— 'Female Masks: Luigi Pirandello's Plays for Women', in *Twentieth-Century European Drama*, ed. by Brian Docherty (Basingstoke: Macmillan, 1994), pp. 13–25

―――― *Luigi Pirandello* (London: Macmillan, 1983)
BASSNETT S., and A. LEFEVERE, eds, *Constructing Culture: Essays on Literary Translation* (Clevedon: Multilingual Matters, 1996)
BASSNETT, S., and J. LORCH, eds, *Luigi Pirandello: A Documentary Record* (Chur, Switzerland, Philadelphia, Pa: Harwood Academic Publishers, 1993)
BATTAGLIA, GIACINTO, *Mosaico: saggi diversi di critica drammatica* (Milan: Guglielmini, 1845)
BEERBOHM, MAX, *Around Theatres* (London: Rupert Hart-Davis, 1953)
BENTLEY, ERIC, *The Pirandello Commentaries* (Evanston, Illinois: Northwestern University Press, 1986)
―――― *Pirandello: Plays* (Evanston, Illinois: Northwest University Press, 1998)
BERNHARDT, SARAH, *The Art of Theatre*, trans. by Henry James Stenning, with a preface by James Agate (London: Geoffrey Bles, 1929)
BIGAZZI, ROBERTO, *I colori del vero: vent'anni di narrativa: 1860–1880* (Pisa: Nistri-Lischi, 1978)
―――― *Le risorse del romanzo: componenti di genere nella narrativa moderna* (Pisa: Nistri-Lischi, 1996)
―――― *Su Verga novelliere* (Pisa: Nistri-Lischi editore, 1975)
BIGGI, MARIA IDA, ed., *Eleonora Duse: viaggio intorno al mondo* (Milan: Skira, 2010).
BINI, DANIELA, 'Enacting the Dissolution of the Self: Woman as One, No One, and One Hundred Thousand', in *Luigi Pirandello: Contemporary Perspectives*, ed. by Gian-Paolo Biasin and Manuela Gieri (Toronto: University of Toronto Press, 1999), pp. 163–88
―――― *Pirandello and his Muse: The Plays for Marta Abba* (Florida: University Press of Florida, 1997)
BLAZINA, SERGIO, *La mano invisibile: poetica e procedimenti narrativi del romanzo verghiano* (Turin: Tirrenia, 1989)
BOTTIGHEIMER, RUTH B., 'Silenced Women in the Grimms' Tales: The "Fit" Between Fairy Tales and Society in Their Historical Context', in *Fairy Tales and Society: Illusion, Allusion, and Paradigm*, ed. by Ruth B. Bottigheimer (Philadelphia: University of Pennsylvania, 1986)
BRAGAGLIA, ANTON GIULIO, 'Pirandello, l'uomo', in *Almanacco letterario Bompiani* (Milan: Bompiani, 1938), pp. 87–88
BRAGAGLIA, LEONARDO, *Interpreti pirandelliani (1910–1969): vita scenica delle commedie di Luigi Pirandello dalle origini ai giorni nostri* (Rome: Trevi, 1969)
―――― *Ruggero Ruggeri in sessantacinque anni di storia del teatro rappresentato* (Rome: Trevi, 1968)
BRANCA, VITTORIO, 'Divina Duse, reciti per me: Suo Pirandello', *Corriere della sera*, 8 October 1986
BRONFEN, ELIZABETH, *Over her Dead Body: Death, Femininity and the Aesthetic* (Manchester: Manchester University Press, 1992)
BRONTË, CHARLOTTE, *The Letters of Charlotte Brontë: With a Selection of Letters by Family and Friends*, ed. by Margaret Smith, 3 vols (Oxford: Oxford University Press, 2000)
BRUMANA, BIANCA MARIA, 'G. Verga e P. Mascagni: continuità e innovazione nella tematica di *Cavalleria rusticana* in rapporto al melodramma italiano dell'Ottocento', in *Famiglia e società nell'opera di G. Verga: atti del convegno nazionale (Perugia 25–26–27 ottobre 1989)*, ed. by Norberto Cacciaglia, Ada Neiger and Renzo Pavese (Florence: Olschki, 1991), pp. 429–36
BRUNI, ARNALDO, 'Modelli e interferenze nell'esordio di Pirandello drammaturgo: *La morsa*', *Cuadernos de filología italiana*, 5 (1998), 175–87
BRUSTEIN, ROBERT, *The Theatre of Revolt* (Guildford: Billing & Sons, 1965)
BUONANNO, GIOVANNA, *International Actresses on the Victorian Stage* (Modena: Il Fiorino, 2002)
BUTTAFUOCO, ANNARITA, *Le mariuccine: storia di un'istituzione laica, l'Asilio Mariuccia* (Milan: Franco Angeli Libri, 1985)

—— 'Vita esemplari: donne nuove di primo Novecento', in *Svelamento Sibilla Aleramo: una biografia intelletuale*, ed. by Annarita Buttafuoco and Marina Zancan (Milan: Feltrinelli, 1988), pp. 139–63

CAESAR, ANN, 'The Branding of Women: Family, Theatre and Female Identity in Pirandello', *Italian Studies*, 45 (1990), 48–63

—— 'Italian Feminism and the Novel: Sibilla Aleramo's *A Woman*', *Feminist Review*, 5 (1980), 79–87 (80)

—— 'Women and the Public/Private Divide: The Salotto, Home and Theatre in Late Nineteenth-Century Italy', in *Gender, Family and Sexuality: The Private Sphere in Italy 1860–1945*, ed. by Perry Willson (Basingstoke: Palgrave Macmillan, 2004), pp. 105–21

—— 'Women Readers and the Novel in Nineteenth-Century Italy', *Italian Studies*, 56.1, 80–97

—— 'Writing by Women in Post-Unification Literary Culture: The Case for De-Segregation', in *Women and Gender in Post-Unification Italy*, ed. by Katharine Mitchell and Helena Sanson (Bern: Peter Lang, 2013), pp. 225–45

CAMILLERI, ANDREA, 'Ibsen', in *Enciclopedia dello spettacolo*, 12 vols (Rome: Le maschere, 1959), VI, pp. 459–75.

—— 'Pirandello e la regia teatrale', in *Atti del congresso internazionale di studi pirandelliani* (Florence: Le Monnier, 1967), pp. 311–15

CANNON, JO ANN, 'The Question of the Frame in Pirandello's Metatheatrical Trilogy', in *Modern Language Studies*, 16.3 (1986), 44–56

CAPUANA, LUIGI, *Gli 'ismi' contemporanei: verismo, simbolismo, idealismo, cosmopolitismo ed altri saggi di critica letteraria ed artistica*, ed. by Giorgio Luti (Milan: Fratelli Fabbri editori, 1973)

—— *Per l'arte*, ed. by Riccardo Scrivano (Naples: Edizioni Scientifiche, 1994)

—— *Studi sulla letteratura contemporanea*, ed. by Paola Azzolini (Naples: Liguori, 1988)

—— *Teatro dialettale siciliano*, 3 vols (Palermo: Alberto Reber, 1911–1912)

CAPUTI, ANTHONY, *Pirandello and the Crisis of Modern Consciousness* (Urbana and Chicago: University of Illinois Press, 1988)

CARETTI, LAURA, 'Capuana, Ibsen e la Duse', in *L'illusione della realtà: studi su Luigi Capuana*, ed. by Michelangelo Picone and Enrica Rossetti (Rome: Salerno, 1990)

—— 'La tarantella di Nora', in *La didascalia nella letteratura teatrale scandinava: testo drammatico e sintesi scenica*, ed. by Merete Kjøller Ritzu (Rome: Bulzoni, 1987), pp. 37–49

CARLSON, MARVIN, *The Italian Shakespearians: Performances by Ristori, Salvini, and Rossi in England and America* (Washington: The Folger Shakespeare Library, 1985)

CASE, SUE-ELLEN, *Feminism and Theatre* (London: Macmillan, 1988)

CASTELLANI, ARRIGO, 'Quanti erano gl'italofoni nel 1861?', *Studi linguistici italiani*, 8 (1982), 3–26

CATTANEO, GIULIO, *Giovanni Verga* (Turin: UTET, 1963)

CAVALLI, ANNAMARIA, *La scienza del romanzo: Romanzo e cultura scientifica tra Ottocento e Novecento* (Bologna: Pàtron, 2006)

CAVARERO, ADRIANA, *For More Than One Voice: Towards a Philosophy of Vocal Expression*, trans. with an intro. by Paul A. Kottman (Stanford: Sanford University Press, 2005)

CAVINA, ENRICA, 'La "crisi femminile" e le istanze dei movimenti emancipazionisti tra il 1870 e la Prima Guerra Mondiale', in: <http://www.gentesdeyilania.org/IT/Downloads/seminari/SibillaAleramo/SibillaAleramoApprofondimento.pdf> [accessed 23 September 2018]

CECCHETTI, GIOVANNI, *Giovanni Verga* (Boston: Twayne Publishers, 1978)

—— *Il Verga maggiore: sette studi* (Florence: La Nuova Italia, 1970)

CENNI, ALESSANDRA, *Gli occhi eroici. Sibilla Aleramo, Eleonora Duse, Cordula Poletti: una storia d'amore nell'Italia della Belle Époque* (Milan: Mursia, 2011)

CHAMBERLAINE, LORI, 'Gender and the Metaphorics of Translation', in *The Translation Reader*, ed. by Laurence Venuti (London, New York: Routledge, 2000), pp. 314–29
CHEMOTTI, SAVERIA, 'La voce e le parole: alcuni modelli della narrativa femminile italiana nel Novecento', in *La galassia sommera: suggestioni sulla scrittura femminile italiana*, ed. by Antonia Arslan and Saveria Chemotti (Padua: Il Poligrafo, 2008), pp. 15–44
CHESLER, PHYLLIS, *Women and Madness* (London: Allen Lane, 1974)
CHIARAMONTE, NICOLA, 'Pirandello and the Contemporary Theatre', *World Theatre*, 16.3 (1967), 224–37
CHISTIANSEN, RUPERT, *Prima Donna: A History* (London: Penguin Books, 1986)
CIRESE, A. M., and L. SERAFINI, *Tradizioni orali non cantate*, ed. by Aurora Milillo (Rome: Ministero per i beni culturali e ambientali, Discoteca di Stato, 1975)
COLERIDGE, MARY ELIZABETH, *Selected Poems of Mary Elizabeth Coleridge*, selected and ed. by Simon Avery (Exeter: Shearsman Books, 2010)
CONTI, B. and A. MORITO, eds, *Sibilla Aleramo e il suo tempo: vita raccontata e illustrata* (Milan: Feltrinelli, 1981)
CORSINOVI, GRAZIELLA, '*Questa sera si recita a soggetto*: il testo. Tra progettazione vitalistica e partitura musicale', in *Testo e messa in scena in Pirandello*, ed. by Enzo Lauretta (Urbino: La Nuova Italia Scientifica, 1986), pp. 105–32
COVATO, CARMELA, *Un'identità divisa: diventare maestra in Italia fra Otto e Novecento* (Rome: Archivio Guido Izzi, 1996)
CURATO, BALDO, 'Il teatro verista italiano', in *Sessant'anni di teatro in Italia: da Giovanni Verga a Ugo Betti* (Milan: Denti, 1947), pp. 31–56
D'AMICO, ALESSANDRO, 'Rendez-vous manqué: Eleonora Duse, Luigi Pirandello', *Théâtre en Europe*, 10 (1986), 98–105
—— 'Il teatro verista e il *grande attore*', in *Il teatro italiano dal naturalismo a Pirandello*, ed. by Alessandro Tinterri (Bologna: Il Mulino, 1990), pp. 25–46
D'AMICO, GIULIANO, 'Marketing Ibsen: A Study of the First Italian Reception, 1883–1891', *Ibsen Studies*, 11.2 (2011), 145–75
—— 'Six Points for a Comparative Ibsen Reception History', *Ibsen Studies*, 14.1 (2014), 4–37
D'AMICO, SILVIO, '*Questa sera si recita a soggetto* di Pirandello, al Quirino', in *Cronache del teatro*, ed. by Eugenio Ferdinando Palmieri and Sandro D'Amico, 2 vols (Bari: Laterza, 1963), I, pp. 90–96
—— *Il teatro italiano* (Milan: Treves, 1932)
—— *Teatro dei fantocci* (Florence: Vallecchi, 1920)
—— *Storia del teatro italiano*, with an intro. by Luigi Pirandello (Milan: Bompiani, 1936)
D'ARONCO, GIANFRANCO, *Le fiabe di magia in Italia* (Udine: Arti grafiche friulane, 1957)
DE BELLA, NINO, *Narrativa e teatro nell'arte di Luigi Pirandello* (Messina-Florence: casa editrice G. D'Anna, 1962)
DEBENEDETTI, GIACOMO, *Verga e il naturalismo* (Milan: Garzanti, 1976)
DE CASTRIS, ARCANGELO LEONE, *Storia di Pirandello* (Bari: Laterza, 1971)
DE DONATO, GIGLIOLA et al., eds, *La parabola della donna nella letteratura italiana dell'Ottocento* (Bari: Adriatica editrice, 1983)
DE FELICE, FRANCESCO, *Storia del teatro siciliano* (Catania: Gianotta, 1956)
DE FRANCISCI, ENZA, 'A Different Leone in *Il giuoco delle parti*', *The Journal of The Pirandello Society of America*, 26 (2013), 33–48
—— 'Eleonora Duse in *Cavalleria rusticana*: Santuzza on the London Stage', *Italian Studies*, 69.1 (2014), 95–110
—— 'The Female Voice: From "Quando si è capito il giuoco" to *Il giuoco delle parti*', *Pirandello Studies*, 33 (2013), 79–90

—— 'Generations (Duse-Abba), Genders (the Performing Female Artist) and Genres (from '"Leonora, addio!"' to *Questa sera si recita a soggetto*), *Pirandello Studies*, 32 (2012), 58–70

—— 'Giovanni Verga's "New Woman" in *La Lupa*', *Modern Language Review*, 110.1 (2015), 149–65

—— '*Liolà* Lost in (its Literal) Translation?' *Pirandello Studies*, 34 (2014), 55–65

—— 'Mariangela in Verga's *La caccia al lupo*: From Page to Stage', *Between: Rivista dell'Associazione del Teoria e Storia Comparata della Letteratura*, 2.4 (2012)

—— 'Pirandello's Actress From Page to Meta-Theatrical Stage: "Leonora, addio!" to *Questa sera si recita a soggetto*', *L'anello che non tiene: Journal of Modern Italian Literature*, 24 (2014), 12–37

—— 'Pirandello's (Futurist?) War of Words', *Pirandello Studies*, 35 (2015), 27–40

—— 'Pirandello's Women: From Page to Stage', *Pirandello Studies*, 28 (2008), 89–99

—— 'Silvia's Silent Voice in *Tutto per bene*', *Pirandello Studies*, 34 (2014), 33–43

—— 'Translating *Sicilianità* in Pirandello's Dialect Play *Liolà*', in *Adapting Translation for the Stage*, ed. by Geraldine Brodie and Emma Cole (London: Routledge, 2017), pp. 223–35

—— 'Verga and Duse: A Silent Partnership in *Cavalleria rusticana* and *In portineria*', in *Eleonora Duse and 'Cenere' ('Ashes')*, ed. by Maria Pia Pagani and Paul Fryer (Jefferson, North Carolina: McFarland and Co., Inc., 2017), pp. 41–55

—— 'Verga and Duse Transposing Silence in "Il canarino del n. 15" and *In portineria*: A prelude to Symbolism?', *The Italianist*, 34.1 (2014), 73–87

DE FRANCISCI, E., and C. STAMATAKIS, eds, *Shakespeare, Italy, and Transnational Exchange: The Early Modern Period to the Present* (New York: Routledge, 2017)

DE GIORGIO, MICHELA, 'Dalla donna nuova alla donna della nuova Italia', in *La grande guerra: esperienza, memoria, immagini*, ed. by Diego Leoni and Camillo Zadra (Bologna: Il Mulino, 1986), pp. 307–29

DE GONCOURT, JULES, *Journal: Mémoires de la vie littéraire 1851–1861* (Fasquelle: Flammarion, 1935)

DE LAURETIS, TERESA, *Alice Doesn't: Feminism, Semiotics, Cinema* (Bloomington: Indiana University Press, 1984)

DELLA TERZA, DANTE, 'Pirandello from Tale to Play: The Case of *Tutto per bene*', *Modern Language Notes*, Italian Issue, 92.1 (January 1977), 63–78

DE MAURO, TULLIO, *Storia linguistica dell'Italia unita* (Rome: Laterza, 1995)

DE ROBERTO, FEDERICO, *Casa Verga e altri sagi verghiani*, ed. by Carmelo Musumarra (Florence: Le Monnier, 1964)

—— *Processi verbali* (Milan: Libreria editrice Galli, 1890)

DI SILVESTRO, ANTONIO, *Le intermittenze del cuore: Verga e il linguaggio dell' interiorità* (Catania: Biblioteca della Fondazione Verga, 2000)

DONATI, CORRADO, *Luigi Pirandello nella storia della critica* (Pesaro: Metauro edizioni, 1998)

DUQUESNEL, FELIX, 'Les Premières', *Le Gaulois*, 1 July 1897

DUSE, ELEONORA, *Lettere d'amore: Eleonora Duse, Arrigo Boito*, ed. by Raul Radice, 16 photographs (Milan: Il Saggiatore, 1979)

EWBANK, INGA-STINA, 'Reading the Brontës Abroad: A Study in the Transmission of Victorian Novels in Continental Europe', in *Reconstructing the Book: Literary Texts in Transmission*, ed. by Maureen Bell et al. (Burlington: Ashgate, 1953), pp. 84–99

FACCIO, RINA PIERANGELI, 'Evoluzione femminile', *Italia femminile*, 45.19 (November 1899)

FALLON, MARIANNE, '*Caccia al lupo* di Verga fra novella e teatro: letture di una dinamica di riscrittura', *Rassegna europea di letteratura italiana*, 20 (2002), 81–98

FANNING, URSULA, 'Angel vs. Monder: Serao's Use of the Female Double', *The Italianist*, 7.1 (1987), 63–87

—— *Gender Meets Genre: Women as Subject in the Fictional Universe of Matilde Serao* (Dublin: Irish Academic Press, 2002)

—— 'Maternal Prescriptions and Descriptions in Post-Unification Italy', in *Women and Gender in Post-Unification Italy*, ed. by Katharine Mitchell and Helena Sanson (Bern: Peter Lang, 2013), pp. 13–37
FARRELL, JOSEPH, 'The Duel and the Code of Honour for Pirandello', *Pirandello Studies*, 28 (2008), 100–10
FERRIS, LESLEY, *Acting Women: Images of Women in Theatre* (Basingstoke: Macmillan, 1990)
FERRONE, SIRO, ed., *La commedia e il dramma borghese dell'ottocento*, Il teatro italiano, 5 (Turin: Einaudi, 1979)
—— *Il teatro di Verga* (Rome: Bulzoni, 1972)
FERRUCCI, CARLO, *La musa ritrosa: Pirandello e Marta Abba* (Bologna: CLUEB, 2010)
FETTERLEY, JUDITH, *The Resisting Reader: A Feminist Approach to American Fiction*, 1st edn (Bloomington: Indiana University Press, 1978)
FINNEY, GAIL, 'Ibsen and Feminism', in *The Cambridge Companion to Ibsen*, ed. by James McFarlane (Cambridge: Cambridge University Press, 2006), pp. 89–105
FORÇADE, EUGÈNE, '*Revue des deux mondes*: October 1848', in *The Brontës: The Critical Heritage*, ed. by Miriam Allott (London: Routledge, 2003), pp. 100–04
FORGACS, DAVID, *Italy's Margins: Social Exclusion and Nation Formation since 1861* (Cambridge: Cambridge University Press, 2014)
FORSYTH, N., and M. HENNARD DUTHEIL DE LA ROCHÈRE, 'Dickens in Francophone Switzerland', in *The Reception of Charles Dickens in Europe*, ed. by Michael Hillington, 2 vols (London: Bloomsbury, 2004), I, pp. 272–80
FUMAGALLI, GIUSEPPE, *Chi l'ha detto?* (Milan: Ulrico Hoepli, 1989)
FUSERO, CLEMENTE, *Eleonora Duse* (Milan: Dall'Oglio editore, 1971)
GARDNER V. and S. RUTHERFORD, eds, *The New Woman and her Sisters: Feminism and Theatre 1850–1914* (Hemel Hempstead: Harvester Wheatsheaf, 1992)
GIBELLINI, PIETRO, 'Tre coltellate per compare Turiddu: Lettura antropologica di *Cavalleria rusticana*', *Strumenti critici*, 8 (1993), 205–23
GILBERT, S. M. and S. GUBAR, *The Madwoman in the Attic: The Woman Writer and the Nineteenth-Century Literary Imagination*, 2nd edn (New Haven: Yale University Press, 2000)
GILMAN, RICHARD, *The Making of Modern Drama: A Study of Büchner, Ibsen, Strindberg, Chekhov, Pirandello, Brecht, Beckett, Handke*, with an intro. by the author (New Haven: Yale University Press, 1999)
GIOANOLA, ELIO, *Pirandello's Story: la vita o si vive o si scrive* (Milan: Jaca Book, 2007)
GIORDANO LOKRANTZ, MARGHERITA, 'Three Unpublished Letters by Henrik Ibsen about the First Performances of *Et dukkehjem* in Italy', *Ibsen Studies*, 2.1 (2002), 59–74
GIUDICE, GASPARE, *Luigi Pirandello* (Turin: UTET, 1963)
—— 'Pirandello e Verga', *Galleria*, 15.1–2 (1965), 19–32
GLUT, DONALD. F, *The Frankenstein Catalog* (North Carolina: McFarland, 1984)
GONZENBACH, LAURA, *Beautiful Angiola: The Great Treasury of Sicilian Folk and Fairy Tales Collected by Laura Gonzenbach*, trans. with an intro. by Jack Zipes (New York: Routledge, 2004)
—— *The Robber with a Witch's Head: More Stories from the Great Treasury of Sicilian Folk and Fairy Tales*, trans. and ed. by Jack Zipes (New York: Routledge, 2004)
GOODMAN, LIZABETH, HELEN SMALL and MARY JACOBUS, 'Madwomen and Attics: Themes and Issues in Women's Fiction', in *Literature and Gender*, ed. by Lizabeth Goodman (New York: Routledge, 1996), pp. 109–44
GRAMSCI, ANTONIO, *Letteratura e vita nazionale* (Rome: Editori Riuniti, 1991)
GRANA, GIANNI, *Profili e letture di contemporanei* (Milan: Marzorati, 1962)
GREENWALD, HELEN, 'Aris moriendi': Reflections on the Death of Mimì', in *The Arts of the Prima Donna in the Long Nineteenth Century*, ed. Rachel Cowgill and Hillary Porris (Oxford: Oxford University Press, 2012), pp 167–85

GRIGNANI, MARIA ANTONIA, 'Incursioni al femminile nei romanzi di Pirandello', in *La donna in Pirandello*, ed. by Stefano Milioto (Agrigento: Centro Nazionale Studi Pirandelliani, 1988), pp. 23–35
—— *Retoriche pirandelliane* (Naples: Liguori, 1993)
GUGLIELMINETTI, MARZIANO, 'Il soliloquio di Pirandello', in *Struttura e sintassi del romanzo italiano del primo novecento* (Milan: Silva, 1964), pp. 63–119
GÜNSBERG, MAGGIE, 'Parla pure, papà: non ti sento', *The Yearbook of the British Pirandello Society*, 8–9 (1988–1989), 91–101
—— *Patriarchal Representations: Gender and Discourse in Pirandello's Theatre* (Oxford: Berg, 1994)
HERCZEG, GIULIO, *Lo stile indiretto libero in italiano* (Florence: G. E. Sansoni editore, 1963)
HUTCHEON, LINDA, *A Theory of Adaptation* (New York: Routledge, 2006)
IBSEN, HENRIK, *Casa di bambola*, trans. by Luigi Capuana (Milan: Kantorowicz, 1894)
—— *Four Major Plays: A Doll's House, Ghosts, Hedda Gabler, The Master Builder*, trans. by James McFarlane and Jens Arup, with an intro. by James McFarlane (Oxford: Oxford University Press, 2008)
—— *Théâtre: Les Revenants, La maison de poupée*, trans. from the Norwegian by Moritz Prozor, with a preface by Édouard Rod, 3rd edn (Paris: Albert Savine, 1892)
JANNUZZI L., and N. LEOTTA, eds, *Verga e il teatro europeo: prove d'autore* (Lecce: Milella, 1992)
JANSEN, STEEN, 'Struttura narrativa e struttura drammatica in *Questa sera si recita a soggetto*', *Rivista italiana di drammaturgia*, 2.6 (December 1977), 55–70
JONES, VERINA R., 'Lucia and her Sisters: Women in Alessandro Manzoni's *I promessi sposi*', in *Women and Italy: Essays on Gender, Culture and History*, ed. by Zygmunt G. Barański and Shirley W. Vinall (London: Macmillan, 1991), pp. 209–23
KNEPLER, HENRY, *The Gilded Stage: The Lives and Careers of Four Great Actresses: Rachel Félix, Adelaide Ristori, Sarah Bernhardt and Eleonora Duse* (London: Constable, 1968)
KÖRNER, AXEL, *Politics of Culture in Liberal Italy: From Unification to Fascism* (New York: Routledge, 2009)
KROHA, LUCIENNE, 'Behind the Veil: A Freudian Reading of Pirandello's *Così è (se vi pare)*', *The Yearbook of the Society for Pirandello Studies*, 12 (1992), 1–21
—— *The Woman Writer in Late-Nineteenth-Century Italy: Gender and the Formation of Literary Identity* (Lewiston: E. Mellen Press, 1992)
LABRIOLA, TERESA, *La quistione femminista* (Rome: Loescher, 1910)
LAURENCE, PATRICIA, 'Women's Silence as a Ritual of Truth: A Study of Literary Expressions in Austen, Brontë and Woolf', in *Listening to Silences: New Essays in Feminist Criticism*, ed. by Elaine Hedges and Shelley Fisher Fishkin (Oxford: Oxford University Press, 1994), pp. 156–67
LAURETTA, ENZO, ed., 'Le novelle per un anno', in *Le novelle di Pirandello: atti del 6° convegno internazionale di studi pirandelliani*, ed. by Stefano Milioto (Agrigento: Centro Nazionale Studi Pirandelliani, 1980), pp. 19–32
LERNER MICHAEL G., 'Édouard Rod and the Introduction of Ibsen into France', *Revue de littérature comparée*, 1 (1969), 69–82
LEO, ULRICH, 'Pirandello between Fiction and Drama', in *Pirandello: A Collection of Critical Essays*, ed. by G. Cambon (Englewood Cliffs, New Jersey: Prentice-Hall, Inc., 1967), pp. 83–90
LEPSCHY, ANNA LAURA, *Narrativa e teatro fra due secoli: Verga, Invernizio, Svevo, Pirandello* (Florence: Olschki, 1984)
—— 'Notes on the Figure of the Actor in Pirandello', *The Yearbook of the British Pirandello Society*, 1 (1981), 1–18
—— 'On Pirandello's Versions of *Liolà*', *Cuadernos de filología italiana*, 16 (2009), 263–73

—— 'Pirandello's Verga', in *Reflexivity: Critical themes in the Italian Cultural Tradition. Essays by Members of the Department of Italian at University College London*, ed. by Prue Shaw and John Took (Ravenna: Longo, 2000), pp. 83–94

—— 'The Treatment of Antefact in Pirandello's Theatre', *Yearbook of the Society for Pirandello Studies*, 11 (1991), 68–90

LEPSCHY, A. L. and G. LEPSCHY, *The Italian Language Today*, 2nd edn (London: Routledge, 1991)

LEVI, CESARE, *Autori drammatici italiani: Giovanni Verga, Roberto Bracco, Marco Praga, Sebatino Lopez* (Bologna: Zanichelli, 1921), pp. 3–16

—— 'Il teatro di Giovanni Verga', *Nuova Antologia di lettere, scienze ed arti*, 6th series (July-August 1920), 141–47

LICASTRO, EMANUELE, *Luigi Pirandello dalle novelle alle commedie* (Verona: Fiorini, 1974)

LIVIO, GIGI, 'Il giuoco delle parti e il grottesco', *Il Castello di Elsinore*, 1 (1988), 49–68

—— *Teatro grottesco del novecento: antologia* (Milan: Mursia, 1965)

—— *Il teatro in rivolta: futurismo, grottesco, Pirandello e pirandellismo* (Milan: Mursia, 1976)

LOCKE, RALPH, 'What Are These Women Doing in Opera?', in *En Traversti: Women, Gender, Subversion, Opera*, ed. by Corinne E. Blackmer and Patricia Juliana Smith (New York: Columbia University Press, 1995), pp. 59–98

LOMBROSO, PAOLA, *Caratteri della femminilità* (Turin: F.lli Bocca, 1909)

LOPEZ, GUIDO, *Marco Praga e Silvio d'Amico: Lettere e documenti (1919–1929)* (Rome: Bulzoni, 1990)

LUCKYL, CHRISTINA, *'A moving rhetoricke': Gender and Silence in Early Modern England* (Manchester: Manchester University Press, 2002)

LUGNE-POË, AURELIEN, *La parade: Sous les étoiles, souvenirs de théâtre (1902–1912)* (Paris: Gallimard, 1933)

—— *Ibsen* (Paris: Les Editions Rieder, 1936)

LUNDELL, TORBORG, 'Gender-Related Biases in the Type and Motif Indexes of Aarne and Thompson', in *Fairy Tales and Society: Illusion, Allusion, and Paradigm*, ed. by Ruth B. Bottigheimer (Philadelphia: University of Pennsylvania Press, 1986), pp. 149–63

LUPERINI, ROMANO, *L'orgoglio e la disperata rassegnazione: natura e società, maschera e realtà nell'ultimo Verga* (Rome: Savelli, 1974)

MACCHIA, GIOVANNI, 'Luigi Pirandello', in *Storia della letteratura italiana*, ed. by Emilio Cecchi e Natalino Sapegno, 9 vols (Milan: Garzanti, 1984), IX, *Il Novecento* pp. 439–92

—— 'Il personaggio sequestrato', in *Omaggio a Pirandello*, ed. by Leonardo Sciascia (Milan: Bompiani, 1987), pp. 85–92

—— *Pirandello o la stanza della tortura* (Milan: Mondadori, 1980)

MACERI, DOMENICO, *Dalla novella alla commedia pirandelliana* (New York: Peter Lang, 1991)

MADRIGNANI, CARLO ALBERTO, 'L'"altro" femminile e la golosità', in *Effetto Sicilia: genesi del romanzo moderno* (Rome: Grafica editrice romana, 2007), pp. 63–72

MALARA, FRANCESCA, *Copioni e drammaturgie di fine ottocento* (Milan: Edizioni universitarie di Lettere Economia Diritto, 2000)

MARCHAND, JEAN-JACQUES, *Edouard Rod et les écrivains italiens: correspondance inédite avec S. Aleramo, L. Capuana, G. Cena, G Deledda, A. Fogazzaro et G. Verga* (Geneva: Droz, 1980)

MARCHI, VIRGILIO, 'Ricordi sul Teatro d'Arte', in *Pirandello capocomico*, ed. by Alessandro D'Amico and Alessandro Tinterri (Palermo: Sellerio, 1987), pp. 407–34

MARIANI, LAURA, *Il tempo delle attrici: emancipazione e teatro in Italia fra Ottocento e Novecento* (Bologna: Monogolfiera, 1991)

—— 'Sibilla Aleramo. Significato di tre incontri col teatro: il personaggio di Nora, Giacinta Pezzana, Eleonora Duse', in *Teatro e Storia*, 2 (1987), 67–133

MARIANI, GAETANO, 'Giovanni Verga', in *Letteratura italiana: i maggiori*, 2 vols (Milan: Marzorati, 1956), II, pp. 1203–74

MARIANI, UMBERTO, *La donna in Pirandello: l'estrema vittima* (Caltanisetta-Rome: Salvatore Sciascia Editore, 2012)

MEITLIS, REBECCA, 'The Adjusted Woman', in *Violetta and Her Sisters. The Lady of the Camellias: Responses to the Myth*, ed. by Nicholas John (London: Faber and Faber 1994), pp. 284–91

MESSINA, MARIA, *Un idillio letterario inedito verghiano: lettere inedite di Maria Messina a Giovanni Verga*, ed. by Giovanni Garra Agosta with an intro. by Concetta Greco Lanza (Catania: Greco, 1979)

MILIOTO, STEFANO, ed., *Pirandello e il teatro del suo tempo* (Agrigento: Centro Nazionale Studi Pirandelliani, 1983)

MINEO, NICOLÒ, 'Famiglia e società nel primo Verga', in *Famiglia e società nell'opera di G. Verga: atti del convegno nazionale (Perugia 25–26–27 ottobre 1989)*, ed. by Norberto Cacciaglia, Ada Neiger and Renzo Pavese (Florence: Olschki, 1991), pp. 3–23

MOESTRUP, JØRN, 'Gli atti unici', in *Gli atti unici di Pirandello (tra narrativa e teatro)*, ed. by Stefano Milioto (Agrigento: Centro Nazionale Studi Pirandelliani, 1978), pp. 337–50

—— 'La diversa funzione di novella e dramma nell'opera di Luigi Pirandello', *Analecta Romana Instituti Danici*, 5 (1965), 199–239

—— *The Structural Patterns of Pirandello's Work*, Études romanes de l'Université d'Odense, 2 (Odense: Odense University Press, 1972)

MITCHELL, KATHARINE, 'Evenings Out: Female Spectators of Opera and Theatre in Late Nineteenth-Century Italy', in *The Formation of a National Audience: Readers and Spectators in Italy, 1750–1890*, ed. by Jennifer Burns and Gabriella Romani (Madison and Teaneck: Fairleigh Dickinson University Press, 2017), pp. 259–80

—— 'La Femme, Fatal or Fallen', *Opera Magazine*, October 2017, pp. 1271–76

—— *Italian Women Writers: Gender and Everyday Life in Fiction and Journalism, 1870–1910* (Toronto: Toronto University Press, 2014)

—— 'Neera's Refiguing of Hysteria as *nervosismo* in *Teresa* and *L'indomani*', *Rethinking Neera. Supplement to The Italianist*, ed. by Katherine Mitchell and Catherine Ramsay-Portolano, 30 (2010), 101–22

—— 'Le traviate: Suffering heroines and the Italian State between the Nineteenth and Twenty-First Centuries', in *Prostitution and Sex Work in Global Visual Media: New Takes on Fallen Women*, ed. by Danielle Hipkins and Kate Taylor (London: Palgrave Macmillan, 2017), pp. 195–217

MOE, NELSON, *The View from Vesuvius: Italian Culture and the Southern Question* (Berkeley: University of California Press, 2002)

MOERS, ELLEN, *Literary Women* (London: W. H. Allen, 1977)

MOLINARI, CESARE, *L'attrice divina: Eleonora Duse nel teatro italiano fra i due secoli* (Rome: Bulzoni, 1985)

—— 'Teorie della recitazione: gli attori sull'attore. Da Rossi a Zacconi', in *Teatro dell'Italia unita: atti dei convegni Firenze 10–11 dicembre 1977, 4–6 novembre 1978*, ed. by Siro Ferrone (Milan: il Saggiatore, 1980), pp. 75–100

MONTI, SILVANA, 'Il teatro di Verga e la società della "Nuova Italia"', *Problemi*, 4–5 (1967), 174–86

MORANDINI, GIULIANA, *... E allora mi hanno rinchiusa: testimonianze dal manicomio femminile*, 2nd edn (Milan: Bompiani, 1977)

MORRIS, PAM, *Literature and Feminism* (Oxford: Blackwell, 1993)

MORONI, GABRIELE, *Verga e il teatro del suo tempo: l'esperimento di 'Cavalleria rusticana'* (Udine: Companotto, 1997)

MULVEY, LAURA, 'Visual pleasure and narrative cinema', *Screen*, 16.3 (1975), 6–18
MUSUMARRA, CARMELO, 'Verga', in *Dizionario critico della letteratura italiana* (Turin: UTET, 1973), pp. 584–89
NAVARRIA, AURELIO, *Annotazioni verghiane e pagine staccate* (Caltanissetta-Rome: Edizioni Salvatore Sciascia, 1976)
NEIGER, ADA, 'La maternità trasgressiva nell'opera verghiana', in *Famiglia e società nell'opera di G. Verga: atti del convegno nazionale (Perugia 25–26–27 ottobre 1989)*, ed. by Norberto Cacciaglia, Neiger Ada, and Pavese Renzo (Florence: Olschki, 1991), pp. 163–73.
NICASTRO, GUIDO, '*Cavalleria rusticana*, ossia una tragedia siciliana', in *Giovanni Verga e il teatro: atti del convegno Catania, 13–15 aprile, Teatro Stabile di Catania* (Catania: Assessorato regionale ai beni culturali e P. I., 1986), pp. 69–79
—— *Teatro e società in Sicilia 1860–1918* (Rome: Bulzoni, 1978)
NIKIFOROV, ALEKSANDR ISAAKOVICH, 'On the Morphological Study of Folklore', trans. with additional notes by Heda Jason, *Linguistica Biblica*, 27–28 (1973), 25–35
NOCCIOLI, GUIDO, *Duse on Tour: Guido Noccioli's Diaries, 1906–07* (Manchester: Manchester University Press, 1982)
OJETTI, UGO, *Alla scoperta dei letterati*, postface by Nicola Merola (Milan: Fratelli Dumolard editori, 1895)
OLIVA, GIANNI, *La scena del vero: lettura e teatro da Verga a Pirandello* (Rome: Bulzoni, 1992)
OLIVER, ROGER W., *Dreams of Passion: The Theatre of Luigi Pirandello* (New York: New York University Press, 1979)
OLSEN, TILLIE, *Silences* (London: Virago, 1980)
O'RAWE, CATHERINE, *Authorial Echoes: Textuality and Self-Plagiarism in the Narrative of Luigi Pirandello* (Oxford: Legenda, 2005)
ORECCHIA, DONATELLA, *La Prima Duse: nascita di un'attrice moderna (1879–1886)* (Rome: Artemide, 2007)
ORVIETO, ADOLFO, '*La Lupa* di G. Verga', *Il Marzocco*, 1.16 (1896)
PAOLUCCI, ANNE, *Pirandello's Theatre: The Recovery of The Modern Stage for Dramatic Art* (Delaware: Griffon House, 2002)
PASCAL, ROY, *The Dual Voice: Free Indirect Speech and its Functioning in the Nineteenth-Century Novel* (Manchester: Manchester University Press, 1977)
PATRUNO, MARIA LUISA, *Verismo e umorismo: poetiche in antitesi* (Bari: Laterza, 1996)
PELLINI, PIERLUIGI, *Naturalismo e verismo* (Florence: La Nuova Italia, 1998)
PERCO, D., and C. BACCHILEGA, 'Female Initiation in Northern Italian Versions of Cinderella', *Western Folklore: Perspectives on the Innocent Persecuted Heroine in Fairy Tales*, 52.1 (1993), 73–84
PERRONI, L., and V. PERRONI, 'Storia de *I Malavoglia*', *Nuova Antologia* (16 March 1940), 105–31, and (1 April 1940), 237–51
PERRONI, VITO, 'Sulla genesi de *I Malavoglia*', *Le ragioni critiche*, 2.6 (October-December 1972), 471–526
PETRONIO, GIUSEPPE, *Pirandello novelliere e la crisi del realismo* (Lucca: Lucentia, 1950)
—— 'Teatro e narrativa in Verga', in *Giovanni Verga e il teatro: atti del convegno Catania, 13–15 aprile, Teatro Stabile di Catania* (Catania: Assessorato regionale ai beni culturali e P. I., 1986), pp. 9–16
PICCINI, GIULIO (Jarro), 'I nervi della Duse', in *Eleonora Duse*, ed. by Leonardo Vergani with the collaboration of Luigi Pizzinelli (Milan: Aldo Martello, 1958), pp. 93–101
PICCITTO, GIORGIO, ed., *Vocabolario siciliano*, with the contribution of the Regione Sicilina and the Consiglio nazionale delle ricerche (Catania: Centro di studi filologici e linguistici siciliani, 1977)
PIERONI BORTOLOTTI, FRANCA, *Alle origini del movimento femminile in Italia 1848–1892* (Milan: Einaudi, 1963)

Pirandello, Andrea, 'Ricordo', in *Pirandello: l'uomo, lo scrittore, il teatrante*, ed. by Fabio Battistini, Maria G. Gregori, Mario Sculatti (Milan: Mazotta, 1987), pp. 144–51

Pitrè, Giuseppe, *Usi, costumi, credenze e pregiudizi del popolo siciliano* (Palermo: L. Pedone Lauriel, 1889)

Plaisance, Michel, 'De la nouvelle au théâtre', in *Pirandello 1867–1957*, ed. by Gerard Genot (Paris: Minard, 1968), pp. 95–113

Pontiero, Giovanni, *Eleonora Duse: In Life and Art* (Frankfurt am Main, Bern, New York: Verlag Peter Lang, 1986).

Pozza, Giovanni, *Cronache teatrali di Giovanni Pozza (1886–1913)*, ed. by Gian Antonio Cibotto (Vicenza: Neri Pozza editore, 1971), pp. 228–32

Praga, Marco, *Cronache teatrali* (Milan: Treves, 1920), pp. 102–12

Praz, Mario, *La carne, la morte e il diavolo nella letteratura romantica* (Florence: Sansoni, 2003 [1930]), pp. 165–246

Prosperi, Giorgio, 'Teatro Verghiano: due restauri', *Rivista italiana di drammaturgia*, 2 (1976), 3–24

Providenti, Elio, 'Note di bibliografia sulle opere giovanili di Luigi Pirandello', *Belfagor*, 23.6 (30 November 1968), 721–40

Pullini, Giorgio, '*Così è (se vi pare)*: dalla novella al dramma', in *Saggi di linguistica e di letteratura in memoria di Paolo Zolli*, ed. by Giampaolo Borghello and others (Padua: Antenore, 1991) pp. 619–28

Puppa, Paolo, *Fantasmi contro giganti: scena e immaginario in Pirandello* (Bologna: Pàtron editore, 1978)

—— 'The Theatre of United Italy', in *A History of Italian Theatre*, ed. by Joseph Farrell and Paolo Puppa (Cambridge: Cambridge University Press, 2006), pp. 223–34

Ragonese, Gaetano, *Interpretazione del Verga: saggi e ricerche*, 2nd edn (Rome: Bulzoni, 1977)

—— 'Verga visto da Pirandello', in *Atti del congresso internazionale di studi pirandelliani, Venezia 2–5 ottobre 1961* (Florence: Le Monnier, 1967), pp. 611–12

Ragusa, Olga, *Luigi Pirandello: An Approach to his Theatre* (Edinburgh: Edinburgh University Press, 1980)

—— '*Tonight We Improvise*: Spectacle and Tragedy', in *A Companion to Pirandello Studies*, ed. by John Louis DiGaetani, foreword by Eric Bentley (New York: Greenwood Press, 1991), pp. 245–58

Rasi, Luigi, *La Duse: con 55 illustrazioni* (Florence: R. Bemporad & Figlio, 1901)

Re, Lucia, 'Eleonora Duse and Women: Performing Desire, Power, and Knowledge', *The Diva in Modern Italian Culture: Italian Studies*, ed. by Katharine Mitchell and Clorinda Donato, 70.3 (2015), 347–63

Robins, Elizabeth, 'On Seeing Madame Bernhardt's *Hamlet*', *North American Review*, 171 (1900), 908–19

Robinson, Paul, 'It's Not Over Till the Soprano Dies', in *New York Times Book Review*, 1 January 1989

Rorman, Brian, *Signifying Nothing: The Semiotics of Zero* (London: Macmillan, 1987)

Rowe, Karen, 'To Spin a Yarn: The Female Voice in Folklore and Fairy Tale', in *The Classic Fairy Tales: Texts, Criticism*, ed. by Maria Tatar, 1st edn (New York: Norton, 1999), pp. 297–308

Russo, Luigi, *Giovanni Verga* (Rome: Laterza, 1995)

—— *I narratori* (Rome: Fondazione Leonardo per la cultura italiana, 1925)

—— *Verga romanziere e novelliere* (Turini: Eri classe unica, 1959)

Rutherford, Susan, *The Prima Donna and Opera 1815–1930* (Cambridge: Cambridge Studies in Opera, 2006)

—— *Verdi, Opera, Women* (Cambridge: Cambridge University Press, 2013)

SANSON, HELENA, *Donne, precettistica e lingua nell'Italia del cinquecento: un contributo alla storia del pensiero linguistico* (Florence: Accademia dell Crusca, 2007)
SANSONE, MATTEO, 'Verga and Mascagni: The Critics' Response to *Cavalleria rusticana*', *Music and Letters*, 71.2 (1 May 1990), 198–214
—— 'Verga, Puccini and *La Lupa*', *Italian Studies*, 44 (1989), 63–76
SAPEGNO, NATALINO, *Ritratto di Manzoni ed altri saggi* (Bari: Latera, 1961), pp. 271–76
SCALINGER G. M., *Ibsen* (Naples: Edizione del priodico fortunio, 1895)
SCARFOGLIO, EDOARDO, *Il libro di Don Chisciotte*, ed. by Carlo Alberto Madrignani (Naples: Liguori, 1990 [1885])
SCHINO, MIRELA, *Il teatro di Eleonora Duse* (Bologna: Il Mulino, 1992)
SCHNEIDER J., and P. SCHNEIDER, *Culture and Political Economy in Western Sicily* (New York: Academic Press, 1976)
SCIASCIA, LEONARDO, *Pirandello e il pirandellismo: con lettere inedite di Pirandello a Tilgher* (Palermo: Cappugli e figli, 1953)
—— *Pirandello e la Sicilia* (Milan: Adelphi, 1996)
SCOGNAMIGLIO, GIUSEPPINA, '*La Lupa* di Giovanni Verga dalla novella alla scena', *Rivista di letteratura teatrale*, 1 (2008), 73–91
SCRIVANO, ENZO, ed., *Pirandello e la drammaturgia tra le due guerre* (Agrigento: Centro Nazionale Studi Pirandelliani, 1985)
SCUDERI, ANTONIO, 'Sicilian dialect theatre', in *A History of Italian Theatre*, ed. by Joseph Farrell and Paolo Puppa (Cambridge: Cambridge University Press, 2006), pp. 257–65
SHAW, GEORGE BERNARD, *The Quintessence of Ibsenism* (London: Constable, 1929)
SHEEHY, HELEN, *Eleonora Duse: A Biography* (New York: Alfred A. Knopt, 2003)
SICA, ANNA, ed., *La drammatica metodo italiano: trattati normative e testi teorici* (Milan: Mimesis, 2013)
—— *The Italian Method of La Drammatica* (Milan: Mimesis, 2014)
SICA, A. and A. WILSON, *The Murray Edwards Duse Collection* (Milan: Mimesis, 2012)
SIGNORELLI, OLGA, *Eleonora Duse* (Rome: Signorelli, 1938)
SIMONCINI FRANCESCA, *Eleonora Duse capocomica* (Rome: Le Lettere, 2011)
—— *Rosmersholm di Ibsen per Eleonora Duse* (Pisa: ETS, 2005)
SIPALA, PAOLO MARIO, 'Due note sul teatro di Verga', *Misure critiche*, 15.55–56 (1985), 43–55
—— 'Il lupo e la volpe', in *Giovanni Verga e il teatro: atti del convegno Catania 13–15 aprile, Teatro Stabile di Catania* (Catania: Assessorato regionale ai beni culturali e P. I., 1986), pp. 37–43
—— *Pirandello dialettale* (Palermo: Palumbo, 1983)
SOGLIUZZO, RICHARD, 'L'arte dell'attore: teoria e pratica', in *La Trilogia di Pirandello: atti del convegno internazionale sul teatro pirandelliano (Agrigento 6–10 dicembre 1976)*, ed. by Enzo Lauretta (Agrigento: Centro Nazionale Studi Pirandelliani, 1977), pp. 149–63
SPIZZO, JEAN, 'Répétition et reformulation du texte pirandellien *Tutto per bene*: de la forme narrative à la forme dramatique', *Revue des études italiennes*, 20 (1974), 74–104
STARKIE, WALTER, *Luigi Pirandello 1867–1936* (Berkeley and Los Angeles: University of California Press, 1965)
STÄUBLE, ANTONIO, *Il teatro intimista: contributo alla storia del teatro italiano del novecento* (Rome: Bulzoni 1975)
STEWENS, DOROTHEA, *Pirandello scrittura e scena* (Agrigento: Centro Nazionale Studi Pirandelliani, 1983)
STONE, KAY, 'Feminist Approaches to the Interpretation of Fairy Tales', in *Fairy Tales and Society: Illusion, Allusion, and Paradigm*, ed. by Ruth B. Bottigheimer (Philadelphia: University of Pennsylvania, 1986), pp. 229–36
—— 'Things Walt Disney Never Told Us', *The Journal of American Folklore: Women and Folklore*, 88.347 (1975), 42–50

SUTCLIFFE, TOM, *Believing in Opera* (London: Faber and Faber, 1996)
SWANN JONES, STEVEN, 'The Innocent Persecuted Heroine Genre: An Analysis of its Structure and Themes', *Western Folklore: Perspectives on the Innocent Persecuted Heroine in Fairy Tales*, 52.1 (1993), 13–41
SYMONS, ARTHUR, *Eleonora Duse* (London: Elkin Mathews, 1926)
TEDESCO, NATALE, *Il cielo di carta: teatro siciliano da Verga a Joppolo* (Palermo: S. F. Flaccovio, 1989)
——'*La Lupa*: La contestualità della novella e delle "scene drammatiche"', in *Giovanni Verga e il teatro: atti del convegno Catania, 13–15 aprile, Teatro Stabile di Catania* (Catania: Assessorato regionale ai beni culturali e P. I, 1986), pp. 101–05
——*Il teatro di Verga e altri saggi* (Palermo: Libreria editrice Gino, 1974)
TERRACINI, BENVENUTO, 'Le *Novelle per un anno* di Luigi Pirandello', in *Analisi stilistica: Teoria, storia, problemi* (Milan: Feltrinelli, 1975), pp. 283–398
TILGHER, ADRIANO, *Il problema centrale: Cronache teatrali 1914–1926*, ed. by Alessandro D'Amico (Genova: Edizioni del teatro stabile, 1973)
——*Studi sul teatro contemporaneo* (Rome: Libreria di Scienze e Lettere, 1928)
——*Voci del tempo: profili di letterati e filosofi contemporanei* (Rome: Libreria di scienze e lettere, 1921)
TINTERRI, ALESSANDRO, 'Le prime messinscene di *Questa sera si recita a soggetto*', in *Testo e messa in scena in Pirandello*, ed. by Enzo Lauretta (Urbino: La Nuova Italia Scientifica, 1986), pp. 133–46
TODOROS, ROBERTA, '*Casa di bambola* tra Luigi Capuana ed Eleonora Duse', *Castello di Elsinore*, 21 (1994), 59–66
TORQUATO, TASSO, *Le prose diverse di Torquato Tasso*, ed. by Cesare Guasti (Florence: Le Monnier, 1875)
TRIFONE, PIETRO, *Malalingua: l'italiano scorretto da Dante a oggi* (Bologna: Il Mulino, 2007)
URSO, SIMONA, 'Ibsen in Italia', in *Scene di fine ottocento: l'Italia fin de siècle a teatro*, ed. by Carlotta Sorba (Rome: Carocci editore, 2004), pp. 193–220
VALLONE, A., 'Le didascalie nel teatro', in *Atti del congresso internazionale di studi pirandelliani, Venezia 2–5 ottobre 1961* (Florence: Le Monnier, 1967), pp. 501–08
VÀRVARO, ALBERTO, '*Liolà* di Luigi Pirandello fra il dialetto e la lingua', *Bollettino del Centro di studi filologici e linguistici siciliani*, 5 (1957), 346–51
VERDIRAME, RITA, 'Il canarino in portineria', in *Giovanni Verga e il teatro: Atti del convegno Catania, 13–15 aprile, Teatro Stabile di Catania* (Catania: Assessorato regionale ai beni culturali e P. I., 1986), pp. 87–99
——'Femme Fatale e Angelo del Focolare nel primo Verga', in *Famiglia e società nell'opera di G. Verga: atti del convegno nazionale (Perugia 25–26–27 ottobre 1989)*, ed. by Norberto Cacciaglia, Ada Neiger, Renzo Pavese (Florence: Olschki, 1991), pp. 225–42
VICENTINI, CLAUDIO, *Pirandello: il disagio del teatro* (Venice: Marsilio, 1993)
VINALL, S. W. and P. S. NOBLE, 'Shrewd and Wanton Women: Adultery in the *Decameron* and the *Heptameron*', in *Women and Italy: Essays on Gender, Culture and History*, ed. by Zygmunt G. Barański and Shirley W. Vinall (London: Macmillan, 1991), pp. 141–72
VON HOFMANNSTHAL, HUGO, *Gabriele D'Annunzio e Eleonora Duse* (Milan: Shakespeare and Company, 1983)
WARNER, MARINA, *Alone of all Her Sex: The Myth and Cult of The Virgin Mary*, new edn (London: Vintage, 2000 [1976])
WEAVER, WILLIAM, *Duse: A Biography with 53 illustrations* (London: Thames and Hudson, 1984)
WHITFIELD, JOHN HUMPHREYS, 'La metamorfosi della novella', in *Atti del congresso internazionale di studi pirandelliani, Venezia 2–5 ottobre 1961* (Florence: Le Monnier, 1967), pp. 735–42

WILLSON, PERRY, *Women in Twentieth-Century Italy* (Basingstoke: Palgrave Macmillan, 2010)
WOOLF, VIRGINIA, *Three Guineas* (New York: Harcourt Brace Jovanovich, 1938)
ZANCAN, MARINA, 'Una donna di Sibilla Aleramo', in *Letteratura italiana: Le opere*, ed. by Alberto Asor Rosa, 4 vols (Turin: Einaudi, 1995), IV, *Il Novecento*, pp. 101–43
ZANGRILLI, FRANCO, *L'arte novellistica di Pirandello* (Ravenna: Longo editore, 1983)
—— 'Pirandello e Verga', in *Pirandello e i classici: da Euripide a Verga* (Florence: Cadmo, 1995), pp. 129–50
ZAPPULLA MUSCARÀ, S., and E. ZAPPULLA, *Le donne del teatro siciliano da Mimì Aguglia a Ida Carrara* (Acireale: La Cantinella, 1995)
—— *Giovanni Grasso: il più grande attore tragico del mondo* (Acireale, Catania: Cantinella, 1995)
—— *Pirandello in guanti gialli* (Caltanisetta — Rome: Salvatore Sciascia, 1988)
—— 'Pirandello traduttore e autotraduttore', in *Pirandello e la parola*, ed. by Enzo Lauretta (Agrigento: Centro Nazionale Studi Pirandelliani, 2000), pp. 133–42
—— *Verga da vedere: teatro, cinema, televisione*, ed. by F. Caffo, S. Zappulla Muscarà and E. Zappulla (Palermo: Regione Siciliana, 2003)
ZIPES, JACK, *The Irresistible Fairy Tale: The Cultural and Social History of a Genre* (Princeton University Press, 2012)
—— ed., *The Oxford Companion to Fairy Tales* (Oxford: Oxford University Press, 2002)
ZOLA, ÉMILE, *Le roman expérimental*, ed. by François-Marie Maurad (Paris: Flammarion, 2006 [1880])
ZUBER-SKERRITT, ORTRUN, ed., *Page to Stage: Theatre as Translation* (Amsterdam: Rodopi, 1984)

INDEX

Aarne, Antti 55, 56
Abba, Marta 2–3, 8, 25–29, 34, 54, 69, 83, 160, 161
Abbate, Carolyn 36
actors:
    grande attore — attrice 5, 8, 25–26, 27, 36, 48, 58, 90
    mattatore 16, 93
    theatre of 16–17
Adorno, Theodor 4
adulteress 1, 120, 150, 159, 162–63
adulterous:
    husband 91
    mother 35, 123
    woman 108
adultery 18, 53–54, 58, 60, 64, 84, 108, 109–10, 113, 114, 130, 137, 162–63
    see also triangular relationships
Aguglia, Mimì 18
Aleramo, Sibilla:
    characters: anonymous narrator in *Una donna* 35, 40–41, 51 n. 41, 161
    journalism: 38
    life 35, 40
    novels:
        Il Passaggio, 40
        Una donna 5, 34, 39, 40–41, 45, 165
    see also Faccio, Rina
Alexander, Alfred 17
Alighieri, Dante 9, 16
Alonge, Roberto 145, 147–48 149–50, 152
Amatangelo, Susan 2, 129
Andò, Flavio 21, 37, 123, 134
Angelini, Franca 54, 65, 149
Apuleius 69
Archer, William 19
Ariosto, Ludovico 9
Asilio Mariuccia 39
audience:
    female 36, 37, 46
    writing for 13–17, 45–48, 94–95, 123–24
Austen, Jane 92, 116, 121
    see also women writers
Austin, Gayle 2, 53, 54, 65, 160

Baldi, Guido 97
Bally, Charles 4
Bang, Herman 19
Bàrberi Squarotti, Giorgio 53–54, 63, 65, 82–83
Barbiera, Raffaello 21

Barsotti, Anna 131–32, 136
Basile, Giambattista 55
Bassein, Beth Ann 53
Bassnett, Susan 3, 5, 19
Battaglia, Giacinto 36
Beerbohm, Max 36
Bembo, Pietro 16
Bentley, Eric 3
Bernard, Catherine 57
Bernardelli, Francesco 69
Bernardini, Adelaide 2
Bernhardt, Sarah 37
Bigazzi, Roberto 60, 96
Bini, Daniela 3, 27, 104, 105, 153, 164
Boccaccio, Giovanni 16, 55, 69
body language 16, 78, 95, 114, 128–29, 153
    external actions 59, 61, 66, 96, 105–06, 127, 129, 137
    physical descriptions 66, 67, 76, 124–25, 127
    see also interior and internal actions
Boito, Arrigo 22, 38, 45, 58
Boutet, Edoardo 21, 43–44, 47
Bragaglia, Anton Giulio 27
Bragaglia, Leonardo 3
Brontë, Charlotte 92, 116, 121, 161
    see also women writers
Bruni, Arnaldo 108
Buttafuoco, Annarita 37–38, 40

Caesar, Ann 3, 35, 39, 162
Camilleri, Andrea 42
Campbell Douglas 83
Campi, Annetta 18
Capuana, Luigi 8, 10, 13, 15–18, 19–20, 21, 29 n. 6, 42–45, 47, 48, 56, 94, 120, 123
Caputi, Anthony 84, 101
Carcano, Giulio 37
Caretti, Laura 45
Carini, Luigi 134
Case, Sue-Ellen 3, 5, 164
Cavarero, Adriana 4
Cenni, Alessandra 41
Chamberlain, Lori 92
Checchi, Tebaldo 38
Chemotti, Saveria 35
Chesler, Phyllis 122
Chiaromonte, Nicola 25
Cibber, Colley 91

Coleridge, Elizabeth 121, 122
commedia dell'arte 16, 83
Congress of Vienna 16

D'Amico, Alessandro 107–08
D'Amico, Giuliano 45
D'Amico, Silvio 11, 70, 84, 105, 148–49, 151
D'Annunzio, Gabriele 9, 22
D'Arcais, Francesco 37
D'Aulnoy, Madame 57
Damiani, Felice 40
damsels in distress 55–58, 53, 159
Dante, *see* Alighieri Dante
death 4, 9, 19, 21, 49 n. 14, 53, 54–55, 56, 58, 60, 65–66, 67, 68, 71, 73–74, 76–77, 78, 80–84, 98–100, 108–10, 116, 124, 132–33, 139, 153
   of a character 32–33 n. 97, 36, 53, 54–56, 69, 72, 81, 83, 84, 87–88 n. 56, 98–100, 108
De Bella, Nino 164
De Castris, Arcangelo Leone 101–02, 153
De Giorgio, Michela 37
De La Force, Charlotte-Rose 55, 57
De Lauretis, Teresa 53
De Mauro, Tullio 16
De Murat, Henriette-Julie 57
De Roberto, Federico 11, 58, 123
De Staël, Madame 91
Della Terza, Dante 112
desire 123, 126, 131, 133 159, 160, 163
   masculine 4
   object of 127, 129, 145
   same-sex 122
Després, Susanne 48
Di Lorenzo, Tina 134
Donati, Corrado 106
Dondini, Cesare 134
dialect 16
   see also Sicilian dialect
Disney, Walt 55
La drammatica 19
duel 58, 63–66, 67–68, 71–73, 94–95, 143–44, 147, 148, 150, 151–53, 163
Dumas, Alexandre 16, 26, 36
Duse, Eleonora 4, 8, 16, 17–22, 26, 27, 29, 34, 36, 37, 38–39, 42–43, 45–49, 54, 58, 59, 68, 83, 86 n. 36, 90, 95, 120, 123, 124, 160, 161, 162, 164–65
   see also actors

Eliot, George 91
emancipation 34, 37–38, 39
   early emancipationists 38, 39, 41–42, 145, 161
   see also feminism, feminist, and women writers

Faccio, Rina 38, 41
   see also Sibilla Aleramo
fairy tale 53, 55, 56–57, 76, 91

characters:
   Cinderella 55
   Rapunzel 54, 55, 77, 84
   Sleeping Beauty 55
   see also damsel in distress, innocent persecuted heroine, and Maiden-in-the-Tower
Fallon Marianne 140
feminism 5, 121
feminist:
   approach 2, 3, 160
   critics 5, 6, 53, 56–57, 90, 92–93, 116, 154, 159–60, 164–65
   early 38–42
   icon 39
   thought 5, 161
   unions 35, 39
   writers 2, 40, 159–60
Ferrari, Paolo 123
Ferris, Lesley 91, 93, 116, 161
Ferrone, Siro 54, 124, 131
Fetterley, Judith 4, 160
Fitzgerald, Zelda 121–22
Flaubert, Gustave 117 n. 13, 121, 160, 162–63
Fojanesi-Rapisardi, Giselda 135
folk 13, 17
folklore 11, 53, 55–58, 60, 125, 126, 127, 128–29
Forgacs, David 122
Foris, Luigi 47
free indirect speech 2, 4, 10, 59, 71, 73, 92, 96, 110, 130, 147, 160

Galletti, Paolo 42
Gardner, Viv 49 n. 1
Giacometti, Paolo 16, 39
Giacosa, Giuseppe 15, 16, 17–18, 20, 58, 59
Gibellini, Pietro 62, 68
Gilbert Sandra 121, 122
Giudice, Gaspare 9, 27, 68
Gonzenbach, Laura 57–58
Goodman, Lizbeth 121, 122
Gounod, Charles, *Faust* (opera) 49 n. 88
Gramsci, Antonio 8, 106
Grana, Gianni 25
Grasso, Giovanni 18
Greppi, Paolina 2
Grignani, Maria Antonietta 2, 105
Grimm, Jacob and Wilhelm 55, 57
Gualdo, Luigi 58
Gubar, Susan 121, 122
Guglielminetti, Marziano 110
Guicciardini, Francesco 9
Günsberg, Maggie 106, 145

Herczeg, Giulio 10
Horkheimer, Max 4

Ibsen, Henrik:
  A Doll's House (*Casa di bambola*) 5, 34, 35, 40, 42–49, 90, 91, 120, 154, 159
    Nora (character) 34, 35, 39, 40, 42–49, 53, 56, 84, 90, 100, 120, 124, 134, 154, 161, 164–65
  Ghosts 48
  The Lady of the Sea 48
impersonality 11–12
  see also *verismo*
innocent persecuted heroine 5, 53, 55–58, 61, 84, 159
interior:
  drama 128
  monologue 96-97, 110
  silence 24-25, 115
interiority:
  discourse of 35, 92
inward-looking perspective 76

Jacobus, Mary 121, 122
Jannuzzi, Lina 13
Jonson, Ben 91

Key, Ellen 40
Kroha, Lucienne 106

Labriola, Teresa 41, 49
Laurence, Patricia 92–93, 116
Leo, Ulrich 103
Leotta, Ninfa 13
Lennartz, Elizabeth 27–28
Levi, Cesare 21, 59, 135, 142
Lhéritier, Marie-Janie 57
Licastro, Emanuele 71, 104, 109
Livio, Gigi 101, 149, 152
Locke, Ralph 36
Lombroso, Cesare 34
Lombroso, Paola 41, 161
Lopez, Sabatino 95
love, see maternal love, romantic love, and sexual love
Lugné-Poë, Aurélien 45, 48
Lugo, Olga 20
Lundell, Torborg 56
Luperini, Romano 132, 140, 142

Macchia, Giovanni 54, 69, 70
Machiavelli, Niccolò 9, 152
Madrignani, Carlo Alberto 123, 159
madwoman 121–22, 154
  see also sexual voice
Maiden-in-the-Tower 55, 69
Majno, Ersilia 39–41
Malara, Francesca 133, 142
Mantegazza, Paolo 34
Manzoni, Alessandro 9, 59
La Marchesa Colombi 35, 117 n. 13, 121
  see also women writers

Marchi, Virgilio 26
Mariani, Anna Laura 39
Mariani, Gaetano 131
Mariani, Umberto 54, 160
Mascagni, Pietro, *Cavalleria rusticana* (opera) 18, 59, 67
maternal:
  instinct 113
  love 45, 66
  role 113
  see also mother
Meitlis, Rebecca 36
Messina, Maria 35
  see also women writers
Mineo, Nicolò 120, 134, 140, 161
Moers, Ellen 91
Moestrup, Jørn 22, 71, 113, 149
Molinari, Cesare 16–17, 19, 21
Monti, Silvana 14–15
Monti, Vincenzo 9
Morandini, Giuliana 122
Moroni, Gabriele 61
Morris, Pam 3
mother:
  of nation-state 37–38
  portrayal of 32–33 n. 97, 43, 52 n. 97, 61, 66, 71, 79, 80–81, 98, 102, 104, 109, 112–13, 120, 129–31, 160, 161
  relationship to son 52 n. 97, 66, 67
  see also adulterous mother, maternal, and motherhood
motherhood 39, 113
Mozzoni, Anna Maria 35
Mulvey, Laura 53
murder 57, 87 n. 50, 140, 147–48
  see also duel
Murray Edwards Collection 39
Musco, Angelo 27, 119 n. 59
muse 4–5, 8, 17, 25, 159
Mussolini, Benito 35
Musumarra, Carmelo 15

Naturalism 13
  Naturalist 10, 23
  naturalistic 20, 162
Naubert, Benedikte 57
Neera 35, 117 n. 13, 121
  see also women writers
Niemann-Raabe, Hedwig 43–44, 45
Nightingale, Florence 91
Nikiforov, Aleksandr Isaakovich 55
novella dialogata 23
  see also *verismo* and impersonality

O'Rawe, Catherine 115
Ojetti, Ugo 14, 66, 122, 127, 129
Oliva, Gianni 94, 143

Oliver, Roger 101, 103
Olsen, Tillie 92
opera 16, 159
    operatic tradition 34, 36–37
    see also Gounod Mascagni, Giuditta Pasta, Puccini, Rossini, Verdi, '"Leonora, addio!"', *Questa sera si recita a soggetto*
Orecchia, Donatella 20
Orvieto, Adolfo 131

Pallanza, Dina 134
parody 53–54, 83
Pasta, Francesco 134
Pasta, Giuditta 36, 37
Pellini, Pierluigi 12
Percoto, Caterina 2
periodicals:
    English:
        The Century Magazine 19, 26, 162
        The Era 19
        The Pall Mall, 19
    French:
        Le Gaulois 18
        Le Temps 24, 43, 78
    Italian:
        L'arte drammatica 21, 42, 47–48
        Carro di Tespi 43–44, 47
        Corriere della sera 18, 20–21, 45–46, 68, 115, 123, 143, 151
        Fanfulla della domenica 58
        Fortunio: Cronaca illustrata della settimana 58
        Gazzetta piemontese 42, 59
        La Gazzetta del Popolo 69
        Gazzetta dei teatri 42
        Giornale d'Italia 39, 143
        Giornale dell'isola 123
        Le Grazie 134
        L'idea nazionale 105, 151
        Illustrazione italiana 42, 47, 107
        Italia femminile 38, 41
        L'Italia del popolo 48
        Il Marzocco 131
        L'ora 18–19
        La Perseveranza 47
        Quadrivio 78
        Rivista nuova di scienze, lettere ed arti 122
        Schiave bianche 40
        Siciliana 134
        La stampa 69
        Unione femminile 40
Perkins Gilman, Charlotte 121
Perodi, Emma 57
Perroni, Lina 13, 86 n. 34
Petrarch (Petrarca, Francesco) 9, 16
Petronio, Giuseppe 13
Pierangeli, Ulderico 40

Pieri, Aliprandi 18, 34 42, 47, 48
Pirandello, Luigi:
    characters:
        Antonio Serra 107
        l'attore brillante 82
        l'attrice caratterista 75, 76–77, 82
        Baldovino 104, 153
        La Barbetti 109, 112
        Clara 148
        Cosmo Laurentano 105, 106
        Cristina 120, 143–44, 147, 148, 151, 163
        La Demente 106
        Donata Genzi 28, 73, 161
        Dorina 82
        Dottor Hinkfuss 70, 74, 75, 83, 84
        Enrico IV 104
        Signora Frola 102–04, 114
        Fulvia (*Come tu mi vuoi*) 146
        Fulvia Corsani 107
        La Generala 71, 74–75, 79, 82
        Ginetta 108, 109
        Gualdi 109
        Guido 144–46, 148, 150, 150–53
        Gubbio 104
        Signora Ignazia 71, 74, 79, 82
        Lando Laurentano 146
        Laudisi 5, 90, 102, 103, 104–05, 106, 116, 144, 145, 153
        Leone 104, 122, 143, 145–48, 150–54, 164
        Lillina Fabris 107
        Lori 107, 108–16, 146, 153, 163
        Manfroni 107, 108, 109, 110, 111–12, 113, 114, 116
        Marta, Ajala 114
        Mattia, Pascal 104
        Maurizio Gueli 107
        Memmo 143, 144, 147
        Miglioritti 148
        Mommina 3, 4, 28, 53, 54–55, 56, 58, 69–84, 159, 160, 163, 164
        Moscarda 104, 106, 146
        Nenè 82
        Palma 108, 109, 110, 111, 113, 114
        Signor Ponza 102–04, 114, 143
        Signora Ponza 4, 5, 90, 102–06, 108–09, 112, 114, 116, 145, 153, 159, 163, 164
        il primo attore 82
        la prima attrice 28, 75, 82, 83, 164
        Silia 120, 122, 143–54, 160, 163, 164
        Silvia 5, 91, 107–13, 115–16, 153, 159, 163, 164
        Totina 79–80, 82
        Verona 107, 108, 109, 110, 111–12
        Verri 2, 54, 56, 68–69, 71–84, 143, 163
    critical essays:
        'L'azione parlata' 23–24, 106
        'Fede e bellezza' 22
        'Femminismo' 5

'Illustratori, attori e traduttori' 25–26
'Novelle e novellieri' 22–23
'Romanzo, racconto, novella' 22
'Soggettivismo e oggettivismo' 9, 22–23
'Teatro e letteratura' 23–24
'Teatro siciliano?' 8–9, 31 n. 49
'L'umorismo' 24–25, 115
  see also *umorismo*
life:
  early career 8–9, 68–69, 101, 107
  intellectual writer 25, 164
  wife 68
  see also Marta Abba and Stefano Pirandello
meta-theatre 8, 12, 29, 54–55, 69, 70, 72, 78, 79, 81, 83, 84, 143, 146, 149, 161, 162, 164
  see also plays (*Questa sera si recita a soggetto*) and characters (Mommina)
novels:
  L'Esclusa 114, 119 n. 67, 162–63
  Il fu Mattia Pascal 9, 10
  Uno, nessuno e centomila 10, 101, 105, 106, 146
plays:
  L'amica delle mogli 27
  Il berretto a sonagli 8
  Ciascuno a modo suo 70
  Come tu mi vuoi 106
  Così è (se vi pare) 4, 6 n. 3, 90–91, 101–06, 108, 112, 114, 116, 144–45, 153, 159, 163, 164
  'U cuccu 22
  Diana e la Tuda, 27
  Enrico IV 69
  L'epilogo 107–08
  La giara 8
  Il giuoco delle parti 4, 6 n. 3, 23, 121, 143–54, 159, 160, 163, 164
  Liolà 3, 8–9, 22, 150
  La morsa: Epilogo in un atto 107–08
  Questa sera si recita a soggetto 2, 3, 4, 6 n. 3, 27–28, 53–55, 56, 58, 68–84, 159, 161, 162, 163, 164
  Trovarsi 28–29, 73, 161
  Tutto per bene 5, 6 n. 3, 9, 91, 107–16, 146, 153, 159, 163, 164
  All'uscita 101
short stories (*Novelle per un anno*):
  'Colloquii coi personaggi' 12
  'Creditor galante' 107
  '"Leonora, addio!"' 2, 3, 4, 6 n. 3, 53, 54, 68–84, 161, 163, 164
  'La paura' 107
  'Personaggi' 12
  'Quando si è capito il giuoco' 4, 6 n. 3, 23, 120, 143–54, 163, 164
  'La Signora Frola e il Signor Ponza, suo genero' 4, 5, 6 n. 3, 90, 101–06, 108, 112, 114, 116, 163, 164
  'La tragedia di un personaggio' 12

'Tutto per bene' 5, 6 n. 3, 9, 91, 107–16, 147, 154, 160, 163, 164
speeches:
  'Discorso di Catania' 9
  'Discorso alla Reale Accademia d'Italia' 9
Pirandello, Stefano 22, 68, 101, 143
Pitrè, Giuseppe 58
Plath, Sylvia 121–22
Poe, Edgar Allan 53
Polese Santarnecchi, Icilio 47–48
Pontiero, Giovanni 22
popular Italian 11
  see also Sicilianised Italian
Potter, Beatrix 91
Pozza, Giovanni 45–47, 131
Praga, Marco 16, 31 n. 49, 107
Primoli, Gegè 20, 95
Prosperi, Girogio 61, 125
Providenti, Elio 107
Prozor, Moritz 43, 44
Puccini, Giacomo:
  characters:
    Butterfly 49 n. 14
    Tosca 36
  life 123
  operas:
    La bohème 49 n. 14
    Tosca 36
Pullini, Giorgio 106
Puppa, Paolo 28, 48, 106, 149

racconto dialogato 10
  see also *verismo* and impersonality
Ragonese, Gaetano 10, 141
Ragusa, Olga 26
Rasi, Luigi 19
relativism 101–02
  relativistic approach 10, 101, 144
  see also *umorismo*
Re, Lucia 37, 39
Realism 22, 99, 124
  see also *verismo*
regional Italian 11
  see also Sicilianised Italian
Reinach, Enrico 20
Reiter, Virginia 123, 134
Risorgimento 37
Ristori, Adelaide 16, 34, 37, 38, 39
  see also actors
Rod, Édouard 12–13, 31 n. 49, 43, 45, 58–59, 123, 133
Romanticism 59, 99, 115
  anti-romantic 129
  romantic love 163
  un-romantic 98–99
Rossi, Cesare 17, 43, 58

Rossi, Ernesto 16
　see also actors
Rossini, Gioachino, *Otello* (opera) 37
Rotman, Brian 93
Ruggeri, Ruggero 27, 107, 114, 143–44, 151
Russo, Luigi 10, 13, 63, 99, 133, 141, 162
Rutherford, Susan 36, 49 n. 1

Salvini, Guido 69–70, 83
Salvini, Tommaso 16
　see also actors
Sanson, Helena 91
Sapegno, Natalino 14, 100, 141
Sardou, Victorien 36
Sbrocchi Leonardo 83
Scalinger, G. M. 47
Scarano, Nicola 12
Schiff, Paolina 35
Schino, Mirella 26, 31 n. 55
Schumann, Clara 92
Schumann, Robert 92
Sciascia, Leonardo 162
script, importance of 83-84
Serao, Matilde 2, 35, 117 n. 13, 155 n. 9
　see also women writers
sexual:
　deviance 122, 134, 163
　liberation 39, 40, 49, 120, 162
　love 165
　monster 121–22
　object 3, 120, 145, 150
　puritan 39
　relationship 40, 55
　voice 120–54
　see also adulteress, adulterous, adultery, desire
Shakespeare, William 27, 92, 93
Shelley, Mary 91, 121, 161
Sica, Anna 19
Sicilian:
　actors 18–19, 31 n. 49
　authors 1, 19–20, 35, 160, 162
　code of honour 135, 87 n. 50
　　see also duel
　community 12, 17, 93–94, 101, 123–24, 135
　dialect 8–9, 11, 14, 18, 19–20, 119 n. 59
　　see also dialect
　peasantry 9
　tales 2, 57–58, 87 n. 45, 95–96, 140, 164
　voice 53–84
　women 54, 120, 142, 163
Sicilianised Italian 11, 14, 60
　see also popular Italian and regional Italian
Sicily 8, 13, 19, 53, 57, 58, 59, 87 n. 50, 94, 120, 124, 161, 163
Signorelli, Olga 32–33 n. 97, 45
silence 2, 91–93, 153
　theatre of 162
　see also interior silence
silent:
　voice 4–5, 90–116, 159, 160, 164
　she-wolf 122, 129, 134
　obedient wife 5, 90–91, 159
　women 91, 116, 121
Silvestro, Antonio 11
Simoncini, Francesca 42–43
Sipala, Paolo Mario 141–42, 162
siren 4–5, 159
Small, Helen 121, 122
Sogliuzzo, Richard 84
soliloquy 76, 103, 110
Spalletti, Gabriella 38
Spizzo, Jean 114
Starkie, Walter 54, 81, 116
Stewens, Dorothea 149
Stone, Kay 57, 58
Swann Jones, Steven 56
symbolist theatre 22, 116 n. 1
　see also silent theatre
Symons, Arthur 18, 19

Talli, Virgilio 26, 106
Tasca, Pier Antonio 123
Tasso, Torquato 9, 91
Teatro d'Arte 2–3, 26
Tedesco, Natale 22, 123–24, 128
Tellini, Gino 142
Terracini, Benvenuto 73
Thompson, Stith 55, 56
Tilgher, Adriano 24, 25, 105, 111, 115, 146
Torelli, Achille 16
Torelli-Viollier, Eugenio 18, 20–21, 58
tragedy 22–23, 59, 63, 64, 68, 71, 75, 78, 92, 106, 125, 162
Treves, Emilio 58, 101, 117 n. 13, 123, 134
triangles 9, 54, 60, 69, 107, 108, 129, 135, 140, 141, 142
triangular relationships 9, 58–59, 68–69, 73, 107, 123, 130, 135, 140, 141
　see also adultery

umorismo 6, 24–25, 101, 115, 63–64
umorista 10, 24, 163
unification of Italy 13, 16, 38, 154, 163
　see also Risorgimento

vedersi vivere 24–25, 115–16
　see also *umorismo*
Verdi, Giuseppe:
　characters:
　　Azucena 69, 80, 88 n. 60
　　Joan of Arc 36
　　Violetta 36

operas:
    La forza del destino 69, 79
    La Traviata 36
    Il Trovatore 69, 80, 83, 88 n. 60
Verdirame, Rita 54
Verdura, Salvatore Paolo 93–94
Verga, Giovanni:
    characters:
        Compare Alfio 15, 56, 58, 60, 62, 64–65, 66, 67, 68, 73, 95, 141, 153
        Assunta 97
        Battista 98, 99
        Bellamà 134, 135, 137, 138, 139–40
        Zio Brasi 61
        Buonocore 138
        Massaro Cola 61, 63
        Mastro Cola 87–88 n. 56
        Compare Camilla 61
        Cardillo 127
        Carlini 95, 96, 97–98, 99, 100, 129, 137, 163
        Zia Filomena 61
        Gilda 95, 96, 97, 98, 100, 125, 129, 160
        Mastro don Gesualdo 99
        Gramigna 156 n. 32
        Don Liborio 119 n. 73
        Lola 56, 58, 60, 62–63, 64, 65, 67–68, 72, 87–88 n. 56, 140, 142
        Lollo 1–2, 134, 135, 136–43
        Lollo's wife 135–43
        La Lupa 120, 122–34, 136, 142
        Malerba 125–26, 135–36
        Màlia 5, 20–21, 48, 73, 90, 95–100, 110, 132, 137, 140, 142, 153, 159, 160, 161, 162, 163
        Mara 123, 128, 130–31, 132, 134
        Mariangela 108, 120, 122, 134, 135–43, 144, 147, 148, 150, 154, 161, 162, 163
        Maricchia 123, 128–30, 133
        Michelangelo 135, 137, 139, 140
        Musarra 138, 139, 140
        Nanni 123–34, 139, 141, 142
        Neli 138, 139, 140
        Padron 'Ntoni 99
        Gnà Nunzia 125, 60–61, 62, 66–67
        Pentolaccia 119 n. 73
        Peppa 156 n. 32
        Gnà Pina 22, 120, 122–34, 136, 137, 139, 140, 141, 142, 144, 145, 154, 161, 162, 163
        Pipuzza 61, 65
        Santa 58–68, 72, 76, 142, 163
        Santuzza 17–20, 21, 42, 48, 53–54, 56, 58–68, 72, 76, 79, 83, 84, 95, 125, 132, 137, 140, 142, 159, 161, 162, 163
        Turiddu 19, 31 n. 49, 56, 58–68, 72–73, 125, 137, 141
        Zango 138
    life:
        vocation for theatre 14–15, 22
        writing for theatre 13–16, 94–95
        younger years 13, 53, 68
    novels:
        I Malavoglia 9, 12, 86 n. 34, 99
        Mastro don Gesualdo 9, 96–97, 99
    plays:
        La caccia al lupo 1–2, 6 n. 3, 63, 107–08, 120, 122, 134–43, 147, 148, 150, 154, 159, 161, 162
        La caccia alla volpe 134
        Cavalleria rusticana 4, 6 n. 3, 13, 15, 17, 18, 19, 20, 22, 26, 36, 53–54, 56, 58–68, 69, 72, 83, 84, 93–95, 96, 100, 123–24, 125, 127, 132, 135, 137, 140, 141, 153, 159, 161, 162
        Dal mio al tuo 14
        La Lupa 6 n. 3, 18, 22, 49, 63, 122–34, 135, 136, 137, 139, 140, 141, 142, 145, 154, 159, 161, 162
        Onore 13
        In portineria 4, 5, 6 n. 3, 15, 20–21, 73, 90, 93–100, 116, 123, 125, 127, 132, 135, 137, 153, 159, 161, 162
        Rose caduche 13
    short stories:
        'Nedda' 12
        Novelle rusticane:
            'Di là del mare' 12
            'Il mistero' 87–88 n. 56
        Novelle sparse:
            'La caccia al lupo' 1–2, 6 n. 3, 122, 134–43
        Per le vie:
            'Il canarino del n. 15' 4, 6 n. 3, 90, 93–100, 110, 116, 129, 135, 161
        Vita dei campi:
            'L'amante di Gramigna' 11, 59, 62, 129, 156 n. 32
            'Cavalleria rusticana' 6 n. 3, 53–54, 56, 58–68, 69, 72, 83, 84, 96, 141, 153, 159, 161
            'Fantasticheria' 12
            'Jeli il patore' 69, 87 n. 45
            'La Lupa' 6 n. 3, 122–34, 135, 136, 141, 142
            'Pentolaccia' 69, 119 n. 73
verismo 6, 11, 163–64
    verista movement 9, 10, 75
    i veristi 8, 9, 10, 12, 13–14, 19, 23, 35–36, 59, 68–69, 71, 107, 162
    see also impersonality and free indirect speech
Vicentini, Claudio 26, 28
violence 131, 153
violent 54, 72, 77–78, 122, 134, 139, 144
virginity 55
    Virgin Mary 58, 68
    virgin/whore dichotomy 91
Von Hofmannsthal, Hugo 48

war:
    First World War 35, 38–39, 151, 154
    inspiration of 24, 78
    Second World War 35
Weaver, William 22, 86 n. 36
Whitfield, John Humphreys 108

Willson, Perry 35, 39, 40, 151
women writers 2, 35–36, 91–92, 96, 110, 117 n. 13, 121, 160–61
Woolf, Virginia 92, 116
  see also women writers

Zampaldi 47
Zancan, Marina 40
Zola, Émile 13
  see also Naturalism
Zorzi 48

www.ingramcontent.com/pod-product-compliance
Lightning Source LLC
LaVergne TN
LVHW061251060426
835507LV00017B/2017